The New Media Theory Reader

D0120688

2012

The New Media Theory Reader

Robert Hassan and Julian Thomas

Open University Press

Open University Press
McGraw-Hill Education
McGraw-Hill House
Shoppenhangers Road
Maidenhead
Berkshire
England
SL6 2QL

email: enquiries@openup.co.uk
world wide web: www.openup.co.uk

and Two Penn Plaza, New York, NY 10121-2289, USA

First published 2006

A catalogue record of this book is available from the British Library

ISBN-10: 0 335 21710 9 (pb)   0 335 21711 7 (hb)
ISBN-13: 978 0335 21710 6 (pb)   978 0335 21711 3 (hb)

Library of Congress Cataloging-in-Publication Data
CIP data applied for

Typeset by RefineCatch Limited, Bungay, Suffolk
Printed in Poland by OZGraf S.A.
www.polskabook.pl

Contents

Extracts

One: Media transitions

Manovich (2002) – 'What is new media?'

This article argues that changes wrought by new media are profound. Qualitatively different to past technologies such as the printing press or photography, emerging media, in combination with computer technology, render a fundamental shift due to an ability to affect all stages of communication. Outlining the interweaving historical trajectories of media and computing, the author traces the eventual convergence of the two technologies, explaining how developments in computers facilitated the ability to store, synthesise and manipulate diverse types of media. This, in turn, creates a new set of possibilities, translating traditional forms of media – such as images, sound and text – into *new* media. conversations December summarizing

Cook (1997) – 'Technological revolutions and the Gutenberg Myth'

Debunking the myth that the invention of movable type led to substantial advances in literacy and learning, Cook highlights the essential roles of both cultural and technological advances in explaining social change. Questioning the revolutionary claims associated with Gutenberg's invention, he contends that the affect of the printing press was mediated by the social, religious and political institutions of the day. Increases in literacy rates were driven more by the imperatives of record-keeping, education and work than the development of movable type, and the availability of large quantities of paper were required before large-scale diffusion of writing became possible. He suggests that this traditional, one-dimensional account of a single technology causing broad social change, as typified by the Gutenberg Myth, is an inadequate model for assessing the current realities of the developing world. The computer has already been the subject of such an analysis, being touted as revolutionising society. Cook warns of such determinism, reiterating the need to consider the multiple influences inherent in any technological innovation.

de Sola Pool (2003) – 'A shadow darkens'

The legal status of new communication technologies remains a contested and complex area. The domains of print, common carriers (for example, telegraph, telephone, post) and radio are covered by different sets of laws with little relation to each other, and laws relating to new electronic modes of communication do not always preserve the same protections afforded to traditional technologies. The author expresses concern over the potential erosion of civil liberties and traditional freedoms which could occur as each of these domains enter the era of electronic communication and as law-makers discern a new regulatory course. Ironically, decentralisation and fragmentation, hallmarks of the new media environment, are at risk of being bound up in a set of restrictive regulatory practices which do not suit the current climate of technological innovation. How do we respond to this challenge? Offering five ingredients vital to the formulation of communication policy, Pool highlights the need to preserve freedom in this process.

Nye (1996) – 'The consumer's sublime'

Americans have a unique psychological attraction to new landscapes and new technologies, or, as Nye puts it, the technological sublime. People marvel, indeed crave, the innovative technologies which transfix and then become a part of the national identity. As each new generation throws up novel objects, the amazement associated with existing technology fades. Gradually, though, places and objects attract attention not according to their functional or productive use, but because of their commercial magnetism and role in promoting consumption. Man-made skyscrapers replace mountain-tops. Drawing on the example of Las Vegas, Nye outlines the landscape of capitalist surrealism upon which the city was founded, where human order replaces the natural world. Indeed, technological logic also permeates natural wonders and tries to dominate them. The Grand Canyon is likened to a theme park: as visitors flock to the natural landform they are greeted with movie theatres, hotels and the constant noise of aircraft hovering overhead. In this environment, however, any appreciation of progress and human accomplishment is overpowered by a rush of sight, sound and movement.

Kelly (1998) – 'The computational metaphor'

The metaphor of computers has become a pervasive means of explaining the world around us. Evolution, DNA, biological reproduction, galaxies, mathematics, emotions and rain forests have all been described in computational terms. But is the pervasiveness of this universal vocabulary, able to describe all manner of phenomena, a welcome development?

Marien (1996) – 'New communications technology: a survey of impacts and issues'

Here Marien provides a balanced assessment of claims made about the emergence of an information society. Offering a list of technologies likely to be disseminated in the near future, he draws on two main schools of thought – enthusiasts and critics – in order to speculate on the human impacts of these developments. Are the changes desirable or undesirable? Who will be the winners and losers? Both camps have widely divergent views, ranging from overt optimism through to grave concern. Similar debates are canvassed and explored in the areas of democracy and governance, work, productivity and employment, education, culture and health. Citing an ironic lack of communication between people harbouring different views, this article implores a more rigorous examination of the realities of the information age and a consideration of effective responses to these changes.

Two: Governing new media

Saunders, Hunter and Williamson (1992) – 'Historicising obscenity law'

The connection between media content and regulation is addressed here in light of laws pertaining to the publication of obscene material. This is not a new occurrence: as far back as 1727 pornography was regarded as a threat to public morality, and the first prosecution of such an offence signified a breaking down of the division between common law courts and spiritual courts, and an expansion of government and criminal law into the area of morality. Their description highlights the particular historical and cultural influences surrounding this transition, and dismisses alternative accounts which follow a single logic and fail to engage with the complex social milieu affecting such a decision.

Owen (1999) – 'The tragedy of broadcast regulation'

According to Owen, although regulation is a creature of democratic process, policy outcomes are inferior to market outcomes. Based on this contention, he suggests the American government's role in regulating the radio and television broadcasting industry has stifled competition and diversity. Organisations set up to monitor these industries operate on two levels, formal and political, but this framework limits any sound economic and technical analysis which should inform policy choice. The end result is a smaller and more homogonous market which perpetuates the status quo, with consumers the eventual loser. The author finishes with a warning that similar structures may inhibit new digital media: most prominently, the internet.

Graham (1998) – 'Broadcasting policy in the digital age'

Public service broadcasting has an important role to play in promoting common knowledge. It provides a source of information about the world around us, informing how we perceive ourselves in relation to the broader society and how we understand community itself. These characteristics are essential in nurturing commonality, as well as tolerance amongst minority groups. However, market-driven broadcasting does not fulfil these goals well: ethical judgement and editorial responsibility often comes second to profitability, and commercial interests may fragment audiences and hinder the provision of accurate and balanced information. Their interest is in making money, not promoting democracy. Broadcasting then, should not be left entirely to the market: some regulations are necessary in order to ensure the values of choice, quality, community and democracy. This task, however, is not an easy one. His point is clear: an active commercial sector, complemented by a healthy universal public broadcasting service – publicly financed, producing its own programs, and supported by legal regulation – is central to the health of a democratic society.

Robins and Webster (1999) – 'From public sphere to cybernetic state'

Robins and Webster cast a critical eye over the role of information and communication technologies in enhancing the government's ability to control political debate. Surveillance, propaganda and social planning depend upon these technologies, they argue, facilitating the development of opinion polling, public relations, news management, political advertising, censorship, and more precise advertising campaigns. Political campaigns, for example, use computers to access demographic details, organise mail-outs, and analyse and target voter groups. The Information Revolution is not a matter of straightforward technological progress, but must be viewed in terms of the phenomena it has helped construct and consolidate: bureaucratic organisations, political and corporate power structures, social engineering, and surveillance and control.

McChesney (2001) – 'Policing the unthinkable'

In spite of deregulation, large and powerful organisations have come to dominate the media industry. Because of this, it is hard for newcomers to enter the market. The content of journalism has also taken a hit: driven by commercial rationale, news is less controversial, focusing on trivial stories about celebrities and crime. New communication media promise emancipation from these trends as they spawn an array of viable competition to the major players. This process is stifled, however, by the existing market power of monopolies, a situation fuelled by government policy which provides them with licences and subsidies. These firms have created what McChesney refers to as a 'commercial media system'. The result is an undermining of civic participation and, most significantly, the restriction of democratic public involvement in the formulation of media policy.

Compaine (2001) – 'The myths of encroaching global media ownership'

Compaine disputes the contention that corporate media ownership has contributed to an attack on democracy, creating unhealthy concentrations of power and control. Yes, company mergers are important and grab the headlines. But underneath lives a dynamic industry: the number of smaller companies is growing, major organisations are breaking up and new players are arriving on the scene. These corporations are, after all, publicly owned. And yes, the media is run according to profit. But claims that they should give the public 'what they want' are too idealistic. In reality, mass media must be financially viable, and making decisions based on audience preference is fundamental to the success of any program. More to the point, he argues, in democracies there is no such thing as a 'universal public interest'.

Three: Properties and commons

Patterson (1968) – 'Copyright in historical perspective'

The legal deliberations surrounding copyright are complex. Although a clearly achieved purpose and a concise definition of the problems to be solved are ideal elements of copyright law, these conditions are rarely attained. Initial laws were introduced in response to the book trade industry's concern in maintaining a monopoly. The contemporary environment is vastly different. Conflicting concepts of freedom of expression versus the protection of ideas as private property, rather than notions of control and censorship, have taken centre stage. Despite this change, the legacy of previous laws has produced confusion over the philosophical basis of copyright: is it about the author's actual work, or his ideas? Does an author have a natural right to protect his work and ideas? As Patterson points out, publishers, and society more generally, create a range of competing, and sometimes complementary, interests. Recognition of these divergent interests, and the essential value of an author's creative work, is crucial in order to more effectively protect an individuals' work.

Boyle (1996) – 'Intellectual property and the liberal state'

Capturing and defining the concept of physical property is not easy. Once conceived of as absolute, the courts were willing to accept property as not only physical, but conceptual. Rights, then, may be restricted to particular interests, or apply in some situations and not others. What, then, are the implications for intellectual property? A number of tasks must be accomplished: the role of information in liberal society must be clarified, and the tension between protecting the private sphere whilst maintaining public debate (in order to avoid an oppressive state), must be addressed. Intellectual property law should also attempt to conceptually reconcile, or at least find a middle ground, between physical and absolute, and relativist and partial, conceptions of the law.

Littman (2001) – 'Choosing metaphors'

The ways people think about and conceive copyright law can impact upon the application of that law. Over the years a range of models have guided the implementation of copyright regulations. In the early 1900s public authors were granted exclusive rights in order to facilitate the dissemination of their work. This evolved into a framework based on the idea of compensation, focusing first on authors', and then copyright owners', ability to make money off their work. This economic model turned into a trade issue, where owners control property as they see fit. This rhetorical manoeuvring has been adopted by various groups in order to achieve their own ends. Most prominently, content owners have been effective in promoting the term 'piracy' in order to reinforce a perception of content owners' control over property. This strategy is exemplified in the domain of music. The result has been a realisation of more control for copyright owners, an occurrence which has flown under the radar of any public discussion.

Lessig (2000) – 'The promise for intellectual property in cyberspace'

It is hard to trace the distribution of and access to material on the internet. At present it is an all or nothing proposition: you can copy or you can't, you have access or you don't. But what if there were a way to accurately track, and therefore regulate and control, access to material? What might be the problems with this? Lessig offers two answers to this latter question. First, intellectual property differs from physical property in fundamental ways. Unlike an object, ideas are consumed in a different manner, whereby their use is not reduced by virtue of others consuming it. Second, if intellectual property were to be monitored via technological means, the guarantee of public use disappears and such tracking would involve a degree of personal invasion. The implications are clear: anonymity and privacy in cyberspace should be preserved, and technological architecture should include the ability to facilitate what Lessig calls an intellectual commons.

Stallman (2002) – 'Why software should not have owners'

Although digital technology enhances the ease with which people can copy and modify information, copyright laws aim to limit this action. Inheriting a legal heritage from printing, the rigid copyright system does not cope well will the flexible and fluid nature of information technologies. The result, according to Stallman, is the enforcement of draconian measures based on existing laws. Aside from the threat of legal punishment, copyright owners have used a number of tactics to support their argument for more control over information: exaggeration and name-calling, claims of natural rights for authors of property, and economic disadvantage. Refuting each of these, he draws on the free software movement to promote the open sharing of software.

Four: Politics of new media technologies

Barry (2001) – 'On interactivity'

In light of the decline in political participation, interactive and networked technologies have been heralded as a key resource in fostering public participation and facilitating an active, empowered citizenry. Drawing a parallel between government and museums of science, Barry argues that techniques which treat people as participants (rather than observers) encourages agency, experimentation, enterprise, democracy and self-regulation. But the effects of an interactive model are not restricted to just one arena: educational, political and broadcasting institutions are being reinvented along similar lines, and the importance of interactive devices is evident in the classroom, marketing and mass media. The emergence of new media and information technologies has important implications for systems of governance because, suggests Barry, politics flows through instruments and practices.

Barber (2000) – 'Three scenarios for the future of technology and strong democracy'

What will be the impact of new technologies on democracy? Barber offers three stark alternatives. In Pangloss, a posture of complacency will mean that existing inequalities are perpetuated as new technologies are controlled and manipulated by current market forces. For Pandora, the proliferation of information and communication technologies is at risk of being appropriated by tyrannical governments, who may use it to covertly monitor and control citizens. In this scenario, the erosion of freedom and privacy, and the potential for government and/or commercial monopolies, are very real possibilities. In a more optimistic prediction, the Jeffersonian world will see these technologies enhancing education and participation in political processes, as well as promoting tolerance and diversity. This piece concludes by suggesting that while technology may facilitate 'strong democracy', this will not eventuate of its own accord: it will depend on the collective will and character of political institutions and their constituents.

Sunstein (2001) – 'Citizens'

Sunstein explores the relationship between freedom, choice, citizenship and consumption, asking how these are affected by new communication technologies. He paints a picture of opportunity as well as limitation. New media has the potential to enhance choice and expand knowledge, but at the same time our own preferences and choices can limit freedom. Unrestricted consumer choice should not be equated with freedom, he says. Governments, too, can seek to inhibit ideas and possibilities via media policy that pursues censorship. In terms of a democratic system, an important distinction needs to be made between the roles of citizen and consumer. It is an error to merge the two, he argues, and political choice cannot be understood solely in terms of people's capacity as consumers. Indeed, it is important to seek to promote a high-quality and diverse communications market, even if consumers are satisfied with programs which satisfy narrow preferences. This is because limitless individual choice does not always support the interests of self-government and citizenship.

Wark (2004) – 'Abstraction/class'

Wark tells the story of class and the appropriation of property, both physical and intellectual. First land, and then information, becomes a form of private property. As corporations monopolise intellectual property – via patents, copyrights and trademarks – and increase their value by communication, a class of people is displaced. But as information becomes the dominant resource, a new class emerges: that of the hacker. Venturing into a new world, they produce new concepts, perceptions and sensations out of raw data, creating possibilities and standing against the ruling class who seek to control innovation. Fact or fiction? You be the judge.

Five: Time and space in the age of information

Carey (1989) – 'Technology and ideology: the case of the telegraph'

Telegraphy does not deserve to be one of the least studied communication technologies, suggests Carey. It spawned the first communications empire and industrial monopoly, was the first product of the science and engineering-based industry, and contributed to significant changes to the nature of language. Separating communication from transportation, the telegraph laid the foundation for the development of future generations of communication technologies. This innovation was not purely physical and technical: it opened up new ways of thinking about communication and enabled the alteration of ideas. In particular, the telegraph had close ties with three ideological developments: first, it changed the form and structure of organisation and management; second, it helped generate new religious and philosophical metaphors; and, third, it affected everyday, ordinary ideas. A critical instrument in the development of a uniform price system, as well as the standardisation of time zones, the telegraph aided a fundamental reconfiguration and reconstruction of practical consciousness and practical activity.

Stein (1999) – 'Reflections on time, time–space compression and technology in the nineteenth century'

The terms 'time–space convergence' and 'time–space compression' have been coined recently in an effort to describe changes to physical advances in the movement of services and information, as well as the social and psychological affects of these developments. But current explanations need to be revised, according to Stein, because they fail to consider how the changes are experienced amongst different sections of society, and the role of new technologies is often exaggerated. Far from being revolutionary, a combination of communication technologies has prefigured contemporary developments, including the telegraph, telephone and railway line. Each added to a sense of a shrinking world at the time, and coincided with novel ways of thinking about physics, psychology, art and music, culminating in the emergence of the term: 'annihilation of space and time'. This phrase, which was adopted around the turn of the nineteenth century in conceptualising this series of progressive, incremental changes, supports Stein's contention that modern accounts are overstated and lack historical perspective.

Green (2002) – 'On the move: technology, mobility, and the mediation of social time and space'

The impact of new technologies has been profound. They have affected our experience of time and the coordination of (work and personal) activities, dislocated individuals from the collective, fragmented interactions, and disrupted current understandings of social relationships. Or so the argument goes. Green draws on the example of mobile telephony in order to question these presuppositions, highlighting the device's role in reinforcing existing patterns found in everyday life. By outlining the mobile phone's use in people's lives and its role in institutional change, Green shows how many temporalities and experiences are relatively enduring, locally continuous and configured according to multiple daily rhythms and situated action. In contrast to grandiose claims about revolutionary change, control of time and mobility is shaped in a more understated manner by local factors and social practice.

Lee and Liebenau (2001) – 'Time and the internet'

Information technology is changing our conceptualisation of time. Constant and instantaneous access, along with the construction of virtual reality environments, is reducing the significance of time as a reference point and eliminating rigid work rhythms. The internet exemplifies the characteristics (and potentialities) of new technologies in altering temporal dimensions in this manner. Lee and Liebenau offer six inter-related effects of the internet which are contributing to this process: a reduction in the duration of attention span, a weakening of the relevance of physical location, a loss of linear continuity, a renegotiation of the structure of deadlines and task cycles, and the ability to manipulate work rhythms and 'busy-ness'.

Eriksen (2001) – 'Speed is contagious'

Things are happening faster: news updates, renovating a house and everyday speech, to name a few. Information technology removes distance, shortens time and fills what gaps are left with an abundance of information. But what are the consequences of this set of developments? In Eriksen's view the casualties are context, understanding and, ultimately, credibility. Although the desire for speed grows the faster an activity gets, increases in processing power and speed do not, ironically, necessarily result in greater efficiency. Simpler tasks may actually save time, because complex technological operations increase the level of expertise and concentration required, whilst also raising the chance of system failure. This new reality, he asserts, creates subtle but serious unintended consequences. Are we able to counter a 'contagious speed' which is running out of control?

Introduction

Introducing new media theory

The study of new media opens up some of the most fascinating and challenging issues in contemporary culture: questions of ownership and control over information and cultural goods; the changing experience of space and time; the political consequences of new communication technologies; the role of governments in global networks; the power of users and consumers to disrupt established economic and business models. All these topics are vital current issues in economic, social and political life; all of them are also difficult to analyse and understand, because the technologies are fluid, the outcomes are uncertain, and the whole field is characterised by rapid innovation and adaptation.

So where to begin if we are looking for a deeper understanding of new media? Neat categorisations are rarely informative when describing the media, neither are they always the best place to begin a theoretical exploration of the subject. The term *new media* raises questions from the outset: what is it that is said to be new? What might be particularly useful about theories of new media? One useful thing would be to help us exercise some analytic caution at a time when so much is attributed to the power of new technologies: well into the second decade of the web, the promise of novelty still functions as a demand for attention, for resources, for special dispensations in the world of academic study as well as in the commercially and politically driven world of the media industries.

In selecting material for this book, we have attempted to encourage some detachment from contemporary new media enthusiasms. First, we encourage readers to pay close attention to that adjective '*new*' and the many meanings it carries. Some writers in this volume see the special quality of new media in its democratic promise; others see it in the individual character of digital communication; others in the transformed social and economic relationships that new media sustain. Second, we aim to draw attention to new media as a historical as well as a contemporary phenomenon. As a number of contributions to this book show, new technologies have a past; and the challenges and problems they present also have histories. Although the term new media is itself a new one, dating back less than 50 years, the issues it raises are not new, and an understanding of contemporary transformations wrought by mobile phones and the internet benefits from an awareness of earlier 'new technologies', such as the printing press, radio and the telegraph. New media, in one form or another, have been with us for centuries.

One further aspect of the new media field is important to note. We have drawn together a reader in new media theory in the absence of any unified body of new media theory. New media theory is not comparable to topics in fields such as aesthetics, history or law where there is a largely agreed core of foundational writing that has shaped a discipline or subject area. Instead, this book draws on many areas of academic work, including cultural history, cultural studies, economics, law, and politics. From our point of view, this is not an undesirable aspect of the field. New media is an exciting and challenging subject of inquiry partly because it is still emerging and adapting from other domains of knowledge. And precisely because studying new media means working across so many areas, claims to authoritative expertise in this field need to be treated with particular caution.

Our assumption in selecting material for this reader is that a broad understanding of the most interesting, important and challenging arguments in this area involves working across a range of disciplines that go beyond the traditional boundaries of media studies and cultural studies. Fresh thinking about new media involves applying, adapting and sometimes connecting knowledge, arguments and skills from those diverse fields; and that means a great deal of writing in the area is necessarily still provisional and tentative. Much of it is also responsive, not to strictly academic problems, but to the pace of change and its sometimes unpredictable directions in the wider world. The eclectic, reactive and provisional nature of new media theory has shaped this reader in the range of our sources and in the volume's organisation. We have structured the book around key problems, issues and arguments rather than foundational texts.

Contemporary contexts for new media theory

Nonetheless, this somewhat artificial perspective can sometimes highlight the nature of change and assist us to understand some of its substantive qualities. Such is the case, we believe, with the development of what are called new media and the theories that have evolved to explain them. It is this approach we take in this introduction to historically situate the developments in computer technologies that underlie new media and the context of economic, social and cultural transformation in which they operate.

The second half of the 20th century, essentially from the end of World War Two until the millennium's closing years, was a period of immense social, political, economic and technological change. This post-war dynamic of change grew rapidly and spread comprehensively; so much so that it was eventually experienced in every register of life and continues to be today. However, within this five-decade phase we can periodise yet more: the world of the 1950s was very different from that of the 1960s, which was, in its turn, markedly different from the crisis-prone 1970s, which itself became something of a shadow of the enterprising and even more change-filled decades that followed. Stephen Toulmin has argued similarly: 'Experience in the last quarter of a century has convinced people that the twenty-first century will resemble the twentieth even less than the twentieth century has resembled the nineteenth' (1992:2).

If change is always with us what then is so different about this 50-year span? Were not the previous 50 years just as transformative of every aspect of life? Well, yes, but in different ways and at a slower rate. War and political strife and economic depression seared the collective and individual consciousness of those who lived through the first half of the 20th century in ways and with an intensity that those born after 1950 would not experience. These were cataclysms made possible by technological transformation, to be sure, but were of a different order and substance. It was change envisioned through an essentially late-19th-century mode of industrialisation that rested on the central pillars of classic modernity. And change was actualised through the power of coal, oil, electricity and the combustion engine. Modernisation and industrialisation were spread through communication and distribution networks that were of similar vintage: through the spatial sinews of railways and macadam roads, and through the 'old media' of telegraphs, telephones and newspapers. Such transformation was, in its own way, revolutionary and signalled that we were living in a globalised (or globalising) world of interdependencies and contiguous effects that inserted themselves into more and more parts of everyday life.

But this was change with a distinct political and economic context. It was a context that served to shape the technological development of the period and made it very different from that which would dominate the latter half of the century. For example, the late-19th-century imperialist order contributed to an almost perpetual state of political crises. Territorial rivalries between the major nation states would eventually provoke two world wars. In terms of the rate and spread of technological development across the world, these were held back by a shift toward an economic and political autarky that emerged especially after the 1914–18 war. A traditionally 'isolationist' USA and the determination by certain European states to protect their own imperial systems through tariffs and protectionism meant that technological change was incremental as opposed to radical and comprehensive. Indeed, many areas of everyday life and culture could be left almost untouched. It was a kind of 'local–global' form of development where the political 'local' still had preponderance over the natural 'global' tendencies of capitalism.

The end of the hot war of 1945 saw a transition into a Cold War between the new superpowers, the USA and the USSR. Military conflict continued, of course, but these were localised and conducted mainly in undeveloped countries under the auspices of Washington–Moscow strategic rivalry. Enmity was ideological in the first instance: between the worldviews of liberal capitalism and totalitarian communism, but it had immensely important spin-offs. Primary among these, in terms of their effects upon economy and society, was the *rapid developments in computer technology*. The Cold War put the immediate exigencies of large-scale military conflict into deep freeze. This released much of the ideological and inventive energies of politicians and scientists. These were channelled in no small part into research and development in computer science (Edwards, 1996). In the USA, politicians and military analysts thought strategically about how to best confront the challenges of the new times. The perceived level of threat was such that they were prepared to do whatever it took to ensure that they could stay ahead of the USSR in terms of technological and scientific development.

Much government largesse was thus conferred on the best and the brightest minds in the universities and the industrial laboratories. Accordingly, in the 1950s, among the many beneficiaries of this intense focus on technological development were men such as Norbert Wiener and J.C.R. Licklider. These were influential scientists who pushed the boundaries of thinking about what humans in conjunction with computers were capable of.

'Conjunction' – meaning 'the state of being joined' – is a key term that characterises how these leading theorists thought about the science of computing. Weiner, a professor of logic and scientist at the Massachusetts Institute of Technology (MIT) pioneered the school of thought he called 'cybernetics'. This was a theory of both control and communication through flows of information in which 'feedback mechanisms' play an essential part. Fundamental to cybernetics was the claim that it applied equally to humans and machines. Information feedback, Wiener argued, would generate automatic processes between the human and the machine (Wiener, 1950). Automatic doors work on this principle. A person approaching such a door alerts a sensor which 'understands' this human action and triggers a mechanism causing it to open. Human and machine create this 'automatic' action through mutual interface – through feedback. Cybernetics was, then, at its very inception, a mode of thought, a form of 'mediation', which was linked to the military concepts of 'command and control'. Its overall purpose was to discover ways in which environments could be engineered and manipulated through human and computer interaction. Wiener saw computers as machines that mirrored what humans were in their essence. In his 1950 book *The Human Use of Human Being: Cybernetics and Society* he was unequivocal about this link:

> [T]he [human] nervous system corresponds to the theory of those machines that consist in a sequence of switching devices in which the opening of a later switch depends on the action of precise combinations of earlier switches leading into it, which open at the same time. This all-or-none machine is called a *digital machine*. It has great advantages for the most varied problems of communication and control.

Equating humans with computers through a system of cybernetics was a powerful hypothesis in the development of computer networking and the systems of communication that would eventually become the internet, the network society and the new media applications that make it possible. For example, J.C.R. Licklider, an intellectual father of the internet, wrote a highly influential paper in 1960 called 'Man–computer symbiosis'. In the introduction to this he wrote:

> Man–computer symbiosis is an expected development in cooperative interaction between men and electronic computers. It will involve very close coupling between the human and the electronic members of the partnership. [. . .] In the symbiotic partnership, men will set the goals, formulate the hypotheses, determine the criteria and perform the evaluations. Computing machines will do the routinizable work that must be done to prepare the way for insights and decisions in technical and scientific thinking. Preliminary analyses indicate that the symbiotic partnership

will perform intellectual operations much more effectively that man alone can perform them.

In both Wiener and Licklider we see two significant and mutually compatible theses on the nature of computing and humans' relations to it. Wiener argues that to be fully modern is to depend on computing power, and Licklider suggests that computing may also reflect our human essence. These perspectives are at the core of post war computer science; and the work of these towering intellectuals in information systems and cybernetics contain basic assumptions regarding people and computer systems that flow directly into the creation of our networked society. Both theorists view humans as fundamentally *processors of information* in a world whose reality becomes apparent only through the interface with numbers. As Theodor Roszak wrote in his book *The Cult of Information*: 'In perfecting feedback and the means of rapid data manipulation, the science of cybernetics was gaining a deeper understanding of life itself as being, at its core, the processing of information' (p. 39). The central challenge for humans aspiring to full modernity, so the logic runs, is to develop information-processing machines that increase in their sophistication, speed and capacity. The more powerful computers become, the more we realise our inner essence, and the more we are able to understand the world around us.

The computer-automated vistas of Wiener and Licklider were becoming a reality in the 1950s and 1960s. The powerful number-crunching capabilities made possible by developments in computing allowed advances in not only atomic weaponry, but also solved some of the mathematical problems of trajectory plotting that had beset engineers of rocketry. Projectiles could now be launched with unprecedented levels of accuracy and power. In the USSR, similar developments in computer science were taking place. So much so that the Soviets stole the march on the Americans in 1957 by launching into space the *Sputnik* satellite. This was the first time that humans had achieved the 'escape velocity' necessary to reach beyond the Earth's atmosphere – and computing power made it possible. The US response to this was to enter into what would become the 'space race' with a commitment by President Kennedy in 1960 to land a man on the moon by the end of the decade. And so yet more funds poured into the universities and the commercial labs to give the USA and the 'free West' the decisive technological edge through computer-based 'solutions' that were shown to have applications across many industries as well as the military.

Away from the worries and concerns of superpower conflict, this confidence in technologically assisted human capabilities gave something of a fresh impetus to the project of modernity. After the destruction of two global wars and the chaos of economic depression, the post-war period opened up into what David Harvey (1989) called the phase of 'high modernity' – at least in the liberal–capitalist west. In the 1960s the rate of innovation in science and technology grew rapidly and the complexity and buoyancy of the globalising economy reflected this. Full employment became the norm in the developed economies of the west, and the growing affluence of society boosted yet further the demand for technologically based solutions. In communications, jet travel became increasingly commonplace, as did use of the telephone for local, national and international networking. A global media was emerging through the mass diffusion of television and transistor radios, allowing people to 'experience' live events such as soccer world cups or the Olympics; or the emergent mediascape brought political/military events such as the Vietnam War much closer to our everyday consciousness. Indeed, much of the planet watched part of this global mediascape as President Kennedy's pledge was kept when astronaut Neil Armstrong stepped onto the Moon in July 1969.

This 'high modernity' was organised and articulated through what might be equally termed a 'high' Fordism. In 1914 in the USA Henry Ford had pioneered his eponymous system of automated production lines using low-skilled labour to mass manufacture the Model T car. His techniques were revolutionary and soon multiplied far beyond the production of cars. Mass production was predicated on mass consumption, which was in turn reliant on mass communication. The technical rationality of micro-planned and micro-managed Fordist principles spread across the emerging 'mass society' to evolve into what Harvey termed 'a whole way of life' (1989:135). As the method grew and became more dominant in the 1950s and 1960s, Fordism evolved into a tightly macro-managed *economic system* through the top-level cooperation between business, organised labour and corporate capitalism. The effect of this in culture, in economy, and in society was to regulate and make fairly predictable the pace of change and the trajectory of change. And so British Prime Minister Harold Wilson's characterisation of the 1960s as being shaped by the 'white heat of the technological revolution' notwithstanding, the reality was one of control and of management. Computer systems experts of the time knew, for example, that the automation of much more of industry would enable it to be more efficient and productive. However, in the context of full employment and high profits, the economic impetus to take such a step (which would be politically sensitive and involve the destruction of many jobs) was simply not strong enough. The concept of the *national economy* was still operating; and the political will to subsidise industries and businesses in the national interest was still dominant. Local–global, then, was still the dominant metaphor to describe the phase of 'high modernity' and 'high Fordism'.

This began to change in the 1970s. High Fordism and the high modernity it helped produce as a 'whole way of life' full of certainties in employment, in modes of consumption and so on, had been maturing and was growing rigid and sclerotic (Kolko, 1988). The system, as it grew in scope and complexity, developed its own internal contradictions. The need for capitalism to 'naturally' expand spatially, and accelerate temporally, was 'artificially' constrained by nation state politics. In Europe and North America, this led directly to pressures of competition from the emerging economies of East Asia and Japan, which were aggressively export oriented. Moreover, falling productivity and falling profits increased the scale of economic crises in the west. These were exacerbated by growing inflationary pressures and, in 1973, the 'oil shock' when the Arab members of OPEC placed an embargo against the USA in particular, which sent world oil prices to unprecedented levels.

The economic and social system of Fordism was in trouble by the mid-1970s. Indeed it was beginning to unravel though growing unemployment, growing uncertainty about the future, and a growing call for wide-ranging 'solutions' from representatives of big business and economic radicals in governments. Ideologues with 'solutions' had, in fact, been growing in influence over the previous decade. These were the 'neoliberals' who argued, after Adam Smith the 18th-century political economist, that markets must be free from 'rigidities' such as tariffs and subsidies. A central demand to be heard from business at the time was that it should be business alone that should decide how and where capital is invested, free from either the sectional interests of organised labour or the narrow political interests of government. In the climate of deep crises, neoliberalism swept like a gale through the 'whole way of life' that had been the system of post-war social, political and economic consensus. Led by political ideologues such as Margaret Thatcher and Ronald Reagan, government began to abnegate its consensus-building role between business and labour, as well as its role as protector and nurturer of the national economy. Economics was to take the leading role and neoliberals identified major increases in productivity and efficiency, across the whole of the economy, as the prime factors in the restructuring of capitalism. The application of computer-based information and communication technologies (ICTs) had long been developing in the commercial sector as spin-offs from military R&D. However during the 1950s, as we saw, the take-up was slow and accumulative because of the political considerations of the consensus approach. By the early 1980s, however, ICTs were seen, as Neil Postman put it, as a 'solution in search of a problem' (1993:17). Automation was thus to be the panacea for the issues of low productivity and efficiency in just about every industry. It was at this time that the mutually reinforcing dynamics of neoliberal globalisation and the revolution in ICTs really got under way.

The 1980s saw a phase of the entrenchment of neoliberal ideas, especially in the polities and economies of the Anglo-American countries. This had a direct flow-on effect into less developed countries through multilateral organisations such as the World Bank and the International Monetary Fund. The restructuring of the world's economies to make them more 'flexible' and productive and efficient was made possible only through the unrestrained application of ICTs across industries and across entire economies. The flow-on to culture and society of rapid computerisation was swift. In something of a homage to Wiener and Licklider's dreams of human–computer 'symbiosis', the middle of the 1980s saw the beginnings of the quaintly termed 'personal computer' (PC) revolution at home and at the workplace. Growing and increasingly flexible 'post-Fordist' economies were now changing rapidly through the introduction of new media technologies that seem to be getting faster and more powerful by the month. Fuelled by the growth of the NSDAQ bubble, the 1990s saw the popularisation of the internet, the growth to behemoth status of corporations such as Microsoft, Intel and Apple, and the realisation of the global 'information economy'. And into our collective consciousness would be inserted, in the form of a verb, the spirit of the information age through neologisms such as Ebay, Amazon, Yahoo! and Google.

It was during this frenetic activity that Manuel Castells observed that: 'The information technology revolution, and the restructuring of capitalism, has induced a new form of society, the network society' (1996:xv). New media technologies were and are central to this process. These are the technologies of 'mediation'; connectable technologies that make networking and the network society possible. Castells further describes the social and economic effects of networks:

Networks are open structures, able to expand without limits, integrating new nodes as long as they are able to communicate within the network, namely as long as they share the same communication codes [. . .] Networks are appropriate instruments for a capitalist economy based on innovation, globalization, and decentralised concentration; for work, workers, and firms based upon flexibility, and adaptability; for a culture of endless deconstruction and reconstruction; for a polity geared towards the instant processing of new values and public moods; and for a social organization aimed at the suppression of space and the annihilation of time.

(1996:470–471)

The notion of what Castells calls 'polity geared toward the instant processing of new values and public moods' is for us a fascinating consideration. How do we make sense of constant, rapid, and often comprehensive new media-driven change? It is a concern that was similarly expressed more recently by Thomas de Zengotita in his book, *Mediated*. In it he claims that: 'The real world is reconstituting itself on a plane that transcends ancient solidarities of nature and custom, craft and industry. The whole process has been accelerated since the invention of modern communication technologies (telegraph, photograph, telephone), and it crossed a qualitative threshold in the past couple of decades, with the rise of new media' (2005:17–18).

The works selected for this reader go to the heart of these qualitative changes – if that, indeed, is what they are. The subtitle of de Zengotita's book is 'how the media shape your world'. Theorising effects of 'new media' is not the same as theorising the effects of a particular media technology such as a DVD player or mobile phone. 'New media' in the context of this book are plural and encompassing in their scope. It takes in a *media or mediated environment* in which any application or process that is networkable or digitisable has its place. This can range from the latest and fastest wireless laptop and digital camera, to the act of shopping with a plastic card – and even this book, which may be bought online, or easily scanned or converted to PDF and made available online. New media technologies are above all connectable, compatible with others, creating in their plurality a highly mediated context which connects to numberless other mediated contexts that users create in their day-to-day life.

It is this evanescent media landscape that the authors in this collection attempt to describe and explain. The extracts give the taste of larger works that look at the nature of technological change The challenge for us as editors was to try to capture, as much as is possible, the kind of role new media has played in the undoubted change that has taken place over the last couple of decades. This has meant taking a range of views on new media theory that do not fall into a 'gee whiz' technophilia or, at the other pole, a sombre technophobia that sees only doom and gloom. Many perspectives are unavoidably situated at some point along this continuum, although they never fall into egregious or unconsidered writing that would place them at either extreme. Importantly, we have chosen to compile this collection in a more subtle and we think more intellectually fruitful way. Several of the works do not, in fact, deal with new media at all, but are perspectives on our relationship (cultural, economic, politic and psychological) with technology. What these do is to provoke other modes of thought that allow us consider, say, the introduction of the telegraph in Canada in the 19th century, as emy Stein does in Part 5, and compare this with the writings – or our experience – of a hyper-mediated world. We can then ask: is there really any qualitative difference? If so, what, and if not, why not? We do not provide 'answers' to this or other questions; only pathways to more questions.

Contents of this reader

The book is organised into five parts, which cover the broad themes we see as being emblematic of the main debates today. We outline the content here in general terms as each part is prefaced by a short discussion on its detail.

Part 1 is called 'Media transitions' and introduces some key ideas about the nature of new media, both in the past and present. Here we try to clarify what is distinctive about contemporary networked, digital communication technologies, and also what we can learn from earlier transformations. We see some of the claims made for new media, survey the extraordinary range of economic, social and political effects attributed to new media, and provide some cultural and historical contexts for understanding these.

Part 2, 'Governing new media', takes up questions, which although flowing directly from some of the issues raised already, are in themselves unique to our era. The acceleration of change has legislators the world over constantly playing catch-up with the social and economic effects that new media are having over the realm of media itself. New ways of delivering 'old' and once relatively stable media such as books, newspapers or television; as well as new ways of organising the content and distribution of these on a global scale is transforming what it means to be a media consumer. 'Content' is more than this or that soap opera, or news programme or sports coverage. To be sure, networking and the imperatives of economic 'efficiency' has the capability to merge it all into a single package, a single product. But the fact that there *is* an important difference underlies the challenges to effectively and democratically govern-ing a new media-generated global mediascape. Content is information, the stuff of the network society, and it is information which shapes our view of the world. The questions, in this context, inescapably become political. Who controls the new media landscape? In what ways are our views of the world being shaped? Who decides what is important in our media lives – the market, the technology, or people themselves through a better informed relationship with a vibrant and diverse media made possible by innovation in media technology?

In Part 3, 'Properties and commons', the central debates about the changing nature of ownership in the network society are introduced. Arguments around the claims and scope of intellectual property have a long history, but have sharpened in the new media environment. The French philosopher Henri Lefebvre argued in his 1991 book *The Production of Space* that space is socially produced. The precise form and function this takes stems from the 'production and reproduction' characteristics of 'each social formation'. In other words, it tends to reflect the power relations of a given society. In the network society a cyberspace is being created by not only commercially oriented applications and processes, but also by people as part of a civil society, creating a 'digital commons' that, supposedly, is free from commercial concerns. The tensions between these concepts of digital space – who owns it, who creates it and for whose benefit – are set to create a central battleground in the courts and in the streets in the early decades of the 21st century.

The overtly political battles of power, control and ownership that the network society has brought into the digital age are discussed in Part 4, 'Politics of new media technologies'. Control and the associated problems of *governmentality*, in the sense that Michel Foucault (1978) used the term as a way of locating and analysing power at the level of the individual, the institution such as the family, workplace and so on – right up to the level of the network society itself – provide a context with which these extracts may be read. The restructuring of society that new media technologies has made possible has reconfigured much of the power geometry that characterised the post-war age. Relatively settled and predictable patterns of power have eroded, throwing open to question the nature of social power and the effectiveness of institutional democratic politics in the network society. What is or should be the role of government in a networked society that is practically transnational? New sources of power are beginning to find a political voice within cyberspace. How do we relate to these shifting forms of power and what does the growing importance of some of them and a relative diminution of others portend for democratic practices in the 21st century?

Finally, new media technologies have compressed time and space to an extent that is claimed by some to be historically unprecedented. The concluding part, 'Time and space in the age of information', looks at what this means in theory and in practice through a range of perspectives. Here we revisit the question of what, if anything, makes digital networks different from, say, the analogue communication networks based on telegraph and telephone that began to emerge as long ago as the late 19th century? The part offers a comparative view of how communications technologies change our relationships with time and space, in previous epochs and in our own, encouraging the reader to think about these relatively neglected social categories.

This reader is not a comprehensive account of the current state of opinion about new media technologies, or the conceptual frameworks that seek to explain them. What we have aimed for is a range of perspectives that are representative, not only of some of the most perceptive thinking on new media technologies, but also of the tremendous *range* of effects that they are having in every realm of life. The extracts themselves are accessible and arranged in such a way as to encourage critical examination and debate around the issues in question. In this way they function as introductions to larger arguments.

References

Castells, M. (1996) *The Rise of the Network Society*, 2nd edn, Cambridge, MA: Blackwell.

Edwards, P.N. (1996) *The Closed World: Computers and the Politics of Discourse in Cold War America*, Cambridge, MA: MIT Press.

Foucault, M. (1978) 'Governmentality', trans. Rosi Braidotti and revised by Colin Gordon, in Graham Burchell, Colin Gordon and Peter Miller (eds) (1991) *The Foucault Effect: Studies in Governmentality*, pp. 87–104, Chicago, IL: University of Chicago Press.

Harvey, D. (1989) *The Condition of Postmodernity*, Oxford: Blackwell.

Kolko, J. (1988) *Restructuring the World Economy*, New York: Pantheon.

Lefebvre, H. (1991) *The Production of Space*, Cambridge, MA: Blackwell.

Licklider, J.C.R. (1960) 'Man–computer symbiosis', *IRE Transactions on Human Factors in Electronics*, HFE-1, March, pp. 4–11.

Postman, N. (1993) *Technopoly*, New York: Vintage.

Roszak, T. (1994) *The Cult of Information: A Neo-Luddite Treatise on High-Tech, Artificial Intelligence, and the True Art of Thinking*, 2nd edn, Berkeley, CA: University of California Press.

Toulmin, S. (1992) *Cosmopolis: The Hidden Agenda of Modernity*, Chicago, IL: University of Chicago Press.

Wiener, N. (1950) *The Human Use of Human Beings: Cybernetics and Society*, Boston, MA: Houghton Mifflin.

Zengotita, T. de (2005) *Mediated: How the Media Shape Your World*, London: Bloomsbury.

Publisher's acknowledgements

The authors and publisher wish to thank the following for permission to use copyright material:

Manovich, L (2001) 'What is New Media?' in *The Language of New Media*, Cambridge, Massachusetts: MIT Press

Cook, S as originally published in Stefik, M (1997) 'Technological revolutions and the Gutenberg myth' in *Internet Dreams: Archetypes, Myths and Metaphors*, Cambridge, Massachusetts: MIT Press

Pool, Ithiel de Sola "A Shadow of Darkness" reprinted by permission of the publisher from TECHNOLOGIES OF FREEDOM: ON FREE SPEECH AN ELECTRONIC AGE by Ithiel de Sola Pool, pp. 1–10, Cambridge, Mass.: Harvard University Press, Copyright © 1982 by the President and Fellows of Harvard College

Nye, D. E (1996) 'The Consumer's sublime' in *American Technological Sublime*, Cambridge, Massachusetts: MIT Press

Kelly, K 'The Computational Metaphor' in *Whole Earth*, Winter 1998

Marien, M (1996) in 'New Communications Technology: a survey of impacts and issues' in *Telecommunications Policy*, Vol. 20, No 5, pp 375–387

Saunders, D; Hunter, I. M and Williamson, D (1992) 'Historicising obscenity law' in *On Pornography: Literature, Obscenity and Law*, London: Macmillan

Owen, B. M "The Tragedy of Broadcast Regulation" reprinted by permission of the publisher from INTERNET CHALLENGE TO TELEVISION by Bruce M. Owen, pp. 79–89, Cambridge, Mass.: Harvard University Press, Copyright © 1999 by the President and Fellows of Harvard College

Graham, A (1998) 'Broadcasting policy in the digital age' in Firestone, C. M and Korzick Garner, A (eds) *Digital Broadcasting and the Public Interest*, Washington, DC: Aspen Institute

Robins, K and Webster, F (1998) 'The cybernetic imagination of capitalism' in Mosoko, V and Wasko, J (eds) *The Political Economy of Information*, Madison, WI: The University of Wisconsin Press

McChesney, R. W (2001) 'Policing the thinkable', Opendemocracy.net

Compaine, B (2001) 'The myths of encroaching global media ownership', Opendemocracy.net

Patterson, L. R (1968) 'Copyright in historical perspective' in *Copyright in Historical Perspective*, Nashville, TN: Vanderbilt University Press

Boyle, J (1996) 'Intellectual property and the liberal state' in *Shamans Software and Spleens: Law and the Construction of the Information Society*, Cambridge, Massachusetts: Harvard University Press

Litman, J (2001) 'Choosing metaphors' in *Digital Copyright: Protecting Intellectual Property on the Internet*, Amherst, New York: Prometheus Books

Lessig, L (2000) 'The promise for intellectual property in cyberspace' in *Code and Other Laws if Cyberspace*, New York: Basic Books

Stallman, R (2002) 'Why software should not have owners' in *Free Software: Free Society*, Boston, Massachusetts: Free Software Foundation

Barry, A (2001) 'On Interactivity' in *Political Machines: Governing a technological Society*, London: Athlone Press

Barber, B. R (2000) 'Pangloss, Pandora or Jefferson? Three Scenarios for the Future of Technology and Democracy' in *A Passion for Democracy: American Essays*, Princeton University Press, pp. 245 – 257

Sunstein, C (2001) 'Citizens' in *Republic.com*, Princeton, New Jersey: Princeton University Press

Wark, M (2004) 'Abstraction/class' in *A Hacker Manifesto*, Cambridge, MA: Harvard University Press

Carey, J (1989) 'Technology and Ideology: the case of the telegraph' in *Communication as Culture*, London: Routledge

Stein, J (1999) 'Reflections on time, time-space compression and technology in the nineteenth century' in Craig, M, Crang, P and May, j (eds) *Virtual Geographies: Bodies, Space and Relations*, New York: Routledge

Green, N (2002) 'On the move: technology, mobility and the mediation of social time and space' in *The Information Society*, 18(4(, pp 281–292

Lee, H and Liebenau, J (2001) 'Time and the internet' in *Time and Society*, 9(1), pp 48–55

Eriksen, T. H (2001) 'Speed is contagious' in *Tyranny of the Moment: Fast and Slow Time in the Age of the Information*, London: Pluto Press

PART 1
Media transitions

An underlying theme of this volume on new media theory is to examine the idea that digital technologies have, over the past quarter-century or so, transformed our world. Undoubtedly, things have changed a lot. If one thinks about what Lev Manovich terms the 'language of new media', that is to say, the words, metaphors and narratives we use routinely to describe our informationalised society, what stands out is a *language* of change that reflects a real-world *process* of change. What is made implicit or explicit in much of this discourse is not change in the ordinary sense of the word, but a rapid and far reaching transformation. The materials collected in this part deal with the nature of this transformation – its scope, its politics, its aesthetic basis, and its multifarious consequences.

We painted a broadbrush picture of these changes in the *Introduction*. But we can also sharpen the focus and go down to the level of the individual and to his or her experiences, to find the same seemingly constant and comprehensive dynamics of change. One only needs to think of the sense impressions gained by simply existing in the developed or developing world, even over the last decade. For example, prior to, say, 1995, the internet was not widely available, and mobile phones were still fairly exotic devices used primarily by businessmen and women and could still make heads turn in the street. Personal computers (PCs) were widely distributed in the workplace, but very much less so in the home. Moreover, they were big and noisy, and not routinely connected to global networks but to a big central inhouse computer, or they were simply standalones. They ran on an MS-DOS operating system with a 386 CPU and had hardly any memory. 'Floppy disks' – an already neglected word as well as technology – were the media they used. Blackberrys, iPods, Bluetooth-enabled wireless laptops, cameraphones, plasma screens, Google, broadband and most, if not all, of what you now see cramming your high street electronics store did not exist. A prototype of eBay, and a clunky PlayStation 1 had only just been launched. We nonetheless thought this was cutting-edge stuff, and felt on the cusp of a surging technological wave.

We still do today. Tutored as well as seduced by industry advertising, the lure of new media for consumers and for business as 'solutions' for almost anything, is more powerful than ever. What this momentum means is that new media-driven change is set only to get faster and more inclusive. That we are living through a phase of technological, economic and cultural change is now undeniable, but what kind of change is it, and is it as widespread and systematic as many theorists argue? As Manovich observes: 'New media may look like media, but this is only the surface' (2002:47). For theorists of new media who argue in such terms, what we are experiencing is something more funda-mental – a Kuhnian 'paradigm shift' (1962/1996). Deep-level computability transforms how we represent life through the ubiquity of mutable digital imagery; and transforms life through the industries, cultures, and institutions that produce and sustain our sense of being in the world.

We have titled this opening part 'Media transitions'. The ideas and arguments contained in it function within the open boundaries of the notion of 'transition', of moving from one paradigm to another, of moving from a world where computers and computer-based media were peripheral, to one where they are central. As with every chapter in this volume, the perspectives are not homologous. New media technologies are seen to represent both threat and opportunity, liberation or trap – or possibly some-thing more nebulous and subtle in between. An extract from Lev Manovich's book *The Language of New Media* opens the collection, and makes the bold argument that what we are experiencing today is 'a [media] revolution [that is] . . . more profound than the previous ones, and we are just beginning to register its initial effects'. Essentially, for Manovich, ubiquitous computing functions as a 'manipulator' and 'weaver' of all cultural forms into 'computer-mediated forms of production, distribution and communication'. In other words, 'new media', in the wide definition Manovich gives the term, is truly a paradigm shift in that it represents a world-historically important convergence of computation and media. S.D. Noam Cook's essay 'Technological revolutions and the Gutenberg Myth' indirectly takes up Manovich's claims for 'revolution' by critically appraising the more widely accepted notion of a revolution that occurred with the invention of Gutenberg's movable-type printing press in the middle of the 15th century. Explaining some of the 'myths' and the realities of the Gutenberg revolution, Cook argues that we are then in a better position to more accurately assess the nature of technological development through digital new media today.

Ithiel de Sola Pool's extract from his *Technologies of Freedom* was originally written in 1983 and represents an early attempt to understand and predict the effects of the 'changed technological base' upon US First Amendment provisions for free speech in the media. Foreshadowing many of the libertarian themes of the 1990s, de Sola Pool sees the 'convergence of delivery mechanisms' for media as both a threat to American traditions of free speech and the opportunity to revitalise it. The author fears that the heavy regulation of the big media monopolies that was a feature of the early years of broadcasting will be grafted onto the new media environment. This is ironic, he argues, because the new environment is oriented towards fragmentation and decentralisation – in other words back to the original 18th-century media environment in which the First Amendment protecting freedoms of speech and the press was crafted.

David E. Nye also provides a thought-provoking essay which discusses our aesthetic and psychological relationship with technology. Its focus is the USA, but it holds relevance, although to a possibly lesser degree, to most developed economies and societies. We tend to stand in awe of technological development, argues Nye. This produces a kind of passivity in respect of the trajectory of technological development (where it is taking us); and an addiction to the constructed and essentially shallow world it represents for us. The simulated (and sublime) world of Las Vegas is examined as a polar extreme of this propensity. As with Cook's essay, this thesis on the psychology of our relationship with technology is able to illuminate the ways in which new media today is revered by theorists and users alike. We reprint in full a short but insightful article by Kevin Kelly which looks at the 'subversive trend' of using the metaphor of the computer or computer logic to describe almost everything. This is the effect, possibly, of the saturation of society by the computer. However, the growth of the computational metaphor in our language, Kelly argues, runs the risk of becoming a self-fulfilling logic, where the more we see the world through the lens of the computational metaphor, then the more we are likely to act on in it this way – to the detriment of other ways.

The final extract is a valuable survey of the numerous and wide-ranging issues that new media technology has raised since the beginnings of the ICT revolution. Written by Michael Marien in 1996 for the journal *Telecommunications Policy*, its incisive discussion of the new media 'transition' and extensive bibliography on theory and practice of information technologies, remains a valuable resource for students wishing to explore this formative phase of the age of information.

References

Kuhn, T. (1962/1996) *The Structure of Scientific Revolutions*, Chicago, IL: University of Chicago Press.

Manovich, L. (2002) *The Language of New Media*, Cambridge, MA: MIT Press.

1.1

What is new media?,
by Lev Manovich

What is new media? We may begin answering this question by listing the categories commonly discussed under this topic in the popular press: the Internet, Web sites, computer multimedia, computer games, CD-ROMs and DVD, virtual reality. Is this all there is to new media? What about television programs shot on digital video and edited on computer workstations? Or feature films that use 3-D animation and digital compositing? Shall we also count these as new media? What about images and text-image compositions – photographs, illustrations, layouts, ads – created on computers and then printed on paper? Where shall we stop?

As can be seen from these examples, the popular understanding of new media identifies it with the use of a computer for distribution and exhibition rather than production. Accordingly, texts distributed on a computer (Web sites and electronic books) are considered to be new media, whereas texts distributed on paper are not. Similarly, photographs that are put on a CD-ROM and require a computer to be viewed are considered new media; the same photographs printed in a book are not.

Shall we accept this definition? If we want to understand the effects of computerization on culture as a whole, I think it is too limiting. There is no reason to privilege the computer as a machine for the exhibition and distribution of media over the computer as a tool for media production or as a media storage device. All have the same potential to change existing cultural languages. And all have the same potential to leave culture as it is.

The last scenario is unlikely, however. What is more likely is that just as the printing press in the fourteenth century and photography in the nineteenth century had a revolutionary impact on the development of modern society and culture, today we are in the middle of a new media revolution – the shift of all culture to computer-mediated forms of production, distribution, and communication. This new revolution is arguably more profound than the previous ones, and we are just beginning to register its initial effects. Indeed, the introduction of the printing press affected only one stage of cultural communication – the distribution of media. Similarly, the introduction of photography affected only one type of cultural communication – still images. In contrast, the computer media revolution affects all stages of communication, including acquisition, manipulation, storage, and distribution; it also affects all types of media – texts, still images, moving images, sound, and spatial constructions.

How shall we begin to map out the effects of this fundamental shift? What are the ways in which the use of computers to record, store, create, and distribute media makes it "new"?

In the section "Media and Computation," I show that new media represents a convergence of two separate historical trajectories: computing and media technologies. Both begin in the 1830s with Babbage's Analytical Engine and Daguerre's daguerreotype. Eventually, in the middle of the twentieth century, a modern digital computer is developed to perform calculations on numerical data more efficiently; it takes over from numerous mechanical tabulators and calculators widely employed by companies and governments since the turn of the century. In a parallel movement, we witness the rise of modern media technologies that allow the storage of images, image sequences, sounds, and text using different material forms – photographic plates, film stocks, gramophone records, etc. The synthesis of these two histories? The translation of all existing media into numerical data accessible through computers. The result is new media – graphics, moving images, sounds, shapes, spaces, and texts that have become computable; that is, they comprise simply another set of computer data. In "Principles of New Media," I look at the key consequences of this new status of media. Rather than focusing on familiar categories such as interactivity or hypermedia, I suggest a different list. This list reduces all principles of new media to five – numerical representation, modularity, automation, variability, and cultural transcoding. In the last section, "What New Media Is Not," I address other principles that are often attributed to new media. I show that these principles can already be found at work in older cultural forms and media technologies such as cinema, and therefore in and of themselves are in sufficient to distinguish new media from old.

How media became new

On August 19, 1839, the Palace of the Institute in Paris was filled with curious Parisians who had come to hear the formal description of the new reproduction process invented by Louis Daguerre. Daguerre, already well known for his Diorama, called the new process *daguerreotype*. According to a contemporary, "a few days later, opticians' shops were crowded with amateurs panting for daguerreotype apparatus, and everywhere cameras were trained on buildings. Everyone wanted to record the view from his window, and he was lucky who at first trial got a silhouette of roof tops against the sky."[1] The media frenzy had begun. Within five months more than thirty different descriptions of the technique had been published around the world – Barcelona, Edinburgh, Naples, Philadelphia, St. Petersburg, Stockholm. At first, daguerreotypes of architecture and landscapes dominated the public's imagination; two years later, after various technical improvements to the process had been made, portrait galleries had opened everywhere – and everyone rushed to have her picture taken by the new media machine.[2]

In 1833 Charles Babbage began designing a device he called "the Analytical Engine." The Engine contained most of the key features of the modern digital computer. Punch cards were used to enter both data and instructions. This information was stored in the Engine's memory. A processing unit, which Babbage referred to as a "mill," performed operations on the data and wrote the results to memory; final results were to be printed out on a printer. The Engine was designed to be capable of doing any mathematical operation; not only would it follow the program fed into it by cards, but it would also decide which instructions to execute next, based on intermediate results. However, in contrast to the daguerreotype, not a single copy of the Engine was completed. While the invention of the daguerreotype, a modern media tool for the reproduction of reality, impacted society immediately, the impact of the computer was yet to be seen.

Interestingly, Babbage borrowed the idea of using punch cards to store information from an earlier programmed machine. Around 1800, J. M. Jacquard invented a loom that was automatically controlled by punched paper cards. The loom was used to weave intricate figurative images, including Jacquard's portrait. This specialized graphics computer, so to speak, inspired Babbage in his work on the Analytical Engine, a general computer for numerical calculations. As Ada Augusta, Babbage's supporter and the first computer programmer, put it, "The Analytical Engine weaves algebraical patterns just as the Jacquard loom weaves flowers and leaves."[3] Thus a programmed machine was already synthesizing images even before it was put to processing numbers. The connection between the Jacquard loom and the Analytical Engine is not something historians of computers make much of, since for them computer image synthesis represents just one application of the modern digital computer among thousands of others, but for a historian of new media, it is full of significance.

We should not be surprised that both trajectories – the development of modern media and the development of computers – begin around the same time. Both media machines and computing machines were absolutely necessary for the functioning of modern mass societies. The ability to disseminate the same texts, images, and sounds to millions of citizens – thus assuring the same ideological beliefs – was as essential as the ability to keep track of their birth records, employment records, medical records, and police records. Photography, film, the offset printing press, radio, and television made the former possible while computers made possible the latter. Mass media and data processing are complementary technologies; they appear together and develop side by side, making modern mass society possible.

For a long time the two trajectories ran in parallel without ever crossing paths. Throughout the nineteenth and the early twentieth centuries, numerous mechanical and electrical tabulators and calculators were developed; they gradually became faster and their use more widespread. In a parallel movement, we witness the rise of modern media that allow the storage of images, image sequences, sounds, and texts in different material forms – photographic plates, film stock, gramophone records, etc.

Let us continue tracing this joint history. In the 1890s modern media took another step forward as still photographs were put in motion. In January 1893, the first movie studio – Edison's "Black Maria" – started producing twenty-second shorts that were shown in special Kinetoscope parlors. Two years later the Lumière brothers showed their new Cinématographie camera/projection hybrid, first to a scientific audience and later, in December 1895, to the paying public. Within a year, audiences in Johannesburg, Bombay, Rio de Janeiro, Melbourne, Mexico City, and Osaka were subjected to the new media machine, and they found it irresistible.[4] Gradually scenes grew longer, the staging of reality before the camera and the subsequent editing of samples became more intricate, and copies multiplied. In Chicago and Calcutta, London and St. Petersburg, Tokyo and Berlin, and thousands of smaller places, film images would soothe movie audiences, who were facing an increasingly dense information environment outside the theater, an environment that no longer could be adequately handled by their own sampling and data processing systems (i.e., their brains). Periodic trips into the dark relaxation chambers of movie theaters became a routine survival technique for the subjects of modern society.

The 1890s was the crucial decade not only for the development of media, but also for computing. If individual brains were overwhelmed by the amount of information they had to process, the same was true of corporations and of governments. In 1887, the U.S. Census Bureau was still interpreting figures from the 1880 census. For the 1890 census, the Census Bureau adopted electric tabulating machines designed by Herman Hollerith. The data collected on every person was punched into cards; 46,804 enumerators completed forms for a total population of 62,979,766. The Hollerith tabulator opened the door for the adoption of calculating machines by business; during the next decade electric tabulators became standard equipment in insurance companies, public utility companies, railroad offices, and accounting departments. In 1911, Hollerith's Tabulating Machine Company was merged with three other companies to form the Computing-Tabulating-Recording Company; in 1914, Thomas J. Watson was chosen as its head. Ten years later its business tripled, and Watson renamed the company the "International Business Machines Corporation," or IBM.[5]

Moving into the twentieth century, the key year for the history of media and computing is 1936. British mathematician Alan Turing wrote a seminal paper entitled "On Computable Numbers." In it he provided a theoretical description of a general-purpose computer later named after its inventor: "the Universal Turing Machine." Even though it was capable of only four operations, the machine could perform any calculation that could be done by a human and could also imitate any other computing machine. The machine operated by reading and writing numbers on an endless tape. At every step the tape would be advanced to retrieve the next command, read the data, or write the result. Its diagram looks suspiciously like a film projector. Is this a coincidence?

If we believe the word *cinematograph*, which means "writing movement," the essence of cinema is recording and storing visible data in a material form. A film camera records data on film; a film projector reads it off. This cinematic apparatus is similar to a computer in one key respect: A computer's program and data also have to be stored in some medium. This is why the Universal Turing Machine looks like a film projector. It is a kind of film camera and film projector at once, reading instructions and data stored on endless tape and writing them in other locations on this tape. In fact, the development of a suitable storage medium and a method for coding data represent important parts of the prehistory of both cinema and the computer. As we know, the inventors of cinema eventually settled on using discrete images recorded on a strip of celluloid; the inventors of the computer – which needed much greater speed of access as well as the ability to quickly read and write data – eventually decided to store it electronically in a binary code.

The histories of media and computing became further entwined when German engineer Konrad Zuse began building a computer in the living room of his parents' apartment in Berlin – the same year that Turing wrote his seminal paper. Zuse's computer was the first working digital computer. One of his innovations was using punched tape to control computer programs. The tape Zuse used was actually discarded 35 mm movie film.[6]

One of the surviving pieces of this film shows binary code punched over the original frames of an interior shot. A typical movie scene   two people in a room involved in some action – becomes a support for a set of computer commands. Whatever meaning and emotion was contained in this movie scene has been wiped out by its new function as data carrier. The pretense of modern media to create simulations of sensible reality is similarly canceled; media are reduced to their original condition as information carrier, nothing less, nothing more. In a technological remake of the Oedipal complex, a son murders his father. The iconic code of cinema is discarded in favor of the more efficient binary one. Cinema becomes a slave to the computer.

But this is not yet the end of the story. Our story has a new twist – a happy one. Zuse's film, with its strange superimposition of binary over iconic code, anticipates the convergence that will follow half a century later. The two separate historical trajectories finally meet. Media and computer – Daguerre's daguerreotype and Babbage's Analytical Engine, the Lumière Cinématographie and Hollerith's tabulator – merge into one. All existing media are translated into numerical data accessible for the computer. The result: graphics, moving images, sounds, shapes, spaces, and texts become computable, that is, simply sets of computer data. In short, media become new media.

This meeting changes the identity of both media and the computer itself. No longer just a calculator, control mechanism, or communication device, the computer becomes a media processor. Before, the computer could read a row of numbers, outputting a statistical result or a gun trajectory. Now it can read pixel values, blurring the image, adjusting its contrast, or checking whether it contains an outline of an object. Building on these lower-level operations, it can also perform more ambitious ones – searching image databases for images similar in composition or content to an input image, detecting shot changes in a movie, or synthesizing the movie shot itself, complete with setting and actors. In a historical loop, the computer has returned to its origins. No longer just an Analytical Engine, suitable only for crunching numbers, it has become Jacquard's loom – a media synthesizer and manipulator.

Principles of new media

The identity of media has changed even more dramatically than that of the computer. Below I summarize some of the key differences between old and new media. In compiling this list of differences, I tried to arrange them in a logical order. That is, the the last three principles are dependent on the first two. This is not dissimilar to axiomatic logic, in which certain axioms are taken as starting points and further theorems are proved on their basis.

Not every new media object obeys these principles. They should be considered not as absolute laws but rather as general tendencies of a culture undergoing computerization. As computerization affects deeper and deeper layers of culture, these tendencies will increasingly manifest themselves.

1 Numerical representation

All new media objects, whether created from scratch on computers or converted from analog media sources, are composed of digital code; they are numerical representations. This fact has two key consequences:

1   A new media object can be described formally (mathematically). For instance, an image or a shape can be described using a mathematical function.

2   A new media object is subject to algorithmic manipulation. For instance, by applying appropriate algorithms, we can automatically remove "noise" from a photograph, improve its contrast, locate the edges of the shapes, or change its proportions. In short, *media becomes programmable*.

Notes

1   Quoted in Beaumont Newhall, *The History of Photography from 1839 to the Present Day*, 4th ed. (New York: Museum of Modern Art, 1964), 18.
2   Newhall, *The History of Photography*, 17–22.
3   Charles Eames, *A Computer Perspective: Background to the Computer Age* (Cambridge, Mass: Harvard University Press, 1990), 18.
4   David Bordwell and Kristin Thompson, *Film Art: An Introduction*, 5th ed. (New York: McGraw-Hill), 15.
5   Eames, *A Computer Perspective*, 22–27, 46–51, 90–91.
6   Ibid., 120.

1.2

Technological revolutions and the Gutenberg Myth,
by S.D. Noam Cook

The dream of a digital network linking people and information around the globe is commonly considered *the* technological revolution of the 1990s, with the shape of the twenty-first century issuing from it. The Internet, the World Wide Web, and their next-generation cousins have captured the imagination of the public and of specialists in numerous fields. What is imagined is nothing short of revolutionary changes in our lives, our society and our world. Ultimately, we are told, the scale of these changes will be even greater than those of the Gutenberg revolution – the changes commonly associated with invention of movable type printing in fifteenth-century Europe.

The new technologies of our time are indeed exciting and powerful. Much good (or much evil) could be done with them. But the claim that we are seeing a new Gutenberg revolution is a dangerous one. It is dangerous because the picture of the Gutenberg revolution found in histories, encyclopedias, and the popular media is historically inaccurate and conceptually misleading. It would have us believe that rapid and far-reaching changes in literacy, learning and social institutions were caused by a single new technology. This is what I call the Gutenberg Myth; it is not accurate history (as we will see below). Yet, the Gutenberg Myth has become the most commonly used model for making predictions about the directions new technologies will take and for identifying what we need to do to avoid being left behind.

As a model for understanding other revolutions the Gutenberg Myth can be dangerously misleading. Using a faulty sense of printing as a way of understanding other powerful innovations guarantees neither their wise development nor responsible use of them. A better model for technological revolutions, especially the digital revolutions going on around us, is suggested by a broader, more realistic understanding of the Gutenberg revolution itself.

The Gutenberg Myth

The appearance of printing has been celebrated as a major step in the advance of technology and the development of western civilization. Charles Babbage, the nineteenth-century inventor of calculating machines, remarked that "the modern world commences with the printing press." Today, it is commonly held that the invention of movable type made possible the mass distribution of the printed word, brought about a string of broad and rapid social advances through an explosion in literacy and learning, and ultimately "democratized knowledge" (Burke 1978). *The McGraw-Hill Encyclopedia of Science and Technology* states that the invention of movable type printing ". . . was one of the most important inventions in human history. It was significant, even revolutionary, in two respects." The first was the principle of movable type itself. "A second and more important aspect [was that it] . . . made it possible to put more information into the hands of more people in less time and at lower cost, and thereby to spread literacy and learning more widely and rapidly than ever before" (Bruno 1987). As historian of science Derek de Solla Price put it, "By 1500 . . . the printed book had become a quite new force. The momentous effect, of course, was that the world of learning, hitherto the domain of a tiny privileged elite, was suddenly made much more accessible to the common man" (de Solla Price 1975, p. 99).

This is the traditional view of the Gutenberg revolution. It is the image that comes to mind when printing is suggested as a model for other technological revolutions. It does not, however, reflect the realities of European history. The process by which the world of learning became "accessible to the common man" entailed several factors in addition to movable type. I will focus on two of them that are particularly central. The first was paper: bringing the printed word to the masses required a medium to print on which was available in quantities and at a cost amenable to "mass distribution." The second factor was literacy: the "common man" needed to be able to read. Neither of these requirements obtained in 1500. These discrepancies point to the need for a richer, more accurate account of the story of movable type and its relationship to the spread of literacy and learning to a broad population in western civilization. It is, after all, the achievement of broad literacy and learning that makes the story of printing revolutionary. This story can begin with the Gutenberg Bible itself.

Gutenberg revisited

The invention of movable type printing is usually credited to Johann Gutenberg of Mainz, Germany, who used it to produce one of the most famous masterpieces of the fifteenth century: the book now called the Gutenberg Bible. As with many important inventions, when, where and by whom the invention actually came about has been the subject of considerable debate. One theory, for example, holds that the first person in Europe to develop movable type was not Gutenberg, but Laurens Janszoon Coster, a contemporary of Gutenberg's living in the Netherlands. (This theory has a good measure of historical merit; as well as a great deal of popularity among the Dutch.) In fact, Gutenberg was not the only person in Europe working on the idea of mechanical printing. It is also quite likely that Gutenberg drew on the work of others in such allied crafts such as metal alloying and casting. Further, it is possible that the work of Gutenberg, Coster, and others in Europe owes a significant debt to the development of print blocks in Asia, which by the fifteenth century had been in common use in China, Japan, and Korea for generations (including their use in the printing of books). With these qualifications in mind, we can take the advent of movable type printing in mid-fifteenth century Europe as a starting point of the "print revolution" associated, symbolically at least, with the printing of the Gutenberg Bible.

The principle of movable type used in printing the Gutenberg Bible is elegantly simple. Gutenberg took as his basic unit the single letter, making type blocks that carried one letter each. The blocks were of standard size in all their dimensions so they could be set one-by-one, in any combination, into consistently straight lines on a flat printing bed in an arrangement of text making up an entire page, which in turn offered a consistently level printing surface. After being used to print any number of copies of that page, the arrangement could be broken down and the type blocks reused. Gutenberg's chief technological accomplishments included developing techniques of metal casting and alloying that made this process economically and technically practical.

In keeping with the principle of movable type, each letter of the Gutenberg Bible was set by hand. The pages, over one thousand of them, were printed one at a time onto hide parchment or rag-fiber paper. Next, in the spirit of the manuscripts of the day, hand illuminations and lettering, details were added to each of the printed pages. Letters at the beginning of chapters, for example, were written in by hand and elaborately illumined and every capital letter in the entire text had a red highlight scribed through it. Finally, the leaves were bound, again by the hand of the craftsman, into large, elegant volumes. The whole project, from casting the first type to binding the final volume, took several years.

Looking at the Gutenberg Bible and at Gutenberg's practice as a craftsman, one does not sense the invention and exploitation of a revolutionary technology but rather the conservative use of an innovative technique for the mechanical production of manuscripts. In fact, the very aim of movable type printing and the technical innovations Gutenberg brought to it were directed at producing volumes that looked as much as possible like manuscripts. Within the printing craft in general, moreover, the same standards of craftsmanship and aesthetics associated with manuscripts were applied to printed books for at least two generations beyond the Gutenberg Bible. Had the new technology not met these old standards, it might well have been dismissed as a failed experiment. Indeed, a judgment like this seems to have been made in China. Type blocks containing a single character were developed, but the Chinese abandoned them in favor of plate blocks containing entire texts; they felt that the type blocks were not sufficiently consistent in shape to produce a printed page that met the high aesthetic standards of their calligraphy. This suggests that the initiation of a technological revolution may often depend on *new* technologies being functionally compatible with *old* craft practices and *traditional* values of the surrounding culture.

Since printing the Gutenberg Bible on fine parchment entailed the use of hundreds of pieces of hide, raw materials alone could be a costly factor. A single copy required the skins of fifty to seventy-five sheep. Likewise, the paper Gutenberg used (most copies were on paper), though less costly than parchment, was nonetheless a valuable commodity. It was produced a single sheet at a time by skilled craftsmen dependent on often scarce supplies of waste rag or scrap from garment manufacture.

Gutenberg's finished product, then, was a marvelously fine piece of craftsmanship, a beautiful and valuable example of the printer's art. And it remains so to the present day. But it was also an artifact for elites, chiefly the aristocracy and the Church. The Word as printed by Gutenberg was not distributed to the masses. In fact, only about two hundred copies of the Gutenberg Bible were ever produced.

Meanwhile, printed books in general remained far too costly for de Solla Price's "common man" well beyond 1500.

Not only were most people in the fifteenth century unable to buy a Gutenberg Bible, they were also unable to read it. This is an essential element in assessing the course of the printing revolution; any potential mass social change associated with printing must be weighed against the extent of mass illiteracy.

Although difficult to define and measure, even a cautious estimate places illiteracy in fifteenth-century Europe at well over 90 percent of the general population. Further, since those who could read were concentrated among clergy, scholars, and aristocrats – and there almost entirely among men – illiteracy in most other segments of society was close to universal. Even among those who could read, not all were schooled in Latin, which was, of course, the language of the Christian Bible.

In the light of such factors. Gutenberg's efforts appear far from revolutionary – indeed, they are quite in keeping with the social, religious, political, and economic institutions of his day.

Printing and mass illiteracy

Even so, printing was much faster and less expensive than the copying of manuscripts. This fact, along with the aesthetic quality of printed texts, came to present a significant challenge to traditional manuscript production. Indeed, the displacement of calligraphy by movable type as the preferred means of creating documents resulted in a dramatic spread of printing technology. By the middle of the sixteenth century, presses were operating in most major centers of Europe and had begun to appear in the Middle East and Asia. In the New World, the first press was established at Mexico City in 1539; the second, a century later in 1638, at Cambridge, Massachusetts.

Within literate communities, the press helped bring about a greater availability of texts and a vastly expanded number of individual titles. It is estimated that some thirty thousand editions were printed in the first fifty years following the advent of the press, equaling the number produced in the previous one thousand years. Moreover, in scholastic communities, the press became a key element in a remarkably rapid growth in the translation and publication of classical texts – a phenomenon that was to fan the glowing coals of the Enlightenment.

By 1650, movable type technology was a fact of life in hundreds of communities throughout Europe. But the spread of the technology did not carry with it a broad social revolution in literacy and learning. Although levels of literacy rose in some sectors of the population (in connection with the Reformation, for example), illiteracy in Europe in general stood at about 80 percent in 1650, and the ability to read and write remained significantly associated with class and gender. At this point, two hundred years after Gutenberg, access to the world of learning was *not* a fact of life for the masses.

In the eighteenth century, illiteracy began to decline at a greater rate. By 1700 it had fallen to between 65 and 70 percent. As the nineteenth century approached, the figure neared 50 percent. Among the factors associated with this improvement was the growing role of reading and writing in work, especially in the trades. In fact, one of the earliest exceptions to the exclusion of literacy to all but social elites was its appearance among the trades. Reading and writing became a growing part of work as the increasing organization of society expanded the need to keep records. Treatises on craft skills, meanwhile, became one of the largest categories of printed books (third after religion and law).

Significantly, the spread of literacy to more people and more classes of people during this period (approximately 1650 to 1800) occurred alongside some rather remarkable changes in both the idea and reality of social equality. The notion that individuals are equal within a human community found strong expression in the political, literary, and philosophical writings of the time. Philosophical propositions like Hobbes's argument that all people are equal in "a state of nature" and Locke's contention that all people are by nature equally free found broader expression in Jefferson's declaration that "all men are created equal" and Rousseau's insistence that social inequalities are unnatural creations of our institutions. Claims of a political right to specific forms of social equality became banners of the American and French Revolutions. Kant gave these themes a stronger moral sense with his argument that all people are (or ought to be) moral equals as legislators within a "kingdom of ends." Similarly, various notions of equality were explored in the art, architecture and music of the period.

Ultimately, this sweeping reevaluation of the idea of equality entailed nothing less than a recasting of what was to be understood as the entitlements of membership in society and the beginnings of a parallel redesign of the social institutions associated with providing and guaranteeing those rights. All this made the spread of literacy, as a prerequisite of citizenship rather than of privilege, more "thinkable," and thus more feasible. The decline in illiteracy during this period, therefore, must be understood as much more the product of changing social, political, and moral values than as a consequence of the continued presence of the centuries-old technology of printing. That is, this aspect of the printing revolution was due more to social than technological factors.

The paper it's printed on

From the time of Gutenberg until the early nineteenth century, paper was the product of costly materials and highly skilled craftsmanship. No major advance had been made in the painstaking, sheet-by-sheet hand work of the ancient craft since it entered Europe from the Islamic world in the twelfth century.

Correspondingly, the value placed on paper is reflected in numerous laws and customs from the time of Gutenberg to the nineteenth century. A 1666 English law, for example, decreed that only wool, being unsuitable for papermaking, could be used in burying the dead. An early New England periodical, in encouraging readers to save rags for papermakers, suggested that each housewife make a rag tag and keep it next to the family Bible – a wonderfully symbolic connection emphasizing the value placed on paper. The *Boston News Letter* printed an announcement in 1769 that ". . . the bell cart will go through Boston about the end of each month . . ." for the purpose of collecting rags. Readers were further encouraged to fulfill their civic duty with the following poem.

Rags are beauties which concealed lie,
But when in paper, how charms the eye!
Pray save your rags, new beauties to discover,
For of paper, truly, everyone's a lover;
By the pen and press such knowledge is displayed
As wouldn't exist if paper was not made.
Wisdom of things, mysterious, divine,
Illustriously doth on paper shine.

In 1776 the Massachusetts General Court required that in each community a person be appointed to collect rags. To conserve paper, it remained until 1818 a punishable offense in England to print newssheets or broadsides larger than 22 by 32 inches (roughly the current size of the *New York Times*).

The search for a reliable, less expensive alternative to rag scrap as the raw material for paper had been unsuccessful – though not for want of effort. Several materials were tried experimentally, including hemp, pine cones, used shingles, potatoes, and asbestos. A particularly imaginative source for rag, itself, was found in the mid-nineteenth century in Egyptian mummies. Shiploads of mummies were sent from Egypt to paper companies in the United States, where their linen wrappings were taken off and recycled, so to speak, into paper. This practice continued for some time, apparently without the intervention of concerned health officials, outraged clergy, or jealous archaeologists. The only competition the papermakers had for the mummies was from the new Egyptian railroad, which, reportedly, used them as fuel.

That mummies could be shipped all the way from Egypt to the United States solely for the use of their wrappings is a gauge of the value and cost of paper at the time (as well as a measure of deficit in respect for the dead). The availability of rag and the cost of paper were clearly serious obstacles to printing on a mass scale well into the nineteenth century.

Mass printing and mass society

Through the course of the nineteenth century, several technological and social innovations combined to produce dramatic changes in printing and literacy. By the turn of the century, wood pulp had been identified as a reliable and plentiful fiber source for papermaking. The first experimental techniques for producing pulp-fiber paper by machine were operational by the 1810s. In the 1840s, a machine designed specifically for the mass production of paper-quality pulp was introduced. By the 1860s, wood pulp paper was being made commercially in mills that could turn out paper at dazzling speed in continuous rolls of indefinite length. The development of machine-made pulp and paper made possible a rapid drop in the cost of paper. The price of newsprint, for example, fell by a factor of ten between the 1860s and 1890s.

Printing itself developed remarkably through the nineteenth century. Steam power was introduced to press operation in 1810. In the middle of the century, the flat reciprocating printing bed was displaced by the development of the stereotype cylinder, the molded and curved printing surfaces now associated with the "rolling press." A major step in the printing craft was made in 1884 with the invention of the linotype.

With this machine, the highly time-consuming hand work of setting type one letter at a time could be replaced by a mechanized operation that cast type by the line. This principle dramatically increased the speed and reduced the cost of typesetting. In doing so, the linotype became an important factor in making possible the mass production of the printed word. With respect to printing technology, meanwhile, the linotype represents a significant step away from the principle of movable type, since it treats the line rather than the single letter as its basic unit.

Resting on expanding notions of social equality a fundamentally important social innovation of the nineteenth century was the introduction of public education. From the middle of the century onward, state-supported elementary education became a reality in country after country. By the end of the century, it was accepted, at least in principle, throughout Western Europe. The parallel decline in illiteracy was dramatic. In 1800, half of the general population was illiterate. By the century's end, the figure was under 10 percent.

With the advent of mass literacy and the development of technologies for the rapid and relatively inexpensive mass production of paper and printed materials, the mass distribution of the printed word became a meaningful and practical possibility. It was not until the latter decades of the nineteenth century, therefore, that the social and technological elements for making "the world of learning . . . accessible to the common" person through printing were fully in place – four hundred years after the appearance of the movable type press.

All of these factors combine to help us sketch out a fuller, more accurate understanding of the printing revolution; they also point to the need for a broader, multi-dimensional model of the structure of technological revolutions to replace the Gutenberg Myth. At the very least, this account of the printing revolution suggests that the traditional, one-dimensional model of new technologies (or a single new material gadget) causing broad social change must be regarded with deep suspicion.

A healthy skepticism about the Gutenberg Myth is also called for in our efforts to understand the social changes associated with new technologies in our own time. Clearly, we need a new model of the structure of technological revolutions in order to assess the role of technological change in our lives and cultures in a way that avoids the political and moral myopia of the Gutenberg Myth. It is to the exploration of some examples of these pitfalls that I now turn.

Illiteracy in the shadow of technology

The story of the spread of literacy and learning in western civilization is an important one, as is the role of the printing press within it. At the same time, the call for making "learning . . . accessible to the common" person is still heard today in the broader context of making literacy and learning accessible to the peoples of the world.

Approximately 90 percent of the illiterate people alive today live in the developing world, where the average level of adult illiteracy is around 40 percent. Many of these countries have literacy programs, and there are internationally sponsored literacy initiatives through the United Nations and private organizations. Progress is being made, but neither the "problem" nor the "solution" is simple. Nor is it simply a matter of technological need. The level of illiteracy in these countries fell by almost

10 percent between 1970 and 1980, yet (because of population trends) the absolute number of illiterate people increased during that period by nearly seventy million.

Just as the Gutenberg Myth fails to capture the realities of western history, so too it fails as a model for assessing the current realities of the developing world: The image of literacy and learning emerging on a mass scale from the introduction of printing technology would, indeed, be a very misleading model for these nations. The situation in the developing world is neither well understood nor effectively addressed by assuming that mass literacy can emerge from the introduction of a single technology. Today, print and other technologies such as computers are readily available, but this has not made it possible to "put more information into the hands of more people . . . and thereby to spread literacy and learning" throughout the developing world (as the McGraw-Hill encyclopedia's formulation of the Gutenberg Myth might suggest).

Exciting new technologies, same old myth

The printing revolution is often evoked as a model for understanding the social importance of new technologies. The structure of technological revolutions implicit in such analogies is typically the Gutenberg Myth: a single technology being the sole cause of rapid and far-reaching social change. Throughout the 1980s, for example, the personal computer was depicted in the popular and scholarly press as single-handedly revolutionizing the whole of society. By the early 1990s the same was being said about the "data superhighway." Not surprisingly such discussions of exciting new technologies reflect the same sorts of historical and conceptual distortions found in nearly all references to the printing revolution.

Conclusion: revolutions recaptured

This brief look at the printing revolution suggests that the structure of technological revolutions is neither simple, technologically determined, nor everywhere the same, either historically or culturally. It is clear that the model of sweeping social change being caused by a single technological innovation is historically and conceptually faulty and misleading. Such changes are not *caused* by the appearance of a single gadget; they are *constituted* in multiple, mutually influencing technological and social innovations. A new model of the structure of technological revolutions must reflect these facts. Moreover, it must be able to embrace the deeply held values that inform our cultures and underlie the choices we make about the direction our technologies ought to take – even when those choices are made by default rather than by design. The technological determinism inherent in the Gutenberg Myth forecloses discussion of just these social, political, and moral values – which are ultimately the only means by which we can distinguish between an appropriate and inappropriate role for any of the exciting new technologies of our day.

1.3

A shadow darkens,
by Ithiel de Sola Pool

Civil liberty functions today in a changing technological context. For five hundred years a struggle was fought, and in a few countries won, for the right of people to speak and print freely, unlicensed, uncensored, and uncontrolled. But new technologies of electronic communication may now relegate old and freed media such as pamphlets, platforms, and periodicals to a corner of the public forum. Electronic modes of communication that enjoy lesser rights are moving to center stage. The new communication technologies have not inherited all the legal immunities that were won for the old. When wires, radio waves, satellites, and computers became major vehicles of discourse, regulation seemed to be a technical necessity. And so, as speech increasingly flows over those electronic media, the five-century growth of an unabridged right of citizens to speak without controls may be endangered.

Alarm over this trend is common, though understanding of it is rare. In 1980 the chairman of the American Federal Communications Commission (FCC) sent a shiver through print journalists when he raised the question of whether a newspaper delivered by teletext is an extension of print and thus as free as any other newspaper, or whether it is a broadcast and thus under the control of the government.[1] A reporter, discussing computerized information services, broached an issue with far-reaching implications for society when she asked, "Will traditional First Amendment freedom of the press apply to the signals sent out over telephone wires or television cables?"[2] William S. Paley, chairman of the Columbia Broadcasting System (CBS), warned the press: "Broadcasters and print people have been so busy improving and defining their own turf that it has escaped some of us how much we are being drawn together by the vast revolution in 'electronification' that is changing the face of the media today . . . Convergence of delivery mechanisms for news and information raises anew some critical First Amendment questions . . . Once the print media comes into the home through the television set, or an attachment, with an impact and basic content similar to that which the broadcasters now deliver, then the question of government regulation becomes paramount for print as well."[3] And Senator Bob Packwood proposed a new amendment to the Constitution extending First Amendment rights to the electronic media, on the assumption that they are not covered now.

Although the first principle of communications law in the United States is the

guarantee of freedom in the First Amendment, in fact this country has a trifurcated communications system. In three domains of communication – print, common carriage, and broadcasting – the law has evolved separately, and in each domain with but modest relation to the others.

In the domain of print and other means of communication that existed in the formative days of the nation, such as pulpits, periodicals, and public meetings, the First Amendment truly governs. In well over one hundred cases dealing with publishing, canvassing, public speeches, and associations, the Supreme Court has applied the First Amendment to the media that existed in the eighteenth century.

In the domain of common carriers, which includes the telephone, the telegraph, the postal system, and now some computer networks, a different set of policies has been applied, designed above all to ensure universal service and fair access by the public to the facilities of the carrier. That right of access is what defines a common carrier: it is obligated to serve all on equal terms without discrimination.

Finally, in the domain of broadcasting, Congress and the courts have established a highly regulated regime, very different from that of print. On the grounds of a supposed scarcity of usable frequencies in the radio spectrum, broadcasters are selected by the government for merit in its eyes, assigned a slice each of the spectrum of frequencies, and required to use that assignment fairly and for community welfare as defined by state authorities. The principles of common carriage and of the First Amendment have been applied to broadcasting in only atrophied form. For broadcasting, a politically managed system has been invented.

The electronic modes of twentieth century communication, whether they be carriers or broadcasters, have lost a large part of the eighteenth and nineteenth century constitutional protections of no prior restraint, no licenses, no special taxes, no regulations, and no laws. Every radio spectrum user, for example, must be licensed. This requirement started in 1912, almost a decade before the beginning of broadcasting, at a time when radio was used mainly for maritime communication. Because the United States Navy's communications were suffering interference, Congress, in an effort at remedy, imposed licensing on transmitters, thereby breaching a tradition that went back to John Milton against requiring licenses for communicating.

Regulation as a response to perceived technical problems has now reached the point where transmissions enclosed in wires or cables, and therefore causing no over-the-air interference, are also licensed and regulated. The FCC claims the right to control which broadcast stations a cablecaster may or must carry. Until the courts blew the whistle, the rules even barred a pay channel from performing movies that were more than three or less than ten years old. Telephone bills are taxed. A public network interconnecting computers must be licensed and, according to present interpretations of the 1934 Communications Act, may be denied a license if the government does not believe that it serves "the public convenience, interest, or necessity."

Both civil libertarians and free marketers are perturbed at the expanding scope of communications regulation. After computers became linked by communications networks, for example, the FCC spent several years figuring out how to avoid regulating the computer industry. The line of reasoning behind this laudable self-restraint, known as deregulation, has nothing to do, however, with freedom of speech.

Deregulation, whatever its economic merits, is something much less than the First Amendment. The Constitution, in Article 1, Section 8, gives the federal government the right to regulate interstate commerce, but in the First Amendment, equally explicitly, it excludes one kind of commerce, namely communication, from government authority. Yet here is the FCC trying to figure out how it can avoid regulating the commerce of the computer industry (an authority Congress could have given, but never did) while continuing to regulate communications whenever it considers this necessary. The Constitution has been turned on its head.

The mystery is how the clear intent of the Constitution, so well and strictly enforced in the domain of print, has been so neglected in the electronic revolution. The answer lies partly in changes in the prevailing concerns and historical circumstances from the time of the founding fathers to the world of today; but it lies at least as much in the failure of Congress and the courts to understand the character of the new technologies. Judges and legislators have tried to fit technological innovations under conventional legal concepts. The errors of understanding by these scientific laymen, though honest, have been mammoth. They have sought to guide toward good purposes technologies they did not comprehend.

"It would seem," wrote Alexis de Tocqueville, "that if despotism were to be established among the democratic nations of our days . . . it would be more extensive and more mild; it would degrade men without tormenting them." This is the kind of mild but degrading erosion of freedom that our system of communication faces today, not a rise of dictators or totalitarian movements. The threat in America, as Tocqueville perceived, is from well-intentioned policies, with results that are poorly foreseen. The danger is "tutelary power," which aims at the happiness of the people but also seeks to be the "arbiter of that happiness."[4]

Yet in a century and a half since Tocqueville wrote, the mild despotism that he saw in the wings of American politics has not become a reality. For all his understanding of the American political system, he missed one vital element of the picture. In the tension between tutelary and libertarian impulses that is built into American culture, a strong institutional dike has held back assaults on freedom. It is the first ten amendments to the Constitution. Extraordinary as this may seem, in Tocqueville's great two volumes there is nowhere a mention of the Bill of Rights!

The erosion of traditional freedoms that has occurred as government has striven to cope with problems of new communications media would not have surprised Tocqueville, for it is a story of how, in pursuit of the public good, a growing structure of controls has been imposed. But one part of the story would have surprised him, for it tells how a legal institution that he overlooked, namely the First Amendment, has up to now maintained the freedom and individualism that he saw as endangered.

A hundred and fifty years from now, today's fears about the future of free expression may prove as alarmist as Tocqueville's did. But there is reason to suspect that our situation is more ominous. What has changed in twentieth century communications is its technological base. Tocqueville wrote in a pluralistic society of small enterprises where the then new mass media consisted entirely of the printed press which the First Amendment protected. In the period since his day, new and mostly electronic media have proliferated in the form of great oligopolistic networks of common carriers and broadcasters. Regulation was a natural response. Fortunately and strangely, as electronics advances further, another reversal is now taking place, toward growing decentralization and toward fragmentation of the audience of the newest media. The transitional era of giant media may nonetheless leave a permanent set of regulatory practices implanted on a system that is coming to have technical characteristics that would otherwise be conducive to freedom.

The causal relationships between technology and culture are a matter that social scientists have long debated. Some may question how far technological trends shape the political freedom or control under which communication takes place, believing, as does Daniel Bell, that each subsystem of society, such as techno-economics, polity, and culture, has its own heritage and axial principles and goes its own way.[5] Others contend, like Karl Marx or Ruth Benedict, that a deep commonality binds all aspects of a culture. Some argue that technology is neutral, used as the culture demands; others that the technology of the medium controls the message.

The interaction over the past two centuries between the changing technologies of communication and the practice of free speech, I would argue, fits a pattern that is sometimes described as "soft technological determinism." Freedom is fostered when the means of communication are dispersed, decentralized, and easily available, as are printing presses or microcomputers. Central control is more likely when the means of communication are concentrated, monopolized, and scarce, as are great networks. But the relationship between technology and institutions is not simple or uni-directional, nor are the effects immediate. Institutions that evolve in response to one technological environment persist and to some degree are later imposed on what may be a changed technology. The First Amendment came out of a pluralistic world of small communicators, but it shaped the present treatment of great national networks. Later on, systems of regulation that emerged for national common carriers and for the use of "scarce" spectrum for broadcasting tended to be imposed on more recent generations of electronic technologies that no longer require them.

Simple versions of technological determinism fail to take account of the differences in the way things happen at different stages in the life cycle of a technology. When a new invention is made, such as the telephone or radio, its fundamental laws are usually not well understood. It is designed to suit institutions that already exist, but in its early stages if it is to be used at all, it must be used in whatever form it proved experimentally to work. Institutions for its use are thus designed around a techno-logically determined model. Later, when scientists have comprehended the funda-mental theory, the early technological embodiment becomes simply a special case. Alternative devices can then be designed to meet human needs. Technology, no longer need control. A 1920s motion picture had to be black and white, silent, panto-mimic, and shown in a place of public assembly; there was no practical choice. A 1980s video can have whatever colors, sounds, and three-dimensional or synthetic effects are wanted, and can be seen in whatever location is desired. In the meantime, however, an industry has established studios, theaters, career lines, unions, funding, and advertising practices, all designed to use the technology that is in place. Change occurs, but the established institutions are a constraint on its direction and pace.

Today, in an era of advanced (and still advancing) electronic theory, it has become possible to build virtually any kind of communications device that one might wish, though at a price. The market, not technology, sets most limits. For example, technology no longer imposes licensing and government regulation. That pattern was established for electronic media a half-century ago, when there seemed to be no alternative, but the institutions of control then adopted persist. That is why today's alarms could turn out to be more portentous than Tocqueville's.

The key technological change, at the root of the social changes, is that communication, other than conversation face to face, is becoming overwhelmingly electronic. Not only is electronic communication growing faster than traditional media of publishing, but also the convergence of modes of delivery is bringing the press, journals, and books into the electronic world. One question raised by these changes is whether some social features are inherent in the electronic character of the emerging media. Is television the model of the future? Are electromagnetic pulses simply an alternative conduit to deliver whatever is wanted, or are there aspects of electronic technology that make it different from print – more centralized or more decentralized, more banal or more profound, more private or more government dependent?

The electronic transformation of the media occurs not in a vacuum but in a specific historical and legal context. Freedom for publishing has been one of America's proudest traditions. But just what is it that the courts have protected, and how does this differ from how the courts acted later when the media through which ideas flowed came to be the telegraph, telephone, television, or computers? What images did policy makers have of how each of these media works; how far were their images valid; and what happened to their images when the facts changed?

In each of the three parts of the American communications system – print, common carriers, and broadcasting – the law has rested on a perception of technology that is sometimes accurate, often inaccurate, and which changes slowly as technology changes fast. Each new advance in the technology of communications disturbs a status quo. It meets resistance from those whose dominance it threatens, but if useful, it begins to be adopted. Initially, because it is new and a full scientific mastery of the options is not yet at hand, the invention comes into use in a rather clumsy form. Technical laymen, such as judges, perceive the new technology in that early, clumsy form, which then becomes their image of its nature, possibilities, and use. This perception is an incubus on later understanding.

The courts and regulatory agencies in the American system (or other authorities elsewhere) enter as arbiters of the conflicts among entrepreneurs, interest groups, and political organizations battling for control of the new technology. The arbiters, applying familiar analogies from the past to their lay image of the new technology, create a partly old, partly new structure of rights and obligations. The telegraph was analogized to railroads, the telephone to the telegraph, and cable television to broadcasting. The legal system thus invented for each new technology may in some instances, like the First Amendment, be a *tour de force* of political creativity, but in other instances it may be less worthy. The system created can turn out to be inappropriate to more habile forms of the technology which gradually emerge as the technology progresses. This is when problems arise, as they are arising so acutely today.

Historically, the various media that are now converging have been differently organized and differently treated under the law. The outcome to be feared is that communications in the future may be unnecessarily regulated under the unfree tradition of law that has been applied so far to the electronic media. The clash between the

print, common carrier, and broadcast models is likely to be a vehement communications policy issue in the next decades. Convergence of modes is upsetting the trifurcated system developed over the past two hundred years, and questions that had
seemed to be settled centuries ago are being reopened, unfortunately sometimes not
in a libertarian way.

The problem is worldwide. What is true for the United States is true, *mutatis
mutandis*, for all free nations. All have the same three systems. All are in their way
deferential to private publishing but allow government control or ownership of carriers and broadcasters. And all are moving into the era of electronic communication.
So they face the same prospect of either freeing up their electronic media or else
finding their major means of communication slipping back under political control.

The American case is unique only in the specific feature of the First Amendment
and in the role of the courts in upholding it. The First Amendment, as interpreted
by the courts, provides an anchor for freedom of the press and thus accentuates
the difference between publishing and the electronic domain. Because of the unique
power of the American courts, the issue in the United States unfolds largely in
judicial decisions. But the same dilemmas and trends could be illustrated by citing
declarations of policy and institutional structures in each advanced country.

If the boundaries between publishing, broadcasting, cable television, and the
telephone network are indeed broken in the coming decades, then communications
policies in all advanced countries must address the issue of which of the three models
will dominate public policy regarding them. Public interest regulation could begin to
extend over the print media as those media increasingly use regulated electronic
channels. Conversely, concern for the traditional notion of a free press could lead to
finding ways to free the electronic media from regulation. The policies adopted, even
among free nations, will differ, though with much in common. The problems in all of
them are very much the same.

The phrase "communications policy" rings oddly in a discussion of freedom
from government. But freedom is also a policy. The question it poses is how to reduce
the public control of communications in an electronic era. A policy of freedom aims at
pluralism of expression rather than at dissemination of preferred ideas.

A communications policy, or indeed any policy, may be mapped on a few central
topics:

> Definition of the domain in which the policy operates
> Availability of resources
> Organization of access to resources
> Establishment and enforcement of norms and controls
> Problems at the system boundaries

The *definition of the domain* of a communications policy requires consideration of
the point at which human intercourse becomes something more than communication. In American law, at some point speech becomes action and thus no longer
receives First Amendment protection. Similar issues arise as to whether under the law
pornography is speech, and whether commercial speech is speech.

The *availability of resources* raises another set of questions. Tools, money, raw materials, and labor are all required in order to carry on communication. The press needs newsprint; broadcasters need spectrum. How much of these can be made available, and at what prices can they be had?

The *organization of access to these resources* can be by a market or by rationing by the state. There may be a diversity of sources of resources, or there may be a monopoly. How much freedom is allowed to those who control the resources to exercise choice about who gets what? Are resources taxed, are they subsidized, or neither? How is intellectual property defined, and how is it protected?

The *exercise of regulation and control* over communication is a central concern in any treatise on freedom. How much control are policy makers allowed to exercise? What are the limitations on them, such as the First Amendment? May they censor? May they license those who seek to communicate? What norms control the things that communicators may say to each other? What is libel, what is slander, what violates privacy or security? Who is chosen to enforce these rules, and how?

The *problems encountered at the system boundaries* include the transborder issues that arise when there is a conflict of laws about communications which cross frontiers. Censorship is often imposed for reasons of national security, cultural protection, and trade advantage. These issues, which have not been central in past First Amendment controversies, are likely to be of growing importance in the electronic era.

From this map of policy analysis can be extracted what social scientists sometimes call a mapping sentence, a brief but formal statement of the problem to be analyzed in this book. It seeks to understand the impact of resource availability, as affected both by technology and by the organization of access to the resources, upon freedom from regulation and control. The specific question to be answered is whether the electronic resources for communication can be as free of public regulation in the future as the platform and printing press have been in the past. Not a decade goes by in free countries, and not a day in the world, without grim oppressions that bring protesters once more to picket lines and demonstrations. Vigilance that must be so eternal becomes routine, and citizens grow callous.

The issue of the handling of the electronic media is the salient free speech problem for this decade, at least as important for this moment as were the last generation's issues for them, and as the next generation's will be for them too. But perhaps it is more than that. The move to electronic communication may be a turning point that history will remember. Just as in seventeenth and eighteenth century Great Britain and America a few tracts and acts set precedents for print by which we live today, so what we think and do today may frame the information system for a substantial period in the future.

In that future society the norms that govern information and communication will be even more crucial than in the past. Those who read, wrote, and published in the seventeenth and eighteenth centuries, and who shaped whatever heritage of art, literature, science, and history continues to matter today, were part of a small minority, well under one-tenth of the work force. Information activities now occupy the lives of much of the population. In advanced societies about half the work force are information processors.[6] It would be dire if the laws we make today governing the dominant mode of information handling in such an information society were subversive of its freedom. The onus is on us to determine whether free societies in the twenty-first century will conduct electronic communication under the conditions of freedom established for the domain of print through centuries of struggle, or whether that great achievement will become lost in a confusion about new technologies.

Notes

1   Charles D. Ferris, quoted in *The Report*, Nov. 14, 1980, p. 11.
2   Nina McCain, *Boston Globe*, Field News Service, Aug. 31, 1980.
3   "Press Freedom – A Continuing Struggle," speech to Associated Press Broadcasters Convention, June 6, 1980; *New York Times*, July 7, 1980, sec. B, p. 3. See also Judge David Bazclon, "The First Amendment and the New Media," *Federal Communications Law Journal* 31.2 (Spring 1979); Bazelen, "The First Amendment's Second Chance," *Channels*, Feb.–Mar. 1982, pp. 16–17; Charles Jackson, Harry M. Shooshan, and Jane L. Wilson, *Newspapers and Videotex: How Free a Press?* (St. Petersburg, Ha.: Modern Media Institute, 1982); John Wicklein, *Electronic Nightmare – The New Communications and Freedom* (New York: Viking, 1981); and an early statement by this author, Ithiel de Sola Pool, "From Gutenberg to Electronics: Implications for the First Amendment," *The Key Reporter* 43.3 (Spring 1978).
4   Alexis de Tocqueville, *Democracy in America* (1840, reprint New York: Knopf, 1945), 11, 316–318.
5   Daniel Bell, *The Cultural Contradictions of Capitalism* (New York: Basic Books, 1975), p. 10.
6   Mark U. Porat and Michael R. Rubin, *The Information Economy*, 9 vols. (Washington, DC Government Printing Office, 1977); Organization for Economic Cooperation and Development, *Information Activities, Electronics and Telecommunications Technologies: Impact on Employment, Growth and Trade* (Paris: 1981).

1.4

The consumer's sublime,
by David E. Nye

In 1845 an American visitor to Niagara Falls stood watch on the piazza of his hotel during a thunderstorm. He later wrote: "The finest thing we have seen yet – and one of the grandest I ever saw – was a thunder storm among the waters . . . the other night, which lighted up the two cascades, as seen from our piazzas, with most magnificent effect. They had a spectral look, as they came out of the darkness and were again swallowed up in it, that defies all description and all imagination."[1] This spectacle combined the mathematical sublime of the vast waterfall with the dynamic sublime of thunder and lightning, creating a still more powerful effect.

In a few years, the gorge at Niagara was spanned by Roebling's railway bridge, which many thought as wonderful as the falls. Two generations later, the falls were illuminated by searchlights. These lights – major attractions of the electrical sublime – received their power from Niagara's new hydroelectric power stations, which themselves became tourist attractions and which provided the theme for the 1901 Pan-American Exposition in Buffalo. The industrial sublime also emerged here, for the factories attracted to the site by cheap electricity drew crowds to witness the wonder of mass production. Thus, a succession of natural and technological sublimes appeared at this one site.

The sublime has persisted as a preferred American trope through two centuries. Aside from the specific characteristics of each form, Americans seem to have a particular affinity for sharp discontinuities in sensory experience, for sudden shifts of perspective, for a broken figure of thought in which the quotidian is ruptured. The psychology of the sublime has long been a recurrent figure of thought as Americans have established their relationship to new landscapes and new technologies. This underlying pattern persists in the descriptions of objects as disparate as Niagara Falls, the Grand Canyon, the Natural Bridge of Virginia, the first railroads, suspension bridges, skyscrapers, city skylines, spectacular lighting, electric advertising, world's fairs, atomic explosions, and the rockets of the space program.

Europeans neither invented nor embraced the vertical city of the skyscraper. Europeans banned or restricted electric signs, and rightly saw the landscape of Times Square as peculiarly American. Europeans did not see atomic explosions as tourist sites. Europeans seldom journeyed to see rockets go into space, but Americans went by the millions.[2] There is a persistent American attraction to the technological sublime.

Not only is the sublime a recurrent figure in American thought; potential sublimity has also justified the creation of new technologies in the first place. This was not merely a matter of the rationalization of new projects, or a simple form of class domination in which an overawed populace acceded to new displays of technological power. There is an American penchant for thinking of the subject as a consciousness that can stand apart from the world and project its will upon it. In this mode of thought, the subject elides Kantian transcendental reason with technological reason and sees new structures and inventions as continuations of nature. Those operating within this logic embrace the reconstruction of the life-world by machinery, experience the dislocations and perceptual disorientations caused by this reconstruction in terms of awe and wonder, and, in their excitement, feel insulated from immediate danger. New technologies become self-justifying parts of a national destiny, just as the natural sublime once undergirded the rhetoric of manifest destiny. Fundamental changes in the landscape paradoxically seem part of an inevitable process in harmony with nature.

After centuries of neglect, the sublime – first described in classical antiquity – reemerged in the eighteenth century in tandem with the apotheosis of reason and the advent of industrialization. This broken figure of thought, which permitted both the imagination of an ineffable surplus of emotion and its recontainment, was not based on a perceived opposition between nature and culture in the ancient world or in Enlightenment England. Nor was there an absolute opposition between the natural and the technological sublime in Jacksonian America. Although there is an undoubted tension between what Leo Marx terms "the machine" and "the garden," Americans looked for sublimity in both realms.[3] Each provided a disruption of ordinary sense perception, and each was interpreted as a sign of national greatness.

At first the sublime was understood to be an emotion almost exclusive to the male sex, women being relegated to the realm of the beautiful, as in Kant's early writings. The mature formulation of Kant's aesthetic held, however, that the sublime was a universal emotion, accessible to all. Yet, in practice, the scenes that elicited the sublime were usually more accessible, and accessible at an earlier time, to men than to women. The explorers who first saw Yosemite and the Grand Canyon were men. The engineers who built the railways, the architects that designed the skyscrapers, and the technicians who created the electrical displays were men. Men created virtually all the central objects of the technological sublime that have been the focus of this study. It was the male gaze of domination that looked out from the railway engine, the skyscraper, and the factory manager's office, surveying an orderly domain. Though women were not absolutely excluded, they were marginal.

Yet women played a vital part in the incorporation of the technological object into ordinary life. Once the initial shock of the sublime object had passed, it was domesticated and made familiar through a process of feminization. The railway engine soon became a "she," and train crews spoke of getting "her" to the station on time. The steel mill became an industrial mother, giving birth to molten ingots. Electricity was usually represented as a woman in statuary and paintings.[4] In the 1950s there was a "Miss Atom Bomb" beauty queen. In 1986 the sophisticated engineering of Eiffel and the copper cladding of Bartholdi merged with laser beams and computer-designed fireworks in the rededication of the Statue of Liberty. Feminization transformed the alien into the familiar and implied the emergence of a new synthetic realm in which the lines between nature, technology, and culture were blurred if not erased.

Feminization tamed technology, preparing the subject to experience new forms of the sublime. Despite its power, the technological sublime always implies its own rapid obsolescence, making room for the wonders of the next generation. The railway of 1835 hardly amazed in 1870, and most Americans eventually lost interest in trains (though that particular "romance" lasted longer than most). During each generation the radically new disappeared into ordinary experience. The shape of the life-world, the envelope of techniques and customs that appeared natural to a child, kept changing.[5] Travelers on the first trains, in the 1830s, felt that their disruptive experience was sublime, and remained in a state of heightened awareness, but the sense of an extraordinary break in experience soon disappeared. Similarly, the wonder of 1855 was to see a freight train cross the suspension bridge over Niagara Gorge. In the 1880s came the Brooklyn Bridge; in the 1930s came the Golden Gate Bridge. Each of these structures was longer than its predecessors, sustaining more weight over a greater span.

The logic of the technological sublime demanded that each object exceed its precursors. Similarly, each world's fair erected more elaborate lighting displays than its predecessors, creating more powerful illusions to satisfy the viewers' increasingly voracious appetite. The first skyscrapers, which had fewer than 15 stories, soon were overshadowed by far larger structures. The once dizzying and disorienting view from atop the Flatiron Building became familiar, and higher towers were needed to upset the sense of "normal" spatial relations. Likewise, the first airplanes to appear over Chicago or New York drew millions out into the streets; yet within 20 years daredevil stunts were necessary to hold the crowd's interest, and by 1960 aviation had passed into the ordinary. Each form of the technological sublime became a "natural" part of the world and ceased to amaze, though the capacity and the desire for amazement persisted.

Although the wonder of one generation scarcely drew a glance in the next, each loss of sublimity prepared the subject for more radical shifts in perspective yet to come. In the early 1950s Las Vegas newspapers complained that a recent round of open-air atomic explosions had been too small: " 'Bigger bombs, that's what we're waiting for,' said one Las Vegas nightclub owner. 'Americans have to have their kicks.' "[6]

Sublime experience is not merely a matter of vision; all the senses are engaged. Burke noted that, although the eye was often dominant, movement, noise, smell, and touch were also important. A city sounds much different at the top of a skyscraper than on the street below. The wind makes one feel more vulnerable out on the open span of a long bridge. The steam locomotive shook the ground and filled the air with an alien smell of steam, smoke, and sparks; the Saturn rocket did much the same thing on a larger scale. The strong contrast between the silence of a rocket's liftoff and the sudden roar that follows a few seconds later is also a vital element in making that spectacle sublime. The sheer size of the crowd attracted to a technological display further arouses the emotions. In each event, the human subject feels that the familiar envelope of sensory experience has been rent asunder.

Most Americans have not interpreted these powerful experiences according to Kant. In the case of the natural sublime, while some well-read individuals deduced from the magnificence of Niagara Falls and the Natural Bridge the existence of a universal moral sense, many early visitors to these sites felt that they proved the existence of God. Technological marvels were even less likely to be "read" in Kantian terms. Most Americans thought that a man-made rupture in ordinary experience proved the potential omnipotence of humanity. A railroad, a skyscraper, or a hydro-electric dam proclaimed the ever-increasing power of technicians, demonstrating their ability to disrupt what had become normal perception and creating the discontinuity that Americans seemed to crave. This radical break in experience became a necessary epiphany; it reinforced the sense of progress. At the same time, the "Americanness" of this epiphany invigorated nationalistic sentiment.

There were occasional dissenters. Since the 1820s some have greeted new technologies with skepticism. Thoreau suggested that the railroad, for all its admirable celerity, nevertheless exemplified a more general development, in which (in Emerson's words) "things are in the saddle and ride mankind."[7] Later, others felt the skyscraper destroyed the scale of the city and reduced the citizen to a stick figure, a featureless pedestrian seen from a great distance. This opposition suggests a contradiction at the heart of the technological sublime that invites the observer to interpret a sudden expansion of perceptual experience as the corollary to an expansion of human power and yet simultaneously evokes the sense of individual insignificance and powerlessness. One is both the all-seeing observer in a high tower and the ant-like pedestrian inching along the pavement below. One can either be outside, terrified by the speed and noise of the railway, or riding triumphantly over the landscape. One may (like the young Lewis Mumford) experience the electrified skyline as an epiphany, or one may (like Claude McKay) feel overwhelmed by the swirling lights of Times Square. Technologies can be perceived as an extension and affirmation of reason or as the expression of a crushing, omnipotent force outside the self. In this bifurcation, those who have the greatest political, economic, and social power are more likely to find themselves inside the panopticon, surveying the vast surround.

Such a division was less evident during the Jacksonian period, when new technologies were embraced by a cross-section of the body politic. In the 1828 parade that celebrated the construction of the Baltimore and Ohio Railroad, representatives of virtually all trades and every social class took part. (Such events contrasted with unruly, spontaneous parades of the unskilled and the working poor.) During the remainder of the nineteenth century, formal parades organized by local elites gradually deleted the skilled worker and the ordinary citizen, focusing instead on engineers, entrepreneurs, and a few elected officials. Even more important, attention shifted away from human beings to technological objects. The huge Corliss Engine became the icon of the 1876 Centennial Exposition. A decade later, few of the millions who saw the inauguration of Brooklyn Bridge or that of the Statue of Liberty heard the speeches. The word was increasingly replaced by massive representations, a process advanced by the electrical sublime at world's fairs and the Hudson-Fulton Celebration of 1909. Gradually the word ceased to be the carrier of sublimity. Reenactments and displays became important before film and television, which proved ill suited to convey the full force of the technological sublime. It had to be seen, heard, and felt in person. The citizen had become less an active participant than a tourist and a consumer – a fact well understood by corporate exhibitors at the New York World's Fair of 1939 and self-evident by the rededication of the Statue of Liberty in 1986.

The classic location of such experiences was the urban metropolis. It possessed the magnificent railway stations, the artificial cliffs and ravines of the new skyline, the skyscraper panoramas that encouraged fantasies of domain, the de-natured industrial districts, and the phantasmagoria of the Great White Way. Each of these offered the visitor a powerful demonstration of what human beings had accomplished. In the view from a skyscraper, in the artificial totality of the factory zone, or in the special effects of the Great White Way, nature had disappeared. The visitor was by turns terrified, exalted, and reduced to insignificance. The new skyscrapers reduced the individual to an insect or a shadow. The new factories contained vast interiors filled with workers whose sheer numbers demonstrated the insignificance and interchangeability of individuals. Electric advertising did not emphasize producers, engineers, architects, or inventors; rather, it paraded the brand names of mass-produced products. Whereas Independence Day had been a once-a-year commemoration, the factory tour and the skyscraper observation platform were open each day and the Great White Way shone every night.

The paradox of the technological sublime is that it pretends to present a legible materialization of the unrepresentable – as though a physical construction could be infinite, as though the boundless could be bounded, as though the shapeless could be shaped. Slavoj Zizek has called the sublime "a unique point in Kant's system, a point at which the fissures, the gap between phenomenon and Thing-in-itself, is abolished in a negative way, because in it the phenomenon's very inability to represent the Thing adequately is inscribed in the phenomenon itself."[8] For Kant the hurricane was not a concretization of reason, but Americans have long thought that new machines are nothing less than that. For Kant the natural sublime object evokes the feeling of enthusiasm, or a pleasure of a purely negative kind, for it finally concerns a failure of representation. In contrast, the American technological sublime is built on a pleasure of a positive kind, for it concerns an apparently successful representation of man's ability to construct an infinite and perfect world.

In the search for this positive pleasure, a "consumer's sublime" has emerged as Americans shop for new sensations of empowerment. Icons of the natural sublime, such as the Grand Canyon, are subjected to this process, and indeed the national parks have far more visitors today than in the early twentieth century. But increasingly they are appreciated not as signs of nature's immeasurable power and sublimity but as contrasts to a civilization that threatens to overwhelm them. The national park thus becomes a species of theme park, making available a relatively unspoiled nature which society has spared from development. In this reconfiguration, part of the Grand Canyon's attraction and interest is that it is threatened by an array of technologies and therefore should be seen immediately before it is further defiled by the smog blowing in from the west, by acid rain, and by the "light pollution" that makes it hard to see the stars at night. The tourist is told to feel pleased if the weather is clear. A fortunate few fill the quotas for river raft trips, although the rapids are more predictable now than in the nineteenth century because the waters of the Colorado are dammed to the immediate north and south of the park. Glen Canyon Dam impounds the silt and rock that once would have been carried through the gorge and replenished its sand banks. It releases water at an even rate, thus slowing the erosion that carved the canyon in the first place. The moderate flow permits the growth of dense foliage where once the plants would have been scoured off the banks by flash floods. The water also is much colder now, since it comes from the deep lake behind the dam, and several species of fish unique to the area, such as the humpback chub, have been driven back to the warmer tributary streams. At the other end of the canyon, a 1984 government report found, unsupervised "use of the remote portions of the Colorado River from Diamond Creek to Lake Mead is increasing dramatically. Boating upriver from Lake Mead is increasingly popular and difficult to regulate."[9] (Environmental protests protected the canyon from another dam within its boundaries.) Noise pollution is also a problem. Overhead, planes and helicopters carrying tourists from Las Vegas and Phoenix can be heard during half of the daylight hours.[10] Five million people came to the park in 1993, and the visitation rate has doubled every decade since 1919. This massive influx greatly exceeds the park's hotel capacity of 3628 hotel rooms and 329 campsites. One feels fortunate to get a room inside the park, fortunate to have good visibility, fortunate if there are not too many planes overhead. In short, the Grand Canyon, if one is lucky, may appear undisturbed and "natural."

Yet the environmental threats to the canyon and the increased visitation are only one side of the problem. In the past the Grand Canyon invited reflection on human insignificance, but today much of the public sees it through a cultural lens shaped by advanced technology. The characteristic questions about the canyon reported by Park Service employees assume that humans dug the canyon or that they could improve it so that it might be viewed quickly and easily. Rangers report repeated queries for directions to the road, the elevator, the train, the bus, or the trolley to the bottom. Other visitors request that the canyon be lighted at night. Many assume that the canyon was produced either by one of the New Deal dam-building programs or by the Indians – "What tools did they use?" is a common question.[11] These remarks reveal a common belief that the canyon is a colossal human achievement that ought to be improved. Visitors enjoy it in its present form, but some see room for improvements: light shows, elevators, roads, tramways, riverboats, luxury hotels at the bottom. The assumption of human omnipotence has become so common that the natural world seems an extension of ourselves, rather than vice versa. These are by no means the opinions of all visitors, of course. Many want no "improvements" in the Grand Canyon, and some hope to see 90 percent of it set aside as a designated wilderness. Yet even the Park Service, which does not want further development, has asked the managers of Disney World for advice on how to deal with the enormous influx of visitors.

Paradigmatic sites of the natural sublime have long been made more accessible by improved transportation, beginning with the Erie Canal. But increasingly advanced technologies not only get people to the site; they also provide alternatives to seeing it. A maximum of 92 people per night are allowed to stay at the Phantom Ranch, at the bottom of the Grand Canyon; but outside the park 525 people per hour can sit in an IMAX theater and watch *The Grand Canyon – The Hidden Secrets*, a 34-minute film shown on a 70-foot screen with six-track Dolby sound. As an additional attraction, the theater advertises "Native Americans in traditional dress on the staff." During the performance guests are encouraged to "enjoy our fast food, popcorn, ice cream" and other snacks. Why bother to hike into the canyon when all the highlights have been prepackaged? Similar theaters now serve Niagara Falls and Yosemite. Their gift shops sell videocassettes, postcards, photographs, slides, maps, guides, and illustrated books. These representations cannot extirpate the sublimity of these sites, but they can make it difficult for tourists, who usually remain for only one day, to rid themselves of their pre-visualizations. Many people experience a natural wonder as incomplete, disappointing, or overrated, and even when the Grand Canyon satisfies it often does so because it lives up to its image.

This egotistical sublime is hardly new. In the nineteenth century it was familiar to Margaret Fuller, to Nathaniel Hawthorne, and to the geologist Clarence Dutton. But this response has become pervasive, signaling the triumph of the consumer's vision, which asks that each object be clearly labeled, neatly packaged, and easily appropriated. Each year several people fall into the Grand Canyon because they venture too close to the edge, and their relatives then sue the Park Service because there were no fences or guard rails – as if a terrifying immensity that people journey great distances to see ought to have hand rails and warning signs; as if the "thing in itself" ought to be equipped with a snack bar; as if the unrepresentable could be projected on a 70-foot screen. The notion of a consumer's sublime is ultimately a contradiction in terms. Not only does it deny the existence of transcendental values that might be deduced from the natural object (that denial was always latent within the technological sublime): it also denies the exaltation, the danger, the difficulty, the immensity, and the otherness of the wild and the nonhuman.

The American fascination with the trope of the technological sublime implies repeated efforts at more and more powerful physical manifestations of human reason. For more than a century it was possible to incorporate each new technology into the life-world. The succession of sublime forms – dynamic technological, geometrical, industrial, electrical – fostered a sense of human control and domination that was radically at odds with the natural sublime. From c. 1820 to c. 1945 this incompatibility, rooted in the difference between Kantian reason and technological reason, was muted. However, the atomic bomb manifested a purely material negativity; it was the ultimate dead end of any attempted representation of the technological "thing in itself." The bomb materialized the end of human technique even as it dematerialized its target. Here the shaped and the bounded works of man merged with the shapeless and the boundless, and Americans first glimpsed the death-world that the technological sublime might portend.

Yet history is not a philosopher's argument. It records not logical developments but a mixture of well-reasoned acts, unintended consequences, accidents, shifting enthusiasms, and delusions. Though by the logic of argument the technological sublime "ought to" have gone into terminal decline after Hiroshima, something more complex occurred instead. While most people dreaded atomic weapons, many embraced the space program and most enjoyed spectacles such as the rededication of the Statue of Liberty. At the same time, Disney transformed the exposition, merging the amusement park with magical corporate displays. These changes marked a nostalgic return to the nineteenth-century technological object and to a sanitized recollection of the city before the diaspora into suburbia. Like the Jacksonians who mingled their awe for natural and man-made wonders, late-twentieth-century Americans seem oblivious to the logical impasses posed by the technological sublime, as their leisure travel increasingly demonstrates. They flock to the Kennedy Space Center, the Empire State Building and other skyscrapers, the Gateway Arch, the Smithsonian Air and Space Museum, Disneyland, and, most recently, Las Vegas.

Unlike the Ford assembly line or Hoover Dam, Disneyland and Las Vegas have no use value. Their representations of sublimity and special effects are created solely for entertainment. Their epiphanies have no referents; they reveal not the existence of God, not the power of nature, not the majesty of human reason, but the titillation of representation itself. The genuine ceases to have any special status; the faked, the artificial, and the copy are the stock-in-trade.

Las Vegas, with more annual visitors than Yellowstone, the Grand Canyon, Niagara Falls, the Empire State Building, and Cape Kennedy combined, exemplifies the full development of the consumer's sublime, which first emerged prominently at the 1939 New York World's Fair. The traditional underpinnings of a city do not exist in Las Vegas. Not the forces of trade nor those of industry nor those of religion nor those of government explain its emergence as a metropolitan area with a population of more than 800,000. One-third of all its jobs are in the hotel and gaming industries, and a good many of the inhabitants who do not work in those industries benefit from tourism indirectly.

Las Vegas's popularity is recent. Begun as a watering hole for westward-bound migrants traveling by horse and wagon, it emerged as a raw railroad town in the early twentieth century. Its spectacular growth began after 1931, when the State of Nevada legalized gambling (which was already prevalent).[12] The construction of Hoover Dam and the establishment of military bases brought in new customers for the casinos. After World War II, the mushrooming population of California and the rest of the Southwest enlarged the clientele further. As casinos grew more spectacular,[13] the city invented its "strip," a long row of lavish hotels decked with the most elaborate lighting west of Times Square and distinguished by an approach to architecture later celebrated by Robert Venturi.[14] In the 1960s air travel made the city accessible to the rest of the nation, and it became a convention and entertainment center as well as a gambling mecca. More than 2100 conventions were held there in 1992, when Las Vegas had more hotel rooms and a higher occupancy rate than London. The more than 21 million visitors stayed an average of four days, gambled more than $430 per person, and produced more than $14.6 billion in revenues.[15] Measured in terms of time or money, Las Vegas has become one of America's most important tourist sites. Built not on production but consumption, not on industry but play, not on the sacred but the profane, not on law but chance, Las Vegas is that rupture in economic and social life where fantasy and play reign supreme, the anti-structure that reveals the structure it opposes.

Neither the slow economy of the 1970s nor the stagnation of the early 1990s affected Las Vegas's surging growth. Long one of the most spectacular sites of the electrical sublime, the city has undergone a multi-billion-dollar development program that includes several skyscrapers and most of the elements once associated with world's fairs and amusement parks. The new casinos combine hotels, gaming rooms, and "Disney-quality" theme parks. The 3000-room Mirage Hotel (1990) cost $630 million. Despite dire predictions that it would never be profitable, it has proved a "cash machine." The Mirage's $30 million, five-story volcano, which erupts several times each hour in front of the hotel, was such a success that in 1993 the owner opened, right next to it, another casino hotel: Treasure Island, where battles between full-size replicas of a pirate ship and a British frigate are staged. Nearby the 4000-room Excalibur (1990), an ersatz castle with hotel towers attached, stresses a pseudo-Arthurian motif, with jousting matches every evening. The Luxor (1993) is a 2500-room pyramid-shaped hotel with a replica of the Sphinx, King Tutankhamen's tomb ("Tut's Hut"), talking robot camels, and a "Nile River" boat ride under the casino, "past murals illustrating the rich history of the Egyptian empire." Circus Circus, which looks like an enormous tent, stages acrobatic acts every hour through the night and contains a $75 million climate-controlled amusement park called Grand Slam Canyon. The film *The Wizard of Oz* provides the motif for the billion-dollar MGM Grand Hotel (1993), the largest in the world. The visitor passes between the golden paws of a 109-foot lion and along a yellow brick road to a 60-foot-high Emerald City, beyond which lie a 33-acre theme park, a 15,200-seat sports area, and eight restaurants.[16] Theme casinos and their amusement parks attract whole families rather than only individuals and couples.[17] They combine fantasies and legends with simulated sublime experiences, including volcanoes, waterfalls, Grand Canyon raft trips, and skyscrapers.[18]

The transformation of Las Vegas into a family theme park in the desert makes it the premiere postmodern landscape – a fantasy world for the middle class. It develops the disembodied illusions of the Great White Way into a multidimensional hyperreality, juxtaposing scenes from fairy tales, history, advertising, novels, and movies to create a dreamscape of disconnected signifiers. At the upscale Forum Shops a cornucopia of designer goods are for sale on a simulated Roman street where the vaulted sky passes from morning to evening to night and "Roman gods come to life in the form of 'animatronic' robots."[19] For those with less cash there are ordinary malls near other casinos and factory outlet stores at the end of the strip. Likewise, Las Vegas stages entertainment for every taste, including Broadway musicals, magic shows, dancing girls, tennis tournaments, world championship boxing matches, demonstrations of virtual reality, and rock concerts. It even recycles elements of the zoo, displaying caged white tigers and tanks full of sharks. This is the landscape of capitalist surrealism, where a man-made order seems to replace the natural order entirely. Visitors experience a potpourri of the technological sublime in a synesthesia of lights, heights, illusions, and fantastic representations. All of these enhance the visceral excitement of gambling, which contains the terror of financial catastrophe and the allure of a huge jackpot.

Whereas the older forms of the technological sublime embodied the values of production, and literally embodied the gaze of the businessman as he surveyed a city from the top of a skyscraper or appreciated steel mills from the window of a passing train, Las Vegas validates the gaze of the consumer, who wants not the rational order of work but the irrational disorder of play. Las Vegas manifests the dream world of consumption. The steamboat, the train, or the Corliss Engine has no role here. The city presents itself as a world entirely without infrastructure and beyond the limitations of nature.[20] The dislocation and the "incoherence" of this landscape are its strongest attractions, suggesting that technology faces no natural or economic constraints. Las Vegas offers visitors an intensification of experience, speeding up time and extending itself round the clock. Its lavishly mirrored interiors, like its landscape of electric signs, destroy normal spatial relations. The aesthetic of Times Square merges here with the automotive strip as the consumer moves along the conveyor belt of images from one fantasy to another. Las Vegas fuses the theme park, the shopping mall, and the casino, presenting itself as the central attraction and other nearby attractions – the Grand Canyon, Hoover Dam, the atomic testing site – as secondary.

The consumer's sublime on offer in Las Vegas anthologizes sublime effects. These effects emphasize not solitary communion with nature but experiences organized for the crowd – not the mountaintop but man-made towers; not three-dimensional order but spatial and temporal disorientation. Kant had reasoned that the awe inspired by sublime objects would make men aware of their moral worth despite their frailties. The nineteenth-century technological sublime had encouraged men to believe in their power to manipulate and control the world. Those enthralled by the dynamic technological, geometrical, electrical, or industrial sublime felt omnipotence and exaltation, counterpointed by fears of individual powerlessness and insignificance. Railways, skyscrapers, bridges, lighting systems, factories, expositions, rockets, and bombs were all extensions of the world of production. Through them, Americans inscribed technological systems on consciousness so that the unrepresentable seemed manifest in human constructions.

But in the consumer's sublime of Las Vegas or Disneyland, technology is put to the service of enacting fantasy. The technological sublime had exhorted the observer to dominate and control nature. It celebrated rationality, substituting technique for transcendental reason, celebrating work and achievement. But the consumer's sublime erases production and excites fantasy. It privileges irrationality, chance, and discontinuity. There had always been an element of escapism in the tours to sublime objects, but there was an uplifting lesson to be drawn from Niagara Falls (God's handiwork) or from a railway, a skyscraper, a factory, or a moon rocket (man's accomplishments). The electrical sublime elided the line between nature and culture and, in the process, dissolved the scale and the three-dimensionality of the landscape; yet it could still serve a vision focused on progress. In contrast, the billions of dollars spent in Las Vegas represent a financial and psychic investment in play for its own sake. The epiphany has been reduced to a rush of simulations, in an escape from the very work, rationality, and domination that once were embodied in the American technological sublime.

Notes

1 George Ticknor, *Life, Letters and Journals of George Ticknor*, cited in Charles Mason Dow, *Anthology and Bibliography of Niagara Falls*, vol. 1 (State of New York, 1921), p. 221.

2 On European intellectuals and their postmodern visions of America see Rob Kroes, "Flatness and Depth," in *Consumption and American Culture.*, ed. D. E. Nye and C. Pedersen (Amsterdam: Free University Press).

3 I believe Professor Marx would agree with this statement.

4 Martha Banta, *Imaging American Women: Idea and Ideals in Cultural History* (Columbia University Press, 1987), p. 761.

5 Don Ihde, *Technology and the Lifeworld: From Garden to Earth* (Indiana University Press, 1990), pp. 21–30.

6 Catherine Caufield, *Multiple Exposures* (University of Chicago Press, 1990), pp. 106–107.

7 Poems of Ralph Waldo Emerson (*Collected Works*, vol. 9) (Houghton Mifflin, 1904), p. 78.

8 Slavoj Zizek, *The Sublime Object of Ideology* (Verso, 1989), pp. 203, 204.

9 National Park Service, *Grand Canyon Natural and Cultural Resource Management Plan,* April 1984.

10 See U.S. Department of the Interior, *Aircraft Management Plan Environmental Assessment, Grand Canyon National Park*, May 1986.

11 These questions had been put so many times that the rangers at the information counters had a list of the twenty most common queries printed up and taped it to the counter in early December 1993. I interviewed five staff members, all of whom confirmed that these were frequently asked questions. It is also common for people to ask where the geysers are and to ask for the location of the "carved stone faces." Some people also want to know if it is true that someone jumped the canyon on a motorcycle.

12 For a history of gambling with a focus on Las Vegas see John M. Findlay, *People of Chance: Gambling in American Society from Jamestown to Las Vegas* (Oxford University Press, 1986).

13 For a survey and a history of Las Vegas's casinos see David Spanier, *Welcome to the Pleasure Dome* (University of Nevada Press, 1992).

14 Robert Venturi, *Learning from Las Vegas: The Forgotten Symbolism of Architectural Form*, revised edition (MIT Press, 1991).

15 Statistics from Las Vegas Chamber of Commerce, *Las Vegas Perspective*. Las Vegas Review Journal, 1993.

16 My descriptions of the hotels are based on visits, brochures, and advertising. See also Sergio Lalli, "Big Projects Boost Vegas," *Hotel and Motel Management* 206, November 4, 1991; "Wynn's World: White Tigers, Blackjack, and a Midas Touch," *Business Week*, March 30, 1992; David B. Rosenbaum, "Resorts: Precast as Big Winner in Vegas" *ERN* 229, July 13, 1992.

17 This fact has interesting financial implications. Surveys already show that Las Vegas attracts mostly middle-class consumers who gamble "voraciously and with less regard for income" than those who go to Atlantic City. In effect, those who visit Las Vegas pay a highly regressive tax for their pleasure. See Mary O. Borg, "An Economic Comparison of Gambling Behavior in Atlantic City and Las Vegas," *Public Finance Quarterly* 18 (1990), no. 3, pp. 291–312.

18 For background information on the new casinos I am indebted to the Las Vegas News Bureau.

19 Mike Weatherford, "Where Dreams Come True," *Nevada*, January–February 1993, pp. 10–14.
20 Though water is used lavishly at the new family resorts, water shortages present a potentially crippling barrier to further development. See John Jesitus, "Growing Gambling Mecca Reacts to Dwindling Supply of Water," *Hotel and Motel Management* 206, November 4, 1991.

1.5

The computational metaphor,
by Kevin Kelly

The least noticed trends are usually the most subversive ones. First on my list for an undetected upheaval is our collective journey toward the belief that the universe is a computer.

Already the following views are widespread: thinking is a type of computation, DNA is software, evolution is an algorithmic process. If we keep going we will quietly arrive at the notion that all materials and all processes are actually forms of computation. Our final destination is a view that the atoms of the universe are fundamentally intangible bits. As the legendary physicist John Wheeler sums up the idea: "Its are bits."

I first became aware of this increasingly commonly held (but not yet articulated) trend at the first Artificial Life Conference in 1987, where biological reproduction and evolution were described by researchers in wholly computer science terms. The surprise wasn't that such organic things could be given mathematical notations, because scientists have been doing that for hundreds of years. The surprise was that biological things could be simulated by computers so well. Well enough that such simulations displayed unexpected biological properties themselves. From this work sprang such fashionable patterns as cellular automata, fractals, and genetic algorithms.

The next step in this trend was to jettison the computer matrix and re-imagine biological processes simply in terms of computer logic. But to do this, first computation had to be stripped from computers as well. Starting with the pioneering work of Von Neumann and Turing, a number of mathematicians concluded that the essential process of computing was so elementary and powerful that it could be understood to happen in all kinds of systems. Or, in other words, the notion of computation was broadened so wide that almost any process or thing could be described in computational terms. Including galaxies, molecules, mathematics, emotions, rain forests and genes.

Is this embrace just a trick of language? Yes, but *that* is the unseen revolution. We are compiling a vocabulary and a syntax that is able to describe in a single language all kinds of phenomena that have escaped a common language until now. It is a new universal metaphor. It has more juice in it than previous metaphors: Freud's dream state, Darwin's variety, Marx's progress, or the Age of Aquarius. And it has more power than anything else in science at the moment. In fact the computational metaphor may eclipse mathematics as a form of universal notation.

This quickening of the new metaphor was made crystal clear recently in the work of mathematicians and physicists who have been dreaming up the next great thing after silicon chips: quantum computers. Quantum computers lie at the convergence of two "impossible" fields, the world of the impossibly small (quantum states), and the world of the impossibly ghostly (bits). Things get strange here very fast, but one thing is strangest of all. In the effort to create mathematical theories of how matter works at levels way below sub-atomic particles, and in the effort to actually build computers that operate in this realm, some scientists have found that using the language of bits best explains the behavior of matter. Their conclusion: Its *are* bits. Young Einsteins such as mathematician/theoretical physicist David Deutsch are now in the very beginnings of a long process of re-describing all of physics in terms of computer theory. Should they succeed, we would see the material universe and all that it holds as a form of computation.

There will be many people who will resist this idea fiercely, for many good reasons. They will point out that the universe isn't really a computer, only that it may act as if it was one. But once the metaphor of computation infiltrates physics and biology deeply, there is no difference between those two statements. It's the metaphor that wins.

And as far as I can tell the computational metaphor is already halfway to winning.

1.6

New communications technology: a survey of impacts and issues,

by Michael Marien

This biblioessay examines a wide range of recent literature to consider the impact and issues raised by new communications technologies. It surveys the extent of the impact of new communications technologies, enthusiasm for and criticism of the information society concept, the effects of television, and the impact of new communications technologies on democracy and governance, work and employment, and education. Copyright © 1996 Elsevier Science Ltd

Introduction: how big a transition?

In an age of multiple transformations, one of the major changes – arguably the most central of all – is the advent of a wide range of new communications technologies. This is resulting in an information society or information age, also described as a knowledge society (Drucker, 1994), a network society (Drucker, 1995), the Third Wave civilization (Toffler, 1995), the intelligent state (Connors, 1993), the infomedia age (Koelsch, 1995), cyberspace (*Time*, Special Issue, 1995) and cybersociety (Jones, 1995).

The information society has emerged gradually throughout the 20th century (Schement/Curtis, 1995). First usage of the term 'information society' appeared only in the late 1970s in Japan. Enthusiasm and dismay regarding this development are not new: consider the extraordinary Spring 1966 special 'Electronic Revolution' issue of *The American Scholar*, with articles by Marshall McLuhan. Buckminster Fuller, Herbert Simon, and many others. There is now a widespread sense, however, that the multi-faceted transformation is accelerating in the mid-1990s, and that much more change lies ahead. Connors (1993) speculates that the information revolution is likely to have run its course by 2005, but is the only observer to see some sort of end. It seems far more likely that the development and dissemination of new information technologies (IT) will continue for the next few decades at least. A vast industry is in place to do just that, and there are many rewards for companies and nations that take the lead, and few barriers to stop them.

In general outlines, we are undergoing a new era of communication that changes the balance between pictures and words (Davies *et al.*, 1990), and moves from relative scarcity of information to hyperabundance in multiple forms. As noted by Daniel Bell (1989), the most crucial fact about the new IT is that it creates a set of changes that pervade all aspects of society and reorganizes all older relationships: it widens arenas, multiplies actors, and increases the velocity and volatility of transactions. Alvin and Heidi Toffler (1993) insist that Third Wave societies run at hyperspeed, although one wonders how much additional speed is desirable, or humanly possible.

In a recent Special Issue of *Futures*, Sardar and Ravetz (1995) declare that "So deep is our collective ignorance of what cybertechnologies are doing to us, that the first urgent task is to discover our ignorance". What sort of revolution this is, and where it is taking us and what we can do about it, they lament, "is as yet completely obscure". This is exaggerated: some of the key technologies, actors, and issues can be identified, which is the purpose of this survey of recent English-language literature. But it is wise to declare 'ignorance' as a starting point – a noteworthy irony in the age of information!

New and prospective technologies

A proper starting point should briefly mention the panoply of communications technologies that are now being disseminated, developed, or expected in the next decade or so. There is no single source that authoritatively describes all of these technologies, and many of the sources listed here may be somewhat out-of-date.

Looking to the near future, Coates *et al.* (1994) state that the art of technology forecasting is still underdeveloped and may well be worsening instead of improving. Many forecasts noted here are propelled by enthusiasm and/or self-interest, and are thus likely to be overstated. Yet other recent IT developments (notably fax machines and the explosive growth of the Internet) were expected by very few observers, if any.

A basic development in the very near future is the merger of computers and telecommunications (Bradley *et al.*, 1993; *Scientific American* Special Issue, 1991), known variously as the information superhighway (Koelsch, 1995), the infobahn (Mitchell, 1995), Integrated Services Digital Network (Horrocks/Scarr, 1993), the telecomputer (Gilder, 1990), the SuperTube (Minow/LaMay, 1995) the National Information Infrastructure (Kahin/Abbate, 1995), the global information utility (Masuda, 1980: 1990), multimedia computing (Laudon *et al.*, 1994), C&C/computers and communications (Makridakis, 1995), universal information systems (Mayo, 1990), integrated information environments (Leebaret, 1991), Omnimedia (Snider/Ziporyn, 1992), and the network of networks (Blackman, 1994; Coates, 1994).

Other interrelated developments and expectations are:

- microprocessor performance doubling every 18 months through 2000 and perhaps beyond (Patterson, 1995; Mayo, 1992);
- ubiquitous computing/embodied reality as dominant mode of computer access over the next 20 years (Weiser, 1991);
- Very Large Scale Integration as key (Horrocks/Scarr, 1993);
- Internet and World Wide Web: explosive growth (Sussman, 1995);
- virtual reality (Durlach/Mavor, 1995; Adam, 1993; Aukstakalnis/Blatner, 1992);

- mirror worlds by end of 1990s (Gelerntner, 1991);
- expert systems widespread by 1998 (Halal, 1993);
- voice-access computers by 2002 (Halal, 1993; Roe/Wilpan, 1994);
- software agents/custom-designed software (Maes, 1995; Leebaert, 1995);
- Global Brain as emergent structure (Mayer-Kress/Barczys, 1995; Pelton, 1989);
- language translators for some vocabularies by 2025 (Coates, 1994);
- global currency by 2025 (Coates, 1994);
- smart cards for most Americans within three years (Belsie, 1993);
- e-mail as dominant telecom media in 15 years (Negroponte, 1995);
- wrist-mounted TV/computer/telephone in 5 years (Negroponte, 1995);
- photonic lightwave transmission systems capability doubling annually for next two decades (Mayo, 1992);
- Universal Information Systems offering any combination, anywhere, anytime (Mayo, 1990);
- public networks enabling access for all by 2007 (Halal, 1993);
- 500-channel cable TV (Brody, 1993);
- home distribution video systems in a few years (Minoli, 1995);
- long-distance charges abolished by 2001 (Lundberg, 1991);
- a global personal communicator by 2010 (Lundberg, 1991);
- wireless cellular services for nearly a half billion people worldwide by 2001 (Zyzman, 1995);
- fiber amplifiers increasing lightwave communication transmission capacities by a factor of 100 (Desurvire, 1992);
- pager use up 15% per annum for next few years (MacLachlan, 1993);
- electronic book under development (Markoff, 1991; Lande, 1991);
- service robotics outstripping industrial robotics before 1995 (Engelberger, 1989);
- robots widespread by 2015 (Makridakis, 1995);
- humanlike androids to perform 'drudge' jobs within 20 years (Caudill, 1992);
- greater-than-human intelligence within 30 years (Vinge, 1993); and
- human equivalence (AI) in desktop computers in 30–65 years (Crevier, 1993);

Some of these developments – perhaps many – will be delayed. A few might not be realized at all, eg Japan's failure to develop Fifth Generation artificial intelligence (Pollack, 1992). But a few might be realized sooner than expected, and some unexpected technologies or technological twists are likely. If, say, only half of the above developments were widespread in the next decade or so, human communications would surely be markedly transformed, for better and worse.

The new technologies will not simply happen. They demand public policies to smooth the way and deal with various problems:

- regulating the degree of competition (Blackman/Schoof, 1994);
- controlling the emerging Microsoft monopoly (Gleick, 1995; Burstein/Kline, 1995);
- providing public access to the Internet (Kahin/Keller, 1995);
- correcting Internet security flaws (Markoff, 1995);
- developing standards for interconnection and interoperability (Kahin/Abbate, 1995);

- considering options for the National Information Infrastructure (National Research Council, 1994a; Office of Technology Assessment, 1994; CPSR, 1993; Dertouzos, 1991);
- developing policy on intellectual property rights (National Research Council, 1993; Dyson, 1995);
- policy for the International Public Network (Harasim, 1993); and
- articulating a Bill of Rights for the Information Age (Glastonbury/LaMendola, 1992).

Ideally, a long-term program, as proposed by Bankes and Builder of the Rand Corporation (1992), could identify high-leverage investments in infotech, expand human rights, and promote an open world society. Muddling through seems far more likely. One way or another, though, we will live in the midst of most of these new communications technologies, as well as others not mentioned here and yet to be imagined by anyone.

Information society enthusiasts

The rapidly-changing configuration of new communications technologies can be roughly grasped, but requires constant updating. We already live in an information society, where most workers are involved in information-related work, involving computers and other new technologies. In the next decade, infotech will affect more people worldwide, at an ever-deeper level. What, then, are the many human impacts that can now be recognized, and, overall, is the information society desirable or undesirable, and for whom? Who gains, and who loses?

The answer to this basic question depends very much on who is consulted. As noted by Rob Kling (1994), the literature on computerization is divided by utopians, anti-utopians, and more empirically-anchored writers. The gulf between utopian enthusiasts and anti-utopian critics is vast; ironically, there is virtually no evidence of any communication! A leading early enthusiast was the late Marshall McLuhan (1964), who identified the transition from 'the mechanical age' to 'the electric age' in *Understanding Media*, and later supplied the visionary 'global village' term that is still widely used. Less well-known in the West is Japan's Yoneji Masuda (1980, 1990), who spelled out a highly optimistic and humanistic ideal of the global information society. Alvin Toffler's best-seller *The Third Wave* (1980) pronounced a 'quantum leap forward' and a 'new civilization', based on a new techno-sphere and info-sphere, demassified media, and working at home in the electronic cottage.

Another best-seller was written by John Naisbitt (1982), who extolled the first of his ten 'megatrends' as the transition from industrial society to information society. In the late 1980s, conservative thinker George Gilder declared the overthrow of matter by the microchip (1989) and the interactive telecomputer replacing the age of television (1990). Joseph Pelton (1989) saw the global brain making the global village a reality and leading to '*Homo electronicus*'.

Among contemporary visionaries, Bill Gates (1995), the Chairman and CEO of Microsoft (and today's wealthiest American), is leading the way, with a rather bland view of the wallet PC, digital cash, and E-books. Other enthusiasts include Nicholas

Negroponte of the MIT Media Lab (1995), Arno Penzias of Bell Labs (1995), Frank Koelsch (1995), Myron C Tuman (1992), and Peter Huber (1994), who notes how our present communications are quite the opposite from the monolithic telescreen of George Orwell's *1984* Big Brother. Howard Rheingold (1993) offers guarded optimism for the 'virtual community' warning that big power and big money may control access. The home for enthusiasts is *Wired* magazine in San Francisco (call 1–800/SO WIRED), which boasted some 250 000 subscribers in late 1995 – only its third year of publication!

To summarize the proclaimed benefits of information society:

- democracy enhanced (Gilder, 1990; Masuda, 1990; Rheingold, 1993);
- education enhanced (Gilder, 1990; Masuda, 1990);
- science enhanced (Rheingold, 1993);
- individualism enhanced (Gilder, 1990; Negroponte, 1995);
- global consciousness/global brain (Pelton, 1989);
- global economy (Masuda, 1980; Koelsch, 1995);
- harmonization when business and technology work together (Penzia, 1995; Negroponte, 1995);
- online literacy to free us from the deadening past (Tuman, 1992);
- more free expression/freedom of thought (Huber, 1994);
- ample means to close rich/poor gap (Penzias, 1995; Gates, 1995);
- thousands of choices; shopper's heaven; friction-free capitalism (Gates, 1995); and
- faster flows, shortening sender/receiver distance and collapsing the 'information float' (Naisbitt, 1982).

The visionaries as a group make no reference to each other or to any of their critics. Nor do they make any effort to provide any suggestive evidence for their hopeful claims.

This survey now turns to the critics, and then to experience with actual infotech impacts in various areas.

Information society critics

The utopian/enthusiasts include techno-leaders (Gates, Negroponte, Penzias, Pelton, Masuda), futurist/business consultants (Toffler, Naisbitt, Koelsch), and political libertarians (Huber, Rheingold, Gilder).

In contrast, the critics are social scientists (Ellul, Estabrooks, Klapp, Kurtzman, Roszak), communications scholars (Haywood, Postman, Winston), political leftists (Brook/Boal, Kroker/Weinstein, Sale), humanists (Birkerts, Slouka), psychologists (Gergen, Kegan), and computer experts with no financial stake (Stoll, Talbott). In contrast to merely making assertions, many of their arguments are amply documented (eg Ellul, Webster/Robins). Several proudly identify themselves as neo-Luddites (Roszak, Sale, Webster/Robins, Brook/Boal).

The most frequent and perhaps most important general complaint is that of information overload or infoglut (Ellul, 1990; Postman, 1992; Roszak, 1986; Klapp,

1986; Stoll, 1995; Kegan, 1994). Even Alvin Toffler (1970) dealt extensively with the stressful impacts of too much information in *Future Shock* (but his later writing ignores this problem). Other concerns:

- absurdity and unreason (Ellul, 1990; Gergan, 1991);
- flying blind/obsessive gambling (Hamelink, 1988);
- undermining humanity and morals (Postman, 1992; Sale, 1995);
- unemployment (Webster/Robins, 1986);
- distraction from reality (Stoll, 1995; Slouka, 1995);
- literacy and creativity diminished (Stoll, 1995; Birkerts, 1994);
- culture of the book declining (Sanders, 1994; Kernan, 1990);
- reduced attention span (Birkerts, 1994);
- technobabble/computerese influencing language (Barry, 1991);
- loss of community; networks as isolating (Stoll, 1995; Birkerts, 1994; Slouka, 1995);
- rich/poor gap aggravated (Stoll, 1995; Haywood, 1995);
- saturated and disconnected self (Gergan, 1991);
- critical discourse diminished; information commodified (Haywood, 1995);
- hyperactive society increases demands on managers and workers; degrading work (Estabrooks, 1988; Brook/Boal, 1995);
- volatile electric economy adding to social instability (Kurtzman, 1993; Cunningham/Porter, 1992);
- cyber-authoritarianism (Kroker/Weinstein, 1994);
- computer dehumanizes many social activities (Forester, 1992); and
- costs of insecure and unreliable computer systems (Ellul, 1990; Forester/ Morrison, 1994).

Television pro and con

Television has been a major social force for nearly 50 years. Thus in some respects it might be overlooked as a 'new' communication technology. But it has been evolving and extending its influence through cable and satellites. And it will further evolve when it is married to computers in the near future.

The impacts of TV, in America at least, are generally considered to be negative, and getting more so. Among recent commentators, there are a few supporters: Neuman (1995) argues that TV has not replaced or diminished literacy; Bianculli (1992) writes that TV has improved substantially and deserves more respect than it gets; Fowles (1992) attacks anti-TV attitudes of TV priggery and asserts that TV is a grandly therapeutic force for nearly all Americans. Contrast these views with the critics:

- TV as principal cause of our demoralization due to too much vicarious experience (Shrader, 1992);
- reduced imagination and corporate domination (O'Neill, 1991);
- an age of missing information when vital knowledge is beyond our reach and lessons of the natural world grow fainter (McKibbon, 1992);

- neglected potential of children's TV (Minow/LaMay, 1995; Palmer, 1988);
- abandonment of public interest TV (Day, 1995; Minow/LaMay, 1995);
- growing corporate control of mass media and cultural industries (Schiller, 1989);
- talk shows bad for mental health (Heaton/Wilson, 1995);
- pursuit of sensation and vulgarity; excessive commercialism (Bogart, 1995);
- considerable expansion of space occupied by advertising (Mattelart, 1991);
- market-driven 'junk journalism' displacing healthier fare (McManus, 1994);
- decrease in quality of TV news due to network cutbacks (Kimball, 1994); and
- growing concentration and globalization of media ownership (Bagdikian, 1992; Smith, 1991; Kobrak/Luey, 1992).

Will the augmented TV of the future be any different? According to Minow and LaMay (1995), who argue that the explosion of cable and new interactive media have increased the violence children are exposed to, the 'SuperTube' is likely to be more of the same without constructive policy intervention.

Democracy and governance: better or worse?

Developments in infotech and the growing role and reach of the mass media create new patterns of human interconnection and a loss of boundaries: as society becomes more complex, the capacity of governing systems becomes overwhelmed (Rosell, 1992; Michael, 1993). Ronfeldt (1992) describes how the modern bureaucratic state is giving way to 'cyberocracy', which may radically affect who rules, how, and why. He warns that "cyberocracy, far from favoring democracy or totalitarianism, may make possible still more advanced, more opposite, and farther apart forms of both". Similarly, Ogden (1994) offers two contrasting scenarios of cyberdemocracy (Jeffersonian networks committed to pluralism and diversity) vs virtual mercantilism of private sector control.

An interesting coalition of Alvin Toffler, George Gilder, Ester Dyson, and Jay Keyworth, working through the Progress and Freedom Foundation allied to Rep. Newt Gingrich, proposes a 'Magna Carta for the Knowledge Age' to facilitate and hasten the transition to a Third Wave economy and a 'vastly smaller' (perhaps by 50% or more) Third Wave government (Dyson, 1994).

There are potentials for infotech enhancement of democracy. Ganley (1992) extols the role that 'personal electronic media' have already played in empowerment. Slaton (1992) reports on 'Televote' experiments for a much more participatory government. And Snider (1994) describes how both direct and mediated democracy can be ideally enhanced by electronic town meetings and interactive multi-media. Potentially, online resources could empower 21st century journalists and the public (Koch, 1991).

But arguments are building that infotech is diminishing democracy. A *Time Magazine* cover story (Wright, 1995) asserts that a 'hyperdemocracy' of too much public feedback has led to impulsive passage of dubious laws and fosters gridlock. Wines (1994) complains that modern communications have made politicians slaves to public opinion. Meanwhile, public opinion rests on a slimmer foundation, as more citizens rely on TV for information at the same time that TV news is being downsized (Cook *et al.*, 1992; Kaniss, 1995), soundbites have radically shrunk (Tierney, 1992), and local TV news is more susceptible to manipulation (Kaniss, 1995). Television makes voters feel informed about public affairs while miseducating the citizenry (Hart, 1994; Iyengar, 1991). At a time when citizens should appreciate the new global reality of increasing complexity, the 'unreality industry' works in the opposite direction (Mitroff/Bennis, 1989).

Work, productivity, employment: better or worse?

One highly popularized enthusiast (Dent, 1995) asserts that infotech is bringing a work revolution that will lead to a 'tidal wave of progress', advancing our standard of living and humanizing our lives. (Characteristically, the argument is made without any documentation.) Another enthusiast, writing in *The Futurist* (Hines, 1994), envisions massive data storage systems helping workers with infoglut, and various AI systems becoming partners with workers by 2010. Penzias (1995) envisions useful employment for all in the approaching 'Era of Harmony'.

There are indeed many potential benefits in computer conferencing/electronic meeting systems (Coates/Jarratt, 1994; Finley, 1991), telecommuting/distributed work (Schepp/Schepp, 1995; Coates/Jarratt, 1994), 'groupware' cooperative working (Lloyd, 1994), networked organizations (Sproull/Kiesler, 1991), and telerobotics (1992). Electronic job recruitment (Kennedy/Morrow, 1994) is already reshaping the job market. Coates (1995) forecasts that distributed work (those working outside the traditional workplace) could grow from 3.5% of today's workforce to 20% by 2005 and 40% by 2020.

Offsetting these benefits are four problems:

- extensive unemployment (Coates, 1995; Rifkin, 1995; Aronowitz/DiFazio, 1994; Mowshowitz, 1994; Bridges, 1994);
- the need for highly skilled employees in a process of continuous learning in complex organizations (Howard, 1995; Adler, 1992; NRC, 1994b);
- ineffective use of infotech: only a few firms are demonstrably better off and many show negative productivity (Morton, 1991); avoiding blind alleys and overambitious claims (Weizer, 1991; NRC, 1994b); full and effective use far from realized (Bikson/Law, 1993); and
- criminal use and abuse of infotech: viruses (Louw/Duffy, 1992); inadequate computer security (NRC, 1991; Lewis, 1995); cellular theft and phone fraud (Stephens, 1995); virtual crimes such as nonexistent properties and stocks (Stephens, 1995); computer extortion and credit card fraud (Moore, 1994, 1995); moles in financial institutions providing access codes (Moore, 1994); global organized crime threatening world financial infrastructure (Raine/Cilluffo, 1994); info-terrorism (Toffler, 1993).

The criminal dimension is difficult to measure and underreported (Lewis, 1995), and frequently ignored because it doesn't fit into conventional categories of analysis. Cybercrime may already be contributing significantly to the chaos and anxiety of our times. And the potential for disruption of work, productivity, and employment itself is high. Necessary responses to this situation may well include an international criminal justice system (Moore, 1995) and hastening the transition to a cashless society to reduce crime (Warwick, 1992). Until security is improved, many Internet users are barricaded behind firewalls (Lewis, 1995).

Education potentials and realities

The educational potentials of infotech are profound and numerous, and it is easy to get into the enthusiast/visionary mode of thought. Seymour Papert (1993) of the MIT Media Lab points to the centrality of the computer in the truly modern school, and to personal media capable of supporting a wide range of intellectual styles. Lewis Perelman (1992) extols hyperlearning technology that will enable virtually anyone to learn anything, anywhere, any time, and goes on to propose the new technology as a total replacement for conventional schools. Within the schools and colleges, the virtual class (Tiffin, 1995) and the virtual classroom (Hiltz, 1994) are seen as the new primary locus of learning. English professor Richard Lanham (1993) claims that electronic expression "has come not to destroy the Western arts and letters, but to fulfill them". The University of the World has been established to disseminate electronic resources to students and faculty worldwide (Becker, 1989), and many global ideas are explored by Rossman (1992) in *The Emerging Worldwide Electronic University*. Dunn (1994) envisions the totally wired campus and signs of the coming virtual university by 2000. Feigenbaum (1989) sees the library of the future as an active intelligent knowledge server. Halal and Liebowitz (1994) point to millions of corporate employees now being trained with interactive multimedia systems, and business is taking the lead in applying electronic technology to a 'K-80' marketplace for learning (Davis/Botkin, 1994). Electronic links for learning are getting better and could still expand greatly (Horner/Roberts, 1991; Palmer, 1993; Office of Technology Assessment, 1993).

But there are sobering cautions. The Office of Technology Assessment (1995) reports that a substantial number of teachers still make little or no use of computers because they lack training. Computer-literacy education often teaches only shallow recognition of jargon and components, and only a few applications (Rosenberg, 1991). A study of school reform in America (Tyack/Cuban, 1995) finds recurring faith in revolutionary electronic pedagogy over the past 70 years (Edison proclaimed that the motion picture would revolutionize education). Birdsall (1994) points to a similar myth of the electronic library over the past 50 years (microfilm was once seen as revolutionizing library services). Meanwhile, librarians are getting technical education at the expense of subject-matter education (American Library Association, 1995), and libraries are suffering from an ever-growing number of increasingly costly periodicals at a time of diminishing library budgets (Rice/Robillard, 1991), and from infoglut in general (ALA, 1995; Kingston, 1989).

Other concerns

Global culture: how engulfing?

In the concluding sentence to *Understanding Media*, Marshall McLuhan (1964) stated that "Panic about automation as a threat of uniformity on a world scale is the projection into the future of mechanical standardization and specialism, which are now past". There is some justification for this view. A study of cultural imperialism (Tomlinson, 1991) concludes that the subject is exaggerated by media theorists and that globalization weakens the cultural coherence of all nation-states. A study of international popular music (Robinson *et al.*, 1991), "the most universal of all the media", found that world musical homogenization is clearly not occurring. And a recent report on global television (Parker, 1995) found that global programs such as CNN newscasts are growing much slower than expected, and that national broadcasting systems are gaining strength. On the other hand, powerful arguments are made for the growth of 'the global cultural bazaar' and 'the global shopping mall' (Barnet/Cavanagh, 1994) and for the force of transnational corporate culture (Schiller, 1992).

Nationalism seriously eroded

It is commonly held that the global economy has weakened the nation-state in many respects. But this argument can also be overstated, as in book titles such as *The Twilight of Sovereignty* (Wriston, 1992) and *The End of the Nation State* (Ohmae, 1995).

Development potentials and realities

Information technology can help to expand access to science and technology for developing countries (Salomon/Sachs-Jeantet, 1994). Expert systems seem to be an especially promising tool for knowledge transfer (Woherem, 1991), and communication satellites can reach out to noncabled rural areas (Hudson, 1990). Mexico is one example of explosive growth in telecoms, both wired and wireless, which opens possibilities for tele-education and stemming the flow of people to over-populated cities (Vajda, 1993). 'Rural area networks' also hold promise for developing poor rural communities in the US (Office of Technology Assessment, 1991). And the role of mass communications in development could be greatly enhanced by operating under a new paradigm of more egalitarian relationships and shared responsibility (Casmir, 1991). But it is cautioned that infotech is not a panacea to Third World nations (Dordick/Wang, 1993), that transnational corporations and the US dominate the new 'informatics' (Gonzalez-Manet, 1992), and that more critical perspectives are needed against yet another instance of Western domination, well-meaning or not (Sussman/ Lent, 1991).

Cities reshaped

Mitchell (1995) sketches the 'City of Bits' as the new capital of the 21st century, and follows with various suggestions for urban design and rethinking the body in space. Intelligent transportation systems seem likely in 21st century urban areas (Diebold Institute, 1995). But Gibbs (1993) cautions against certain forms of telematics infrastructure that may lock an urban area into particular types of development.

Health care facilitated

Medical informatics will assist surgery and dental care, provide large databases and data interchange to greatly increase the speed and efficiency of research, and dramatically enhance the sharing of health knowledge by medical personnel and patients (Pickover, 1995; McNerney/Bezold, 1995). The potential of electronic health care services to the home is being realized at a time when prohibitive health care costs force more consideration of home care economies (Jones, 1995). But computerized decision support could accelerate an ongoing decline in medical autonomy and status (Weaver, 1991). And medical histories on smart cards and health database organizations pose threats to privacy (Donaldson/Lohr, 1994).

Privacy invaded

Some excellent reports on privacy were published in the 1980s and deserve mention here: several studies by the Office of Technology Assessment (1985, 1986), a warning about 'dossier society' as the other side of the information economy (Laudon, 1986), and a comparative study of surveillance in Germany, Sweden, France, Canada and the US (Flaherty, 1989). The former chairman of the US Privacy Protection Commission warns that "silently but relentlessly the computer is making it easy for big business and government to erode our right to be let alone" (Linowes, 1989). More recent literature explores legal issues of the information age (Branscomb, 1994), the need for better privacy safeguards (Ware, 1993), the loss of privacy from new telephone services (Dutton, 1992; Marx, 1994), and privacy principles and codes of ethics for industry (Smith, 1994; Mason et al., 1995). A new approach to information-handling based on new advances in cryptography, whereby one gives different pseudonyms to different organizations, is proposed to end the 'dossier society' threat (Chaum, 1992).

Consuming enhanced

The credit card industry is spreading worldwide and could well be a major threat to privacy (Ritzer, 1995). Ritzer also points to how growing credit card use facilitates consumption, and how these cards have become 'instruments of bondage' for many people, embedding them in the consumer society. Many activities now undertaken at shopping malls will soon be efficiently undertaken at the information mall (Sheth/ Sisodia, 1993). Software mogul Bill Gates (1995) envisions the electronic marketplace as the universal middleman: "market information will be plentiful and transaction costs low. It will be a shopper's heaven". Snider and Ziporyn (1992) idealistically propose a new type of consumerism based on an age of 'Omnimedia' and independent consumer information companies. The advent of E-money will facilitate "buying sprees at the virtual mall" (Levy, 1994).

Truth-seeking made difficult

Increasing complexity and turbulence, along with more access to multiple points of view, make truth-telling more difficult (Michael, 1993). This growing uncertainty can

only be aggravated by the new possibilities of creating, recombining, and transforming visual images (Mitchell, 1992), and by the advent of virtual reality, which may well
erode our sense of what is real (Heim, 1993: Cartwright, 1994: Jones, 1995).

A culture of peace obstructed?

The laudable notion of building a culture of peace appears confined to Federico
Mayer and UNESCO. A massive campaign on many fronts would be necessary to
advance it, preferably combined with some reinvented notion of the public interest as
a governing ethic in television broadcasting (Day, 1995). According to Day, trends
are moving away from this ideal. Another ominous trend is the growth of video games
largely based on themes of aggression and violence, and now a part of the daily
experience of many children (Provenzo, 1991).

Evolution accelerated

The executive editor of *Wired* has recently articulated a complex theory of the rise of
neo-biological civilization replacing the old world of mechanistic control (Kelly,
1994). Another recent view holds that the merging of humans and machines will
create Meta-man, a global superorganism and a powerful new image of ourselves
(Stock, 1993). Both views are in the visionary/enthusiast school of positive thinking
about infotech.

Conclusion: getting a grip on the real road ahead

Above all else, this survey should clearly impress any reader that our ignorance about
infotech and its impacts is vast, and the infoglut demonstrated here should rightfully
be unsettling.

No one has a good, up-to-date grasp of the emerging technologies. The enthusi-
astic advocates have no communication with the critics and the empiricists. Communications scholars are notably unhelpful, with the vast majority losing themselves
in behaviorist trivia and minutia. There are remarkably few journals in this area, and
no yearbooks to survey the 'knowledge industry' in its broadest dimensions (in contrast, the travel industry has several yearbooks). Futurists and their publications have
made many contributions (often on the upbeat/enthusiast side), but still largely focus
on single topics rather than broad patterns and frameworks.

Weighing the pros and cons of information society in general, as well as impacts
in specific areas, the skeptical and negative views appear to have at least as much
intellectual foundation as the positive views – and perhaps much more. The key is to
separate potentials and promising experiments from reality, and to look at *all* impacts.
Democracy has the potential to be enhanced by infotech, but present trends suggest
erosion by TV. Work and productivity have the potential to be enhanced, but misuse
of infotech and criminal activity raise questions about productivity, and the social
costs of unemployment may be vast. Infotech applications to education have vast
potential, yet the technology is still not used well and the learning climate in many
schools is being strained by budget cuts, violence, and bureaucracy. The potentials for

enhanced health care seem immense. The potentials for growing privacy invasion also seem immense. And there is a wide variety of opinions on the pros and cons of infotech aiding development, enhancing consumption, reshaping cities, and accelerating evolution in very new directions.

No answers can be offered here, only more questions. This survey is both too long and too short. The reader is thanked for enduring to the ambiguous end; yet, much more could be included. Somehow, we need to get a grip on the emerging information society: the ever-unfolding panoply of technologies, the actual and potential impacts, the pros and cons of what we are doing, and alternative policies to promote the public interest. This survey suggests the beginnings of what must be done: an ongoing, timely, and comprehensive survey of all relevant thinking worldwide on this momentous global development, with resulting information arrayed in a variety of formats. Think about it.

Bibliography

Adam, JA (1993) 'Virtual reality is for real' (Special Report) *IEEE Spectrum* 30 (10) (October) 22–29

Adler, PS (ed) (1992) *Technology and the Future of Work* Oxford University Press, New York (April) 336 pages

American Library Association, Library Instruction Round Table (1995) *Information for a New Age: Redefining the Librarian* Libraries Unlimited, Englewood, CO (February) 192 pages

Aronowitz, S, and DiFazio, W (1994) *The Jobless Future: SciTech and the Dogma of Work* University of Minnesota Press, Minneapolis, MN (October) 392 pages

Aukstakalnis, S, and Blatner, D (1992) *Silicon Mirage: The Art and Science of Virtual Reality* Peachpit Press, Berkeley, CA, 317 pages

Bagdikian, BH (1992) *The Media Monopoly* (Fourth Edition) Beacon Press, Boston, MA, 288 pages

Bankes, S, and Builder, C (1992) 'Seizing the moment: harnessing the information society' *The Information Society* 8 (1) (January–March) 1–59

Barnet, RJ, and Cavanagh, J (1994) *Global Dreams: Imperial Corporations and the New World Order* Simon and Schuster, New York, 480 pages

Barry, JA (1991) *Technobabble* MIT Press, Cambridge, MA, 268 pages

Becker, J (1989) 'The concept of a University of the World' *The Information Society* 6 (3) 83–92

Bell, D (1989) 'The third technological revolution: and its possible consequences' *Dissent* 36 (2) (Spring) 164–176

Belsie, L (1993) 'Smart cards connect customers' *The Christian Science Monitor* (13 August) 8

Bianculli, D (1992) *Teleliteracy: Taking Television Seriously* Continuum Publishing Co. New York, 315 pages

Bikson, TK, and Law, SA (1993) 'Electronic mail use at the World Bank: messages from users' *The Information Society* 9 (2) (April–June) 89–124

Birdsall, WF (1994) *The Myth of the Electronic Library: Librarianship and Social Change in America* Greenwood Press, Westport, CT, 206 pages

Birkerts, S (1994) *The Gutenberg Elegies: The Fate of Reading in an Electronic Age* Faber and Faber, Winchester, MA (December) 231 pages. Fawcett Columbine paperbound edition, New York (November 1995)

Blackman, C, and Schoof H (eds) (1994) 'Competition and convergence' (Special Issue) *Telecommunications Policy* 18 (8) (November) 571–667

Bogart, L (1995) *Commercial Culture: The Media System and the Public Interest* Oxford University Press. New York (January) 384 pages

Bradley, SP *et al.* (1993) *Globalization, Technology and Competition: The Fusion of Computers and Telecommunications in the 1990s* Harvard Business School Press, Boston, MA, 392 pages

Branscomb, AW (1994) *Who Owns Information? From Privacy to Public Access* Basic Books, New York (June) 241 pages

Bridges, W (1994) *JobShift: How to Prosper in a Workplace Without Jobs* Addison-Wesley, Reading, MA (October) 257 pages

Brody, H (1993) 'Information highway: the home front' *Technology Review* **96** (6) (August–September) 30–40

Brook, J, and Boal, IA (eds) (1995) *Resisting the Virtual Life: The Culture and Politics of Information* City Lights Books, San Francisco, CA (June) 278 pages

Burstein, D, and Kline, D (1995) *Road Warriors: Dreams and Nightmares along the Information Highway* Dutton/Penguin, New York (November) 466 pages

Cartwright, GF (1994) 'Virtual or real? The mind in cyberspace' *The Futurist* **28** (2) (March–April) 22–26

Casmir, FL (ed) (1991) *Communication in Development* Ablex Publishing Co, Norwood, NJ, 352 pages

Caudill, M (1992) *In Our Own Image: Building an Artificial Person* Oxford University Press, New York. 242 pages

Chaum, D (1992) 'Achieving electronic privacy' *Scientific American* **267** (2) (August) 96–101

Coates, JF (1994) 'The highly probably future: 83 assumptions about the year 2025' *The Futurist* **28** (4) (July–August) 7-page insert

Coates, JF (1995) 'Work and pay in the twenty-first century: an impending crisis' *Employment Relations Today* (Spring) 17–22

Coates, JF, and Jarratt, J (1994) 'White collar productivity: key to future competitiveness' *The Future at Work* **9** (November) 8 pages

Coates, JF *et al.* (1994) 'Technological forecasting: 1970–1993' *Technological Forecasting and Social Change* **47** (1) (September) 23–33

Computer Professionals for Social Responsibility (1993) *Serving the Community: A Public Interest Vision of The National Information Infrastructure* Computer Professionals for Social Responsibility, Palo Alto, CA, 30 pages

Connors, M (1993) *The Race to the Intelligent State: Towards the Global Information Economy of 2005* Blackwell Business, Oxford, UK, and Cambridge, MA, 221 pages

Cook, PS *et al.* (1992) *The Future of News: Television–Newspapers–Wire Services–Newsmagazines* Wilson Center Press, Washington, and Johns Hopkins University Press, Baltimore, 270 pages

Crevier, D (1993) *AI: The Tumultuous History of the Search for Artificial Intelligence* Basic Books, New York, 386 pages

Cunningham, S. and Porter, AL (1992) 'Communication networks: a dozen ways they'll change our lives' *The Futurist* **26** (1) (January–February) 19–22

Davies, D *et al.* (1990) *The Telling Image: The Changing Balance between Pictures and Words in a Technological Age* Oxford University Press. Oxford, UK, 166 pages

Davis, S, and Botkin, J (1994) *The Monster under the Bed: How Business is Mastering the Opportunity of Knowledge for Profit* Simon and Schuster. New York (September) 189 pages

Day, J (1995) *The Vanishing Vision: The Inside Story of Public Television* University of California Press. Berkeley, CA (October) 443 pages

Dent, HS. Jr (1995) *Job Shock: Four New Principles Transforming our Work and Business* St Martin's Press, New York (March) 295 pages

Dertouzos, ML (1991) 'Building the information marketplace' *Technology Review* **94** (1) (January) 28–40

Desurvire, E (1992) 'Lightwave communications: the fifth generation' *Scientific American* **266** (1) (January) 114–121

Diebold Institute for Public Policy Studies (1995) *Transportation Infrastructures: The Development of Intelligent Transportation Systems* Praeger, Westport, CT (May) 207 pages

Donaldson, MS, and Lohr KN (eds) (1994) *Health Data in the Information Age: Use, Disclosure, and Privacy* National Academy Press, Washington, DC (April) 257 pages

Dordick, HS, and Wang, G (1993) *The Information Society: A Retrospective View* Sage Publications, Newbury Park, CA, 168 pages

Drucker, PF (1994) 'The age of social transformation' *The Atlantic Monthly* **274** (5) (November) 53–80

Drucker, PF (1995) *Managing in a Time of Great Change* Truman Talley Books/Dutton, New York (November) 371 pages

Dunn, SL (1994) 'The challenge of the nineties in US higher education: from Camelot to the 21st century' *Futures Research Quarterly* **10** (3) (Fall) 35–55

Durlach, NI, and Mavor, AS (eds) (1995) *Virtual Reality: Scientific and Technological Challenges* National Academy Press, Washington, DC (January) 542 pages

Dutton, WH (1992) 'The social impact of emerging telephone services' *Telecommunications Policy* **16** (5) (July) 377–387

Dyson, E (1995) 'Intellectual value' *Wired* **3** (7) (July) 136–141

Dyson, E, Gilder, G, Keyworth, J, and Toffler, A (1994) 'A Magna Carta for the knowledge age' *New Perspectives Quarterly* **11** (4) (Fall) 26–37

Ellul, J (1990) *The Technological Bluff* (translated by Bromiley, GW) William B Eerdmans Publishing Co, Grand Rapids, MI, 418 pages

Engelberger, JF (1989) *Robotics in Service* MIT Press, Cambridge, MA, 248 pages

Estabrooks, M (1988) *Programmed Capitalism: A Computer-Mediated Global Society* ME Sharpe, Armonk, NY, 205 pages

Feigenbaum, EA (1989) 'Toward the library of the future' *Long Range Planning* **22** (1) (February) 118–123

Finley, M (1991) 'The best of all possible meetings' *Across the Board* **28** (9) (September) 40–45

Flaherty, DH (1989) *Protecting Privacy in Surveillance Societies: The Federal Republic of Germany, Sweden, France, Canada, and the United States* University of North Carolina Press, Chapel Hill, NC, 483 pages

Forester, T (1992) 'Megatrends or megamistakes? What ever happened to the Information Society?' *The Information Society* **8** (3) (July–September) 133–146

Forester, T, and Morrison, P (1994) *Computer Ethics: Cautionary Tales and Ethical Dilemmas in Computing* (Second Edition) MIT Press, Cambridge, MA (January) 347 pages

Fowles, J (1992) *Why Viewers Watch: A Reappraisal of Television's Effects* (Revised Edition) Sage Publications, Newbury Park, CA, 280 pages

Ganley, GD (1992) *The Exploding Political Power of Personal Media* Ablex Publishing Co, Norwood, NJ, 181 pages

Gates, B (1995) *The Road Ahead* Viking, New York (November) 286 pages

Gelernter, D (1991) *Mirror Worlds, or the Day Software Puts the Universe in a Shoebox . . . How It Will Happen and What It Will Mean* Oxford University Press, New York, 237 pages

Gergen, KJ (1991) *The Saturated Self: Dilemmas of Identity in Contemporary Life* Basic Books, New York, 295 pages

Gibbs, D (1993) 'Telematics and urban economic development policies: time for caution?' *Telecommunications Policy* **17** (4) (May–June) 250–256

Gilder, G (1989) *Microcosm: The Quantum Revolution in Economics and Technology* Simon and Schuster, New York, 426 pages

Gilder, G (1990) *Life After Television* Whittle Direct Books, Knoxville, TN, 86 pages

Glastonbury, B, and LaMendola, W (1992) *The Integrity of Intelligence: A Bill of Rights for the Information Age* St Martin's Press, New York, 206 pages

Gleick, J (1995) 'Making Microsoft safe for capitalism' (Cover Story) *The New York Times Magazine* (5 November) 50–57

Gonzalez-Manet, E (1992) *Informatics and Society: The New Challenges* Ablex Publishing Corp, Norwood, NJ, 201 pages

Halal, WE (1993) 'The information technology revolution: computer hardware, software, and services into the 21st century' *Technological Forecasting and Social Change* 44 (1) (August) 69–86

Halal, WE, and Liebowitz, J (1994) 'Telelearning: the multimedia revolution in education' *The Futurist* 28 (6) (November–December) 21–26

Hamelink, CJ (1988) *The Technology Gamble. Informatics and Public Policy: A Study of Technology* Ablex Publishing Corp, Norwood, NJ, 117 pages

Harasim, LM (ed) (1993) *Global Networks: Computers and International Communication* MIT Press, Cambridge, MA, 411 pages

Hart, RP (1994) *Seducing America: How Television Charms the Modern Voter* Oxford University Press, New York (May) 230 pages

Haywood, T (1995) *Info-Rich/Info-Poor: Access and Exchange in the Global Information Society* Bowker/Saur, West Sussex, UK (April) 274 pages

Heaton, JA, and Wilson, NL (1995) *Tuning in Trouble: Talk TV's Destructive Impact on Mental Health* Jossey-Bass, San Francisco (September) 284 pages

Heim, M (1993) *The Metaphysics of Virtual Reality* Oxford University Press, New York, 175 pages

Hiltz, SR (1994) *The Virtual Classroom: Learning Without Limits via Computer Networks* Ablex Publishing Corp, Norwood, NJ, 384 pages

Hines, A (1994) 'Jobs and infotech: work in the information society' *The Futurist* 28 (1) (January–February) 9–13

Horner, VM (ed) (1991) 'Electronic links for learning' (special issue) *Annals of The American Academy of Political and Social Science* 514 (March) 1–174

Horrocks, RJ, and Scarr, RWA (1993) *Future Trends in Telecommunications* John Wiley, Chichester, UK, and New York, 452 pages

Howard, A (ed) (1995) *The Changing Nature of Work* Jossey-Bass, San Francisco (July) 590 pages

Huber, P (1994) *Orwell's Revenge: The 1984 Palimpsest* The Free Press, New York (November) 374 pages

Hudson, HE (1990) *Communication Satellites: Their Development and Impact* The Free Press, New York, 338 pages

Iyengar, S (1991) *Is Anyone Responsible? How Television Frames Political Issues* University of Chicago Press, Chicago, 195 pages

Jones, MG (1995) *Electronic House Calls: 21st Century Options* Consumer Interest Research Group, Washington (June) 27 pages

Jones, SG (ed) (1995) *CyberSociety: Computer-Mediated Communication and Community* Sage Publications, Thousand Oaks, CA (January) 241 pages

Kahin, B, and Abbate. J (eds) (1995) *Standards Policy for Information Infrastructure* MIT Press, Cambridge, MA (October) 653 pages

Kahin, B, and Keller J (eds) (1995) *Public Access to the Internet* MIT Press. Cambridge, MA (September) 390 pages

Kaniss, P (1995) *The Media and the Mayor's Race: The Failure of Urban Political Reporting* Indiana University Press. Bloomington. IN (February) 395 pages

Kegan R (1994) *In Over Our Heads: The Mental Demands of Modern Life* Harvard University Press, Cambridge, MA (May) 396 pages

Kelly, K (1994) *Out of Control: The Rise of Neo-Biological Civilization* Addison-Wesley, Reading, MA (June) 521 pages

Kennedy, JL, and Morrow, TJ (1994) *Electronic Job Search Revolution: Win with the New Technology that's Reshaping Today's Job Market* John Wiley, New York, 207 pages

Kernan, A (1990) *The Death of Literature* Yale University Press, New Haven, CT, 230 pages

Kimball, Penn (1994) *Downsizing the News: Network Cutbacks in the Nation's Capital* Woodrow Wilson Center Press. Washington, and Johns Hopkins University Press, Baltimore (March) 181 pages

Kingston, JA (1989) 'Where information is all, pleas arise for less of it' *The New York Times* 9 July, E9

Klapp, OE (1986) *Overload and Boredom: Essays on the Quality of Life in the Information Society* Greenwood Press, Westport, CT, 174 pages

Kling, R (1994) 'Reading "all about" computerization: how genre conventions shape nonfiction social analysis' *The Information Society* 10 (3) (July–September) 147–172

Kobrak, F, and Luey, B (eds) (1992) *The Structure of International Publishing in the 1990s* Transaction Publishers, New Brunswick, NJ, 240 pages

Koch, T (1991) *Journalism for the 21st Century: Online Information, Electronic Databases, and the News* Greenwood/Praeger, Westport, CT, 374 pages

Koelsch, F (1995) *The Infomedia Revolution: How it is Changing our World and your Life* McGraw-Hill Ryerson. Toronto (February) 358 pages

Kroker, A, and Weinstein, M (1994) *Data Trash: The Theory of the Virtual Class* St Martin's Press, New York (November) 165 pages

Kurtzman, J (1993) *The Death of Money: How the Electric Economy has Destabilized the World's Markets and Created Financial Chaos* Simon and Schuster, New York, 256 pages. Paperbound edition from Little Brown Back Bay Books

Lande, N (1991) 'Toward the electronic book' *Publishers Weekly* (20 September) 28–30

Lanham, RA (1993) *The Electronic Word: Democracy, Technology, and the Arts* University of Chicago Press, Chicago, 285 pages

Laudon, KC (1986) *Dossier Society: Value Choices in the Design of National Information Systems* Columbia University Press, New York, 421 pages

Leebaert, D (ed) (1991) *Technology 2001: The Future of Computing and Communications* MIT Press, Cambridge, MA, 392 pages

Leebaert, D (ed) (1995) *The Future of Software* MIT Press, Cambridge, MA, (February) 300 pages

Levy, S (1994) 'E-money' *Wired* 2 (12) (December) 174–179

Lewis, PH (1995) 'Security is lost in cyberspace' *The New York Times* 22 February, D1

Linowes, DF (1989) *Privacy in America: Is your Private Life in the Public Eye?* University of Illinois Press, Urbana, IL, 190 pages

Lloyd, P (ed) (1994) *Groupware in the 21st Century: Computer Supported Cooperative Working toward the Millennium* Praeger, Westport, CT (November) 307 pages. Published in UK by Adamantine Press

Louw, E, and Duffy, N (1992) *Managing Computer Viruses* Oxford University Press, Oxford, UK, and New York, 171 pages

Lundberg, O (1991) 'The perils of being a visionary: one man's vision' *InterMedia* 19 (1) (January–February) 33–39

MacLachlan, SL (1993) 'Pagers' sophistication keeps sales growing' *The Christian Science Monitor* 23 August, 7

Maes, P (1995) 'Intelligent software' *Scientific American* (September) 84–86

Makridakis, S (1995) 'The forthcoming information revolution: its impact on society and firms' *Futures* **27** (8) (October) 799–821

Markoff, J (1991) 'Is the electronic book closer than you think?' *The New York Times* 29 December, E5

Markoff, J (1995) 'Discovery of Internet flaws is setback for on-line trade' *The New York Times* 11 October, A1

Marx, GT (1994) 'New telecommunications technologies require new manners' *Telecommunications Policy* **18** (7) (October) 538–551

Mason, RO *et al.* (1995) *Ethics of Information Management* Sage Publications, Thousand Oaks. CA (July) 327 pages

Masuda, Y (1990) *Managing in the Information Society: Releasing Synergy Japanese Style* Basil Blackwell, Oxford, UK, and Cambridge, MA, 168 pages (New edition of *The Information Society as Post-Industrial Society* Institute of the Information Society, Tokyo, and World Future Society, Bethesda, MD, 1980)

Mattelart, A (1991) *Advertising International: The Privatisation of Public Space* Routledge, London and New York (First published in Paris in 1989)

Mayer-Kress, G, and Barczys, C (1995) 'The global brain as an emergent structure from the worldwide computing network, and its implications for modeling' *The Information Society* **11** (1) January–March 1–27

Mayo, JS (1990) 'The telecommunications revolution of the 1990s' *Vital Speeches of the Day* **57** (5) (15 December) 151–155

Mayo, JS (1992) 'R&D in the third millennium: requirements and challenges' *Vital Speeches of the Day* **59** (1) (15 October) 26–29

McKibbon, B (1992) *The Age of Missing Information* Random House, New York (Brief version in *The New Yorker* 9 March 1992 40–80)

McLuhan, M (1994) *Understanding Media: The Extensions of Man* MIT Press, Cambridge, MA (October) 365 pages (30th Anniversary reissue of 1964 McGraw-Hill edition)

McManus, JH (1994) *Market-Driven Journalism: Let the Citizen Beware?* Sage Publications, Thousand Oaks. CA (April) 243 pages

McNerney, WJ, and Bezold, C (1995) *Health Care Innovation: A Vision for the 21st Century* Institute for Alternative Futures, Alexandria, VA (August) 6 pages

Michael, DN (1993) 'Governing by learning: boundaries, myths and metaphors' *Futures* **25** (1) (January-February) 81–89

Minoli, D (1995) *Video Dialtone Technology: Digital Video over ADSL, HFC, FTTC, and ATM* McGraw-Hill, New York (June) 495 pages

Minow, NN and LaMay, CL (1995) *Abandoned in the Wasteland: Children, Television, and the First Amendment* Hill and Wang, New York (July) 237 pages

Mitchell, WJ (1992) *The Reconfigured Eye: Visual Truth in the Post-Photographic Era* MIT Press, Cambridge, MA, 273 pages

Mitchell, WJ (1995) *City of Bits: Space, Place, and the Infobahn* MIT Press, Cambridge, MA (September) 225 pages

Mitroff, II, and Bennis, W (1989) *The Unreality Industry: The Deliberate Manufacturing of Falsehood and What it is Doing to our Lives* Birch Lane Press/Carol Publishing Group, New York, 218 pages

Moore, RH, Jr (1994) 'Wiseguys: smarter criminals and smarter crime in the 21st century' *The Futurist* **28** (5) (September–October) 33–37

Moore, RH, Jr (1995) 'Twenty-first century law to meet the challenge of twenty-first century organized crime' *Futures Research Quarterly* **11** (1) (Spring) 23–46

Morton, MSS (1991) *The Corporation of the 1990s: Information Technology and Organizational Transformation* Oxford University Press, New York, 331 pages

Mowshowitz, A (1994) 'Virtual organization: a vision of management' *The Information Society* **10** (4) (October–December) 267–288

Naisbitt, J (1982) *Megatrends: Ten New Directions Transforming our Lives* Warner Books. New York, 290 pages

National Research Council, Computer Science and Telecoms Board (1994) *Information Technology in the Service Society: A Twenty-First Century Lever* National Academy Press. Washington, 270 pages

National Research Council. NRENAISSANCE Committee (1994) *Realizing the Information Future: The Internet and Beyond* National Academy Press, Washington, 301 pages

National Research Council, Office of International Affairs (1993) *Global Dimensions of Intellectual Property Rights in Science and Technology* National Academy Press, Washington, 442 pages

National Research Council, System Security Study Committee (1991) *Computers at Risk: Safe Computing in the Information Age* National Academy Press, Washington, 303 pages

Negroponte, N (1995) *Being Digital* Alfred A Knopf, New York (February) 243 pages

Newman, SB (1995) *Literacy in the Television Age: The Myth of the TV Effect* Ablex Publishing Corp, Norwood, NJ (Spring) 233 pages

Office of Technology Assessment, US Congress (1985) *Federal Government Information Technology: Electronic Surveillance and Civil Liberties* US Government Printing Office, Washington

Ibid (1986) *Electronic Record Systems and Individual Privacy* US Government Printing Office, Washington

Ibid (1991) *Rural America at the Crossroads: Networking for the Future* US Government Printing Office, Washington

Ibid (1993) *Adult Literacy and New Technologies: Tools for a Lifetime* US Government Printing Office, Washington

Ibid (1994) *Electronic Enterprises: Looking to the Future* US Government Printing Office, Washington, 188 pages

Ibid (1995) *Teachers and Technology: Making the Connection* US Government Printing Office, Washington, 304 pages

Ogden, MR (1994) 'Politics in a parallel universe: is there a future for cyberdemocracy' *Futures* **26** (7) (September) 713–729

Ohmae, K (1995) *The End of the Nation State: The Rise of Regional Economies* The Free Press, New York (June) 214 pages

O'Neill, J (1991) *Plato's Cave: Desire, Power, and the Specular Functions of the Media* Ablex Publishing Corp, Norwood, NJ, 206 pages

Palmer, EL (1988) *Television and America's Children: A Crisis of Neglect* Oxford University Press, New York, 194 pages

Palmer, EL (1993) *Toward a Literate World: Television in Literacy Education – Lessons from the Arab Region* Westview Press, Boulder, CO, 170 pages

Papert, S (1993) *The Children's Machine: Rethinking School in the Age of the Computer* Basic Books, New York, 241 pages

Parker, R (1995) *Mixed Signals: The Prospects for Global Television* Twentieth Century Fund Press, New York (August) 103 pages

Patterson, DA (1995) 'Microprocessors in 2020' *Scientific American* (September) 62–67

Pelton, JN (1989) 'Telepower: the emerging global brain', *The Futurist* 23 (5) (September–October) 9–14

Penzias, A (1995) *Harmony: Business, Technology & Life After Paperwork* Harper Business, New York (April) 178 pages

Perelman, LJ (1992) *School's Out: Hyperlearning, The New Technology, and the End of Education* William Morrow, New York, 368 pages (Paperback edition from Avon Books, October 1993)

Pickover, CA (ed) (1995) *Future Health: Computers and Medicine in the Twenty-first Century* St Martin's Press, New York (November) 184 pages

Pollack, A (1992) ' "Fifth generation" became Japan's lost generation' *The New York Times* 5 June, D1

Postman, N (1992) *Technopoly: The Surrender of Culture to Technology* Alfred A Knopf, New York, 222 pages

Provenzo, EF, Jr (1991) *Video Kids: Making Sense of Nintendo* Harvard University Press, Cambridge, MA, 184 pages

Raine, LP, and Cilluffo, FJ (eds) (1994) *Global Organized Crime: The New Empire of Evil* Center for Strategic and International Studies, Washington (November) 185 pages

Rheingold, H (1993) *The Virtual Community: Homesteading on the Electronic Frontier* Addison-Wesley, Reading, MA, 325 pages (Paperback edition from Harper Perennial)

Rice, PO, and Robillard, JA (eds) (1991) *The Future of Serials: Proceedings of the North American Serials Interest Group* The Haworth Press, Binghamton, NY, 260 pages

Rifkin, J (1995) *The End of Work: The Decline of the Global Labor Force and the Dawn of the Post-Market Era* Tarcher/ Putnam, New York (January) 350 pages

Ritzer, G (1995) *Expressing America: A Critique of the Global Credit Card Society* Pine Forge Press/Sage Publications, Thousand Oaks, CA (January) 240 pages

Robinson, DC *et al.* (1991) *Music at the Margins: Popular Music and Global Cultural Diversity* Sage Publications, Newbury Park, CA, 312 pages

Roe, DB, and Wilpon, JG (eds) (1994) *Voice Communication between Humans and Machines* National Academy Press, Washington, 548 pages

Ronfeldt, D (1992) 'Cyberocracy is coming' *The Information Society* 8 (4) (October–December) 243–296

Rosell, SA (1992) *Governing in an Information Society* Institute for Research on Public Policy, Montreal, 167 pages

Rosenberg, R (1991) 'Debunking computer literacy' *Technology Review* 94 (1) (January) 58–65

Rossman, P (1992) *The Emerging Worldwide Electronic University: Information Age Global Higher Education* Greenwood Press, Westport, CT, 169 pages

Roszak, T (1994) *The Cult of Information: A Neo-Luddite Treatise on High-Tech, Artificial Intelligence, and the True Art of Thinking* (second edition) University of California Press, Berkeley, CA, 267 pages (First published in 1986)

Sale, K (1995) *Rebels Against the Future: The Luddites and their War on the Industrial Revolution; Lessons for the Computer Age* Addison-Wesley, Reading, MA (May) 320 pages

Salomon, JJ *et al.* (eds) (1994) *The Uncertain Quest: Science, Technology, and Development* United Nations University Press, Tokyo (April) 532 pages. Also see Wesley-Tanakovic, I (1994) *Expanding Access to Science and Technology: The Role of Information Technologies* United Nations University Press, Tokyo (February) 462 pages

Sanders, B (1994) *A is for Ox: Violence, Electronic Media, and the Silencing of the Written Word* Pantheon Books, New York (October) 269 pages

Sardar, Z, and Ravetz, JR (eds) (1995) 'Cyberspace: to boldly go' (Special Issue) *Futures* 27 (7) (September) 695–796

Schement, JR, and Curtis, T (1995) *Tendencies and Tensions of the Information Age: The*

Production and Distribution of Information in the United States Transaction Publishers, New Brunswick, NJ (January) 285 pages

Schepp, D, and Schepp, B (1995) *The Telecommuter's Handbook: How to Earn a Living without Going to the Office* (second edition) McGraw-Hill, New York (August) 207 pages

Schiller, HI (1989) *Culture, Inc.: The Corporate Takeover of Public Expression* Oxford University Press, New York, 201 pages

Schiller, HI (1992) *Mass Communications and American Empire* (second edition, updated) Westview Press, Boulder, CO, 214 pages

Scientific American (1991) 'Communications, computers and networks' (Special Issue) *Scientific American* **265** (3) (September) 62–166

Sheridan, TB (1992) *Telerobotics, Automation, and Human Supervisory Control* MIT Press, Cambridge, MA, 393 pages

Sheth, JN, and Sisodia, RS (1993) 'The information mall' *Telecommunications Policy* **17** (5) (July) 376–389

Shrader, WK (1992) *Media Blight and the Dehumanizing of America* Praeger, New York, 184 pages

Slaton, CD (1992) *Televote: Expanding Citizen Participation in the Quantum Age* Praeger, New York, 226 pages

Slouka, M (1995) *War of the Worlds: Cyberspace and the High-Tech Assault on Reality* Basic Books, New York (August) 185 pages

Smith, A (1991) *The Age of Behemoths: The Globalization of Mass Media Firms* A Twentieth Century Fund Paper Priority Press, New York, 83 pages (Distribution by Brookings Institution)

Smith, HJ (1994) *Managing Privacy: Information Technology and Corporate America* University of North Carolina Press, Chapel Hill, NC (June) 297 pages

Snider, J (1994) 'Democracy on-line: tomorrow's electronic electorate' *The Futurist* **28** (5) (September–October) 15–19

Snider, J, and Ziporyn, T (1992) *Future Shop: How New Technologies Will Change the Way We Shop and What We Buy* St Martin's Press, New York. 316 pages

Sproull, L, and Kiesler, S (1991) *Connections: New Ways of Working in the Networked Organization* MIT Press, Cambridge, MA, 212 pages

Stephens, G (1995) 'Crime in cyberspace: the digital underworld' *The Futurist* **29** (5) (September–October) 24–28

Stock, G (1993) *Metaman: The Merging of Humans and Machines into a Global Superorganism* Simon and Schuster, New York, 365 pages

Stoll, C (1995) *Silicon Snake Oil: Second Thoughts on the Information Highway* Doubleday, New York (March) 247 pages

Sussman, G (ed) (1991) *Transnational Communications: Wiring the Third World* Sage Publications. Newbury Park, CA, 327 pages

Sussman, V (1995) 'Gold rush in cyberspace' (Cover Story) *U.S. News & World Report* 13 November, 72–83

Talbott, SL (1995) *The Future Does Not Compute: Transcending the Machines in Our Midst* O'Reilly and Associates, Sebastopol, CA (June) 481 pages

Tierney, J (1992) 'Sound bites become smaller mouthfuls' *The New York Times* 23 January, A1

Tiffin, J, and Rajasingham, L (1995) *In Search of the Virtual Class: Education in an Information Society* Routledge, London (August) 204 pages

Time Magazine (1995) 'Welcome to cyberspace' (Special Issue) *Time* Spring, 88 pages

Toffler, A (1980) *The Third Wave* William Morrow and Company, New York, 544 pages.

Toffler, A, and Toffler, H (1993a) 'Societies at hyper-speed' *The New York Times* 31 October, E17

Toffler, A, and Toffler, H (1993b) *War and Anti-War: Survival at the Dawn of the 21st Century* Little Brown and Co. Boston, 302 pages

Toffler, A, and Toffler, H (1995) 'Getting set for the coming millennium' *The Futurist* 29 (2) (March–April) 10–15

Tomlinson, J (1991) *Cultural Imperialism: A Critical Introduction* Johns Hopkins University Press, Baltimore, MD, 187 pages

Tuman, MC (1992) *Word Perfect: Literacy in the Computer Age* University of Pittsburgh Press, Pittsburgh, PA, 150 pages

Tyack, D, and Cuban, L (1995) *Tinkering Toward Utopia: A Century of Public School Reform* Harvard University Press, Cambridge, MA (September) 184 pages

Vajda, SA (1993) 'The growth and expansion of telecoms in Mexico' *InterMedia* 21 (4–5) (August–September) 8–13

Vinge, V (1993) 'Technological singularity' *Whole Earth Review* 81 (Winter) 88–95

Ware, WH (1993) 'The new faces of privacy' *The Information Society* 9 (3) (July–September) 193–211

Warwick, DR (1992) 'The cash-free society' *The Futurist* 26 (6) (November–December) 19–22

Weaver, RR (1991) *Computers and Medical Knowledge: The Diffusion of Decision Support Technology* Westview Press, Boulder, CO, 142 pages

Webster, F, and Robins, K (1986) *Information Technology: A Luddite Analysis* Ablex Publishing Co, Norwood, NJ, 387 pages

Weiser, M (1991) 'The computer for the 21st century' *Scientific American* 265 (3) (September) 94–104

Weizer, N *et al.* (1991) *The Arthur D. Little Forecast on Information Technology and Productivity: Making the Integrated Enterprise Work* John Wiley, New York, 272 pages

Wines, M (1994) 'Washington really is in touch: we're the problem' *The New York Times* 16 October, E1

Winston, B (1986) *Misunderstanding Media* Harvard University Press, Cambridge, MA. 419 pages

Woherem, EE (1991) 'Expert systems as a medium for knowledge transfer to less developed countries' *Science and Public Policy* 18 (5) (October) 301–309

Wright, R (1995) 'Hyperdemocracy' (Cover Story) *Time* 23 January, 15–21

Wriston, WB (1992) *The Twilight of Sovereignty: How the Information Revolution is Transforming the World* Charles Scribner's Sons/Macmillan, New York, 192 pages

Zysman, GI (1995) 'Wireless networks' *Scientific American* (September) 68–71

PART 2

Governing new media

This part of the reader is concerned with the complex relations between new media and government. On the one hand, as we saw in the *Introduction*, many writers see the new media of the present as a distinctive product of the nationally driven military techno-logical competition of the 1950s and 1960s. On the other, new media are also widely seen as creatures of globalisation, resistant to national laws and regulations. Govern-ments are long used to controlling the distribution or communication of cultural goods: it is, for example, broadcasting which is generally strictly controlled, not the making of television programmes. The classification and circulation of tangible cultural goods, such as books, magazines, films, and sound recordings have also often been controlled through laws regulating the importation of such works across national boundaries. But when these goods cease to be tangible objects, and become instead no more than a stream of signals being transmitted down a cable or through the atmosphere, the regulatory task becomes substantially more challenging.

Governments persist in seeking to exercise controls over new media broadly similar to those which regulate old media; part of the reason is that citizens in most countries continue to expect governments to control offensive or dangerous media and communi-cations. But there is a strong view held by many that such efforts are a waste of time, economically costly and technically futile. This perspective may be summed up in the famous mid-1990s' line 'the Net interprets censorship as damage and routes around it', attributed to the internet pioneer and free speech advocate John Gilmore.

Gilmore's view of the fundamental value of free expression is widely held. It is worth comparing the approach of some of the writers in this part to that of Andrew Barry in Part 4. While many writers conceptualise the relationship between government and technology as a case of intervention in the private realm – whether necessary, counter-productive, or doomed to failure – Barry suggests ways in which the focus can switch to the formative, citizen-making role of new technologies. New media are shaped by government; they also shape civic life.

Since censorship looms so large in debates over new media, we have included an alternative perspective here, taken from Saunders, Hunter and Williamson's illuminating historical study of pornography and obscenity law. The view they present may be usefully contrasted with that of de Sola Pool and other writers in the technological–libertarian tradition: instead of seeing censorship as an untoward governmental intrusion into a domain of legitimate private choice, they characterise the emergence of obscenity law as a response to the unplanned interactions of several historical forces, including developments in printing technology and the book trade: 'Obscenity law first emerged in a complex technical environment formed by the overlap of a new governmental distinction between public and private spheres and the spread of a specific cultural technology and competence' (1992:51).

A further degree of complexity arises here around the relations between old and new media, and the highly differential approaches of governments to them. The emergence of what are now considered older electronic media – radio and television – in the mid-20th century coincided with the expansion of western governments' liberalising ambition. In many countries those industries remain highly regulated, harnessed to national cultural and social policy goals. New networked media, by the same token, have emerged and in the main continue to operate outside this domain, while increasingly competing with it. Bruce M. Owen presents a media economist's view of the legacy of government's long era of regulating broadcast media. In Owen's view, government intervention has reduced the capacity and efficiency of the broadcasting industry, and the choices it has been able to offer consumers: 'So restrictive and distorting has been the effect of regulatory policy that it is almost impossible to imagine what broadcasting would have been like had it developed in a free market environment, except that there would have been a lot more of it a lot sooner.' Owen points to the commercial and political pressures which give rise to costly over-regulation, and notes that there is no reason why new digital media should be immune from these very same dynamics.

Andrew Graham adopts a different approach to the policy legacy of broadcasting in the extract from his work included here. Making a case for the continued role of what he terms 'public service broadcasting' in the digital age, he emphasises the economic, social and political benefits of what he calls 'common knowledge'. Common knowledge is essential to public debate in democracies: it is 'what everyone knows everyone knows'. Further, the media are a major source of contemporary common knowledge, if not the only one. Public service media, the argument runs, have a crucial role in aiming not merely to inform people, or communicate news, or to attract audiences: they must also 'extend the understanding and experience of those who watch and listen'. Market-driven media alone will not serve democracy or citizenship well. For Kevin Robins and Frank Webster, this failure has already occurred. For them the 'public sphere' has become a rationalised 'cybernetic state' which comprises a 'programmed market and a regulated and coded consumer society'.

The question then becomes one of whether old media rules should or could be remodelled along the lines of the relative freedoms accorded new media. Here Robert McChesney and Ben Compaine conduct a lively debate over the relevance of new media freedoms for old media policy. Does the efflorescence of new media mean the end of old media regulations, rendering irrelevant special rules such as those regarding takeovers and acquisitions? Are the media integrating, globalising and concentrating, as the economic and technological forces of convergence drive further restructuring and policy liberalisation? Speaking about the United States, McChesney makes the important point, echoing Owen, that the media landscape does not reflect the dynamics of the market but is a corrupt dispersal of privileges and licences. Neither do the problems stop with old media: many new technologies have been developed with public sub-sidies. McChesney's conclusion is that the threat to democracy from new media is such that independent and non-commercial media will be more important than ever in the years to come, and it is vital that media and communications policy itself be democratised.

Ben Compaine addresses McChesney's arguments directly. Compaine's point is that globalisation and deregulation have not in fact produced more concentrated global media sector: in his view, there is only one genuinely global media company. In diverse and complex societies with no single 'public interest', markets actually provide an important democratic constraint on media companies.

2.1

Historicising obscenity law,
by David Saunders, Ian M. Hunter and Dugald Williamson

Literary histories of obscenity law – the work of what we have termed 'censorship historians' – identify the person who creates and the person who is prosecuted. This identification is manifest in the attachment of post-Romantic criticism to the figure of the transgressive author (or text), said to embody the whole impetus of human development against the repressive powers of law and state. This identification is so profoundly established that these literary histories do not pause to digest the fact that the bulk of obscenity prosecutions have been of printers, publishers and booksellers, not of writers.

It was thus as a printer and bookseller, not as a writer, that an individual was first convicted of obscene publication. [In Chapter 2 we noted that] in 1727, with *Rex* v. *Curll*, the court of King's Bench created the offence of obscene libel, conceptualised as a disturbing of the King's peace by virtue of an obscene publication which does harm to public morality.[1] In 1724, the London printer, bookseller, pamphleteer, journalist, publicist, employer of hacks, pirate and pornographer Edmund Curll was charged in relation to the publication of *Venus in the Cloister; or, the Nun in her Smock*, an English translation of Jean Barrin's *Vénus dans le cloître*, together with certain other works. For the first time, obscene publication appeared within the purview of the common law, entering the criminal justice system and thereby gaining a new social generality as the object of governmental responsibility. With the sentencing of Curll in 1727, obscene publication gained legal recognition as a danger which, left unchecked by the custodial and legal powers of the sovereign, could morally harm the population at large. In effect, the judges in Curll's case adopted a new disposition of public morality, transferring a specific form of immorality from sin to crime and shifting its control from religious to legal regulations.

This shift marked a significant mutation in the existing division of jurisdiction between the temporal or common law courts and the spiritual or ecclesiastical courts which, hitherto, had dealt with matters pertaining to personal morality and sex (hence their popular appellation as the Bawdy Courts).[2] The spiritual courts had traditionally carried the responsibility for dealing with 'personal' offences *pro custodia morum* of the community and *pro salute animae* of the offender, that is, for the sake of reforming the sinner. The judges did not slip obscene publication across this jurisdictional boundary without a deal of debate about the existing demarcation of competence between the different courts and about the indications and counter-indications of such precedents as were to hand, notably *Rex* v. *Sir Charles Sedley* 1663 and *Regina* v. *Read* 1707. A solid tussle was conducted within the terms of a specific common law procedure – the construction, extension and application of precedent. This is just one sign that the judges' action was anything but automatic and driven by Puritan morality or by a reflex repression of sexual expressivity.

Curll's defence to the charge ran within established boundaries and rested, one would think, on a solid precedent in *Read*. In 1707 the King's Bench had quashed a conviction on the grounds that a written publication which did not defame some actual person was not a criminal matter. As Curll's counsel said of *Read*:

> [T]here was an information for a libel in writing an obscene book called *The Fifteen Plagues of a Maidenhead*, and after conviction it was moved in arrest of judgement that this was not punishable in the Temporal Courts; and the opinion of Chief Justice Holt was so strong with the objection, that the prosecutor never thought fit to stir it again.
>
> (*Rex* v. *Curll*, pp. 849–50)

Yet this defence failed against an evidently successful analogy drawn by the Attorney General: just as 'particular acts of fornication are not punishable in the Temporal Courts, and bawdy houses are' (p. 850), so the action of obscene publication – if it 'tends to disturb the civil order of society' or reflect upon morality – should be considered by the court in the same terms as the running of a bawdy house.

In this unforeseen reorganisation of the institutions of moral regulation, the common law courts acquired a new responsibility: regulation of the field of obscene publication. In its early modern configuration, this field was organised around an equally unforeseen yet potent liaison between certain literate products of a confessional practice concerned with instilling an ever more detailed sense of the erotic and the sinful, and a commercial book trade beginning to exploit that same developing erotic sensitivity but for ends quite other than grace. The once specialist genre of libertine anti-clerical erotica was thereby redirected to a new audience, as English translation and publication established new circulations for works such as *Vénus dans le cloître*. In Chapter 2, in considering the question of this new audience, we thus suggested that what pushed Curll's publication across the threshold into the domain of criminal law was the formation of a new and less specialised public with a disposition for pornography in English.

This particular expansion of government and criminal law into the area of public morality did not involve an abstract specification of the existence of a public with a propensity for corruption. Without the definite means of becoming corrupt, in other words without the communications technology of the book and without the dissemination of a particular cultural competence – print literacy – a public which might be corrupted by obscene publications could not actually exist. Hence the significance of one judge's observation that '[t]he spiritual Courts punish only personal spiritual defamation by words; if it is reduced to writing, it is a temporal offence' (p. 850). More pointed still is the contrast drawn by Justice Reynolds between *Sedley*, where

Sir Charles had 'only exposed himself to the people then present, who might choose whether they would look upon him or not', and the action of Curll, whose 'book goes all over the kingdom' (p. 851). The notion of the new distributional force of print, and the judges' suspicion that print exercises a certain type of direct impact upon its readers, swings the case against Curll. This had not been the decision in *Read*, and the divergence of these two decisions at common law, separated by only twenty years, says something of the instability of the pornographic field from the very start. The court in *Curll* thus set itself to weigh up whether a publication of obscene literature, the distribution and reading of *Venus in the Cloister*, could disturb the King's peace as surely as the actions of Sedley, friend of Rochester, had been found to do in 1663. In the earlier case, along with the public display of nakedness on the balcony, the defendant had, as Chief Justice Fortescue remarked in *Curll*, exercised a physical force in throwing out bottles and pissing down upon the people's heads.

Aside from the telling contrast with our own times when, in the Williams Report (1979), *books* fall by their essential nature as 'writing' into the realm of free 'choice' whereas *photographs* are excluded on the grounds of the coercive immediacy of their impact, what is the historical and theoretical interest of Curll's case for subsequent law on obscenity?[3] The judges in *Curll* realised a complex piece of lawmaking which – as the offence of obscene libel – was to endure in English criminal law for 232 years, until the Obscene Publications Act of 1959. The creation of this new offence and the judicial initiative to use the criminal law for the moral government of the kingdom were contingent on an unpredictable conjunction of legal and cultural factors: the *Sedley* precedent whereby the common law declared itself competent – as *custos morum* of all the king's subjects – to indict on the grounds of a subversion of public morals; the rise of the distribution of printed works and a rapid expansion of the cultural capacity – discursive literacy – needed to consume them; the emergence of a less specialist interest in erotic writings and the formation of a system of supply, for instance by a pornographer, printer and bookseller such as Curll, of a market providing for this new 'personal' interest.

It is in this conjunction of otherwise unrelated factors – legal, governmental, cultural, technological and commercial – that the contingency of the early modern pornographic field is displayed. Set against this background of unplanned circumstances, the attempt to account for the first emergence of the crime of obscene publication in terms of some general movement of consciousness of which the law was the pliant instrument – typically an access of 'Puritan' repressiveness – promises only a loss of historical specificity and a reduced descriptive capacity. Certainly, an expansion of the sphere of government occurred through the mechanism of the criminal law. But this unanticipated reorganisation of the institutions regulating public morality resulted from a characteristic piece of common law innovation, building up from gritty example and particularity of circumstance. The court was confronted by the possibility of a crime involving a disturbance of the peace where there was no use of physical force and a libel where no one was libelled. The question of how such an act could have become intelligible as a crime, as it evidently did with *Curll*, calls for analysis in terms of quite local circumstances, not grand philosophical schemes.

In Curll's case, a printed and published writing was recognised as constituting an obscene libel and made the object of a criminal sanction on the grounds that – left unchecked – such a publication would harm public morality and disturb the social balance by libelling the honour of the king through an exposure of his subjects to the imperious force of printed obscenity. By the time of the Obscene Publications Act of 1857 and *Hicklin* in 1868, things are very different. By then, a work counted as obscene is treated as a toxic substance having 'a tendency . . . to deprave and corrupt those whose minds are open to such immoral influences, and into whose hands a publications of this sort may fall'. If the publication is dangerous enough to be deemed a social risk and thus made subject to preventive legal regulatory measures, it is no longer as an action liable to disturb the king's peace. Rather, it has become a dangerous substance, a commodity capable of inducing the user who comes from what is deemed a category of vulnerable and non-competent persons to deviate from known norms of moral and physical health. What nineteenth-century obscenity law targetted as an essential object of government responsibility was no longer an act of sedition endangering the social balance, but a dangerous poison inducing moral and medical harm. To underscore such transformations is to break with the received pattern of historiography that has been imposed on English obscenity law. We have in mind accounts such as St John-Stevas (1956), Hyde (1964), Rolph (1969), Thomas (1969) and Robertson (1979). These are unitary narratives which construct a history of the legal relations of erotic writing in terms of a single trans-historical struggle between repressive external controls – censorship, obscenity law, police – and an essential subjectivity which seeks individual expression in writing the truth about sex.

What is the problem with such accounts? It is not just that they write the history backwards from the present as if a single logic, a single dark and shining path led from Ezekiel to D. H. Lawrence (Robertson, 1979) or from ancient Greece to the First Amendment and Arthur Schlesigner Jr (Widmer, 1970). More importantly, the received historiography does no justice to the substantive changes in the social organisation of subjectivity. The medicalised morality and moralised medicine which created and so minutely managed the nineteenth-century sexual personality – and thus directly informed the obscenity law of that time and cultural milieu – register a high degree of historical particularity. In our present study, historical transformations of subjectivity are taken as a necessary starting point for any attempt to put the record straight concerning the objectives and norms of obscenity law. The difference should be clear between a history which recognises the historically distinctive but impermanent arrangement of sexual, moral, medical and legal attributes in nineteenth-century England and one – the received historiography of the censorship historians – that assumes a timeless sexual subject upon which, except at rare moments of emancipation, more or less the same censorious law eternally impinges in more or less the same repressive manner. No doubt the notion of a transhistorical sexuality is convenient, providing both origin and destiny for the traditional history of erotic writing, whether for the author behind the work, the reader in front of it or the historian wanting to write his or her single story of repression.

By contrast, we have emphasised the historical and cultural differences between a crime of obscene publication defined within a series comprising sin, sedition, disturbance of the king's peace, print technology and a crime of obscene publication defined within a series comprising moral offence, medical harm, abortificients, lotteries, the Post Office, unregulated poisons and mutoscopes allowing universal access. In foregrounding the fact of historical difference, we directly confront those two trad-itional periodisations of English obscenity law which tie the emergence of that law either to the alleged excess of puritan moral conscientiousness or to the supposedly overweaning power of Victorian moralism. In each case, the received historiography underestimates the technical complexity and historical particularity of the legal-cultural arrangements, just as it underestimates the possibility – if, that is, it even suspects it – that western sexuality is less the locus of an essential human truth than a specialised cultural artefact into which so much work has gone. Not the least important element of this work has been a remarkable alteration in the relations between literature and sex. It is to this theme – a quite unforeseen transformation of the concerns and content of aesthetic literature and the problems which this transformation posed for obscenity law – that we now turn.

Notes

1   For the detail of the record, we note the following factual errors in accounts of Curll's case. Thomas (1969, p. 82) names the three judges as Raymond, Fortescue and Reynolds. The first of these names is wrong; it should be Mr Justice Probyn. The Williams Report (1979, p. 167) has the Chief Justice say that 'if it were not for the case of Read, he would see little difficulty in it'. In fact these are the words of the Attorney General prosecuting, in response to the opening by Curll's coun-sel, Mr Marsh. The error arises from a mis-reading of a vocative at the head of the concluding paragraph of the Attorney's statement ('Chief Justice, I think this is a case of very great consequence, though if it was not for the case of *The Queen* v. *Read*, I should make no great difficulty of it.') The Chief Justice is responding to this statement, so we can take the Attorney's 'Chief Justice' to refer to him, not to signal the reporter's identification of the speaker.
2   On these courts, see Chapter 8, 'The Bawdy Courts', in Hill (1964). On the state and functions of the eccelesiastical courts at the start of the eighteenth century, see Archer (1956).
3   Reynolds (1975, p. 222) warns against too much reliance on early obscenity decisions since 'the eighteenth-century legal precedents for punishment of obscene publication have politics as their basis, not close legal reasoning'. Curll had published the memoirs of John Ker, a spy in the service of Queen Anne, which reflected unfavourably on the House of Hanover. According to Reynolds (p. 221), George II intervened in the case by having Chief Justice Fortescue replaced by Francis Page, 'the "hanging judge" notorious in Pope's poems, Johnson's *Life of Savage*, and Fielding's *Tom Jones*'. With Page's appointment, the court rapidly and unanimously found in favour of punishing Curll.

2.2

The tragedy of broadcast regulation,
by Bruce M. Owen

If it were not for the failure of government policy, American consumers would have had much more and more diverse radio and television much sooner than they did, supported by vigorous competition. Sadly, not only has broadcast regulation been wrong-headed and harmful, it has been largely unnecessary.

Broadcast regulation began in earnest in 1927, when the Radio Act nationalized the airwaves. From the beginning, regulatory policies were heavily influenced by and therefore beneficial to the industry they regulated. This was by design. In close cooperation with Herbert Hoover and the Commerce Department from 1921 to 1929, the industry did much to encourage and to engineer its own regulation. Government intervention in those years may have reduced risk and encouraged investment in the new radio medium. For these reasons, some defend early government intervention. But continued regulation had no such good effects or rationale. Certainly the advent of television in the late 1940s was attended by none of the confusion, risk, and uncertainty that attended the birth of radio, and thus provided no justification for the restrictive measures imposed on the industry.

The government has almost always acted to restrict and restrain both competition and output in television markets in order to protect the economic interests of members of the industry. The government has permitted technological change to happen only very slowly for the same reason. In this respect the FCC has behaved no differently than various now-defunct federal regulatory agencies such as the Civil Aeronautics Board and the Interstate Commerce Commission.

Regulation is an invention and creature of the democratic process. Regulatory agencies never make important decisions in a political vacuum, as a court might. They consult with executive agencies, the White House, and several congressional committees (the House and Senate Commerce committees, among others) before announcing any major decision. Interested industry groups must lobby not only the agency concerned but also other agencies and elected representatives with a stake in the outcome as well. What comes out of this process is some sort of compromise, or perhaps consensus. And that, of course, is what representative government is all about.

The difficulty is that political outcomes, however procedurally democratic, are not market outcomes – and for economic affairs, market outcomes are generally better for consumers than political consensus. For that reason, ideally, the political process is substituted for the market process only when the market has failed badly, or would fail, but for the intervention.

As the FCC itself has demonstrated in recent years by gradually deregulating some parts of the television industry, there is no reason to suppose that unregulated television markets will fail. Regulators have probably known this for many years. But then, why regulate? The answer is that having begun to regulate, the government created a set of economic interests that stand to lose from deregulation. They stand to lose because deregulation means increased competition from new sellers and the destruction of incumbents' rents. So the rationale for continued regulation and the suppression of market forces is not market failure but the protection of clients whose existence or status is attributable to the government's prior actions.

Allocation of room in the airwaves for digital television stations provides a good illustration of these issues. Some policymakers have proposed giving every television broadcaster one free digital channel in exchange for its conventional channel. Then Senator Bob Dole, Representative Barney Frank, and other legislators opposed this so-called giveaway to broadcasters and argued that the broadcasters should be required to pay for their new digital channels. Is it a windfall to a broadcaster to be handed a free digital channel in exchange for its current analog one? There is no easy answer. On the one hand, the conventional channels were originally given to broadcasters without charge. On the other hand, present-day broadcasters are not the same entities who got those free licenses. Current broadcasters have had to pay previous owners tens or hundreds of millions of dollars for their channels. The original windfall was capitalized into the market value of each channel, and any owner after the first has paid full value for it. Thus, to take away the present channels while requiring broadcasters to pay for the new digital ones would be arguably an unfair "taking" of private property.

Digital television actually presents two problems: (1) allocating spectrum in an efficient manner that maximizes economic welfare and (2) ensuring that everyone involved is treated fairly. An effective solution to problem (1) would maximize the size of the pie available to be divided in solving problem (2). Often, however, there is no practical way to compensate those that lose from efficient changes. The lack of a mechanism to compensate losers is one of many reasons why the political process and regulatory agencies in particular are so resistant to change, even change that would make society as a whole better off. The issue arises in many other contexts. For example, an inability to decide how to compensate the owners of obsolete facilities has delayed the introduction of competition in the supply of telephone service and electricity.

Bigger pie or bigger slice?

One of the easiest public policy choices is one that makes some people better off while leaving no one worse off. But seldom do such "Pareto superior" choices present themselves. Very often, the welfare of some can be advanced only at the expense of others. One way to approach the more difficult choices is to ask whether the pie as a whole is made bigger by some policy choice, or whether it is merely being divided in a different way. If the welfare of society as a whole is increased, it may be worthwhile to make the move, even though some groups are made worse off. Such policies are especially attractive if there exists a mechanism by which some of the winners' gains can be taxed away and used to compensate the losers. Too often, there is no such mechanism, and in a representative system of government it is not difficult for groups of potential losers to block action on plans that would hurt them.

For three-quarters of a century, the federal government has specified in great detail the way in which the airwaves can be used, for what purpose, and by whom. These rules fill 1,330 pages in the Code of Federal Regulations, and every one of them affects the ability of communication firms to compete and to adopt innovative methods of using the airwaves. And yet no change is possible without the elaborate and ponderous process of winning the government's approval.

Like other agencies, the FCC operates on two levels. One is formal, even ritualistic, following the dictates of due process as defined by the Constitution, the Administrative Procedures Act, and various court decisions. There are notices and comment periods, and reply comments, and petitions for reconsideration, and documents with titles like "Sixth Further Notice of Proposed Rulemaking and Notice of Inquiry in the Matter of the Assignment of Frequencies in the Fixed Satellite Service." Sometimes there are hearings, which may be organized either like court proceedings or like congressional committee hearings.

The other level is political. Congress created the Federal Communications Commission in 1934 and delegated to it certain regulatory functions (to regulate telephone and telegraph common carriers, allocate radio frequencies, license radio and television stations, and so on) that were too complex to handle through ordinary legislation. As such, the FCC, like other federal regulatory agencies, is an arm of Congress. The President appoints its members, who must be approved by the Senate, and Congress appropriates the agency's operating funds. The FCC's main political function is accommodating diverse interests. The building of coalitions of interests, usually blocking coalitions, is the meat and potatoes of regulatory policymaking.

Nowhere in either of these two levels of operation – the formal and the political – is there much room for sound economic and technical analysis of the policy choices that will best serve the public. This is not to say that we need agencies peopled by an elite cadre of technocrats or economists tasked to serve the public interest as best they can without regard to process or politics. That would be exceedingly undemocratic, and there could be no guarantee that the technocrats would get the answers right. Most of the time, the technocrats would have little or no basis on which to guess what the right answer might be. If regulation of the communication industry is required, the FCC is the kind of regulator we need and deserve.

But do we need to regulate the broadcast industry? What market failure is so serious in this industry (as compared, say, with book or newspaper publishing or computer software manufacturing) that the guiding hand of government is required to protect consumers against market outcomes? Very simply, there is none. Segments of the industry have substantial market power. But this power is protected most closely not by natural barriers to entry, but by federal and state governments, whose permission is required by new entrants. At present, the airwaves do not have well-defined private property rights that would prevent serious externalities in their private ownership and use. But the reason is not that such rights cannot be defined; it is that the government has prevented their development. Broadcast regulation is an emperor with no clothes.

Naked or not, the regulators are not about to run away and hide. The FCC will not go the way of abolished regulatory agencies like the CAB and the ICC. Any attempt to understand why the communication industry has the structure it has, much less any attempt to predict its future, must take the FCC and the political system whose interests it serves into account.

Uncle Sam as Mary Shelley

It is difficult to say much that is good about the role of regulation in the later history of broadcasting. So restrictive and distorting has been the effect of regulatory policy that it is almost impossible to imagine what broadcasting would have been like had it developed in a free market environment, except that there would have been a lot more of it a lot sooner. While it is possible to understand the underlying political motivation, the details of broadcast regulation in America are a Frankenstein's monster hardly more sensible than the Internal Revenue Code.

There have been two central difficulties. First, the government has assumed responsibility for determining all of the structure and much of the behavior of the broadcasting industry. This central planning role is not workable. Markets, even very imperfect ones, seem to do better than planners at serving consumers' needs, and markets are far more easily revolutionized by innovation than are regulatory fiefs. Second, because regulation is an element of representative government, its goal has rarely been efficient outcomes. Instead, the goal has been to reconcile and arbitrate interest group positions. But neither consumers nor those industries or technologies that would exist but for the rules can organize effective interest groups. Hence the government ends up catering chiefly to those economic interests that it has created or nurtured in the past. The result is a strong tendency to perpetuate the status quo, to protect economic rents, and to avoid undue competition.

The first of these problems is probably best illustrated by the collapse of Soviet economic central planning. The second problem can be illustrated by considering a few of the more famous broadcasting rules. Several have been mentioned already: the government's accommodation to RCA chief David Sarnoff in the matter of FM radio spectrum assignments after World War II, and the chain broadcasting rules set up to protect stations from networks. In effect, the chain broadcasting rules increased the cost and reduced the efficiency in the broadcasting industry. Although the rules shifted profits from networks to broadcasters, they also reduced the overall amount of profits to be divided. The network "duopoly" rule, mentioned in Chapter 4 in connection with NBC's divestiture of the Blue Network, probably had an adverse effect on industry performance as well. When one company owns two networks or channels, it tries not to duplicate the programming on them or to serve the same audience. Instead, as with the BBC, each channel will be aimed at a different kind of listener or viewer. For this reason, the network duopoly rule probably reduced program content diversity in broadcasting, although it may have increased competition in advertising markets.

The chain broadcasting rules were upheld on appeal to the Supreme Court in the 1943 Networks case (National Broadcasting Company, Inc. v. United States, 319 U.S. 190 (1943)). On this occasion Felix Frankfurter invented out of whole cloth the scarcity rationale for broadcast regulation, reading into history the false assumption that government regulation (beyond the Radio Act of 1912) was necessary to prevent "chaos" on the airwaves. Behind Frankfurter's synthetic justification for broadcast regulation, and behind the views of many influential lawmakers and opinion leaders then and since, lies a deep suspicion that broadcasting is too powerful a social force to leave unregulated, whatever the economics of it may be. Frankfurter wrote his opinion at a time when the public well remembered the power that radio conferred on demagogues such as Father Coughlin and Huey Long. Other nations have generally taken a similar view; indeed, until recently, most kept broadcasting a state monopoly.

The notion that broadcasting has too much social importance to be left to the market is ironic: the fear of powerful media arises from the fact that the broadcast media have been so highly concentrated – a consequence of regulation, not of any natural feature of radio or television technology. Spectrum could have been bought and sold with no greater difficulty than land, and is no more scarce. Now that concentration in broadcasting has been greatly reduced, probably the greatest remaining "demand" for regulation comes from the industry itself, as it seeks to manipulate the government to acquire or retain economic rents.

The government has a variety of "ownership" rules, some of them now codified by the Telecommunications Act of 1996. There are limitations on the percentage of subscribers any cable operator can serve. There are limitations on the percentage of the population that jointly owned TV and radio stations may serve, both nationally and in any given city. Some of these rules make sense as antitrust policy, although the same result could probably be reached through direct application of the antimerger law (Clayton Act §7). But many make no sense at all, reflect the obsolescent concern with media social power, and simply inhibit industry performance. For example, there is no anticompetitive effect that arises from ownership of broadcast stations in more than one city, and probably there are economies in such ownership. There is no reason for this limitation. The same applies with particular force to restrictions on the sizes of cable MSOs, a subject discussed in Chapter 7.

Two particularly painful episodes of broadcast regulation began in 1970. The FCC adopted the Prime Time Access Rule (PTAR) and the Financial Interest and Syndication Rule (FISR). Just as the chain broadcasting rules were at bottom an attempt to shift profits from networks to stations, these rules were attempts to shift profits from networks to Hollywood studios and other programming interests by eliminating more efficient competitors.

The Prime Time Access Rule made it unlawful for any network-affiliated TV station to show network programs (as opposed to programs purchased from syndicators or produced locally) between 7:00 P.M. and 8:00 P.M., except for a half-hour of network news. This bizarre regulation spawned a programming industry that was devoted to cheap game shows and made stars of Vanna White and Alex Trebeck. The network programming that was replaced was of higher "quality" in the sense that more viewers watched it. (The reason that network affiliates previously broadcast network programming in this period was that network programming generated greater profits.) PTAR reduced overall TV audience size.

The Financial Interest and Syndication Rule made it unlawful for any network to have ownership interests in the prime-time series programs that it aired or to engage in the business of syndicating network reruns to TV stations. This rule made it impossible for the networks to finance or underwrite program production in exchange for an equity interest in the show. The Hollywood studios stepped in to provide such financing, but at a higher cost than the networks. (The studios individually were smaller than the networks and thus less efficient risk bearers. In addition, the networks were in a position to optimize program schedules, which the studios were not.) The effect was to increase the cost of producing programs, while increasing the profits of Hollywood studios.

Both PTAR and FISR were repealed in 1995, the latter after a scathing analysis by the Seventh Circuit Court of Appeal. The government's own analysis of the rules at the time of their repeal admits their adverse effects. Starting as early as 1980, staff studies had repeatedly condemned these rules, and they were universally treated with derision by scholars. And yet it took twenty-five years to repeal rules that were supported by no one but the Motion Picture Association of America (MPAA) and related Hollywood interests, including a certain former president of the Screen Actors' Guild named Ronald Reagan. The point is not to disparage the MPAA, which was after all remarkably effective; it is to highlight the process that permits small groups with strong interests to govern regulatory outcomes, especially when it comes to preventing change.

The Internet: a fat new target

On July 1, 1997, President Bill Clinton announced a new government policy toward the Internet. The policy was characterized as "hands off" – that is, minimizing government regulation and taxation. At the same time, the policy was promotional. The White House championed the Internet as an engine for the growth of transactional commerce as well as a vehicle for U.S. export sales of related computer equipment and software. The Internet, the President implied, would bring extraordinary high-tech benefits to American citizens – praise reminiscent of the pronouncements made at the time cable television was "deregulated" in 1984.

In spite of the government's "hands-off" pronouncement, regulation surely looms in the future of the Internet, for several reasons. First, the development of video or other entertainment delivery on the Internet will economically threaten the current television industry, which will quickly call upon the government to bring the Internet further within the regulatory ambit. The effect of this would be to attenuate the Internet's ability to threaten broadcasters – by no means a far-fetched possibility, as the cable industry knows to its chagrin. Broadcasters were able to delay the growth of cable for years by such means.

Second, the government may be the solution to some of the problems of excessive risk and lack of standardization that today delays the commercial exploitation of

digital technology. In other words, the government may do for the Internet what
Secretary Hoover did for radio – make the technology safe for business. Just as they
did in the 1920s, major industry players may seek government help

Third, boisterous hyperbole is an important element of successful new Internet
technologies. The government's overblown prediction of what the Internet can
achieve, however, has created expectations that the Internet industry may be unable to
meet. The government is prematurely licking its chops at the prospect of the social
benefits, including tax revenues, that will result from Internet growth and commercial-
ization. Some of those benefits are already being distributed to schools, hospitals, and
the poor by overeager politicians. Businesses associated with the Internet are benefit-
ing from a variety of preferences mandated by the government in order to encourage
the growth of digital media. For example, Internet service providers and users are
spared telephone access fees that might otherwise be imposed on them. If expectations are disappointed (and perhaps even if they are not), the government is likely to
become disenchanted or impatient and to demand something in return, especially if
there is an identifiable commercial enterprise or group to blame for the lack of
performance.

The first forays into Internet regulation have already occurred: the 1996 Telecommunications Act mandates subsidies for Internet access by certain groups at the
expense of certain other groups, the national security agencies have attempted
to impose "key escrow" requirements on users of cryptographic software, and (in
September 1997) the government proposed requiring that personal computers be
equipped with the "V-chip," a move intended to regulate objectionable TV
programming.

Conclusion

Restrictions of competition and limitations on spectrum availability may have facilitated the early development of radio. But these government policies did not cease after
the developmental period, and they have had significant adverse effects on consumers
for more than half a century. First radio and then television channels were limited,
leaving unsatisfied consumer demand for programming. The legal establishment succeeded in inventing the required rationalizations. Such anticonsumer policies have not
arisen simply from errors of judgment; they are a reflection of the workings of the
political process, which requires regulators to take account of important economic
interest groups. New digital media such as the Internet are not immune from this
process.

2.3

Broadcasting policy in the digital age,
by Andrew Graham

Citizenship, culture, and community

The argument, so far, has been that there is a case for public service broadcasting so as to make good the deficiencies of the market in providing what well-informed *consumers*, acting either individually or in aggregate, would wish to buy over the longer term. A quite separate argument arises from the fact that there are parts of our lives to which the market is simply not relevant. To be more concrete, we watch television and listen to the radio, not just as consumers, but also as *citizens*.

Our citizenship carries with it three separate implications. First, as citizens we have rights. This includes the right to certain core information about our own society. Thus almost everyone would agree that anyone is entitled to *know without having to pay for it* such basic things as the key items of news, their legal rights, who their Member of Congress is, etc. It is immediately obvious that the market makes no provision for this (any more than it does for basic education or primary health care for the poor). Moreover, there is a danger that, in the absence of appropriate public policy, the new technology of the Internet and Intranets will create a world in which there is high-quality commercially provided information but only poor-quality information in the public domain. In this new context the informational role of a public service broadcaster operating universally is therefore more important than ever. As the local public library declines, so the public broadcaster must fill the gap – and for zero charge at the margin.

Second, as citizens we have views about society that cannot be captured just in our buying and selling. In particular, in a wide-ranging investigation carried out in 1994 and 1995, the Bertelsmann Foundation working with the European Institute for the Media found that in all ten countries covered by its study people expected and wanted "socially responsible television."[1] Moreover, they concluded that "responsibility in programming has a chance only if and when it has been defined and constantly pursued as a strategic aim in the management [of the broadcaster]."[2] It is difficult to see how both profitability and responsibility can be constant strategic aims at the same time. In the competitive marketplace profitability is bound to take priority.

Third, as citizens we are members of a community. It has been said that while we are all individual we are also all individual *somebodies*. In other words our sense of our own identity derives from how we see ourselves in relation to society and where we "locate" ourselves within it. Stated simply, there is intrinsic value to individuals if they have a sense of community – to be alienated is literally to lose a part of oneself.

The crucial importance of broadcasting in this context is that for the great majority of people it is today their major source of information about the world beyond that of family, friends, and acquaintances. Television provides not only the hard facts, but also the fuzzy categories – the social, ethnic, psychological, etc., concepts within which we must make sense of the world. It also supplies a set of fantasies, emotions, and fictional images with which we construct our understanding (or misunderstanding) of all those parts of society beyond our immediate surroundings. It is therefore part not just of how we see ourselves in relation to the community, or communities, within which we are embedded, but also part of how we understand the community itself – and indeed part of where the very idea of community arises and is given meaning.

The general importance of community and of a common culture to the well-being of a society and its citizens is widely recognized. Culture and community provide a common frame of reference in terms of which to comprehend the history, present, and future of one's society and of one's own place within it, and so to make sense of the decisions one has to take both as an individual and as a citizen. Moreover, the texts, practices, and traditions that make it up function as sources of aesthetic and moral understanding and empowerment, as well as providing a focus for communal identification.

There is little doubt that in today's society the viewing of television is part of what creates any sense of commonality that we may have. This is true as much of low as of high culture. The latest episode of a soap opera or a recent football match can function as a topic upon which all members of the society can form an opinion or converse with one another regardless of the differences in their life-style, social class, or status group. Given that any society must embody such sociocultural differences, the value of a community where people have things in common and can interact on that basis is or should be obvious. Indeed the winning of the World Cup by France in 1998, watched on television by almost the entire nation, is already being credited with a more tolerant and inclusive approach to the immigrant community in France. Commonality has generated the overlap from one community to another.

The value of commonality, the value of shared experience, the value of self-identity, and the value provided by non-stereotypical portrayal of other cultures are not considerations that do, or could, enter into the transactions of the marketplace – but they are values nonetheless. For all of these reasons there is a case for public service broadcasting, one of whose objectives would be the provision of those broadcasts to which we are entitled as citizens.

Fragmentation

This general point about commonality takes on added importance as well as a different form in the context of a pluralist society, such as the United States in the late 1990s. As the processes of technological, economic, and social change increase in rapidity, traditional forms of social unity can break down, and new subcultures based on partially overlapping but less widely shared and equally deep commitments to certain forms or styles of life (ones based on class, region, religion, race, sexual orientation, and so on) can proliferate. To this must be added the near certainty that a "free market" in broadcasting based on an abundance of channels would itself fragment audiences and, by so doing, increase the sense of separateness. In such a context, the risks of socio-cultural fragmentation are high, and so is the value of any medium by means of which that fragmentation could be fought.

As technology fragments the market, it is therefore entirely appropriate for U.S. public service broadcasting in the 1990s to contribute towards the (re)construction and maintenance of a common national culture – not a single dominant culture, but a set of shared values that are accommodating enough to accept on equal terms as many as possible of the minority group cultures that go to make up such a pluralist society, and thereby minimize its tendency towards fragmentation. What would be shared by the members of such a culture would *not* be belief in a particular form of life, but rather an understanding of the lives of other citizens, together with a shared acknowledgment of their worth or validity. And it is this latter requirement that specifies the sense in which the various subcultures are accepted within (form part of) a common culture on equal terms with one another.

The importance of one or more public service broadcasters in this process would be that by broadcasting informed and accurate representations of minority cultures, they would help to maintain the culture's shared emphasis upon respect for human life – it would do so by disseminating the knowledge that forms the essential basis for acknowledging those aspects of the minority cultures that make them worthy of respect. Indeed in modern society, the key way of ensuring the legitimation of a given subculture by conferring a public profile upon it is through television.

One final area under the heading of citizenship and community where a public service broadcaster might play a special role is in the broadcasting of national events. Here, the idea would be that a public service broadcaster should be given the responsibility to broadcast events which, going beyond questions of purely subculture-specific interests, are of genuinely national interest. The events in question would include happenings anywhere in the world that are of significance to virtually anyone (e.g., the collapse of the Berlin Wall) or to the United States in particular (e.g., the U.S. athletics team in the Olympic Games), as well as events in the United States that are primarily of importance to its citizens (e.g., the inauguration of the president). The idea would not be to stop the commercial stations from covering such events, but to ensure (especially as we move into pay-per-view) that events which are constitutive of citizenship are also available free at the point of view. Such broadcasting would help to maintain a sense of national identity that transcends more local communal identifications and allows individuals to understand themselves as members of a particular nation.

Democracy and the mass media

It is a basic principle of democratic society that votes should not be bought and sold. This alone is sufficient justification for broadcasting not being entirely commercial. As President Clinton put it, "Candidates should be able to talk to voters based on the strength of their ideas, not the size of their pocketbooks."[3] By the same token, broad-casting should not be directly under the control of the state. There has to be a source of information that can be trusted to be accurate in its news, documentaries, and current affairs programs and to be impartial among differing social and political views. It is a necessary, but not sufficient condition, for this to be possible that some at least of the broadcasters be independent of any political party and of any business interest.

It is not enough, however, for truth to be upheld. It must also be available – and available to all. In other countries with strong public service broadcasting traditions, it is fundamental that they are *nationally available* and *easily accessible*. Moreover, their tradition of dedicated public service provides the basis for trust without which much information is just propaganda; and their independence from governmental and commercial or marketplace pressures has, on the whole, made it more capable of representing unpopular or otherwise unpalatable truths.

These arguments are not, however, absolute ones, but contingent upon behavior. A number of supposedly "public service" broadcasters have been little more than mouthpieces for the state. The reputation of the PSBs is not therefore automatic – they have to continue to be *earned*.

On the other side of the coin, it should also not be assumed (as it often is) that commercial broadcasting is necessarily freer of politics than public service broadcast-ing just because one is public and one is commercial. In France, the close connection between Canal Plus and Mitterrand has already been noted. In Italy, the interventions have been far more blatant. In the March 1994 elections, Berlusconi used his three TV stations reaching 40 percent of the Italian audience to give unremitting support to his own political party, Forza Italia, and the wider grouping of the Freedom Alliance. Subsequent research showed not only that there was a bigger swing to the right (3.5 percent more) among Berlusconi viewers than in the electorate in general, but also that this swing could not be explained by the fact that viewers of Berlusconi channels were *already* more right wing. Viewers of these channels were found to be middle of the road and only shifted their voting *after* watching the Berlusconi channels.[4] Then, of course, after the election, the government *was* Berlusconi and in the referendum on whether Berlusconi should be obliged to sell off two of its three TV networks, Finin-vest used its networks to support the "Vote No" campaign. Fininvest carried 520 spots for the Vote No campaign as compared with only 42 for the "Vote Yes" cam-paign, which was effectively forced off the air because its slots were placed in such disadvantageous positions.[5]

Common knowledge

So far the arguments about the relationship between the mass media and democracy strongly reinforce the case for public service broadcasters existing as major sources of independent, accurate, and impartial information. However, the ideas of accurate information and of impartiality need to be seen in a wider context. Although it is not often recognized, society depends critically on the existence of "common knowledge" – what everybody knows that everybody knows. Most of the time the existence of such knowledge is taken for granted. However, it plays a role in society that is both more profound and more important than at first it seems.

The influence of common knowledge is more profound than it might seem because *any* debate requires some common knowledge – at a minimum, it has to be agreed upon what is being debated. Moreover, in modern societies the media is one major way in which common knowledge is *created*. The influence of common knowledge is also more important than it might seem because almost all solutions to problems require the *extension* of common knowledge. In order to be *agreed upon*, solutions have to be based on a common understanding of the situation. Common knowledge is therefore a *precondition* of many coordination problems in democratic societies.

Agreeing on solutions and agreeing on correct solutions are not, however, the same thing. Or to put the same point another way, knowledge, which implies that what is known is true, is not the same as belief, which may or may not be true. The "power of the witch doctor" may have been thought of as common knowledge, but strictly speaking it was only "common belief." Another more contemporary example that displays both the power of the media and the danger and inefficiency of inaccurate "common knowledge," if that contradiction may be used, comes from the experience reported by the British Labor Member of Parliament Dianne Abbott. When visiting a school in the United Kingdom she asked what number the pupils would dial in an emergency. The answer from many was "911" – yet the U.K. emergency number is 999!

This example also illustrates that "knowledge" and "information" need to be understood as including much more than is dealt with by news programs. It also covers the discussions of news, trends, and images that are to be found on radio phone-in shows, chat shows, and so on, as well as the scientific and cultural matters typically dealt with by programs such as those on the Discovery channel, not to mention the lifestyles presented in so many contemporary fictional creations.

Furthermore, central to the idea of the democratic society is that of the well-informed and self-determining individual; but, if individuals are to be genuinely autonomous, it is not sufficient for them merely to receive information (no matter how much and how impartially presented), they must be able to *understand* it. They must be able to make sense of it in ways that relate to their own lives and decisions. Neither facts on the one hand nor opinions on the other (although both are important) are sufficient; for neither are utilizable by those who absorb them unless they are made the subject of reasoned analysis – unless, in other words, they are not merely transmitted but presented (organized and submitted to informed and coherent criticism from as many perspectives as possible) in a way which allows them to be understood and thereby incorporated into the audience's own judgments. Information without "organizing insights" is just noise.

The media has therefore a double responsibility. First, programs need to handle information in such a way to increase understanding and create knowledge. Second, programs need to ensure, as far as possible, that such knowledge correctly represents the world as we know it.

It is worth noting here the sharp contrast between talk shows on commercial and on public service channels. In April 1996, the New York radio station WABC fired a talk-show host named Bob Grant, but this was only after twenty-five years of regular attacks on blacks, Hispanics, and other minorities. An ABC producer was asked whether Bob Grant's remarks were an example of free speech that should be protected under the First Amendment or whether they were verbal pollution. His reply was "If the person has good ratings a station has to overlook the garbage that he spews out." The same producer added, "[In the United States,] radio is the only serious soapbox the racists have. Our advertisers are aware that hate sells their products."[6]

The editorial responsibility that is so obviously lacking in this case is not surprising. If the product sells and makes a profit, that is all that is required. Ethical judgments, even where the only ethical requirement is a respect for evidence, is not part of its natural domain. Its *purpose* is to make money, not to sustain democracy, nor to expand common knowledge nor to extend the tastes and capacities of its audience.

Purposes matter. Almost all societies allow children to attend a single school for many years. The school is therefore the monopoly provider of both information and understanding – and at a particularly formative stage in a person's life. Yet an equivalent commercial monopoly, even later in life, is strongly resisted. The reason is that schools and commerce have different objectives. The *purpose* of a school is not to indoctrinate, but to educate. Indeed the exception proves the rule. In the rare number of cases when people do object to the influence of schools it is usually because the school is suspected of peddling a particular point of view to the detriment of education.

Closely related to this is what can be described as the "Yes, Minister" problem (after the famous U.K. TV show of that name). Someone has a piece of information. You may know that they have it and you may know that the information would be useful to you. However, you may not know what question to ask to elucidate that information. As the "Yes, Minister" program brought out so well, some civil servants like being in that kind of position, because information is power and power is not always given up easily. Typically the way in which this problem has been handled in the past has been through education. The *purpose* of educators is to empower other people and they want to teach people what questions to ask and how to use information to understand the world. Such an assumption cannot be made of the commercial world. The purpose of the commercial world is to make a profit. Nothing wrong in that, but it is different.

In brief, if democracy (and the role of its citizens) is left just to the market, democracy and its citizens will be poorly served. There will be a gap in broadcasting; a fully functioning democracy requires public service broadcasting to fill that gap. Moreover, one key principle for public service broadcasters to follow on this count is that they should aim to extend the understanding and experience of those who watch or listen. It is important to emphasize that this core principle is not restricted in its application to certain types of current affairs or documentary programming (although of course it does apply to them). Drama, soap operas, chat shows, children's programs, and situation comedies could all contribute to empowering as large a body of the citizenry as possible.

Public service broadcasters performing this function would therefore provide a central forum – the public space – within which society could engage in the process of extending its common knowledge as well as in illuminating and either reaffirming, questioning, or extending its already existing values.

Rules-based intervention versus public service broadcasting

The arguments above provide a strong case for thinking that broadcasting should not be left just to the market. There is therefore a *prima facie* case for intervention, but such arguments provide no guidance on the form that intervention should take. Why, one has to ask, could market failures not be dealt with by regulation, as occurs, for example, in the case of health and safety legislation?

The answer to this question is in two parts. First, it can be agreed that in some cases regulation is appropriate. For example, if the *only* concern of public policy were that child pornography should not be broadcast, then rules banning this activity could make an important contribution. The same is true of concentration. If the goal is to stop a single person or organization controlling a large part of the media, then laws limiting cross-ownership of media outlets have an important role to play. In short, the Federal Communications Commission (FCC) can play an important role – if it chooses to do so.

However, the second answer is far more important. In the particular case of broadcasting, rules-based intervention is necessary but not sufficient, especially not in the new environment of the late 1990s.

The first reason why rules are insufficient is that many of the issues concerning broadcasting are qualitative rather than quantitative in nature. This is self-evidently true of quality itself, but it applies equally to the discussion above of the importance of maintaining a sense of community as well as valuing a democratic society. These broad principles, which should guide part of broadcasting, could not be incorporated in any precise set of rules – indeed it is the impossibility of doing so that differentiates qualitative from quantitative assessments.[7]

The need to make qualitative judgments creates difficulties for all countries, but especially so in the United States where any attempt to *impose* such judgments on commercial companies is regarded as unconstitutional. Of course, it might, nevertheless, still be possible to design a legislative framework containing clear principles and for the *judgments* about the principles to be delegated to a broadcasting authority. However, once rules are discretionary, a new set of issues arises. The regulators, unable to appeal to a firm rule, may give in to pressure from those they are regulating. If so, the apparent attraction of rules-based intervention is much diminished. Similarly, if producers are required to act in necessarily loosely defined ways and in ways that are *against* their commercial interests, it may be more efficient to establish a public body charged with explicitly non-commercial goals than to police a complex and imprecise set of regulations. To put the same point another way, trying to achieve multiple and complex objectives via regulation is just writing a blank check for the lawyers.

The second reason why rules are insufficient is that rules are, at best, negative – especially when regulating *against* strong commercial forces. While regulation may, therefore, be able to protect standards, for example by *preventing* the display of excessive violence or sexual material considered offensive, it is much less well suited to *promoting* quality. This point is central. At numerous points in the earlier argument it has been shown that *purposes* matter. But purposes are about *doing* things – educating, informing, and entertaining, for example. Such purposes cannot possibly be achieved by rules because rules cannot make things happen. This is of great importance because, in the case of broadcasting it has been shown that there are gaps in the system which require *positive* pressure to correct them. This is why, corresponding to each area in which the market would fall down, it has been possible above to identify one or more primary *objectives* that a public service broadcaster should pursue. To offset market failure, it should aim to expand quality and to extend individuals' ideas of what they can achieve; to meet the requirements of citizenship it should provide for the needs of community (or communities); and to sustain democracy it should extend common knowledge and empower those that watch it or listen to it.

Moreover, none of these objectives is genre specific. Neither enrichment, nor our ideas of community, nor common knowledge are restricted to some "high-brow" ghetto. What will matter most of the time are not the *kinds* of programs that are made, but how they are made – hardly the task for a regulator.

Nevertheless, at the risk of repetition, it should be emphasized that the structure of broadcasting envisaged here would *include* some regulation. Indeed one fundamental point of this section is that, in the particular case of broadcasting, regulation and direct public provision can be and should be complementary to one another. Equally important is that the particular mix of regulation and public provision should change as the context changes.

In the late 1990s in the United States, as elsewhere, there are two reasons why this context is altering in ways that make rules-based intervention less effective. First, there is technological change. At the moment, the government (via the FCC) retains the ability to allocate frequencies and so regulation can be enforced. However, as satellite broadcasting (including from outside the borders of the United States) and Internet TV become more widespread, such regulation becomes more difficult. Second, the spread of the new media means that citizens will increasingly rely on television (or whatever the TV becomes) for their information. And, as shown above, good information cannot be produced via rules.

The answer to such problems is not to conclude that regulation is impossible, but to reconsider the objectives and to see whether there is some other way of influencing the market. One obvious possibility is to use public service broadcasting. If so, public service broadcasting will become more, rather than less, important as the technology develops.

One final point about the role of a public service broadcaster remains to be underlined. Each of the three grounds for public service broadcasting – the need to promote high-quality broadcasting, the need to generate a sense of community, and the need for citizens to have and understand the information essential for the functioning of democracy – exist independent of the particular set of choices made *now*.

Suppose, purely hypothetically, that everyone today had full information and full autonomy and that they chose a particular (narrow) mix of programs. This outcome would then have occurred without market failure. Nevertheless, given the potential interdependence between the broadcasting offered and the preferences of consumers, there would still remain the requirement that the *next* generation of consumers should be presented with a diverse, informative, and enriching range of programs so that *their* right to exercise *their* choice with full information and full autonomy would be ensured. The market, left to itself, would not guarantee this right. Consumers whose tastes were unexposed to, and underdeveloped by, a richer fare would not and could not demand programs that did not exist, and so producers, for their part, would experience no unfilled demand. There would be no driving force towards better quality.

Similarly, suppose – again hypothetically – that the interaction of today's consumers with the market produced a myriad of channels, each with its own format, each differentiated (however marginally) from the others, presenting an endless stream of diverse information and diverse lifestyles without apparent connection. Here again there would remain the case, many would say the imperative need, to present within one universally available channel the idea of a society (or societies) with which future generations of individuals could identify if they so wished. We cannot choose to belong to a society unless a society exists to which we may choose to belong. To deny future generations this would be to deny them a choice, not just between brand A and brand B, but about how they might wish to lead their lives and the kinds of people they might wish to become.

On all three grounds (quality, community, and democracy), therefore, a major argument for public service broadcasting today is that it provides an insurance policy for the desires, needs, and rights of the generations of tomorrow. Moreover, this is not an insurance policy that any form of rules-based intervention will provide. What is required, especially within the increasingly deregulated environment of the late 1990s, is one or more public service broadcasters, widening and extending choice, both by its own existence and by its influence on other broadcasters.

There is much misunderstanding on this question of choice. It is clear that the fear of censorship and, in particular, of hidden censorship, has loomed large in the minds of many of the critics of public service broadcasting. In the United States in particular such fears are written deep into the Constitution – no discussion of U.S. broadcasting is complete without reference to the First Amendment. Similarly, in the United Kingdom, such fears are a major reason for criticism of the BBC, which is seen by some as elitist and paternalistic. These fears and criticisms were understandable in the past when spectrum scarcity prevailed and when, as a result, access to televisual media was, as the critics would have said, exclusively under the control of either state-funded or state-authorized institutions. But this will not be the broadcasting world of the next century. Satellite, cable, and video mean that private televisual media will expand considerably irrespective of the role played by public broadcasters and so, in this new world, provided only that the costs are met and the general law of the land is respected, no one will be *denied* making or seeing anything they wish. On the contrary, in the face of the new technology which threatens excessive fragmentation, the loss of common knowledge, and low quality, it will be the existence of a public service broadcaster that *widens choice* and which, through its commitment to provide understanding, gives the *means to make the choice for oneself*. Thus a vibrant commercial system *plus* a context influenced by public service broadcasting would be the very opposite of elitism, paternalism, or censorship.

In other words, public production and public broadcasting is needed for the health of the *whole* system. Thus public service broadcasting is central, not an optional add-on. In short, such a public service broadcaster is a real public good and the true justification for public funding is not the financing of a particular corporation, but the financing of choice, quality, and public information throughout the system as whole.

Just as in the nineteenth century no one thought that regulation could *provide* public libraries, so in the twenty-first century regulation cannot provide public service broadcasting. Public service broadcasting exists to meet goals that are not those of the market and no amount of regulation can make the market pursue such goals. Thus while public service broadcasters have no *right* to exist, there are *purposes for their existence*.

Policy suggestions

The arguments above have set out the case for public service broadcasting. If this is to exist, what form (or forms) should it take? No attempt will be made here to answer this question in detail. Nevertheless, the arguments above plus the particular context of the United States suggest certain key principles.

First, and most important of all, there has to be a public service broadcasting *institution*. Trying to impose public service obligations on the commercial channels is hopeless in the U.S. context. As noted in the Bertelsmann study mentioned above, socially responsible television occurs only when it is a constant strategic aim of the management of the broadcaster. Moreover, as Henry Geller argues, the "play or pay" option always was a non-starter – any commercial broadcaster will always spend as little as possible on the public service slots that have been imposed upon it.[8] Even in the U.K. context such public service obligations only worked (a) because U.K. regu-lators can make qualitative judgments (not possible in the United States), (b) because the BBC is very large and so able to influence the system as a whole (not applicable to the United States), and (c) because the U.K. system has in the past contained an element of monopoly profit so there was scope for the commercial broadcasters to act "non-commercially" (but even this is rapidly disappearing). In short, instead of legal regulations or obligations there must be direct public provision.

Second, as emphasized earlier, legal regulations can play a complementary role. In particular, depending on the structure chosen, regulations on both the national commercial channels and on cable TV could insist on a "must carry" clause as well as on a "must display prominently" clause so that in the world of digital television the viewer can easily find the public service broadcasts on his/her EPG. In saying this it must, of course, be noted that a "must carry" clause is fundamentally different from a system in which commercial broadcasters are required to reserve a certain number of hours for public service broadcasting, *but hours which they then fill*. What is implied here is that they would be required to broadcast material *produced by the public service broadcaster(s), which, with adequate funding, should be of high quality*.

Third, the institution must be publicly financed. The analogy with club member-ship was made above – and for the nation the club is everyone and with no opting out. What is more, the fixed costs must be met collectively, but with consumption of the services free at the point of use (for all the reasons given above).

Fourth, the scale of such a broadcaster must be substantial and it must not spread its investments too thinly. In particular, if such a broadcaster were to transmit its own programs nationally it should not at the same time aim at providing a proliferation of channels. Both of these points follow from the requirement that there must be sufficient funds to meet the high fixed costs that quality requires – and if it is not to be high quality, why bother?

Fifth, if one of its key roles is to provide the core public information to which all citizens are entitled, and without which there will be a nation of the information-rich and the information-poor, then it must be universal in its reach. It must therefore be nationally available (another reason why it must be substantial in scale and why "must carry" clauses could be so important).

Sixth, it must make some of its own programs (though not necessarily all). This is because so many of the public service objectives are *not genre specific*. Neither enrichment, nor our ideas of community, nor common knowledge are restricted to some "highbrow" ghetto. What will matter most of the time are not the *kinds* of programs that are made, but how they are made. There must therefore be an institution whose *purpose* is the making of public service programs. The argument is exactly analogous with the reasons why we have schools and universities. They have purposes quite different from those of the market and these values and purposes – just like any others – require an institutional context if they, and the individuals committed to them, are to prosper.

One final suggestion remains to be made. It has been argued above (and by many others before) that television is uniquely well placed to provide the new public space within which the issues of the day can be debated. Digital television dramatically reinforces these possibilities both by creating the potential for interactivity and by increasing the availability of the spectrum. What is more, here there is genuine scope for (a) television to be local, and (b) for low-cost entry. Web-based TV does offer wholly new possibilities for deliberative discourse. Nevertheless here also there is scope for an extremely important public service element. The evidence is overwhelming in favor of the view that constructive debate occurs best when someone acts as a moderator so that some degree of order is maintained and so that someone sometimes, gently and tactfully, summarizes and/or poses the next question. Carrying out this task of editing, facilitating, and moderating in ways intended to be democratic is self-evidently a public interest activity.

In other words, entirely complementary to the public service broadcasting institution recommended above would be the training of individuals to act as the new public interest moderators. At the risk of repetition it must be emphasized that there is no implicit censorship here – multiple commercial sites where anything that the market will support and tolerate would, and should, still exist. But alongside this, it is recommended that there should be some sites, run locally, but possibly supported centrally by funds and training from the public service broadcaster (as well as by other quasi-public or not-for-profit organizations), whose function would be the promotion of local democracy and local participation.

Summary and conclusions

Who needs public service broadcasting in a digital era? The answer is that we all do and that the new technology *increases*, not *decreases*, this need. The reasons are, first, that there is a real danger that if broadcasting were left just to the market it would become excessively concentrated; second, that even if this were not the case, commercial broadcasting on its own would fail to produce the form of broadcasting which people individually or as citizens and voters collectively require; and, third, that there is no set of rules or regulations or laws which could entirely correct the deficiencies of a purely commercial system. This is for the simple but powerful reason that rules are necessarily negative. They have the capacity only to stop the undesirable. They cannot promote the desirable.

The only way to counteract fully the deficiencies of a purely commercial system is through the existence of a broadcaster that has as its driving force the ethos of public service broadcasting. In the context of the United States such a public service broadcaster would fulfill four crucial and interrelated roles.

First, it would act as a counterweight to possible monopolization of ownership and yet fragmentation of audiences in the private sector. Second, because its purposes are different, it would widen the choices that consumers individually and collectively will face. Third, provided that, via one means or another, it were universal in its reach, it would be the only sure way of protecting against the emergence of the information-rich and the information-poor. Fourth, and most important of all, it is essential that in a democratic society the issues of the day should be debated not just in terms of the values of the market, but also in terms of the public interest.

There could be more than one such public service broadcaster – since competition *within* the public sector is also healthy. But this would only be sensible if funding on a very large scale were available. Moreover, if it were, then it would be essential that one of them be vertically integrated. This follows from two considerations. First, there is the need for public service broadcasting to be concerned with the full range of broadcasting (training, production, scheduling, and broadcasting). Second, public services values and the commitment to quality can only be maintained, developed, and passed on within an institutional framework that persists.

Equally important is that, alongside any public service broadcaster, there should be an active commercial sector. Each improves the other. The commercial sector keeps the public sector competitive; the public sector raises quality and keeps the commercial sector honest.

In brief, such public service broadcasting is not an optional add-on. It is central to the health of all broadcasting and, beyond this, to the health of a democratic society.

Notes

1   B.P. Lange and R. Woldt, "The Results and Main Conclusions of the International Comparisons," in *Television Requires Responsibility* (Gütersloh: Bertelsmann Foundation Publishers, 1995), 463–502.
2   I. Hamm and F. Harmgarth, "Responsibility of Television – An Introduction," in *Television Requires Responsibility* (Gütersloh: Bertelsmann Foundation Publishers, 1995), 5–7.
3   President Bill Clinton at the National Press Club, 11 March 1997.
4   C. Gallucci, "How Many Votes Did TV Change?" L'Espresso, 11 November 1994.
5   "One Voice on Italy TV," Free Press-Journal of the Campaign of Press and Broadcasting Freedom (London: July/August 1995).

6   Quoted in R. Williams, *Normal Service Won't Be Resumed* (Sydney: Allen & Unwin, 1996), 92.

7   Some of the problems of regulating public utilities where there is an element of quality are discussed in L. Rovizzi and D. Thompson, Price-Cap *Regulated Public Utilities and Quality Regulation in the U.K.* (London: Centre for Business Strategy, Working Paper Series No 111, London Business School, 1991). However, the authors frequently mean not "quality," but "standards" and therefore treat quality as quantifiable, a confusion that the English language has been designed to avoid!

8   Henry Geller, "Public Interest Regulation in the Digital TV Era," in R. G. Noll and M. E. Price, *A Communications Cornucopia: Markle Foundation Essays on Information Policy* (Washington, D.C.: The Brookings Institution, 1998).

2.4

From public sphere to cybernetic state,
by Kevin Robins and Frank Webster

The growth of a 'programmed' market, of a regulated and coded consumer society, is a fundamentally cultural phenomenon. The stimulation of needs, the recording of tastes, the surveillance of consumption, all reflect a more rationalised and regulated way of life. (This does not, of course, imply the necessary success of such strategies, nor does it deny the ability of individuals to derive pleasure and creativity from consumer goods.) We want now to turn to a second set of forces that have been central to the historical development of the 'information society'. We are referring to the role of information and communications resources in the political process. Here too we can trace the tendency towards combined planning and control, and here too this has been of profound significance for the cultural life of modernity.[1]

We have referred to Anthony Giddens' argument that the state, and particularly the nation state, has always been propelled into the business of surveillance and information gathering. Giddens suggests that 'storage of authoritative resources is the basis of the surveillance activities of the state', and such surveillance, he argues, entails 'the collation of information relevant to state control of the conduct of its subject population, and the direct supervision of that conduct'. The storage of authoritative resources and control depends upon 'the retention and control of information or knowledge'.[2] Information and communications, capabilities have been fundamental to the state and the political sphere in a number of respects. First, they have been indispensable prerequisites for administrating and co-ordinating – maintaining the cohesion and integrity – of complex social structures. Second, they have played an important part in policing and controlling 'deviant' members of the internal population, and in the surveillance of external (potential enemy) populations. And, third, they have been central to the democratic process of political debate in the public sphere. In the following discussion we want to outline the specific shape and force that these various information functions have assumed in political life during this century.

Our historical account of the relation between information and the political system gives rise to a number of observations that can usefully be detailed at the outset. First, we should emphasise again that neither planning nor surveillance depends upon technological support. Thus, Theodore Roszak notes what the English Utilitarians recognised early in the nineteenth century, 'the persuasive force of facts and figures in the modern world': 'All the essential elements of the cult of information are there – the facade of ethical neutrality, the air of scientific rigor, the passion for technocratic control. Only one thing is missing: the computer'.[3] And the principles of disciplinary surveillance, too, have non-technological and Benthamite origins in the architecture of the Panopticon. The issue we are addressing is fundamentally about relations of power – though, having said that, we must emphasise that technologies have increasingly been deployed in the twentieth century to render the exercise of power more efficient and automatic. Our second point is that the functions of administration and control have increasingly coalesced, and regulatory and disciplinary tendencies have increasingly expressed themselves through the calculative and 'rational' machinery of administration. Third, we argue that the idea of a democratic 'conversation' in the public sphere has given way to that of the instrumental and 'efficient' Scientific Management of political life. Along with this, surveillance has become associated with a transformation of the political identity and rights of the internal population, and comes to be directed against the 'enemy within'. Finally, we argue that, although there has always been an information politics, a particularly important moment in these processes occurred early in the twentieth century and was associated with the project of Taylorism.

To clarify these arguments, let us begin with the ideal role of information and communications in democratic political theory. In his classic account of the emergence of the bourgeois public sphere, Habermas describes the historical convergence of democratic principles, the new channels of communication and publicity, and the Enlightenment faith in Reason.[4] The public sphere is the forum, open equally to all citizens, in which matters of general and political interest are debated and ideas exchanged. It remains distinct and separate from the state, and, indeed, insofar as it is the locus of critical reasoning, it operates as a curb on state power. The fundamental principles are that 'opinions on matters of concern to the nation and publicly expressed by men outside the government . . . should influence or determine the actions, personnel, or structure of their government', and that 'the government will reveal and explain its decisions in order to enable people outside the government to think and talk about those decisions'.[5] Such democratic discussion within the frontiers of the extended nation state depends necessarily upon an infrastructure of communication and publicity. Indeed, it is only on this basis that the idea of a public can have any meaning. It is through these media that channels of communication and discourse, and access to information resources, are assured. On this basis the public use of reasoning could be assured. Gouldner describes the bourgeois public sphere as 'one of the great historical advances in rationality'.[6]

That was the aspiration, though many critics of Habermas have doubted whether the bourgeois public sphere – and the 'ideal speech situation' that it presupposes – were ever significant historical realities. For the present argument, however, these objections are not important. What concern us now are the subsequent transformations of the public sphere, which do have manifest historical palpability. One process that occurs is the intrusion of market and commodity relations into the public sphere, and this results in the transformation of reasoning into consumption.[7] But perhaps even more important has been that process through which political debate has come to be regulated by large corporate bodies and by the state ('refeudalisation' is

Habermas's term for it). The 'public' is then 'superseded, managed and manipulated by large organisations which arrange things among themselves on the basis of technical information and their relative power positions', and what results is 'the dominance of corporative forms within which discussion is not public but is increasingly limited to technicians and bureaucrats', with the public now becoming 'a condition of organisational action, to be instrumentally managed – i.e. manipulated'.[8] What Habermas and Gouldner both discern is the technocratic and administrative rationalisation of political life, the Scientific Management of the public sphere and of public information and communication. Gouldner goes further, however, in recognising that this rationalising tendency is, ironically, already present in the very foundations of the public sphere. He demonstrates that

> the means to bring about the communicative competence that Habermas requires for rational discourse presuppose precisely the centralisation and strengthening of that state apparatus which increasingly tends to stifle rather than facilitate the universalisation of the rational, uninhibited discourse necessary for any democratic society.[9]

The most important cultural change with regard to the public sphere is the historical shift from a principle of political and public rationality, to one of 'scientific' and administrative rationalisation. As Anthony Giddens argues, there are problems in the very scale and complexity of the modern nation state. Social integration depends upon a strengthening and centralisation of the state, and one aspect of this is the development and regulation of communication and information resources. The rationale and justification of such tendencies become a 'technical' matter of 'efficient' management and administration over the extended territory of the nation state. On this basis, political debate, exchange and disagreement in the public sphere can come to seem 'inefficient', an inhibiting and disturbing obstacle to the rational management of society. Rational and informed discourse in the public sphere gives way to rational Scientific Management of society by technicians and bureaucrats. In this process, the very nature and criteria of rationality have been transformed. In the first case, appeal is made to the reason and judgement of the individual citizen. In the second, it is made to the scientific rationality of the expert, and to the rationality of the social system. The more 'objective' rationality of Scientific Management seems to promise a more 'efficient' democratic order than the often inarticulate and irrational citizen. Reason thus becomes instrumental, the mechanism for administrating, and thereby effectively controlling, the complex social totality. The Enlightenment ideal of Reason gives birth to what Castoriadis calls the 'rationalist ideology': the illusion of omnipotence, the supremacy of economic 'calculus', the belief in the 'rational' organisation of society, the new religion of 'science' and technology.[10]

This technocratic tendency is, of course, reflected in the positivist philosophy of Saint-Simon and Comte, which, as Gouldner persuasively argues, was inimical to the ideal of a politics open to all and conducted in public, and which maintained that public affairs were in fact scientific and technological problems, to be resolved by professionals and experts.[11] But it is with a later form of practical sociology, that associated with the extension of the principles of Scientific Management to the wider society, that such social engineering assumed its most sustained form and that the systematic exploitation of information and communications resources was taken up in earnest. And an emblematic figure here was Walter Lippmann. Scientific Management, especially when placed within the conditions of industrial democracy, embodied in the factory regime what progressive thinkers such as Walter Lippmann envisioned within society at large.[12]

Lippmann points to two dilemmas of the modern mass society. The first refers to the political competence of citizens in democratic society: 'The ideal of the omni-competent, sovereign citizen is, in my opinion, such a false ideal. It is unattainable. The pursuit of it is misleading. The failure to produce it has produced the current disenchantment'.[13] The second dilemma is that society has attained 'a complexity now so great as to be humanly unmanageable'.[14] The implication is that central government has been compelled to assume responsibility for the control and co-ordination of this increasingly diffuse social structure. And this entails 'the need for interposing some form of expertness between the private citizen and the vast environment in which he is entangled'.[15] As in the Taylorist factory, this depends on 'systematic intelligence and information control'; the gathering of social knowledge, Lippmann argues, must necessarily become 'the normal accompaniment of action'.[16] If social control is to be effective, the control of information and communication channels is imperative. With the Scientific Management of social and political life through the centralisation of communications and intelligence activities, 'persuasion . . . become[s] a self-conscious art and a regular organ of popular government' and the 'manufacture of consent improve[s] enormously in technique, because it is now based on analysis rather than rule of thumb'.[17]

What is especially important here, we believe, is the association of public opinion theory with the study of propaganda in contemporary political discourse. Propaganda has commonly, and common-sensibly, been seen as inimical to rational political debate, as a force that obstructs public reasoning. In the context, however, of the social complexity and citizen 'incompetence' observed by Lippmann, propaganda assumed the guise of a more positive social force in the eyes of many social and political thinkers in the early decades of the century. An increasingly pragmatic and 'realistic' appraisal of the political process suggested that 'in a world of competing political doctrines, the partisans of democratic government cannot depend solely upon appeal to reason or abstract liberalism'.[18] It became clear that 'propaganda, as the advocacy of ideas and doctrines, has a legitimate and desirable part to play in our democratic system'.[19] The very complexity of the modern nation state is such that a 'free market' of ideas and debate must be superseded by the management and orchestration of public opinion. Harold Lasswell makes the point succinctly:

> The modern conception of social management is profoundly affected by the propagandist outlook. Concerted action for public ends depends upon a certain concentration of motives. . . . Propaganda is surely here to stay; the modern world is peculiarly dependent upon it for the co-ordination of atomised components in times of crisis and for the conduct of large scale 'normal' operations.[20]

Propaganda is understood here in terms of the regulation and control of channels of communication and information in democratic societies. At one level, this is a matter of disseminating and broadcasting certain categories of information.[21] At another level, it is a matter of restricting access to specific categories of information. As Walter Lippmann makes clear, 'without some form of censorship, propaganda in the strict sense of the word is impossible. In order to conduct a propaganda there must be some barrier between the public and the event'.[22] For Lippmann, propaganda and censorship are complementary, as forms of persuasion and public opinion management. There has been a shift from the idea of an informed and reasoning public, to an acceptance of the massage and manipulation of public opinion by the technicians of public relations. The state function has increasingly come to subsume and regulate the democratic principle; and this to the point that it now seems indissociable from that principle.[23]

We have spent some time in outlining the development of rationalised political management and information control because we feel, again, that this is an important historical context for the development of new information and communications technologies. Through the impetus of Scientific Management, and the development of propaganda and public opinion research, it became clear that social planning and control depended upon the exploitation of information resources and technologies. This was the historical moment of the Information Revolution. The most recent technological developments – in space and satellite technologies, data processing, and in telecommunications – extend what was in reality a fundamentally political 'revolution' in information (and communication) management. It was this historical conjuncture that spawned the 'modern' industries and bureaucracies of public relations, propaganda, public (and private) opinion polling, news management, image production and advocacy, political advertising, censorship and 'official' secrecy, think tanks, and so on. More recent innovations have come with the increase in scale and the exploitation of technological resources.

While information management took on its major features in the period between the wars, in recent decades its growth and spread have been accelerating dramatically. Ironically, however, more information management has been accompanied by a reluctance to admit of its existence. Consider, for example, the enormous expansion and extension of the advertising industry since 1945.[24] Not only has advertising grown massively in economic worth, but it has also extended its reach to incorporate a battery of new informational and communications activities, ranging from consultancy to public relations, direct mail to corporate imagery. In tandem have developed the phenomena of 'junk mail' and free local 'newspapers', innovations designed to reach more, and to more precisely find, potential consumers. Along with these extensions into new products and new markets has come about an improved professionalism amongst practitioners (clear evidence of which is the proliferation of courses in advertising, PR and marketing available in the education system) and a notable increase in the precision of their 'campaigns' (careful market research using social science techniques such as survey samples, focus groups, etc., computerised recording and analysis of data, and carefully 'targeted' audiences).

Further evidence of the growing trend towards managing opinion, and something which reaches deep into the political domain, is the dramatic rise in Britain of lobbying concerns that penetrate Whitehall to extend the influence of their paymasters. A key constituent of this strategy is the hiring of parliamentarians by interested parties. Indeed, Adam Raphael estimated that one-third of British members of parliament are paid 'consultants',[25] with over half having commercial interests either as paid consultants, directors or shareholders.

An important rationale for the deployment of new information technologies is, then, the regulation of political life and the engineering of public opinion. Jeremy Tunstall describes the technological streamlining of political management in the United States: election campaigns 'are now managed via computers'; electronic mailing permits 'separate mailing shots . . . targeted at particular occupational groups or types of housing area'; electronic databases provide political and demographic information.[26] In Britain, too, electioneering is increasingly a matter of electronic techniques, with the development of software programmes to analyse voter groups and behaviour, detailed scrutiny of carefully selected subjects prior to product launch,[27] the growth of targeted mail, and computerised planning of campaigns.[28]

Conclusion

'Is closer and closer social control the inevitable price of "progress", a necessary concomitant of the continued development of modern social forms?'[29] We believe that this is indeed the case. Against those who see the new communications technologies as the basis for a coming 'communications era',[30] and the new information technologies as the panacea for our present 'Age of Ignorance',[31] our own argument is that their development has, in fact, been closely associated with processes of social management and control. The scale and complexity of the modern nation state has made communications and information resources (and technologies) central to the maintenance of political and administrative cohesion.

The 'Information Revolution' is, then, not simply and straightforwardly a matter of technological 'progress', of a new technological or industrial revolution. It is significant, rather, for the new matrix of political and cultural forces that it supports. And a crucial dimension here is that of organisational form and structure. Communication and information resources (and technologies) set the conditions and limits to the scale and nature of organisational possibilities. What they permit is the development of complex and large-scale bureaucratic organisations, and also of extended corporate structures that transcend the apparent limits of space and time (transnational corporations). They also constitute the nervous system of the modern state and guarantee its cohesion as an expansive organisational form. Insofar as they guarantee and consolidate these essential power structures in modern society, information and communication are fundamental to political administrative regulation, and consequently to the social and cultural experience of modernity.

The exploitation of information resources and technologies has expressed itself, politically and culturally, through the dual tendency towards social planning and management, on the one hand, and surveillance and control on the other. In historical terms, this can be seen as the apotheosis of Lewis Mumford's megamachine: technology now increasingly fulfils what previously depended upon bureaucratic organisation and structure. But the central historical reference point is the emergence, early in the twentieth century, of Scientific Management (as a philosophy both of industrial

production and of social reproduction). It was at this moment that 'scientific' planning and management moved beyond the factory to regulate the whole way of life. At
this time, the 'gathering of social knowledge' became 'the normal accompaniment of
action', and the manufacture of consent, through propaganda and opinion management, was increasingly 'based on analysis rather than on rule of thumb'.[32] If, through
Scientific Management, the planning and administration of everyday life became
pervasive, it also became the pre-eminent form and expression of social control.
Planning and management were, necessarily and indissociably, a process of surveillance and of manipulation and persuasion. To the extent that these administrative and
dominative information strategies were first developed on a systematic basis, it was at
this historical moment, we believe, that the 'Information Revolution' was unleashed.
New information and communications technologies have most certainly advanced,
and automated, these combined information and intelligence activities, but they
remain essentially refinements of what was fundamentally a political-administrative
'revolution'.

Recent innovations in information and communications technologies have generally been discussed from a narrow technological or economic perspective. It has
been a matter of technology assessment or of the exploitation of new technologies to
promote industrial competitiveness and economic growth. This, in the light of our
discussion, seems a partial and blinkered vision. The central question to be raised in
the context of the 'Information Revolution' today, is, we believe, the relation between
knowledge/information and the system of political and corporate power. For some,
knowledge is inherently and self-evidently a benevolent force, and improvements in
the utilisation of knowledge are demonstrably the way to ensure social progress.[33]
Information is treated as an instrumental and technical resource that will ensure the
rational and efficient management of society. It is a matter of social engineering by
knowledge professionals and information specialists and technocrats. For us, the
problems of the 'information society' are more substantial, complex, and oblique.

This, of course, raises difficult political and philosophical issues. These are the
issues that Walter Lippmann comes up against when he recognises in the Great
Society 'that centralisation of power which deprives [citizens] of control over the use
of that power', and when, he confronts the disturbing awareness that 'the problems
that vex democracy seem to be unmanageable by democratic methods'.[34] They are
the issues that Lewis Mumford addresses when he argues that 'the tension between
small-scale association and large-scale organisation, between personal autonomy and
institutional regulation, between remote control and diffused local intervention, has
now created a critical situation'.[35] And they are the monumental issues that concern
Castoriadis in his analysis of instrumental reason and the 'rationalist ideology, those
myths which, more than money or weapons, constitute the most formidable obstacles
in the way of the reconstruction of human society'.[36]

Among the significant issues to be raised by the new information technologies are
their relation to social forms of organisation, their centrality to structures of political
power, and their role in the cultural logic of consumer capitalism. Sociological analysis is naïve, we believe, when it treats the new telecommunications, space, video
and computing technologies as innocent technical conceptions and looks hopefully to
a coming, post-industrial utopia. Better to look back to the past, to the entwined

histories of reason, knowledge and technology, and to their relation to the economic development of capitalism and the political and administrative system of the modern nation state.

Notes

1 Philip Corrigan and Derek Sayer, *The Great Arch: English State Formation as Cultural Revolution*, Oxford, Blackwell, 1985.

2 Anthony Giddens, *A Contemporary Critique of Historical Materialism, vol. 1, Power, Property and the State*, London, Macmillan, 1981, p. 94.

3 Theodore Roszak, *The Cult of Information*, Cambridge, Lutterworth Press, 1986, p. 156.

4 Jürgen Habermas, *Strukturwandel der Öffentlichkeit*, Darmstadt, Luchterhand, 1962.

5 Hans Speier, 'Historical Development of Public Opinion', *American Journal of Sociology*, 1950, vol. 55, January, p. 376.

6 Alvin Gouldner, *The Dialectic of Ideology and Technology*, London, Macmillan, 1976; cf. Nicholas Garnham, 'The Media and the Public Sphere', in Peter Golding, Graham Murdock and Philip Schlesinger (eds), *Communicating Politics: Mass Communications and the Political Process*, Leicester, Leicester University Press, 1986, pp. 37–53.

7 Jurgen Habermas, *Strukturwandel der Offentlichkeit*, Darmstadt, Luchterhand, 1962, p. 194.

8 Alvin Gouldner, *The Dialectic of Ideology and Technology*, London, Macmillan, 1976, pp. 139–40.

9 Paul Piccone, 'Paradoxes of Reflexive Sociology', *New German Critique*, 1976, no. 8, Spring, p. 173.

10 Cornelius Castoriadis, 'Reflections on "Rationality" and "Development"', *Thesis Eleven*, 1984/85, no. 10/11.

11 Alvin Gouldner, *The Dialectic of Ideology and Technology*, London, Macmillan, 1976, pp. 36–37.

12 Samuel Haber, *Efficiency and Uplift: Scientific Management in the Progressive Era, 1890–1920*, Chicago, University of Chicago Press, 1964, pp. 90, 93, 97–98.

13 Walter Lippmann, *The Phantom Public*, New York, Harcourt, Brace and Co., 1925, p. 39.

14 Walter Lippmann, *Public Opinion*, London, Allen and Unwin, 1922, p. 394.

15 Ibid., p. 378.

16 Ibid., p. 408.

17 Ibid., p. 248.

18 William Albig, *Public Opinion*, New York, McGraw-Hill, 1939, p. 301.

19 Harwood L. Childs, *Public Opinion: Nature, Formation and Role*, Princeton, NJ, Van Nostrand, 1965, p. 282.

20 Harold D. Lasswell, 'The Vocation of Propagandists' in *On Political Sociology*, Chicago: University of Chicago Press, (1934) 1977, pp. 234, 235.

21 Edward Bernays refers to this as 'special pleading' and Harold Lasswell writes of the function of advocacy, suggesting that as an advocate the propagandist can

think of himself as having much in common with the lawyer'. Indeed, according to Lasswell, society 'cannot act intelligently' without its 'specialists on truth'; 'unless these specialists are properly trained and articulated with one another and the public, we cannot reasonably hope for public interests'. Edward L. Bernays. *Crystallising Public Opinion*, New York, Boni and Liveright, 1923; Harold D. Lasswell, *Democracy Through Public Opinion*, Menasha, Wis., George Banta Publishing Company (The Eleusis of Chi Omega, 1941, vol. 43, no. 1, Part 2), pp. 63, 75–76.

22 Walter Lippmann, *Public Opinion*, London, Allen and Unwin, 1922, p. 43.
23 As Francis Rourke observes 'public opinion [has] become the servant rather than the master of government, reversing the relationship which democratic theory assumes and narrowing the gap between democratic and totalitarian societies'. Francis E. Rourke, *Survey and Publicity: Dilemmas of Democracy*, Baltimore, Johns Hopkins Press, 1961, p. xi.
24 John Sinclair, *Images Incorporated: Advertising as Industry and Ideology*, London, Croom Helm, 1987, pp. 99–123.
25 Adam Raphael, 'What Price Democracy?', *Observer* (Colour Supplement), 1990, 14 October, pp. 7–47.
26 Jeremy Tunstall, 'Deregulation is Politicisation', *Telecommunications Policy*, 1985, vol. 9, no. 3, September, p. 210.
27 See the exceptionally informative article by Bernice Marrin, 'Symbolic Knowledge and Market Forces at the Frontiers of Postmodernism: Qualitative Market Researchers (Britain)' in Hans Kellner and Peter Berger (eds), *Hidden Technocrats: The New Class and New Capitalism*, New Brunswick, Transaction, 1992, pp. 111–56.
28 Cf. Bob Franklin, *Packaging Politics: Political Communications in Britain's Media Democracy*, London, Edward Arnold, 1994.
29 James B. Rule, *Private Lives and Public Surveillance*, London, Allen Lane, 1973, p. 43.
30 Tom Stonier, 'Intelligence Networks, Overview, Purpose and Policies in the Context of Global Social Change', *Aslib Proceedings*, 1986, vol. 38, no. 9, September.
31 Michael Marien, 'Some Questions for the Information Society', *The Information Society*, 1984, vol. 3, no. 2.
32 Walter Lippmann, *Public Opinion*, London, Allen and Unwin, 1922, pp. 408, 248.
33 Kenneth E. Boulding and Lawrence Senesh, *The Optimum Utilisation of Knowledge: Making Knowledge Serve Human Betterment*, Boulder, Col., Westview Press, 1983.
34 Walter Lippmann, *The Phantom Public*, New York, Harcourt, Brace and Co., 1925, pp. 189–90.
35 Lewis Murnford, 'Authoritarian and Democratic Technics', *Technology and Culture*, 1964, vol. 5, no. 2.
36 Cornelius Castoriadis, 'Reflections on "Rationality" and "Development" '; *Thesis Eleven*, 1984/85, no. 10/11, p. 35.

2.5

Policing the thinkable,
by Robert W. McChesney

The global media are integrating and their ownership is concentrating in fewer hands. This process threatens to undermine democracy. We need more independent and non-commercial media to challenge the corporate stranglehold on the culture.

Over the past two decades, as a result of neoliberal deregulation and new communication technologies, the media systems across the world have undergone a startling transformation. There are now fewer and larger companies controlling more and more, and the largest of them are media conglomerates, with vast empires that cover numerous media industries.

Media industries are barely competitive in the economic sense of the term. The giants do compete ferociously, but they do so under the rules of oligopolistic markets, meaning they have far greater control over their fate than those in truly competitive markets. It also means that it is extremely difficult, if not impossible, for newcomers to enter these markets as viable players.

By most theories of liberal democracy, such a concentration of media power into so few hands is disastrous for the free marketplace of ideas, the bedrock upon which informed self-government rests. The key to making markets work in the consumers' interest is that they be open to newcomers, but the present conglomerate-dominated markets are not even remotely competitive in the traditional sense of the term.

This is not a new problem for capitalist media. In fact, in the United States, it was nothing short of a crisis a century ago, as one-newspaper towns and chain newspapers terminated competition in the American newspaper market, then the primary purveyor of journalism. Journalism at the time was still quite partisan, whence the political crisis that resulted from virtual monopoly. It was one thing for newspapers to be opinionated when there were several in a community and it was relatively easy to enter the market. It was quite another thing to have opinionated journalism when there were monopoly newspapers and they stridently advocated the political positions of their owners and major advertisers.

We report, you decide

The solution to this problem was the birth of professional journalism, based on the idea that news should not be opinionated. To cite the slogan for Murdoch's US Fox News Channel: "We report, you decide." In theory news would be produced by trained professional editors and reporters, free of the political bias of owners and advertisers, who would concede control over editorial matters to the professionals.

Readers could trust the news, and not worry about the paucity of local newspapers. Of course, professional journalism was hardly neutral – it tended to volley within the walls of elite opinion and call that neutrality. Even after professionalism became the rule in the United States by mid-century, it was never pristine. But it did serve to make the concentrated ownership of media appear less significant than it would otherwise have been.

In the past 15 years, the autonomy granted professional journalists has come under sustained attack. As many of the major newspaper chains and TV networks have been gobbled up – at high prices – by the giant conglomerates, the traditional deal between owners and journalists has made less and less business sense. Why, accountants ask, should a firm's news division generate less profit than its film studio, its music division, or its TV networks?

Accordingly, newsrooms have increasingly been subjected to commercial rationalisation: reduced staff, less controversial and labour intensive investigative reporting, and more easy-to-cover but trivial stories about celebrities, crime and royal families. News is increasingly pitched to the upscale audience desired by advertisers; in the United States, business news has therefore become a huge part of the overall news, while labour news has fallen from view. The measure of the decline in professional journalism is indicated in every major study of journalists over the past decade. Anecdotally, one need only read the laments of former journalists to see that something fundamental has taken place.

New media provides competition?

With the decline of professionalism as a protection against concentrated control over the media, a new reason to keep things as they are has emerged: the internet will set us free. New digital technologies are so powerful that they will provide a platform for a massive wave of new media competitors who will slay the existing giant corporate media dinosaurs. A golden age of competition is returning.

It is true that the internet is changing a great deal about our lives. In certain media industries, especially music and book publishing, it is forcing a thoroughgoing re-evaluation of the reigning business models. But the evidence so far is emphatic: the internet is not going to launch viable commercial competitors to the existing media giants. Their existing market power trumps the possibilities of the new technologies. There is a plus side for internet journalism; people can access news media from across the planet. But sustaining doing good journalism requires resources and institutional support. There is nothing in the technology or the market that provides either of these to internet upstarts.

Not behind closed doors

A key reason the internet will not set us free is the thoroughly corrupt nature of communication policy making in the United States, and, to varying extents, world-wide. New technologies – often developed by public subsidy – could be used to provide for a new sector of commercial and non-commercial media if public policies were so inclined. But they are not, and they are not for a reason: important licences and subsidies are routinely doled out to media corporations behind closed doors – in the public's name but without the public's informed consent.

In the United States, for example, the premier licences for monopolistic rights to broadcasting frequencies on the scarce airwaves have been provided at no charge to a handful of corporations including Disney, Viacom and News Corporation. A trained chimpanzee could make millions with VHF TV licenses in New York, Chicago, and Los Angeles. Someone with the cunning of a Rupert Murdoch or a Sumner Redstone can do far better than that.

This points to the daunting task that faces those who wish to challenge the cor-porate media status quo. The nature of our media industries results not from some natural "free" market but from explicit government policies and subsidies. As the media firms have grown larger, their power over government policymakers has turned into a vice-grip. They alone control the means of communication, meaning they can shape the manner in which debates over media policy are disseminated and understood.

Global media system

The internet is not all that has changed in the past decade. There has emerged a global commercial media system during the same period. Twenty years ago, one thought of media systems as national phenomena first, with imports a secondary consideration. Today this is reversed. We must see the global system first, then make allowances for differences between nations and regions. This global media system is an indispensable part of the rise of global neoliberal capitalism. Indeed, it would difficult to imagine "globalisation" without the emergence of the international commercial media system. Through these systems transnational firms have access to unprecedented markets, broadcasting content that inevitably supports the values necessary to keep the system ticking.

At the top of the global media system is a tier of fewer than ten transnational giants – AOL Time Warner, Disney, Bertelsmann, Vivendi Universal, Sony, Viacom and News Corporation – that together own all the major film studios and music companies, most of the cable and satellite TV systems and stations, the US television networks, much of global book publishing and much, much, more. By 2001 nearly all of the first tier firms rank among the 300 largest corporations in the world, several among the top 50 or 100. As recently as 20 years ago, one would have been hard-pressed to find a single media company among the 1,000 largest firms in the world. Or, to consider the growth of the media sector in another manner, consider the AOL – Time Warner merger, the largest in business history. That deal, valued at around $160 billion, was nearly 500 times larger than any media deal in history.

The global media system is rounded out by a second tier of 60–80 firms. Most of them are powerhouses in North America or Europe, but several are based in Asia and a few in Latin America. These firms are competitors in some markets but are often collaborators, partners and customers in other markets. They are all wed to the neo-liberal deregulatory model that has permitted them to grow wealthy and profitable. The governments of the United States and its trusty sidekick, Britain, have dedicated themselves to the advancement of these firms' global operations. In many nations, these powerhouses and four or fewer other firms dominate the media systems.

Profit over public service

Although the global media system produces much of value, it is deeply flawed when measured by a democratic yardstick. Journalism tends to assume and support the patterns described above for the United States, undermining civic participation and encouraging business domination of social life. Notions of public service invariably fall before the altar of profit, as Andrew Graham argued in the first issue of **openDemocracy**. The collapsing of professional standards in journalism, as Jean Seaton suggested in her contribution, is one of the inevitable outcomes.

Public service broadcasting finds itself the square peg in a neoliberal hole, and survives as an increasingly commercialised affair only because it is popular, not because it can be justified in market ideology. The great strength of the commercial system is its ability to generate commercially marinated light entertainment, which suits perfectly the sort of depoliticised and inegalitarian society as exists in neoliberalism's spawning ground, the United States.

The media giants themselves assert that their power permits them to stand up to huge governments with large armies and report the tough stories that would otherwise be neglected. The record, however, points to the contrary. The annual lists of reporters who have been arrested, beaten, harassed, and murdered worldwide include precious few employees of the media giants. They are mostly freelance reporters or journalists working with small-scale media. The media giants might claim that this is because tyrannical thugs fear them, but then one would expect to see the media giants aggressively pursuing the stories that put those valiant journalists in hot water. They aren't.

Consider the case of China, where the corporate media lust for a massive market locked in by a police state has seen News Corporation, Disney, Viacom and all the rest trade in their scruples for a crack at the jackpot. A jackpot that Murdoch seems to have won. The moral of the story is clear: the global media giants use their market power to advance their interests and the wealth of their shareholders, and to preclude any public involvement in democratic media policy making. It is a poison pill for democracy.

The solution follows from the critique. We need to democratise media policy-making, and take it from the hands of the self-interested media corporations. We need to determine how to establish a well-funded viable and healthy non-profit and non-commercial media sector, independent of big business and government. We need to maintain a strong and vibrant non-commercial public broadcasting service that provides a full range of programming to the entire population. We need strict ownership and public interest regulations for media firms that are granted broadcast or cable licences. And we need policies that promote the creation of small commercial media as well as media workers' trade unions. In combination, these reforms would go a long way toward democratising our media systems and blasting open the corporate grip over our political cultures. It is not necessarily the most important task for those who favour a more egalitarian, democratic and humane world, but it is nonetheless indispensable. It will not be an easy task, but that makes it no less important.

2.6

The myths of encroaching global media ownership,
by Benjamin Compaine

Media conglomerates are not as powerful as they seem, for even corporations must respect the discipline of the market. A diverse media reflects the plurality of publics in modern society. This is democracy in action.

Is corporate media ownership leading to a dangerous, undemocratic concentration of power and editorial control? In my view it is not. The democracy of the marketplace may be flawed but it is, if anything, getting better, not worse. The first question that must be addressed to fully discuss media ownership and its consequences is: what are the empirical facts?

I try to report these in my book, *Who Owns the Media? Competition and Concentration in the Mass Media.*

Take **Robert McChesney's** opening statement and the very basis for his thesis – that there are fewer and larger companies controlling more and more. This is wrong. Certainly a casual reading of the headlines would lead to this assumption. The merger of Time with Warner and then with America Online got headlines. But the incremental growth of smaller companies from the bottom does not make headlines. Nor do break-ups and divestitures usually get front-page treatment. Nor do the arrival of new players or the shrinkage of old players.

In 1986 there was a list of the fifty largest media companies and there is still a list of the top fifty. And the current fifty account for little more of the total of media pie today than in 1986. In 1986, for example, CBS, Inc. was the largest media company in the US, with sizeable interests in broadcasting, magazine and book publishing. In the following decade it sold off its magazines, divested its book publishing, and was not even among the ten largest US media companies by the time it agreed to be acquired by Viacom. Conversely, Bertelsmann, though a major player in Germany in 1986, was barely visible in the US. By 1997 it was the third largest player in the US. Companies such as Amazon.com, Books-A-Million, Comcast and C-Net were nowhere to be found on a list of the largest media companies in 1980. Others, such as Allied Artists, Macmillan, and Playboy Enterprises either folded or grew so slowly as to fall out of the top ranks. It is a dynamic industry.

More channels, more choice – and more owners

Overall, an index of economic concentration of the fifty largest media industry players, where one thousand is the bottom range of oligopolistic tendencies, stood at two hundred and sixty-eight in the US in 1997, up only marginally from two hundred and six in 1986. That was before AOL and Time Warner or CBS and Viacom merged, but it was also before Ziff broke itself up or Thomson, the owner of more newspapers than any other company in North America, sold off most of its holdings to several established as well as newer players.

There is also the reality that "getting bigger" needs context. Because all developed economies grow, enterprises that grow larger are often simply staying still in relative terms. Or the growth looks less weighty than it would in absolute terms. For example, measured by revenue, Gannett was the largest US newspaper publisher in 1986, its sales accounting for 3.3% of all media revenue that year. In 1997, helped by major acquisitions, its revenue had grown 69%. But the US economy had grown by 86%, leaving Gannett behind. And the media industry had grown by 188%, making a "bigger" Gannett "smaller," with under 2% of total media revenue. There are many similar stories.

There is no doubt that some sectors of the media industry are more concentrated than ten or twenty years earlier – but with little economic or social impact. There are fewer newspaper publishers in the US, but then again the newspaper industry has been contracting in size for decades, and faces far more competition from other media than in its heyday early in the twentieth century. Circulation has fallen steadily, as has its share of advertising. One can't expect a dying industry to do anything but consolidate.

On the other hand, the broadcasting industry in the US, as much of Europe, has become far more competitive. This may not seem evident at first glance, but it is absolutely true. From the 1950s to 1986 US households had access to only three commercial networks. In 1986 News Corp took the risk of putting together a fourth network where others had failed. It was aided by two regulatory decisions that would seem counter-intuitive in promoting competition: a single firm was permitted to own twelve instead of the previous limit of seven local broadcast licenses. This allowed News Corp. to assemble a core of stations in larger markets that gave it a viable start in ensuring a base of an audience.

The Federal Communications Commission also waived a regulation that prohibited TV networks from owning its programming. The original regulation was supposed to foster competition, but was fatal to the economics of a fledging network. News Corp bought 20th Century Fox. With these two pieces in place, the Fox network was the first new and successful alternative to the Big 3 in thirty years. It also showed the way for three other large media players to start two networks. Today there are six commercial broadcast networks controlled by five corporate owners.

From the point of view of the media consumer, then, there is more choice on television. In addition, nearly every household in the US that so desires subscribes to either cable or satellite services, providing them with scores of programming choices from dozens of owners.

The Internet effect

Nor should the Internet glibly be written off as a promise unfulfilled. At this writing, the Internet as a commercial medium for a mass audience is barely seven years old. Only in 1994 did Netscape launch the first commercially promoted user-friendly browser. It was even later that AOL opened itself to the Internet, completely under-mining the proprietary online model that had been central to the business model it shared with CompuServe and Prodigy.

So the Internet today is analogous in both maturity of content and format as was radio in roughly 1928, or television in about 1952. They evolved mightily in all dimensions and the Internet will as well. But rather than seeing the glass as half empty today, it is half – if not more – filled. Certainly the incumbent media companies are going to want to be involved. Not to would be derelict in their fiduciary duties to the employees and stockholders (see below). But the Internet is and will remain a low cost conduit of all manners of players. There's an old adage – "freedom of the press is available only to anyone who owns one." The alternative was often the sound of one's voice at Hyde Park Corner or flyers handed out at a rally. Make no mistake: an advocate of a cause with a dial-up Internet connection and 10mb of space for a Web site on a server cannot easily challenge Disney for audience attention. But as Matt Drudge proved in "breaking" the Monica Lewinsky affair, an individual or small group has access to the world and, with a little work and less money, can actually find an audience. As has historically been true, news or information of real value has a way of getting picked by the mainstream media.

In cumulative small ways the Internet is having a large impact. Less than a decade ago the number of AM or FM radio signals an individual could receive varied from under a half dozen in rural towns to perhaps forty to fifty stations in the largest cities in the US. They provided a variety of news, talk and public affairs and a limited range of culture primarily in the form of music. Today, anyone with an Internet connection and appliance (in the form of a PC or dedicated Internet radio) has access to thousands of programmers. Some are the same old players – Disney, Infinity, the old government-run stations in much of the world. But there is a plethora of newer, Internet-only options. They have not had to invest in government-sanctioned licenses and generally have no limits on their speech (depending on where domiciled) short of outright pornography and slander. Down the road wireless Internet connects will add to its mobility.

Realguide.com provides links to 2500 real time audio streams from around the world. Many are over-the-air stations. The single jazz or classical music station in one market is now supplemented by over one hundred and thirty jazz and nearly one hundred classical others globally. While the vast majority is in English, eighty-two are in Spanish, sixty-three in German, even nine in Icelandic. The audiences, as meas-ured in the US, are heaviest for those stations that are Internet-only. The NetRadio group outdraws stations owned by Disney and other traditional broadcasters. This suggests that the Internet-only broadcasters are doing a better job of understanding their audiences and/or promoting themselves.

The restraint of the market

The notion of the rise of a handful of all-powerful transnational media giants is also vastly overstated. There is only one truly global media enterprise, Australia's News Corporation. In the past decade Germany's Bertelsmann has expanded beyond its European base to North America. And that's it. The substantial global presence of all others is primarily the output of the same Hollywood studios that have distributed their films globally for decades. Nothing new there. Some owners and names have changed: Universal has gone from MCA (US) to Matsushita (Japan) to Seagrams (Canada) to Vivendi (France). But in each case the principal media holding of each owner has been little more than this studio. AOL Time–Warner receives only one-fifth of its revenue from outside the US – and that primarily from Warner Bros. Disney, Viacom and Sony also owe most of their non-North America media revenue to films, a non-event in terms of change over the past few decades.

The number of media companies is only part of the picture. Who actually owns and controls the companies? How do editorial, pricing and programming decisions get made? For the most part, ownership of the media, especially in the US, is extremely democratic. Most of the largest media companies are publicly owned. Through their pension funds teachers in California own parts of Dow Jones and Viacom. The owners of Fidelity's mutual funds had a vested interest in nine per cent of CBS and eight per cent of AOL in 1998. Although these large institutions tend to vote their shares for management's proposals, the media companies have a legal obligation to consider the best interest of their stockholders. When a steel worker or payroll clerk retires, their well-being is directly affected by the financial decisions of their pension funds and investments.

Finally, this leads to a need to understand what motivates media management decision-making. In 1947, AJ Liebling, a fierce critic of the American press, nonetheless understood that in its very commercialism and profit-seeking the media caters to its audience, not to the political or culture whims of its owners and managers. Liebling wrote, "The American press has never been monolithic, like that of an authoritarian state. One reason is that there is always money to be made in journalism by standing up for the underdog . . . His wife buys girdles and baking powder and Literary Guild selections, and the advertiser has to reach her." While stated in impolitic terms by today's correctness, its essence rings true.

That is, the media – certainly in the US and to varying degrees elsewhere – tends to be run not to promote an ideology but to seek profit. To do that, it needs to understand what its audiences expect, what they will respond to. It does tend to make media institutions followers more than leaders. But as a graveyard of entrepreneurs and government regulators with good intentions have learned, mass media cannot be sustained only by meaning well. While there may be a role on the edge for some government or other non-commercial media to promote otherwise non-economically viable approaches, the vast majority of media can exist only if it can sustain itself. No newspaper ever folded because of lack of something to write about, but only for a lack of circulation and therefore advertising. Writers, artists, graphics designers, producers and editors want and need profitable employers to provide livable wages, appropriate equipment, sufficient travel and similar resources.

Cultural elitists distort the picture

This tyranny of the marketplace also means that many media critics and, for lack of a better term, cultural elitists, complain that the public doesn't get what they, the critics, think they *should* get from the media. Should newspapers be more serious, less fluff? With circulation declining as it is, can newspapers afford to cater to a much smaller cadre of readers? Could they then afford any level of quality? Or should we look to the Internet as the vehicle of niche audiences?

That cultural bias of many media critics is evidenced in their view of the Fox Network and the Fox News channel on cable. After years of lamenting the hegemony and cookie-cutter programming of the three US networks, critics expected that a new network would provide the "quality" programming they wanted for "the people." News Corp's Fox did provide a very noticeably different approach in programming – but it was aimed more down-market than the other networks. Fox News, again taking a different approach from CNN and the news operations of the older networks, proclaimed, "We report, you decide." The critics called it politically conservative. A growing audience found it refreshing. Both Foxes clearly added to the long-desired policy goal of diversity of US programming. If it's not what the elitists had in mind, well, be careful what one wishes for – it may come to pass.

It is not generally known that in the 1980s VCRs spread in much of Western Europe faster than in the US. This was in contrast to most technologies, from radio to TV, cable, PCs and the Internet, which tend to catch on faster in North America. Why? In most European countries, broadcasting was generally controlled directly or indirectly by government agencies. There were only two or three channels. Viewers were often offered high culture or low production-value programming. Viewership was hence lower than in the US. The VCR was a taste of choice: rent a video and become your own programmer. In the US, where programming was more democratic via the decisions of the marketplace and the remote control device – and where cable was already providing more choice – the VCR was less obviously needed.

The structure of the media is not perfect. Individual decisions by editors, publishers, and owners are not always those that someone else, with different standards, would make. There are awful policy mistakes made, as when the US Congress supported the lobbying efforts of the broadcasters to be given digital spectrum at no cost. But even that is democracy at work: there were other large constituencies lobbying against the give-away.

In democracies, there is no universal "public interest." Rather there are numerous and changing "interested publics" which fight battles issue by issue, in legislative corridors, regulatory commission hearings and ultimately at the ballot box. That it is sloppy and imperfect is beside the point. To loosely paraphrase Winston Churchill, it works better than any alterative that's been tried or proposed. The media, in all its forms, may be increasingly important in our world. But it is not concentrating or becoming any more monopolistic than it was in the twentieth century. Its owners are not cynical manipulators, who undermine the public's better judgement. Our democracy may be flawed, but it is still in charge, not suborned by the news and programmes produced by the media conglomerates.

PART 3

Properties and commons

This part focuses on one of the most fraught problems surrounding new media: the question of the ownership and control of new media products. How much freedom do users of digital music or films have to copy, share or modify the works they buy? Is there room in the information economy for a commons, where work might be productively and creatively shared?

Intangible information goods are often described as *intellectual property*, although this is a generic term which includes a wide variety of different kinds of exclusive rights, ranging from patented inventions to trade marks to plant varieties. New media often fall within the scope of copyright law, which protects certain categories of cultural and information work, including literary works, films, music, games and software. While copyright is technical and often abstruse, the implications of the arguments that have recently developed around it are profound for the circulation of information in contemporary societies and the accessibility of new media.

We emphasised in the general introduction to this reader the fact that new media are, in large part, the products of liberal capitalist economies. New media industries produce commodities in huge volumes for consumer markets: text, music, and audiovisual entertainment, news and information are typical new media products. The software and hardware that enable people to use these electronic products are also critical elements in the new media industries. The publishers and producers of these works are in the same position as publishers of sheet music in the 19th century: the profitability of their business depends on preserving exclusive rights over the works they control. But sheet music, like books, tapes, and so many other cultural goods, are not hard for other people to copy and distribute, so the battle against piracy has always been a key part of the copyright story. Digital environments introduce another level of complexity; controlling the distribution of music in printed form may have been a constant battle, but it was probably easier than controlling the circulation of digital files over the global internet.

In the 1990s many observers of the emerging internet believed it marked the end of copyright. Copyright, the idea was, would be shortly rendered irrelevant by perfect digital reproduction, ubiquitous public networks, and ever decreasing prices for ever more powerful hardware. The view was not radically different from similar claims made about the impact of earlier technologies – the photocopier, the video recorder, the audio cassette. But in the 1990s those industries that depended on copyright reacted quickly to claims that copyright was threatened. Governments responded by accepting the need for substantially modified policies. And this drive to change copyright law coincided with the liberalisation and privatisation of telecommunications around the world and a concomitant shift to privately funded public networks.

The new media were understood in the terms of the time: an 'information superhighway'. In the USA, the idea of the 'National Information Infrastructure', circa 1995, was not the internet as we now know it, but a vision for a gigantic cable television network, with 1000 channels. The technology of the 1990s was seen, perhaps inevitably, through the prism of old media, and subscription television in particular. Unlike the old academic and military internet, the new one would be built by the private sector, which would only invest the billions necessary if the regulatory structures for commerce and security, including copyright, were in place in advance.

In this part, we provide an overview of some of the current debates, prefaced by Lyman Ray Patterson's brief discussion summarising his study of copyright in historical perspective. Patterson emphasises the unsatisfactory compromises and shifts in emphasis of US copyright law. His account points to an underlying theme in much writing about copyright: the complexity of a legal structure with multifarious and unstable objectives. While there is no doubt that any copyright law must strike balances, contain tensions and find compromises between competing interests, the picture emerging from Patterson's account is of a legal structure which lacks coherence.

James Boyle explores these complexities of copyright law further in his discussion of its relationship to broader traditions of liberal political theory. The problem, perhaps, is that copyright law simply cannot be easily mapped onto liberal philosophical arguments about equal justice, or a benign balance of public and private rights. For Boyle, copyright law must fail because it is required to do too much. Jessica Litman provides a more concrete and more political analysis of the debates surrounding the rewriting of US copyright law in the 1990s. Litman's account is interesting because she looks at the language of debate around copyright and how it has changed over time. From a sequence of highly specific arguments about the nature of the copyright 'bargain' between rights-holders and consumers, the copyright debate evolved into claims around 'incentives' for the producers of copyright works. Inevitably, the incentives for producers are found to be lacking, and governments find themselves seeking ways of strengthening protection for cultural goods. Whether it is, in fact, in the public interest to make these goods more expensive, harder to access, and more difficult to share or modify is rarely examined in any detail.

The two final pieces in this section explore more radical possibilities. Lawrence Lessig makes the case for a public domain, or commons, for digital works. He writes also about what happens when copyright law – and implicitly governments – fail to secure the public interest in workable legislation. As he points out, private rules, written into the code of our digital media products, may easily replace public legislation, with a cost to hard won consumer rights. Finally, Richard Stallman, a pioneer of the 'free software' movement, discusses the promise of alternative models of software distribution, breaking away from the copyright model altogether.

3.1

Copyright in historical perspective,
by Lyman Ray Patterson

Copyright can most usefully be viewed as a legal concept – a series of ideas formulated and directed to a common end. The ideas vary in their degree of definiteness, ranging from the general to the specific, for they manifest both the ends to be achieved and the means of achieving those ends. The general ideas are principles expressing the ends to be achieved; the specific ideas are rules, expressing the means of achieving those ends. The principles are directed to the purposes to be served, the rules are directed to the resolution of problems in order to achieve those purposes. Legal concepts are thus ideally formulated in terms of purposes to be achieved and problems to be resolved.

The purposes, however, are not always clearly defined, and the problems are not always agreed upon. As the history of copyright illustrates, purposes and problems vary according to whose interest is being served. Moreover, they change with new developments. The changes, however, do not necessarily result in the appropriate development of rules. Almost certainly they do not if principles have not been properly formulated, for of the two groups of ideas, principles and rules, principles are by far the more important. It is the choice of principles that determines whether a legal concept is to have the degree of consistency necessary for a unified whole, or whether it is to consist primarily of a series of fragmented rules.

The concept of copyright is more nearly of the latter than the former category, for there is no set of clearly defined principles for copyright. Our ideas of copyright are a heritage of history – few modern statutes are based on an English statute enacted in 1709; fewer still have a direct lineage that goes back to a Star Chamber Decree of 1586. And familiarity with ideas often breeds confidence in their soundness that investigation would undermine: that which is historically sound is not always logically defensible.

Herein lies the value of a historical perspective. The historical context removes obstacles – long-continued acceptance of certain ideas, self-interest, and the pressing need to resolve immediate problems – which may be present when analysis occurs in a wholly contemporary context. And it yields a basis for employing the logic of experience. The historical perspective thus provides the opportunity to compare the ideas of copyright and the problems to which those ideas were directed in origin and development with the ideas of the concept and the problems of today. A brief summary brings into focus the early problems.

Copyright began in the sixteenth century as a device for maintaining order among members of the book trade organized as the Stationers' Company. Supported by laws of press control and censorship, it developed and existed as the private concern of these guild members for a hundred and fifty years. As such, it was the basis of a monopoly in the book trade.

With the demise of censorship, the private copyright of the members of the book trade, no longer supported by governmental sanctions, failed in its purpose of protecting published works. To restore order to the trade, Parliament was finally prevailed upon to enact a copyright statute, modelled on the stationer's copyright, but without its two most objectionable features, its limitation to members of the company, and its perpetual existence. The statutory copyright was available to anyone, and it was limited to two terms of fourteen years each. Instead of an instrument of monopoly, as the stationer's copyright had been, the statutory copyright was intended to be a trade-regulation device.

The developments following the enactment of the statute created the principle source of discontent for copyright. This was the ill-considered transformation of a protection for publishers created by the Stationers' Company into a corresponding right for the author created by law. This change of a copyright to protect members of a guild into an author's legal right was a consequence of the booksellers' efforts to continue their monopoly. Their efforts resulted in a misunderstanding of the Statute of Anne and at the same time they sowed the seeds of the idea that copyright was a natural right of the author.

They almost succeeded, because they framed their issues in the courts so as to preclude the judges from distinguishing the several interests involved: the interests of the author, the publisher, and the public. In this respect, the booksellers were aided by the fact that the courts had no role in the early development of copyright. The common-law courts were thus at a disadvantage because they were dealing in a common-law context with a statute based on a concept developed by a group of private individuals. The courts accepted the ideas presented by the booksellers and applied them, but not as the booksellers desired. The result, not surprisingly, was a confusion of ideas.

In its origin and development, then, there were two fundamental problems to which copyright was directed. In origin, the problem was to provide order in the book trade for the members of a guild organization which had a monopoly of the trade. In development, the problem came to be to destroy the monopoly of the book trade subsequently developed by a small group of men controlling copyrights.

Today, the problem of copyright has taken on new dimensions. The United States of the twentieth century bears little resemblance to England of the sixteenth and eighteenth centuries. In relation to copyright, the basic difference is freedom of the press and speech rather than press control and censorship. Copyright is no longer an instrument used to control and suppress ideas for the benefit of the government; nor is it an instrument used by a private group of monopolists to control the book trade; it is used to protect the expression of ideas for profit. The modern context thus creates a fundamental contradiction for copyright law. A society which has freedom of expression as a basic principle of liberty restricts that freedom to the extent that it vests ideas with legally protected property interests. The contradiction arises from sound, although competing, policies – to enable the author to benefit from his work and to make publication feasible, thereby promoting learning. And the resolution of the conflicts created by the competing policies requires a careful delineation of the rights to be had in connection with published works in terms of principles rather than merely in terms of rules. Thus, the problem of copyright today is how best to reconcile the interests of three groups – authors, who give expression to ideas; publishers, who disseminate ideas; and the members of the public, who use the ideas.

The contradiction of protecting ideas as private property in a society devoted to freedom of expression has been rationalized away with assurances that copyright does not protect ideas, but only the expression of ideas. The rationalization, however, will not stand up in light of the concept of copyright as it exists today. While in origin copyright was a publisher's right giving the publisher protection against the piracy of his manufactured work, it has today developed so as to give protection to the content of the work as well. Here is another irony of copyright law – in a society where there was no freedom of ideas, copyright protected only against piracy; in a society where there is freedom of ideas, copyright protects against plagiarism. Copyright, begun as protection for the publisher only, has come to be protection for the work itself.

The development is due in no small measure to the confusion of ideas resulting from the events in eighteenth-century England, and the confusion has continued. The ideas – that copyright is a monopoly; that copyright is primarily an author's right; that the author has natural rights in his works which must be limited by statute – once stated by the courts, became a fixed part of the heritage of copyright. They were taken over in this country and used almost indiscriminately. And they served as an inadequate substitute for analysis of the several interests in published works and a consideration of how to deal with them appropriately. The emphasis of the law-makers, both judges and legislators, on copyright as a monopoly and as an author's right and the issues created by this emphasis have hindered a clear-cut analysis of copyright ideas. Copyright history thus gives us reason to pause: Is the concept as presently constituted best suited to resolve the fundamental problems of reconciling the interests, conflicting in some respects, compatible in others, of the author, the publisher, and society?

There are three ideas of copyright relevant to the modern concept that the history of copyright crystallizes. The first has to do with monopoly, an idea which had its origins in the booksellers' control of the book trade in eighteenth-century England. In dealing with the monopoly problem of copyright, the real source of the monopoly danger is generally ignored. That source, of course, is not the author, but the pub-lishers. It is the publisher, not the author, who would control the book trade; and it is the publisher, not the author, who desires protection against economic competition. Yet, the problem has been obscured because the availability of the copyright to the publisher is screened behind the idea of copyright as only an author's right.

This fact raises the second problem which history develops. Is copyright an appropriate concept to accommodate the interest of both the publisher and the author? The development of copyright implies not. Copyright changed from a pub-lisher's right to an author's right for reasons that had little to do with the interest of the author. The change, brought about by publishers in an effort to perpetuate their monopoly, has continually obscured the difference between the interest of the publisher and the interest of the author in the author's work.

The interests of the author and the publisher, of course, coincide in the economic benefit to be derived from the publication of the work. Beyond this point, however, their interests may well conflict. The author, as creator of his work, has an interest in maintaining its integrity and protecting his personality and reputation, a creative interest which the publisher does not share. Yet, apart from copyright, the common law offers little protection for the creative interest.

The legal recognition of such interest in the author is neither logically unsound nor undesirable; it is only historically precluded. The booksellers in eighteenth-century England prevailed upon the courts to accept the idea that all rights of copyright are derived from the author. The courts, however, upon accepting the idea that the rights of the publisher conferred by copyright were derived from the author, limited the rights to those defined by statute. In so doing, they not only limited the rights of the author – they left no basis for distinguishing between the interest of the author and that of the publisher. The judges did not suggest what more careful analysis might have made apparent: to recognize common-law rights of the author would not necessarily have been inconsistent with the limitation of the rights of publishers.

If the author invariably retained the copyright, there would be fewer problems, for copyright gives the owner complete protection. But the author does not, invariably – indeed, he seldom retains the copyright. And the subtle irony is that the scope of copyright, supposedly broadened in the author's interest, may very well serve to defeat that interest. Yet, the courts have here overlooked a basic point. Since the statutes have dealt with the economic aspect of copyright, they have left to the courts the power, as yet unused, to deal with the creative interest as justice requires.

Finally, there is a third idea of copyright which has been given little explicit consideration, an idea that was irrelevant when copyright was first developed by the Stationers' Company in the time of censorship and press control. This is the interest of the individual user and thus of society. The interest of society in copyright has now long been acknowledged – the Statute of Anne was "An act for the encouragement of learning," and the Constitution empowers Congress to establish copyright "to promote science and useful arts." But these ideas have traditionally been applied so that society is an indirect rather than a direct beneficiary. The exclusive rights conferred on the copyright owner have served to limit the rights of the individual, although pleas for copyright protection, so that, ostensibly, the public will not be deprived of an adequate supply of books go back to the seventeenth century.

From a legal standpoint, the individual's right to use a copyrighted work is minimal. By and large, when he purchases a book, it is his chattel and no more; the work itself is owned by the copyright owner. And only the nebulous and uncertain doctrine of fair use, the idea that one may reproduce a small part of a copyrighted work for a limited purpose, protects the individual who wishes to extend his use of the work beyond the reading of it.

This problem has lately taken on enlarged significance. The limited ability of the individual a few years ago to reproduce a book has been changed by the availability of high-speed copying machines. The change has made copyright owners – that is, publishers – look to the long-continued concept of monopoly in the guise of property rights to protect their interest. A more subtle and significant point is overlooked. However slight the danger, the failure to recognize the individual user's right results in a limitation upon the freedom of expression. The copyright owner's complete control of his work, based on the notion of the expression of ideas for profit, allows him to control that work completely. A vestige of the heritage of censorship in the law of copyright remains in the interest of profit.

These three ideas – the danger of monopoly from the publisher rather than the author, the differing interests of the publisher and the author, and the rights of the individual user – are the forgotten ideas of copyright. But simple as they are, they are fundamental, and they are the basis for the principles necessary for an integrated concept of copyright.

From the fact that the danger of the monopoly of copyright is the monopoly of the publisher rather than the author, it follows that the basic function of copyright is to protect the publisher – not against the author or the individual user, but against other publishers. This suggests that copyright should be limited again to its traditional function of protecting the entrepreneur, not the work itself. Thus, the first basic principle of copyright is that a copyright owner has a right as against an economic competitor to the exclusive reproduction of a work in its original or derivative form.

To the extent that copyright protects the publisher, it also protects the author. But there is little reason to limit the author's protection to that of the publisher. Indeed, to provide the author additional protection would be effectively to limit the monopoly of the publisher's copyright. And herein lies the essential value of recognizing the author's creative interest in his works. The second principle of copyright, then, should be that an author retains an inalienable right to protect the integrity of his work and his reputation in connection therewith.

And, finally, the limitation of the publisher's protection against economic competitors would constitute a recognition of the right of the individual to make whatever use of a copyrighted work he desires, except for competing profits. The third principle of copyright is that the right of individuals to the use of a copyrighted work for personal, private, or reasonable uses shall not be impaired.

The interrelationship of these ideas suggests a major reason for the unsatisfactory law of copyright and at the same time a reason for the way in which it developed. The characteristic is a rigidity in dealing with copyright problems resulting from the application of rules without guiding principles. Copyright is a concept used to deal with exceedingly complex issues, issues which require careful distinctions based upon a perceptive awareness of the problems, an understanding of purpose, and an appreciation of function.

The distinctions were not made, the purposes not clearly understood, and the functions not appreciated. Copyright was dealt with in absolute, not relative terms.

The reason can be found in the history of copyright. Copyright was developed as a private concept by a private group; subsequently, it was embodied in a statute. When copyright problems were finally brought to the common-law courts, the task of the courts was not to develop a law, but to construe a statute, and to construe a statute for a particular purpose: to destroy an opprobrious monopoly.

In this country, from the beginning, copyright was a statutory concept, not one of common law. And the judges in copyright cases felt themselves bound by the language of the statutes. There was, in the light of history as they understood it, little room to make careful distinctions, analyze problems, and define function. Their task was to resolve disputes under the statute, not to formulate guiding principles.

The implication is clear. Copyright is too complex a matter, too delicate a subject, to be dealt with by statutes alone. Copyright statutes have provided rules, not principles, and if the principles necessary to a sound body of copyright law are to be formulated, the judges must accomplish the task. History shows the consequences to be expected if they fail. More important, however, history gives them an adequate basis upon which to proceed, to recognize the limited function of copyright, to protect the author's creative interest, and to give due regard to the rights of the individual's use of a copyrighted work.

3.2

Intellectual property and the liberal state,
by James Boyle

Like information, property plays a vital role in liberal state theory. That role imposes certain conflicting requirements on the concept of property itself.[1] Legal realism, Lockean political theory, critical legal thought, and law and economics have all stressed – each in its own vocabulary – the idea that property is perhaps the most important mechanism we use in our attempt to reconcile our desire for freedom and our desire for security.[2] How can we be free and yet secure from other people's freedom, secure and yet free to do what we want to do?[3] The most obvious way to deal with this apparent contradiction is to conceive rights of security "in a manner that both makes them appear to be absolute and negates the proposition that they restrict the legitimate freedom of action of others. Thus if we define liberty as free actions that do not affect others at all, and rights as absolute protections from harm, the contradiction vanishes."[4] The traditional Blackstonian definition of property does just that. But there are irresoluble conceptual tensions in any such formulation, a point which has considerable relevance to intellectual property law, as we will see later. Kenneth Vandevelde states the problem in the following way:

> At the beginning of the nineteenth century, property was ideally defined as absolute dominion over things. Exceptions to this definition suffused property law: instances in which the law declared property to exist even though no "thing" was involved or the owner's dominion over the thing was not absolute. Each of these exceptions, however, was explained away. Where no "thing" existed, one was fictionalized. Where dominion was not absolute, limitations could be camouflaged by resorting to fictions, or rationalized as inherent in the nature of the thing or the owner . . . As the nineteenth century progressed, increased exceptions to both the physicalist and the absolutist elements of Blackstone's conception of property were incorporated into the law . . . This dephysicalization was a development that threatened to place the entire corpus of American law in the category of property. Such conceptual imperialism created severe problems for the courts. First, if every valuable interest constituted property, then practically any act would result in either a trespass on or a taking of, someone's property, especially if property was still regarded as absolute. Second, once property had swallowed

the rest of American law, its meaningfulness as a separate category would disappear. On the other hand, if certain valuable interests were not considered property, finding and justifying the criteria for separating property from non-property would be difficult.[5]

To the extent that there was a replacement for this Blackstonian conception, it was the familiar "bundle of rights" notion of modern property law, a vulgarization of Wesley Hohfeld's analytic scheme of jural correlates and opposites, loosely justified by a rough and ready utilitarianism and applied in widely varying ways to legal interests of every kind. The euphonious case of LeRoy Fibre Co. v. Chicago, Milwaukee & St. Paul Ry. is used in many a first-year law school class to illustrate the conceptual shift.[6] Could a flax maker be found guilty of contributory negligence for piling his stacks of flax too close to the tracks? The majority bridled at the very thought. The flax maker was piling his flax on his own property, after all. "The rights of one man in the use of his property cannot be limited by the wrongs of another . . . The legal conception of property is of rights. When you attempt to limit them by wrongs, you venture a solecism." Though the majority's circular reasoning carried the day, it is Oliver Wendell Holmes's (partial) concurrence that pointed to the future.[7] Rather than imagining an absolute sphere of rights surrounding the property lines like a glass bubble, Holmes was happy to remove the flax-piling entitlement from the bundle of property rights for whatever swathe of the property was "so near to the track as to be in danger from a prudently managed engine." He also directed a few sanguine, if vaguely crocodilian, comments toward the majority on the subject of their concern about the apparent relativism of his concept of property: "I do not think we need trouble ourselves with the thought that my view depends upon differences of degree. The whole law does so as soon as it is civilized. Negligence is all degree – that of the defendant here degree of the nicest sort; and between the variations according to distance that I suppose to exist and the simple universality of the rules in the Twelve Tables or the Leges Barbarorum, there lies the culture of two thousand years."[8]

Presumably, the majority consoled itself with the fact that its concern with absolutism and universality was two thousand years out of date. In any event, the writing was on the wall. Property was no longer conceived of as absolute, no longer a guaranteed trump against the interests of the majority or the state, no longer related to any physical thing. Indeed, so thoroughly had the conception been relativized that courts were willing to admit that there could be property rights restricted to particular interests, to be asserted against one person, rather than another, and only in some situations and moments. But if this is the case, where is our shield against other people or the state? If the flax-piling entitlement can be stripped from seventy yards of the LeRoy Fibre Company merely because there would be utilitarian benefits to letting the railroad run unmolested, then why not from one hundred yards, or from the whole thing? Instead of an absolute, unchanging, and universal shield against the world, property is now merely a bundle of assorted entitlements that changes from moment to moment as the balance of utilities changes. It seems that the modern concept of property has given us a system that works on the day-to-day level, but only at the price of giving up the very role that property was supposed to play in the liberal vision.

Thus when we turn to *intellectual* property, an area which throughout its history has been less able to rely on the physicalist and absolutist fictions which kept the traditional concept of property going, we will see an attempt not only to clothe a newly invented romantic author in robes of juridical protection, but to struggle with, mediate, or repress one of the central contradictions in the liberal world view. This, then, is the redoubled contradiction of which I spoke earlier. If it is to protect the legitimacy and intellectual suasion of the liberal world view, intellectual property law (and indeed, all law that deals with information) must accomplish a number of tasks simultaneously. It must provide a conceptual apparatus which appears to mediate the various tensions associated with the role of information in liberal society. Thus, for example, it must give some convincing explanation as to why a person who recombines informational material from the public sphere is not merely engaging in the private appropriation of public wealth. It must explain how it is that we can motivate individuals – who are sometimes postulated to be essentially self-serving, and sometimes to be noble, idealistic souls – to produce information. If the answer is, "by giving them property rights," it must also explain why this will not diminish the common pool, or public domain, so greatly that a net decrease in the production of information will result. (Think of overfishing.) It must reassure us that a realm of guarded privacy will be carved out for the private sphere and at the same time explain how it is that we can have a vigorous sphere of public debate and ample information about a potentially oppressive state. It must do all of this within a vision of justice that expects formal equality within the public sphere, but respect for existing disparities in wealth, status, and power in the private. And all of these things must be accomplished while we are using a concept of property which must avoid the conceptual impossibilities of the physicalist, absolutist conception, but which at the same time is not too obviously relativist, partial, and utilitarian.

Notes

1   See Frances Philbrick, "Changing Conceptions of Property in Law," 86 *University of Pennsylvania Law Review* 691 (1938); Joseph W. Singer, "The Legal Rights Debate in Analytical Jurisprudence from Bentham to Hohfeld," 1982 *Wisconsin Law Review* 975; Kenneth Vandevelde, "The New Property of the Nineteenth Century: The Development of the Modern Concept of Property," 29 *Buffalo Law Review* 325 (1980).

2   To put it in the simplest terms possible, property is a strong barrier against potentially dangerous other people but, at least since the decline of classical legal thought, a weaker barrier against the state. See also Poletown Neighborhood Council v. Detroit, 304 N.W.2d 455 (Mich. 1981); Hawaii Housing Authority v. Midkiff, 467 U.S. 229 (1984). Constitutional rights, by contrast, are generally a stronger barrier against the state but a weak barrier against "private" parties. Or, as one of my colleagues puts it, the full panoply of Constitutional restraints applies to the actions of the dogcatcher in Gary, Indiana, but not to Exxon or General Motors. The best explanation of property as a mediator between freedom and security comes from Singer, "The Legal Rights Debate," and I am indebted to his analysis.

3   See Thomas Hobbes, *Leviathan*, 189–190 (C. B. McPherson ed., 1976); John

Stuart Mill, *On Liberty*, 70–85 (1975); James Boyle, "Thomas Hobbes and the Invented Tradition of Positivism: Reflections on Language, Power, and Essentialism," 135 *University of Pennsylvania Law Review* 383 (1987); Duncan Kennedy, "The Structure of Blackstone's Commentaries," 28 *Buffalo Law Review* 205, 209–221 (1979).

4   Singer, "The Legal Rights Debate," 980.

5   Vandevelde, "The New Property," 328–329.

6   232 U.S. 340 (1914).

7   If the railroad had a duty not to cause the destruction of only that property kept at a reasonably safe distance from the track, where was the wrong? To put it another way, why isn't the majority venturing a solecism by allowing the "wrong" of the flax stacker (in stacking the flax by the tracks) to limit the "rights" of the railroad company to operate its property?

8   Rust v. Sullivan, 500 U.S. 354 (1991).

3.3

Choosing metaphors,
by Jessica Litman

A public domain work is an orphan. No one is responsible for its life. But everyone exploits its use, until that time certain when it becomes soiled and haggard, barren of its previous virtues. Who, then, will invest the funds to renovate and nourish its future life when no one owns it? How does the consumer benefit from that scenario? The answer is, there is no benefit.

– Jack Valenti[1]

The copyright law on the books is a large aggregation of specific statutory provisions; it goes on and on for pages and pages. When most people talk about copyright, though, they don't mean the long complicated statute codified in title 17 of the U.S. Code. Most people's idea of copyright law takes the form of a collection of principles and norms. They understand that those principles are expressed, if sometimes imperfectly, in the statutory language and the case law interpreting it, but they tend to believe that the underlying principles are what count. It is, thus, unsurprising that the rhetoric used in copyright litigation and copyright lobbying is more often drawn from the principles than the provisions.

One can greatly overstate the influence that underlying principles can exercise over the enactment and interpretation of the nitty-gritty provisions of substantive law. In the ongoing negotiations among industry representatives, normative arguments about the nature of copyright show up as rhetorical flourishes, but, typically, change nobody's mind. Still, normative understandings of copyright exercise some constraints on the actual legal provisions that the lobbyists can come up with, agree on, convince Congress to pass, and persuade outsiders to comply with. The ways we have of thinking about copyright law can at least make some changes more difficult to achieve than others.

Lawyers, lobbyists, and scholars in a host of disciplines have reexamined and reformulated copyright principles over the past generation, in ways that have expanded copyright's scope and blinded many of us to the dangers that arise from protecting too much, too expansively for too long. That transformation has facilitated the expansion of copyright protection and the narrowing of copyright limitations and exceptions.

At the turn of the century, when Congress first embraced the copyright confer-ence model that was to trouble us for the rest of the century, the predominant meta-phor for copyright was the notion of a quid pro quo.[2] The public granted authors limited exclusive rights (and only if the authors fulfilled a variety of formal condi-tions) in return for the immediate public dissemination of the work and the eventual dedication of the work in its entirety to the public domain.[3]

As the United States got less hung up on formal prerequisites, that model evolved to a view of copyright as a bargain in which the public granted limited exclusive rights to authors as a means to advance the public interest. This model was about compensa-tion:[4] it focused on copyright as a way to permit authors to make enough money from the works they created in order to encourage them to create the works and make them available to the public. That view of the law persisted until fairly recently.

If you read books, articles, legal briefs, and congressional testimony about copy-right written by scholars and lawyers and judges fifty years ago, you find widespread agreement that copyright protection afforded only shallow and exception-ridden con-trol over protected works. Forty, thirty, even twenty years ago, it was an article of faith that the nature of copyright required that it offer only circumscribed, porous protec-tion to works of authorship. The balance between protection and the material that copyright left unprotected was thought to be the central animating principle of the law. Copyright was a bargain between the public and the author, whereby the public bribed the author to create new works in return for limited commercial control over the new expression the author brought to her works. The public's payoff was that, beyond the borders of the authors' defined exclusive rights, it was entitled to enjoy, consume, learn from, and reuse the works. Even the bounded copyright rights would expire after a limited term, then set at fifty-six years.

A corollary of the limited protection model was that copyright gave owners con-trol only over particular uses of their works.[5] The copyright owner had exclusive rights to duplicate the work. Publishing and public performance were within the copyright owner's control. But copyright never gave owners any control over reading, or private performance, or resale of a copy legitimately owned, or learning from and talking about and writing about a work, because those were all part of what the public gained from its bargain. Thus, the fact that copyright protection lasted for a very long time (far longer than the protection offered by patents); the fact that copyright protec-tion has never required a government examination for originality, creativity, or merit; and the fact that copyright protects works that have very little of any of them was defended as harmless: because copyright *never* took from the public any of the raw material it might need to use to create new works of authorship, the dangers arising from overprotection ranged from modest to trivial.

There was nearly universal agreement on these points through the mid-1970s. Copyright was seen as designed to be full of holes. The balance underlying that view of the copyright system treated the interests of owners of particular works (and often those owners were not the actual authors) as potentially in tension with the interests of the general public, including the authors of the future; the theory of the system was to adjust that balance so that each of the two sides got at least as much as it needed.[6] In economic terms, neither the author nor the public was entitled to appropriate the entire surplus generated by a new work of authorship.[7] Rather, they shared the proceeds, each entitled to claim that portion of them that would best encourage the promiscuous creation of still newer works of authorship.

If you're dissatisfied with the way the spoils are getting divided, one approach is to change the rhetoric. When you conceptualize the law as a balance between copyright owners and the public, you set up a particular dichotomy – some would argue, a false dichotomy[8] – that constrains the choices you are likely to make. If copyright law is a bargain between authors and the public, then we might ask what the public is getting from the bargain. If copyright law is about a balance between owners' control of the exploitation of their works and the robust health of the public domain, one might ask whether the system strikes the appropriate balance.[9] You can see how, at least in some quarters, this talk about bargains and balance might make trouble. Beginning in the late 1970s and early 1980s, advocates of copyright owners began to come up with different descriptions of the nature of copyright, with an eye to enabling copyright owners to capture a greater share of the value embodied in copyright-protected works.[10]

In the last thirty years, the idea of a bargain has gradually been replaced by a model drawn from the economic analysis of law, which characterizes copyright as a system of incentives.[11] Today, this is the standard economic model of copyright law, whereby copyright provides an economic incentive for the creation and distribution of original works of authorship.[12] The model derives a lot of its power from its simplicity: it posits a direct relationship between the extent of copyright protection and the amount of authorship produced and distributed – any increase in the scope or subject matter or duration of copyright will cause an increase in authorship; any reduction will cause a reduction.

The economic analysis model focuses on the effect greater or lesser copyright rights might have on incentives to create and exploit new works. It doesn't bother about stuff like balance or bargains except as they might affect the incentive structure for creating and exploiting new works. To justify copyright limitations, like fair use, under this model, you need to argue that authors and publishers need them in order to create new works of authorship,[13] rather than, say, because that's part of the public's share of the copyright bargain. The model is not rooted in compensation, and so it doesn't ask how broad a copyright would be appropriate or fair; instead it inquires whether broader, longer, or stronger copyright protection would be likely to lead to the production of more works of authorship.

The weakness in this model is that more and stronger and longer copyright protection will always, at the margin, cause more authors to create more works – that's how this sort of linear model operates. If we forget that the model is just a useful thought tool, and persuade ourselves that it straightforwardly describes the real world, then we're trapped in a construct in which there's no good reason why copyrights shouldn't cover everything and last forever.

Lately, that's what seems to have happened. Copyright legislation has recently been a one-way ratchet, and it's hard to argue that that's bad within the confines of the conventional way of thinking about copyright. In the past several years we've seen a further evolution. Copyright today is less about incentives or compensation than it is about control.[14] What ended up persuading lawmakers to adopt that model was the conversion of copyright into a trade issue: The content industries, copyright owners argued, were among the few in which the United States had a favorable balance of trade. Instead of focusing on American citizens who engaged in unlicensed uses of copyrighted works (many of them legal under U.S. law), they drew Congress's attention to people and businesses in other countries who engaged in similar uses. The United States should make it a top priority, they argued, to beef up domestic copyright law at home, and thus ensure that people in other countries paid for any use of copyrighted works abroad. United States copyright law does not apply beyond U.S. borders, but supporters of expanded copyright protection argued that by enacting stronger copyright laws, Congress would set a good example for our trading partners, who could then be persuaded to do the same. Proponents of enhanced protection changed the story of copyright from a story about authors and the public collaborating on a bargain to promote the progress of learning, into a story about Americans trying to protect their property from foreigners trying to steal it.

That story sold. It offered an illusion that, simply by increasing the scope and strength and duration of U.S. copyright protection, Congress could generate new wealth for America without detriment or even inconvenience to any Americans. That recasting of the copyright story persuaded Congress to "improve" copyright protection and cut back on limitations and exceptions.[15]

The upshot of the change in the way we think about copyright is that the dominant metaphor is no longer that of a bargain between authors and the public. We talk now of copyright as property that the owner is entitled to control – to sell to the public (or refuse to sell) on whatever terms the owner chooses. Copyright has been transformed into the right of a property owner to protect what is rightfully hers. (That allows us to skip right past the question of what it is, exactly, that ought to be rightfully hers.) And the current metaphor is reflected both in recent copyright amendments now on the books and in the debate over what those laws mean and whether they go too far.

One example of this trend is the piecemeal repeal of the so-called first sale doctrine, which historically permitted the purchaser of a copy of a copyrighted work to sell, loan, lease, or display the copy without the copyright owner's permission, and is the reason why public libraries, video rental stores, and art galleries are not illegal.[16] The first sale doctrine enhanced public access to copyrighted works that some were unable to purchase. Because the first sale doctrine applies only to copies of a copyrighted work, it became increasingly irrelevant in a world in which vast numbers of works were disseminated to the public through media such as television and radio, which involved no transfer of copies. Copyright owners who did distribute copies of their works, however, lobbied for the first sale doctrine's repeal. Congress yielded to the entreaties of the recording industry to limit the first sale doctrine as it applied to records, cassette tapes and compact discs in 1984, and enacted an amendment that made commercial record rental (but not loan or resale) illegal.[17] After the computer software industry's attempts to evade the operation of the first sale doctrine – by claiming that their distribution of software products involved licenses rather than sales[18] – received an unenthusiastic reception in court,[19] Congress partially repealed the first sale doctrine as it applied to computer programs.[20] Bills to repeal the first sale doctrine for audio/visual works were introduced in Congress,[21] but never accumulated enough support to be enacted. The actual bites these laws took out of the first sale doctrine were small ones, but in the process, the principle that the doctrine represents has been diminished.

If we no longer insist that people who own legitimate copies of works be permitted to do what they please with them, that presents an opportunity to attack a huge realm of unauthorized but not illegal use. If copyright owners can impose conditions on the act of gaining access, and back those conditions up with either technological devices, or legal prohibitions, or both, then copyright owners can license access to and use of their works on a continuing basis. Technological fences, such as passwords or encryption, offer some measure of control, and enhanced opportunities to extract value from the use of a work. The owner of the copyright in money management software, for example, could design the software to require purchasers of copies to authorize a small credit card charge each time they sought to run the program. The owner of the copyright in recorded music could release the recording in a scrambled format, and rent access to descramblers by the day. Technological controls, though, are vulnerable to technological evasion, which is where the part about legal controls comes in.

When copyright owners demanded the legal tools to restrict owners of legitimate copies of works from gaining access to them, Congress was receptive. Copyright owner interests argued that, in a digital age, anyone with access to their works could commit massive violations of their copyrights with a single keystroke by transmitting unauthorized copies all over the Internet. In order for their rights to mean anything, copyright owners insisted, they were entitled to have control over access to their works – not merely initial access, but continuing control over every subsequent act of gaining access to the content of a work.[22] Thus, to protect their property rights, the law needed to be amended to prohibit individuals from gaining unauthorized access to copyrighted works.[23]

Augmenting copyright law with legally enforceable access control could completely annul the first sale doctrine. More fundamentally, enforceable access control has the potential to redesign the copyright landscape completely. The hallmark of legal rights is that they can be carefully calibrated. Copyright law can give authors control over the initial distribution of a copy of a work, without permitting the author to exercise downstream control over who gets to see it. Copyright law can give authors control over the use of the words and pictures in their books without giving them rights to restrict the ideas and facts those words and pictures express. It can give them the ability to collect money for the preface and notes they add to a collection of Shakespeare's plays without allowing them to assert any rights in the text of those plays. It can permit them to control reproductions of their works without giving them the power to restrict consumption of their works. Leaving eye-tracks on a page has never been deemed to be copyright infringement.

Copyrighted works contain protected and unprotected elements, and access to those works may advance restricted or unrestricted uses. Access controls are not so discriminating. Once we permit copyright owners to exert continuing control over consumers' access to the contents of their works, there is no way to ensure that access controls will not prevent consumers from seeing the unprotected facts and ideas in a work. Nor can we make certain that the access controls prevent uses that the law secures to the copyright owner, while permitting access when its purpose is to facilitate a use the law permits. If the law requires that we obtain a license whenever we wish to read protected text, it encourages copyright owners to restrict the availability of licenses whenever it makes economic sense for them to do so. That, in turn, makes access to the ideas, facts, and other unprotected elements contingent on copyright holders' marketing plans, and puts the ability of consumers to engage in legal uses of the material in those texts within the copyright holders' unconstrained discretion. In essence, that's an exclusive right to use. In other words, in order to effectively protect authors' "exclusive rights" to their writings, which is to say, control, we need to give them power to permit or prevent any use that might undermine their control. What that means is that a person who buys a copy of a work may no longer have the right to read and reread it, loan it, resell it, or give it away. But the law has been moving away from that principle for years.

A second example of this trend is the campaign to contract the fair use privilege. Fair use was once understood as the flip side of the limited scope of copyright.[24] The copyright law gave the copyright holder exclusive control over reproductions of the work, but not over all reproductions.[25] The justifications for fair use were various; a common formulation explained that reasonable appropriations of protected works were permissible when they advanced the public interest without inflicting unacceptably grave damage on the copyright owner. Fair use was appropriate in situations when the copyright owner would be likely to authorize the use but it would be a great deal of trouble to ask for permission, such as the quotation of excerpts of a novel in a favorable review or the use of selections from a scholarly article in a subsequent scholarly article building on the first author's research. Fair use was also appropriate in situations when the copyright owner would be unlikely to authorize, such as parodies and critiques, under a justification Prof. Alan Latman described as "enforced consent." The social interest in allowing uses that criticized the copyright owner's work, for example, outweighed the copyright owner's reluctance to permit them. Fair use was appropriate whenever such uses were customary, either under the implied-consent rubric or as a matter of enforced consent. Fair use was finally asserted to be the reason that a variety of uses that come within the technical boundaries of the exclusive rights in the copyright bundle, but were difficult to prevent, like private copying, would not be actionable.[26]

Recent reformulations of the fair use privilege, however, have sought to confine it to the implied assent justification. Where copyright owners would not be likely to authorize the use free of charge, the use should no longer be fair. The uses that were permitted because they were difficult to police are claimed to be a subset of the impliedly permitted uses; should copyright owners devise a mechanism for licensing those uses, there would, similarly, no longer be any need to excuse the uses as fair.[27] In its most extreme form, this argument suggests that fair use itself is an archaic privilege with little application to the digital world: where technology permits automatic licensing, legal fictions based on "implied assent" become unnecessary.[28] Limiting fair use to an implied assent rationale, moreover, makes access controls seem more appealing. Thus, the fact that access controls would make no exception for individuals to gain access in order to make fair use of a work is said to be unproblematic. Why should fair use be a defense to the act of gaining unauthorized access?

By recasting traditional limitations on the scope of copyright as loopholes, proponents of stronger protection have managed to put the champions of limited protection on the defensive. Why, after all, should undesirable loopholes not now be plugged? Instead of being viewed as altruists seeking to assert the public's side of the copyright bargain, library organizations, for example, are said to be giving aid and comfort to pirates. Instead of being able to claim that broad prohibitions on technological devices are bad technological policy, opponents of the copyright-as-control model are painted as folks who believe that it ought to be okay to steal books rather than to buy them. And when educators have argued that everyone is losing sight of the rights that the law gives the public, they have met the response that the copyright law has never asked authors to subsidize education by donating their literary property.

Then there's the remarkable expansion of what we call piracy. Piracy used to be about folks who made and sold large numbers of counterfeit copies. Today, the term "piracy" seems to describe *any* unlicensed activity – especially if the person engaging in it is a teenager. The content industry calls some behavior piracy despite the fact that it is unquestionably legal. When a consumer makes a noncommercial recording of music by, for example, taping a CD she has purchased or borrowed from a friend, her copying comes squarely within the privilege established by the Audio Home Recording Act. The record companies persist in calling that copying piracy even though the statute deems it lawful.[29]

People on the content owners' side of this divide explain that it is technology that has changed penny-ante unauthorized users into pirates, but that's not really it at all. These "pirates" are doing the same sort of things unlicensed users have always done – making copies of things for their own personal use, sharing their copies with their friends, or reverse-engineering the works embodied on the copies to figure out how they work. What's changed is the epithet we apply to them.

If we untangle the claim that technology has turned Johnny Teenager into a pirate, what turns out to be fueling it is the idea that *if* Johnny Teenager were to decide to share his unauthorized copy with two million of his closest friends, the *effect* on a record company would be pretty similar to the effect of some counterfeit CD factory's creating two million CDs and selling them cheap. Copyright owners are worried, and with good reason. But, in response to their worry, they've succeeded in persuading a lot of people that any behavior that has the same effect as piracy must *be* piracy, and must therefore reflect the same moral turpitude we attach to piracy, even if it is the same behavior that we all called legitimate before. Worse, any behavior that *could potentially cause the same effect* as piracy, even if it doesn't, must also be piracy. Because an unauthorized digital copy of something *could* be uploaded to the Internet, where it *could* be downloaded by two million people, even making the digital copy is piracy. Because an unauthorized digital copy of something could be used in a way that could cause all that damage, making a tool that makes it *possible* to make an unauthorized digital copy, even if nobody ever actually makes one, is itself piracy, regardless of the reasons one might have for making this tool. And what could possibly be wrong with a law designed to prevent piracy?

My argument, here, is that this evolution in metaphors conceals immense sleight of hand. We as a society never actually sat down and discussed in policy terms whether, now that we had grown from a copyright-importing nation to a copyright-exporting nation, we wanted to recreate copyright as a more expansive sort of control.

Instead, by changing metaphors, we somehow got snookered into believing that copyright had always been intended to offer content owners extensive control, only, before now, we didn't have the means to enforce it.

Notes

1   *Copyright Term Extension Act: Hearing on H.R. 989 Before the Subcommittee On Courts and Intellectual Property of the House Committee on the Judicary*, 104th Cong., 1st sess. (June 1, 1995) (testimony of Jack Valenti, Motion Picture Association of America).

2   *See* Jessica Litman, *The Public Domain*, 39 Emory Law Journal 965, 977–92 (1990).

3   *See, e.g., London v. Biograph*, 231 F. 696 (1916); *Stone & McCarrick v. Dugan Piano*, 210 F. 399 (ED La 1914).

4   I'm indebted to Professor Niva Elkin-Koren for this insight. See Niva Elkin-Koren, *It's All About Control: Copyright and Market Power in the Information Society* (7/00 draft).

5   *See, e.g., U.S. Library of Congress Copyright Office, Report of the Register of Copyright on the General Revision of the U.S. Copyright Law* 6, 21–36 (1961).

6   *See, e.g.,* Chaffee, *Reflections on the Law of Copyright*, 45 Columbia Law Review 503 (1945); Report of the Register of Copyrights, note 5 above, at 6.

7   Economists would say that the authorship of a new work creates a benefit that exceeds the costs of authoring it. That is the reason why the public benefits when authors create new works. The excess benefit is a surplus. It falls to the law to determine how that surplus should be allocated. Classically, copyright law accorded the author a portion of the surplus thought to be necessary to provide an incentive to create the work and reserved the remaining benefit to the public.

8   *See, e.g.,* Jane C. Ginsburg, *Authors and Users in Copyright*, 45 Journal of the Copyright Society of the USA 1 (1997).

9   *See* Benjamin Kaplan, *An Unhurried View of Copyright* 120–22 (Columbia University Press, 1967); Stephen Breyer, *The Uneasy Case for Copyright: A Study of Copyright in Books, Photocopies and Computer Programs*, 84 Harvard Law Review 281 (1970).

10 One series of writings explored the possibility of characterizing copyright as a natural right, on the theory that works of authorship emanated from and embodied author's individual personalities. *See, e.g.,* Edward J. Damich, *The Right of Personality: A Common Law Basis for the Protection of the Moral Rights of Authors*, 23 Georgia Law Review 1 (1988); Justin Hughes, *The Philosophy of Intellectual Property*, 77 Georgetown Law Journal 287 (1988); John M. Kernochan, *Imperatives for Enforcing Authors' Rights*, 11 Columbia-VLA Journal of Law & the Arts 587 (1987). Ignoring for the moment that, at least in the United States, the overwhelming majority of registered copyrights were corporately owned, these thinkers posited the model of author who creates all works from nothing. The parent/progeny metaphor was popular here – authors were compared with mothers or fathers; their works were their children. Therefore, the argument

went, they were morally entitled to plenary control over their works as they would be over their children.

11 *See, e.g.*, Paul Goldstein, *Derivative Rights and Derivative Works in Copyright*, 30 Journal of the Copyright Society 209 (1982); Wendy J. Gordon, *Fair Use as Market Failure: A Structural and Economic Analysis of the Betamax Case and Its Predecessors*, 82 Columbia Law Review 1600 (1982); William M. Landes and Richard Posner, *An Economic Analysis of Copyright*, 18 Journal of Legal Studies 325 (1989).

12 *See, e.g.*, Dennis Karjala, *Copyright in Electronic Maps*, 35 Jurimetrics Journal 395 (1995); Alfred C. Yen, *When Authors Won't Sell: Parody, Fair Use and Efficiency in Copyright Law*, 62 University of Colorado Law Review 1173 (1991).

13 *See* Wendy J. Gordon, *Toward a Jurisprudence of Benefits: The Norms of Copyright and the Problems of Private Censorship*, 57 University of Chicago Law Review 1009, 1032–49 (1990); Litman, note 2 above, at 1007–12.

14 Again, I'm indebted to Professor Elkin-Koren for the taxonomy. *See* Elkin-Koren, note 4 above.

15 I have told that story in some detail in Jessica Litman, *Copyright and Information Policy*, 55 Law & Contemporary Problems (Spring 1992), at 185.

16 *See* 17 USCA § 109; see generally John M. Kemochan, *The Distribution Right in the United States of America: Review and Reflections*, 42 Vanderbilt Law Review 1407 (1989).

17 Record Rental Amendment of 1984, Pub. L No 98–450, 98 Stat 1727 (1984) (codified as amended at 17 USCA §§ 109, 115).

18 *See* Pamela Samuelson, *Modifying Copyrighted Software: Adjusting Copyright Doctrine to Accommodate a Technology*, 28 Jurimetrics Journal 179, 188–89 (1988).

19 In *Vault Corp. v. Quaid Software, Ltd.*, 847 F2d 255 (5th Cir 1988), the court rejected such a license and the state law purporting to enforce it because the court found it to be inconsistent with federal copyright law, which gives purchasers of copies of computer programs the rights that the shrink-wrap license attempted to withhold.

20 Computer Software Rental Amendments Act of 1990, Pub. L. No. 101–650, 104 Stat 5089, 5134 §§ 801–804 (codified at 17 USC § 109). Like the Record Rental Act, the CSRA prohibits commercial software rental, but not resale, gift, or loan.

21 *See* S. 33, 98th Cong, 1st sess. (January 25, 1983), in 129 Cong. Rec. 590 (January 26, 1983); H.R. 1029, 98th Cong., 1st sess. (January 26, 1983), in 129 Cong. Rec. H201 (January 27, 1983); Home Video Recording, Hearing Before the Senate Committee on the Judiciary, 99th Cong. 2d sess. (1987).

22 *See* Jane C. Ginsburg, *Essay: From Having Copies to Experiencing Works: The Development of an Access Right in U.S. Copyright Law*, in Hugh Hansen, ed., *U.S. Intellectual Property: Law and Policy* (Sweet & Maxwell, 2000).

23 I discuss the access-control amendments extensively in chapter 9. As enacted, they prohibit individuals from circumventing any technological devices designed to restrict access to a work, and make it illegal to make or distribute any tool or service designed to facilitate circumvention. *See* 17 U.S.C. § 1201. The law imposes substantial civil and criminal penalties for violations. *See* 17 U.S.C. §§ 1203, 1204.

24 *See, e.g.*, Alan Latman, *Study # 14: Fair Use 6–7* (1958), reprinted in 2 Studies on Copyright, Studies on Copyright 778, 784–85 (Arthur Fisher Memorial Edition, 1963).

25 *See Folsom* v. *Marsh*, 9 Fed Cas. 342 (1841); H. Ball, The Law of Copyright and Literary Property 260 (Bender, 1944); L. Ray Patterson, *Understanding Fair Use*, 55 Law and Contemporary Problems (Spring 1992), at 249.

26 *See generally* Latman, note 24 above at 7–14, 2 Studies on Copyright at 785–92; Lloyd Weinreb, *Commentary: Fair's Fair: A Comment on the Fair Use Doctrine*, 105 Harvard Law Review 1137 (1990).

27 *See, e.g.*, Jane C. Ginsburg, note 8 above, at 11–20 (1997); *American Geophysical Union v. Texaco*, 60 F.3d 913 (2d Cir. 1995).

28 *See, e.g.*, Torn W. Bell, *Fared Use v. Fair Use: The Impact of Automated Rights Management on Copyright's Fair Use Doctrine*, 76 N. Carolina Law Review 101 (1998).

29 *See, e.g., Music on the Internet: Is There an Upside to Downloading? Hearing Before the Senate Judiciary Committee*, 106th Cong., 2d sess. (July 11, 2000) (remarks of Hilary Rosen, RIAA).

3.4

The promise for intellectual property in cyberspace,
by Lawrence Lessig

It all depends on whether you really understand the idea of trusted systems. If you don't understand them, then this whole approach to commerce and digital publishing is utterly unthinkable. If you do understand them, then it all follows easily.

Ralph Merkle, quoted in Stefik, "Letting Loose the Light" (1996)

Given the present code of the Internet, you can't control well who copies what. If you have a copy of a copyrighted photo, rendered in a graphics file, you can make unlimited copies of that file with no effect on the original. When you make the one-hundredth copy, nothing indicates that it is the one-hundredth copy rather than the first. There is very little in the code as it exists now that regulates the distribution of and access to material on the Net.

This problem is not unique to cyberspace. We have already seen a technology that presented the same problem; a solution to the problem was subsequently built into the technology.[1] Digital audio technology (DAT) tape was a threat to copyright, and a number of solutions to this threat were proposed. Some people argued for higher penalties for illegal copying of tapes (direct regulation by law). Some argued for a tax on blank tapes, with the proceeds compensating copyright holders (indirect regulation of the market by law). Some argued for better education to stop illegal copies of tapes (indirect regulation of norms by law). But some argued for a change in the code of tape machines that would block unlimited perfect copying.

With the code changed, when a machine is used to copy a particular CD, a serial number from the CD is recorded in the tape machine's memory. If the user tries to copy that tape more than a limited number of times, the machine adjusts the quality of the copy. As the copies increase, the quality is degraded. This degradation is deliberately created. Before DAT, it was an unintended consequence of the copying technologies – each copy was unavoidably worse than the original. Now it has been reintroduced to restore a protection that had been eroded by technology.

The same idea animates Stefik's vision, though his idea is not to make the quality of copies decrease but rather to make it possible to track and control the copies that are made.[2]

Think of the proposal like this. Today, when you buy a book, you may do any number of things with it. You can read it once or one hundred times. You can lend it to a friend. You can photocopy pages in it or scan it into your computer. You can burn it, use it as a paperweight, or sell it. You can store it on your shelf and never once open it.

Some of these things you can do because the law gives you the right to do them – you can sell the book, for example, because the copyright law explicitly gives you that right. Other things you can do because there is no way to stop you. A book seller might sell you the book at one price if you promise to read it once, and at a different price if you want to read it one hundred times, but there is no way for the seller to know whether you have obeyed the contract. In principle, the seller could sell a police officer with each book to follow you around and make sure you use the book as you promised, but the costs would plainly be prohibitive.

But what if each of these rights could be controlled, and each unbundled and sold separately? What if, that is, the software itself could regulate whether you read the book once or one hundred times; whether you could cut and paste from it or simply read it without copying; whether you could send it as an attached document to a friend or simply keep it on your machine; whether you could delete it or not; whether you could use it in another work, for another purpose, or not; or whether you could simply have it on your shelf or have it and use it as well?

Stefik describes a network that makes such unbundling of rights possible. He describes an architecture for the network that would allow owners of copyrighted materials to sell access to those materials on the terms they want and would enforce those contracts.

The details of the system are not important here[3] (it builds on the encryption architecture I described in chapter 4), but its general idea is easy enough to describe. As the Net is now, basic functions like copying and access are crudely regulated in an all-or-nothing fashion. You generally have the right to copy or not, to gain access or not.

But a more sophisticated system of rights could be built into the Net – not into a different Net, but on top of the existing Net. This system would function by discriminating in the intercourse it has with other systems. A system that controlled access in this more fine-grained way would grant access to its resources only to another system that controlled access in the same way. A hierarchy of systems would develop, and copyrighted material would be traded only among systems that properly controlled access.

In such a world, then, you could get access, say, to the *New York Times* and pay a different price depending on how much of it you read. The *Times* could determine how much you read, whether you could copy portions of the newspaper, whether you could save it on your hard disk, and so on. But if the code you used to access the *Times* site did not enable the control the *Times* demanded, then the *Times* would not let you onto its site at all. In short, systems would exchange information only with others that could be trusted, and the protocols of trust would be built into the architectures of the systems.

Stefik calls this "trusted systems," and the name evokes a helpful analog. Think of bonded couriers. Sometimes you want to mail a letter with something particularly valuable in it. You could simply give it to the post office, but the post office is not a terribly reliable system; it has relatively little control over its employees, and theft and loss are not uncommon. So instead of going to the post office, you could give your letter to a bonded courier. Bonded couriers are insured, and the insurance is a cost that constrains them to be reliable. This reputation then makes it possible for senders of valuable material to be assured about using their services.

This is what a structure of trusted systems does for owners of intellectual property. It is a bonded courier that takes the thing of value and controls access to and use of it according to the orders given by the principal.

Imagine for a moment that such a structure emerged generally in cyberspace. How would we then think about copyright law?

An important point about copyright law is that, though designed in part to protect authors, its protection was not to be absolute – the copyright is subject to "fair use," limited terms, and first sale. The law threatened to punish violators of copyright laws – and it was this threat that induced a fairly high proportion of people to comply – but the law was never designed to simply do the author's bidding. It had public purposes as well as the author's interest in mind.

Trusted systems provide authors with the same sort of protection. Because authors can restrict unauthorized use of their material, they can extract money in exchange for access. Trusted systems thus achieve what copyright law achieves. But it can achieve this protection *without the law doing the restricting*. It permits a much more fine-grained control over access to and use of protected material than law permits, and it can do so without the aid of the law.

What copyright seeks to do using the threat of law and the push of norms, trusted systems do through the code. Copyright orders others to respect the rights of the copyright holder before using his property. Trusted systems give access only if rights are respected in the first place. The controls needed to regulate this access are built into the systems, and no users (except hackers) have a choice about whether to obey these controls. The code displaces law by codifying the rules, making them more efficient than they were just as rules.

Trusted systems in this scheme are an alternative for protecting intellectual property rights – a privatized alternative to law. They need not be exclusive; there is no reason not to use both law and trusted systems. Nevertheless, the code in effect is doing the work that the law used to do. It implements the law's protection, through code, far more effectively than the law did.

What could be wrong with this? We do not worry when people put double bolts on their doors to supplement the work of the neighborhood cop. We do not worry when they lock their cars and take their keys. It is not an offense to protect yourself rather than rely on the state. Indeed, in some contexts it is a virtue. Andrew Jackson's mother, for example, told him, "Never tell a lie, nor take what is not your own, nor sue anybody for slander, assault and battery. Always settle them cases yourself."[4] Self-sufficiency is often seen as a sign of strength, and going to the law as a sign of weakness.

There are two steps to answering this question. The first rehearses a familiar but forgotten point about the nature of property; the second makes a less familiar, but central, point about the nature of intellectual property. Together they suggest why perfect control is not the control that law has given owners of intellectual property.

The limits on the protection of property

The realists in American legal history (circa 1890–1930) were scholars who (in part) emphasized the role of the state in what was called "private law."[5] At the time they wrote, it was the "private" in private law that got all the emphasis. Forgotten was the "law," as if "property" and "contract" existed independent of the state.

The realists' aim was to undermine this view. Contract and property law, they argued, was *law* that gave private parties power.[6] If you breach a contract with me, I can have the court order the sheriff to force you to pay; the contract gives me access to the state power of the sheriff. If your contract with your employer says that it may dismiss you for being late, then the police can be called in to eject you if you refuse to leave. If your lease forbids you to have cats, then the landlord can use the power of the courts to evict you if you do not get rid of the cats. These are all instances where contract and property, however grounded in private action, give a private person an entitlement to the state.

No doubt this power is justified in many cases; to call it "law" is not to call it unjust. The greatest prosperity in history has been created by a system in which private parties can order their lives freely through contract and property. But whether justified in the main or not, the realists argued that the contours of this "law" should be architected to benefit society.[7]

This is not communism. It is not an attack on private property. It is not to say that the state creates wealth. Put your Ayn Rand away. These are claims about the relationship between private law and public law, and they should be uncontroversial.

Private law creates private rights to the extent that these private rights serve some collective good. If a private right is harmful to a collective good, then the *state* has no reason to create it. The state's interests are general, not particular. It has a reason to create rights when those rights serve a common, rather than particular, end.

The institution of private property is an application of this point. The state has an interest in defining rights to private property because private property helps produce a general, and powerful, prosperity. It is a system for ordering economic relations that greatly benefits all members of society. No other system that we have yet devised better orders economic relations. No other system, some believe, could.[8]

But even with ordinary property – your car, or your house – property rights are never absolute. There is no property that does not have to yield at some point to the interests of the state. Your land may be taken to build a highway, your car seized to carry an accident victim to the hospital, your driveway crossed by the postman, your house inspected by health inspectors. In countless ways, the system of property we call "private property" is a system that balances exclusive control by the individual against certain common state ends. When the latter conflict with the former, it is the former that yields.

This balance, the realists argued, is a feature of all property. But it is an especially important feature of intellectual property. The balance of rights with intellectual property differs from the balance with ordinary real or personal property. "Information," as Boyle puts it, "is different."[9] And a very obvious feature of intellectual property shows why.

When property law gives me the exclusive right to use my house, there's a very good reason for it. If you used my house while I did, I would have less to use. When the law gives me an exclusive right to my apple, that too makes sense. If you eat my apple, then I cannot. Your use of my property ordinarily interferes with my use of my property. Your consumption reduces mine.

The law has a good reason, then, to give me an exclusive right over my personal and real property. If it did not, I would have little reason to work to produce it. Or if I did work to produce it, I would then spend a great deal of my time trying to keep you away. It is better for everyone, the argument goes, if I have an exclusive right to my (rightly acquired) property, because then I have an incentive to produce it and not waste all my time trying to defend it.[10]

Things are different with intellectual property. If you "take" my idea, I still have it. If I tell you an idea, you have not deprived me of it.[11] An unavoidable feature of intellectual property is that its consumption, as the economists like to put it, is "non-rivalrous." Your consumption does not lessen mine. If I write a song, you can sing it without making it impossible for me to sing it. If I write a book, you can read it (please do) without disabling me from reading it. Ideas, at their core, can be *shared* with no reduction in the amount the "owner" can consume. This difference is fundamental, and it has been understood since the founding.

Jefferson put it better than I:

> If nature has made any one thing less susceptible than all others of exclusive property, it is the action of the thinking power called an idea, which an individual may exclusively possess as long as he keeps it to himself, but the moment it is divulged, it forces itself into the possession of every one, and the receiver cannot dispossess himself of it. Its peculiar character, too, is that no one possesses the less, because every other possess the whole of it. He who receives an idea from me, receives instruction himself without lessening mine; as he who lites his taper at mine, receives light without darkening me. That ideas should freely spread from one to another over the globe, for the moral and mutual instruction of man, and improvement of his condition, seems to have been peculiarly and benevolently designed by nature, when she made them, like fire, expansible over all space, without lessening their density at any point, and like the air in which we breathe, move, and have our physical being, incapable of confinement or exclusive appropriation. Inventions then cannot, in nature, be a subject of property.[12]

Technically, Jefferson is confusing two different concepts. One is the possibility of excluding others from using or getting access to an idea. This is the question whether ideas are "excludable"; Jefferson suggests that they are not. The other concept is whether my using an idea lessens your use of the same idea. This is the question of whether ideas are "rivalrous";[13] again, Jefferson suggests that they are not. Jefferson believes that nature has made ideas both nonexcludable and nonrivalrous, and that there is little that man can do to change this fact.[14]

But in fact, ideas are not both nonexcludable and nonrivalrous. I can exclude people from my ideas or my writings – I can keep them secret, or build fences to keep people out. How easily, or how effectively, is a technical question. It depends on the architecture of protection that a given context provides. But given the proper technology, there is no doubt that I can keep people out.

What I cannot do, however, is change the nature of my ideas as "nonrivalrous" goods. No technology (that we know of) will erase an idea from your head as it passes into my head. No technology will make it so that I cannot share your ideas with no harm to you. My knowing what you know does not lessen your knowing of the same thing. That fact is given in the world, and it is that fact that makes intellectual property different. Unlike apples, and unlike houses, ideas are something I can take from you without diminishing what you have.

It does not follow, however, that there is no need for property rights over expressions or inventions.[15] Just because you can have what I have without lessening what I have does not mean that the state has no reason to create rights over ideas, or over the expression of ideas.

If a novelist cannot stop you from copying (rather than buying) her book, then she has very little incentive to produce more books. She may have as much as she had before you took the work she produced, but if you take it without paying, she has no monetary incentive to produce more.

Now in fact, of course, the incentives an author faces are quite complex, and it is not possible to make simple generalizations about the incentives authors face.[16] But generalizations do not have to be perfect to make a point: even if some authors write for free, it is still the case that the law needs some intellectual property rights. If the law did not protect the author at all, there would be fewer authors. The law has a reason to protect the rights of authors, *at least insofar as doing so gives them an incentive to produce*. With ordinary property, the law must both create an incentive to produce and protect the right of possession; with intellectual property, the law need only create the incentive to produce.

This is the difference between these two very different kinds of property, and this difference affects fundamentally the nature of intellectual property law. While we protect real and personal property to protect the owner from harm and give the owner an incentive, we protect intellectual property only to ensure that we create a sufficient incentive to produce it. "Sufficient incentive," however, is something less than "perfect control." And in turn we can say that the ideal protections of intellectual property law are something less than the ideal protections for ordinary or real property.

This difference between the nature of intellectual property and ordinary property was recognized by our Constitution, which in article I, section 8, clause 8, gives Congress the power "to promote the Progress of Science and useful Arts, by securing for limited Times to Authors and Inventors the exclusive Right to their respective Writings and Discoveries."

Note the special structure of this clause. First, it sets forth the precise reason for the power – to promote the progress of science and useful arts. It is for those reasons, and those reasons only, that Congress may grant an exclusive right – otherwise known as a monopoly. And second, note the special temporality of this right: "for limited Times." The Constitution does not allow Congress to grant authors and inventors permanent exclusive rights to their writings and discoveries, only limited rights. It does not give Congress the power to give them "property" in their writings and discoveries, only an exclusive right over them for a limited time.

The Constitution's protection for intellectual property then is fundamentally different from its protection of ordinary property. I've said that all property is granted subject to the limit of the public good. But even so, if the government decided to nationalize all property after a fifteen-year term of ownership, the Constitution would require it to compensate the owners. By contrast, if Congress set the copyright term at fifteen years, there would be no claim that the government pay compensation after the fifteen years were up. Intellectual property rights are a monopoly that the state gives to producers of intellectual property in exchange for their producing intellectual property. After a limited time, the product of their work becomes the public's to use as it wants. This *is* Communism, at the core of our Constitution's protection of intellectual property. This "property" is not property in the ordinary sense of that term.

And this is true for reasons better than tradition as well. Economists have long understood that granting property rights over information is dangerous (to say the least).[17] This is not because of leftist leanings among economists. It is because economists are pragmatists, and their objective in granting any property right is simply to facilitate production. But there is no way to know, in principle, whether increasing or decreasing the rights granted under intellectual property law will lead to an increase in the production of intellectual property. The reasons are complex, but the point is not: increasing intellectual property's protection is not guaranteed to "promote the progress of science and useful arts" – indeed, often doing so will stifle it.

The balance that intellectual property law traditionally strikes is between the protections granted the author and the public use or access granted everyone else. The aim is to give the author sufficient incentive to produce. Built into the law of intellectual property are limits on the power of the author to control use of the ideas she has created.[18]

A classic example of these limits and of this public use dimension is the right of "fair use." Fair use is the right to use copyrighted material, regardless of the wishes of the owner of that material. A copyright gives the owner certain rights; fair use is a limitation on those rights. Under the right of fair use, you can criticize this book, cut sections from it, and reproduce them in an article attacking me. In these ways and in others, you have the right to use this book independent of how I say it should be used.

Fair use does not necessarily work against the author's interest – or more accurately, fair use does not necessarily work against the interests of authors as a class. When fair use protects the right of reviewers to criticize books without the permission of authors, then more critics criticize. And the more criticism there is, the better the information is about what books people should buy. And the better the information is about what to buy, the more people there are who will buy. Authors as a whole benefit from the system of fair use, even if particular authors do not.

The law of copyright is filled with such rules. Another is the "first sale" doctrine. If you buy this book, you can sell it to someone else free of any constraint I might impose on you.[19] This doctrine differs from the tradition in, for example, Europe, where there are "moral rights" that give the creator power over subsequent use.[20] I've already mentioned another example – limited term. The creator cannot extend the term for which the law will provide protection; that is fixed by the statute and runs when the statute runs.[21]

Taken together, these rules give the creator significant control over the use of what he produces, but never perfect control. They give the public some access, but not complete access. They are balanced by design, and different from the balance the law strikes for ordinary property. They are constitutionally structured to help build an intellectual and cultural commons.

The law strikes this balance. It is not a balance that would exist in nature. Without the law, and before cyberspace, authors would have very little protection; with the law, they have significant, but not perfect, protection. The law gives authors something they otherwise would not have in exchange for limits on their rights, secured to benefit the intellectual commons as a whole.

Private substitutes for public law

But what happens when code protects the interests now protected by copyright law? What happens when Mark Stefik's vision is realized, and when what the law protects as intellectual property can be protected through code? Should we expect that any of the limits will remain? Should we expect code to mirror the limits that the law imposes? Fair use? Limited term? Would private code build these "bugs" into its protections?

The point should be obvious: when intellectual property is protected by code, nothing requires that the same balance be struck. Nothing requires the owner to grant the right of fair use. She might, just as a bookstore allows individuals to browse for free, but she might not. Whether she grants this right depends on whether it profits her. Fair use becomes subject to private gain.[22]

As privatized law, trusted systems regulate in the same domain where copyright law regulates, but unlike copyright law, they do not guarantee the same public use protection. Trusted systems give the producer maximum control – admittedly at a cheaper cost, thus permitting many more authors to publish. But they give authors more control (either to charge for or limit use) in an area where the law gave less than perfect control. Code displaces the balance in copyright law and doctrines such as fair use.

Some will respond that I am late to the party: copyright law is already being displaced, if not by code then by the private law of contract. Through the use of click-wrap, or shrink-wrap, licenses, authors are increasingly demanding that purchasers, or licensees, waive rights that copyright law gave them. If copyright law gives the right to reverse-engineer, then these contracts might extract a promise not to reverse-engineer. If copyright law gives the right to dispose of the book however the purchaser wants after the first sale, then a contract might require that the user waive that right. And if these terms in the contract attached to every copyright work are enforceable merely by being "attached" and "knowable" then already we have the ability to rewrite the balance that copyright law creates. Already, through contract law, copyright holders can defeat the balance that copyright law intends.

I agree that this race to privatize copyright law through contract is already far along, fueled in particular by decisions such as Judge Frank Easterbrook's in *ProCD v Zeidenberg*[23] and by the efforts in some quarters to push a new uniform code that would facilitate these contracts.[24]

But contracts are not as bad as code. Contracts are a form of law. If a term of a contract is inconsistent with a value of copyright law, you can refuse to obey it and let the other side get a court to enforce it. The ultimate power of a contract is a decision by a court – to enforce the contract or not. Although courts today are relatively eager to find ways to enforce these contracts, there is at least hope that if the other side makes its case very clear, courts could shift direction again.[25]

The same is not true of code. Whatever problems there are when contracts replace copyright law, the problems are worse when code displaces copyright law. Again – where do we challenge the code? When the software protects in a particular way without relying in the end on the state, where can we challenge the nature of the protection? Where can we demand balance when the code takes it away?

The rise of contracts modifying copyright law (due in part to the falling costs of contracting) and the rise of code modifying copyright law (promised as trusted systems become all the more common) raise for us a question that we have not had to answer before. We have never had to choose whether authors should be permitted perfectly to control the use of their intellectual property independent of the law, for such control could only be achieved through law.[26] The balance struck by the law was the best that authors could get. But now the code gives authors a better deal. And thus we must now decide whether this better deal makes public sense.

Some argue that it does, and that this increased power to control use in fact is not inconsistent with fair use.[27] Fair use, these commentators argue, defined the rights in an area where it was not possible to meter and charge for use. In that context, fair use set a default rule that parties could always contract around. The default rule was that use was free.

But as the limits of what it is possible to meter and charge for changes, the scope of fair use changes as well.[28] If it becomes possible to license every aspect of use, then no aspect of use would have the protections of fair use. Fair use, under this conception, was just the space where it was too expensive to meter use. By eliminating that space, cyberspace merely forces us to recognize the change in the context within which fair use functions.

There are then, from this view, two very different conceptions of fair use.[29] One conception views it as inherent in the copyright – required whether technology makes it possible to take it away or not; the other views it as contingent – needed where technology makes it necessary. We can choose between these two conceptions, if indeed our constitutional commitment is ambiguous.

A nice parallel to this problem exists in constitutional law. The framers gave Congress the power to regulate interstate commerce and commerce that affects interstate commerce.[30] At the founding, that was a lot of commerce, but because of the inefficiencies of the market, not all of it. Thus, the states had a domain of commerce that they alone could regulate.[31]

Over time, however, the scope of interstate commerce has changed so that much less commerce is now within the exclusive domain of the states. This change has produced two sorts of responses. One is to find other ways to give states domains of exclusive regulatory authority. The justification for this response is the claim that these changes in interstate commerce are destroying the framers' vision about state power.

The other response is to concede the increasing scope of federal authority, but to deny that it is inconsistent with the framing balance.[32] Certainly, at the founding, some commerce was not interstate and did not affect interstate commerce. But that does not mean that the framers intended that there must always be such a space. They tied the scope of federal power to a moving target; if the target moves completely to the side of federal power, then that is what we should embrace.[33]

In both contexts, the change is the same. We start in a place where balance is given to us by the mix of frictions within a particular regulatory domain: fair use is a balance given to us because it is too expensive to meter all use; state power over commerce is given to us because not all commerce affects interstate commerce. When new technology disturbs the balance, we must decide whether the original intent was that there be a balance, or that the scope of one side of each balance should faithfully track the index to which it was originally tied. Both contexts, in short, present ambiguity.

Many observers (myself included) have strong feelings one way or the other. We believe this latent ambiguity is not an ambiguity at all. In the context of federal power, we believe either that the states were meant to keep a domain of exclusive authority[34] or that the federal government was to have whatever power affected interstate commerce.[35] In the context of fair use, we believe that either fair use is to be a minimum of public use, guaranteed regardless of the technology,[36] or that it is just an inefficient consequence of inefficient technology, to be removed as soon as efficiency can be achieved.[37]

But in both cases, this may make the problem too easy. The best answer in both contexts may be that the question was unresolved at the time: perhaps no one thought of the matter, and hence there is no answer to the question of what they would have intended if some central presupposition had changed. And if there was no original answer, we must decide the question by our own lights. As Stefik says of trusted systems – and, we might expect, of the implications of trusted systems – "It is a tool never imagined by the creators of copyright law, or by those who believe laws governing intellectual property cannot be enforced."[38]

The loss of fair use is a consequence of the perfection of trusted systems. Whether you consider it a problem or not depends on your view of the value of fair use. If you consider it a public value that should exist regardless of the technological regime, then the emergence of this perfection should trouble you. From your perspective, there was a value latent in the imperfection of the old system that has now been erased.

But even if you do not think that the loss of fair use is a problem, trusted systems threaten other values latent in the imperfection of the real world. Consider now a second.

The anonymity that imperfection allows

I was a student in England for a number of years, at an English university. In the college I attended, there was a "buttery" – a shop that basically sold alcohol. During the first week I was there I had to buy a large amount of Scotch (a series of unimaginative gifts, as I remember). About a week after I made these purchases, I received a summons from my tutor to come talk with him in his office. When I arrived, the tutor asked me about my purchases. This was, to his mind, an excessive amount of alcohol, and he wanted to know whether I had a good reason for buying it.

Needless to say, I was shocked at the question. Of course, formally, I had made a purchase at the college, and I had not hidden my name when I did so (indeed, I had charged it on my college account), so formally, I had revealed to the college and its agents my alcohol purchases. Still, it shocked me that this information would be monitored by college authorities and then checked up on. I could see why they did it, and I could see the good that might come from it. It just never would have occurred to me that this data would be used in this way.

If this is an invasion, of course it is a small one. Later it was easy for me to hide my binges simply by buying from a local store rather than the college buttery. (Though I later learned that the local store rented its space from the college, so who knows what deal they had struck.) And in any case, I was not being punished. The college was just concerned. But the example suggests a more general point: we reveal to the world a certain class of data about ourselves that we ordinarily expect the world not to use.

Trusted systems depend on such data – they depend on the ability to know how people use the property that is being protected. To set prices most efficiently, the system ideally should know as much about individuals and their reading habits as possible. It needs to know this data because it needs an efficient way to track use and so to charge for it.[39]

But this tracking involves a certain invasion. We live now in a world where we think about what we read in just the way that I thought about what I bought as a student in England – we do not expect that anyone is keeping track. We would be shocked if we learned that the library was keeping tabs on the books that people checked out and then using this data in some monitoring way.

Such tracking, however, is just what trusted systems require. And so the question becomes: Should there be a right against this kind of monitoring? The question is parallel to the question of fair use. In a world where this monitoring could not effectively occur, there was, of course, no such right against it. But now that monitoring can occur, we must ask whether the latent right to read anonymously, given to us before by imperfections in technologies, should be a legally protected right.

Julie Cohen argues that it should, and we can see quite directly how her argument proceeds.[40] Whatever its source, it is a value in this world that we can explore intellectually on our own. It is a value that we can read anonymously, without fear that others will know or watch or change their behavior based on what we read. This is an element of intellectual freedom. It is a part of what makes us as we are.[41]

Yet this element is potentially erased by trusted systems. These systems need to monitor, and this monitoring destroys anonymity. We need to decide whether, and how, to preserve values from today in a context of trusted systems.

This is a matter of translation.[42] The question is, how should changes in technology be accommodated to preserve values from an earlier context in a new context? It is the same question that Brandeis asked about wiretapping.[43] It is the question the Court answers in scores of contexts all the time. It is fundamentally a question about preserving values when contexts change.

In the context of both fair use and reading, Cohen has a consistent answer to this question of translation. She argues that there is a right to resist, or "hack," trusted systems to the extent that they infringe on traditional fair use. (Others have called this the "Cohen Theorem.") As for reading, she argues that copyright management schemes must protect a right to read anonymously – that if they monitor, they must be constructed so that they preserve anonymity. The strategy is the same: Cohen identi- fies a value yielded by an old architecture but now threatened by a new architecture, and then argues in favor of an affirmative right to protect the original value.

The problems that perfection makes

These two examples reveal a common problem – one that will reach far beyond copyright. At one time we enjoy a certain kind of liberty, but that liberty comes from the high costs of control.[44] That was the conclusion we drew about fair use – that when the cost of control was high, the space for fair use was great. So too with anonymous reading: we read anonymously in real space not so much because laws protect that right as because the cost of tracking what we read is so great.

When those costs fall, the liberty is threatened. That threat requires a choice – do we allow the erosion, or do we erect other limits to re-create the original space for liberty?

The law of intellectual property is the first example of this general point. The architectures of property will change; they will allow for a greater protection for intellectual property than real-space architectures allowed; and this greater protection will force a choice on us that we do not need to make in real space. Should the architecture allow perfect control over intellectual property, or should we build into the architecture an incompleteness that guarantees a certain aspect of public use? Or a certain space for individual freedom?

Ignoring these questions will not make them go away. Pretending that the framers answered them is no solution either. In this context (and this is just the first) we will need to make a judgment about which values the architecture will protect.

Choices

I've argued that cyberspace will open up at least two important choices in the context of intellectual property: whether to allow intellectual property in effect to become completely propertized (for that is what a perfect code regime for protecting intel- lectual property would do), and whether to allow this regime to erase the anonymity latent in less efficient architectures of control. These choices were not made by our framers. They are for us to make now.

I have a view, in this context as in the following three, about how we should exercise that choice. But I am a lawyer, trained to be shy about saying "how things ought to be." Lawyers are taught to point elsewhere – to the framers, to the United Nations charter, to an act of Congress – when arguing about how things ought to be. Having said that there is no such authority here, I feel as if I ought therefore to be silent.

Cowardly, not silent, however, is how others might see it. I should say, they say, what I think. So in each of these four applications (intellectual property, privacy, free speech, and sovereignty), I will offer my view about how these choices should be made. But I do this under some duress and encourage you to simply ignore what I believe. It will be short, and summary, and easy to discard. It is the balance of the book – and, most importantly, the claim that *we* have a choice to make – that I really want to stick.

Anonymity

Cohen, it seems to me, is plainly right about anonymity, and the Cohen Theorem inspirational. However efficient the alternative may be, we should certainly architect cyberspaces to ensure anonymity – or more precisely, pseudonymity – first. If the code is going to monitor just what I do, then at least it should not know that it is "I" that it is monitoring. I am less troubled if it knows that "14AH342BD7" read such and such; I am deeply troubled if that number is tied back to my name.

Cohen is plainly right for a second reason as well: all of the good that comes from monitoring could be achieved while protecting privacy as well. It may take a bit more coding to build in routines for breaking traceability; it may take more planning to ensure that privacy is protected. But if those rules are embedded up front, the cost would not be terribly high. Far cheaper to architect privacy protections in now rather than retrofit for them later.

The commons

An intellectual commons I feel much more strongly about.

We can architect cyberspace to preserve a commons or not. (Jefferson thought that nature had already done the architecting, but Jefferson wrote before there was code.[45]) We should choose to architect it with a commons. Our past had a commons that could not be designed away; that commons gave our culture great value. What value the commons of the future could bring us is something we are just beginning to see. Intellectual property scholars saw it – long before cyberspace came along – and laid the groundwork for much of the argument we need to have now.[46] The greatest work in the law of cyberspace has been written in the field of intellectual property. In a wide range of contexts, these scholars have made a powerful case for the substantive value of an intellectual commons.[47]

James Boyle puts the case most dramatically in his extraordinary book *Shamans, Software, and Spleens*.[48] Drawing together both cyberspace and noncyberspace questions, he spells out the challenge we face in an information society – and particularly the political challenge we face.[49] Elsewhere he identifies our need for an "environmental movement" in information policy – a rhetoric that gets people to see the broad range of values put at risk by this movement to propertize all information.[50]

We are far from that understanding just now, and this book, on its own, won't get us much closer. It is all that I can do here to point to the choice we will have to make, and hint, as I have, about a direction.

Notes

1   See Joel R. Reidenberg, "Governing Networks and Rule-Making in Cyberspace," *Emory Law Journal* 45 (1996): 911.

2   In *Shifting the Possible* (142–44), Stefik discusses how trusted printers combine four elements – print rights, encrypted online distribution, automatic billing for copies, and digital watermarks – in order to monitor and control the copies they make.

3   Ibid.

4   David Hackett Fischer, *Albion's Seed: Four British Folkways in America* (New York: Oxford University Press, 1989), 765.

5   See *American Legal Realism*, edited by William W. Fisher III et al. (New York: Oxford University Press, 1993), 98–129; John Henry Schlegel, *American Legal Realism and Empirical Social Science* (Chapel Hill: University of North Carolina Press, 1995). For a nice modern example of the same analysis, see Keith Aoki, "(Intellectual) Property and Sovereignty: Notes Toward a Cultural Geography of Authorship," *Stanford Law Review* 48 (1996): 1293.

6   See Fried, *The Progressive Assault on Laissez-Faire*, 1–28; see also Jael P. Trachtman ("The international Economic Law Revolution," *University of Pennsylvania Journal of International Economic Law* 17 [1996]: 33, 34), who notes that many realists and critical legal theorists have asserted that "private law" is an oxymoron.

7   Judges have also made this argument; see *Lochner v New York*, 198 US 45, 74 (1905) (Justice Oliver Wendell Holmes Jr. dissenting).

8   This is the epistemological limitation discussed in much of Friedrich A. von Hayek's work: see, for example, *Law, Legislation, and Liberty*, vol. 2 (Chicago: University of Chicago Press, 1978).

9   Boyle, *Shamons, Software, and Spleens*, 174.

10 I am hiding a great deal of philosophy in this simplified utilitarian account, but for a powerful economic grounding of the point, see Harold Dernsetz. "Toward a Theory of Property Rights," *American Economics Review* 57 (1967): 347.

11 For a wonderfully clear introduction to this point, as well as a complete analysis of the law, see Robert P. Merges et al., *Intellectual Property in the New Technological Age* (New York: Aspen Law and Business, 1997), ch. 1.

12 Thomas Jefferson, letter to Isaac Mcpherson, August 13, 1813, reprinted in *Writings of Thomas Jefferson, 1790–1826*, vol. 6, edited by H. A. Washington (1854), 180–81, quoted in *Graham v John Deere Company*, 383 US 1, 8–9 n.2 (1966).

13 For the classic discussion, see Kenneth J. Arrow, "Economic Welfare and the Allocation of Resources for Invention," in *The Rate and Direction of Inventive Activity: Economic and Social Factors* (Princeton, N.J.: Princeton University Press, 1962), 609, 616–17.

14 For a powerfully compelling problematization of the economic perspective in this context, see Boyle, "Intellectual Property Policy Online," 35–46. Boyle's work evinces the indeterminacy that economics ought to profess about whether increasing property rights over information will also increase the production of information.

15 Some will insist on calling this "property"; see Frank H. Easterbrook," Intellectual Property Is Still Property," *Harvard Journal of Law and Public Policy* 13 (1990): 108.

16 This is the message of Justice Stephen Breyer's work on copyright, for example, "The Uneasy Case for Copyright."

17 For an extensive and balanced analysis, see William M. Landes and Richard A. Posner, "An Economic Analysis of Copyright Law," *Journal of Legal Studies* 18 (1989): 325, 325–27, 344–46. These authors note that because ideas are a public good – that is, an infinite number of people can use an idea without using it up – ideas are readily appropriated from the creator by other people. Hence, copyright protection attempts to balance efficiently the benefits of creating new works with the losses from limiting access and the cost of administering copyright protection; copyright protection seeks to promote the public benefit of advancing knowledge and learning by means of an incentive system. The economic rewards of the marketplace are offered to authors in order to stimulate them to produce and disseminate new works (326). See also Posner, *Law and Literature*, 389–405.

18 These limits come from both the limits in the copyright clause, which sets its purposes out quite clearly, and the First Amendment; see, for example, *Feist Publications, Inc. v Rural Telephone Service Co.*, 499 US 340, 346 (1991).

19 The "first sale" doctrine was developed under § 27 of the former Copyright Act (17 USC [1970]) and has since been adopted under § 109(a) of the present Copyright Act; see *United States v Goss*, 803 F2d 638 (11th Cir 1989) (discussing both versions of the Copyright Act).

20 Europeans like to say that "moral rights" have been part of their system since the beginning of time, but as Professor Jane C. Ginsburg has shown with respect to France, they are actually a nineteenth-century creation; see "A Tale of Two Copyrights: Literary Property in Revolutionary France and America," *Tulane Law Review* 64 (1990): 991.

21 Or so it is argued in *Eldred v Reno* (DDC filed January 4, 1999).

22 It is useful to compare the protection that copyright gives to the protection of trade secret law. All of the protection of trade secret law comes, in a sense, from the architectural constraints I have described. One is always permitted, that is, to reverse-engineer to discover a trade secret; see *Kewanee Oil Company v Bicron Corporation*, 416 US 470, 476 (1974): "A trade secret law . . . does not offer protection against discovery by fair and honest means, such as by independent invention, accidental disclosure, or . . . reverse engineering."

23 B6 F3d 1447 (7th Cir 1996): see also Easterbrook, "Intellectual Property Is Still Property," 113–14. For an excellent account of the debate, see Charles R. McManis, "The Privatization (or 'Shrink-Wrapping') of American Copyright Law," *California Law Review* 87 (1999): 173, 183.

24 This is a reference to the recent battle to draft what was originally called the Uniform Commercial Code 2B, and more recently the Uniform Computer Information Transactions Act (UCITA). By essentially ratifying the click-wrap agreement, this code would facilitate online mass consumer contracts governing the sale of "online information." This move has been widely criticized: see "Symposium: Intellectual Property and Contract Law for the Information Age: The Impact of Article 2B of the Uniform Commercial Code on the Future of Information and Commerce," *California Law Review* 87 (1999): 1; Lawrence Lessig, "Pain in the OS," *The Industry Standard*, February 5, 1999, available at http://www.thestandard. com/articles/display/D, 1449,3423,00.html (visited May 30, 1999). My criticism is that while the rhetoric of this move is grounded in the

"freedom of contract," the code actually does nothing to ensure that the contracting process produces understanding of the terms of the contract by both parties to the contract. The incentives created by provisions like the "Restatement (Second) of Contracts" (§ 211) are not present in the UCITA, UCITA presupposes that if the consumer had a chance to understand, he understands. But from an efficiency perspective, let alone a justice perspective, the consumer is not the cheapest understanding producer. The code simply ratifies the contract that the seller proposes. This is not "freedom of contract," but contract according to whatever the seller says. For a useful analysis, see Walter A. Effross, "The Legal Architecture of Virtual Stores: World Wide Web Sites and the Uniform Commercial Code," *San Diego Law Review* 34 (1997): 1263, 1328–59.

25 See William W. Fisher III. – "Compulsory-Terms in-Internet-Related Contracts," *Chicago-Kent Law Review* 73 (1998). Fisher catalogs public policy restrictions on freedom of contract, which he characterizes as "ubiquitous."

26 An argument is raging about whether, even through law, this modification of the default copyright law should be permitted. Mark A. Lemley has catalogued the provisions of the Copyright Act that are arguably put at risk by contracting behaviour; see "Beyond Preemption: The Law and Policy of Intellectual Property Licensing: *California Law Review 87* (1999): 111; see also A. Michael Froomkin, "Article 2B as Legal Software for Electronic Contracting – Operating System or Trojan Horse?," *Berkeley Technology Law Journal* 13 (1998): 1023; Michael J. Madison, "Legal-War: Contract and Copyright in the Digital Age," *Fordham Law Review* 67 (1998): 1025; David Nimmer et al., "The Metamorphosis of Contract into Expand," *California Law Review* 87 (1999): 17; Pamela Samuelson, "Intellectual Property and Contract Law for the Information Age: Foreword," *California Law Review* 87 (1999): 1. The questions Lemley raises, however, cannot be easily raised when it is the code that protects the intellectual property interest: Maureen A. O'Rourke, "Copyright Preemption After the ProCD Case: A Market-Based Approach," *Berkeley Technology Law Journal* 12 (1997): 53.

27 See Tom W. Bell, "Fair Use vs. Fared Use: The Impact of Automated Rights Management on Copyright's Fair Use Doctrine," *North Carolina Law Review* 76 (1998): 557, 581–84. Bell argues that technology will prove more effective than fair use in curing the market failure that results when transaction costs discourage otherwise value-maximizing uses of copyrighted work; see also the White Paper observation that "it may be that technological means of tracking transactions and licensing will lead to reduced application and scope of the fair use doctrine" (74).

28 See Bell, "Fair Use vs. Fared Use," 582–84; U.S. Department of Commerce, Task Force – Working Group on Intellectual Property Rights, "Intellectual Property and the National Information Infrastructure," 66 n.228, notes the difficulty of defining the bounds of the fair use doctrine.

29 For a foundational modern work on the nature of fair use, see Wendy J. Gordon, "Fair Use as Market Failure: A Structural and Economic Analysis of the Betamax Case and Its Predecessors," *Columbia Law Review* 82 (1982): 1600. A more recent work by William Fisher ("Reconstructing the Fair Use Doctrine," *Harvard Law Review* 101 (1988): 1659, 1661–95) considers both the efficiency and utopian goals of copyright law.

30 See *Gibbons v Ogden*, 22 US 1 (1824) (striking down New York's grant of a monopoly of steamboat navigation on the Hudson River as inconsistent with the federal Coasting Act of 1793): *McCulloch v Maryland*, 17 US 316 (1819) (pronouncing that Congress has the power to do what is "necessary and proper" to achieve a legitimate end, like the regulation of interstate commerce).

31 See Bernard C. Gavit, *The Commerce Clause of the United States Constitution*, (Bloomington, Ind.: Principia Press, 1932), 84.

32 See *Pensacola Telegraph Company v Western Union Telegraph Company*, 96 US 1, 9 (1877).

33 As one commentator put it near the turn of the century: "If the power of Congress has a wider incidence in 1918 than it could have had in 1789, this is merely because production is more dependent now than then on extra-state markets. No state liveth to itself alone to any such extent as was true a century ago. What is changing is not our system of government, but our economic organization"; Thomas Reed Powell, "The Child Labor Law, the Tenth Amendment, and the Commerce Clause," *Southern Law Quarterly* 3 (1918): 175, 200–201.

34 See Alexis de Tocqueville, *Democracy in America*, vol. 1 (New York: Vintage, 1990), 158–70, on the idea that the framers' design pushed states to legislate in a broad domain and keep the local government active.

35 See *Maryland v Wirtz*, 392 US 183, 201 (1968) (Justice William O. Douglas dissenting: the majority's bringing of employees of state-owned enterprises within the reach of the commerce clause was "such a serious invasion of state sovereignty protected by the Tenth Amendment that it . . . [was] not consistent with our constitutional federalism"); *State Board of Insurance v Todd Shipyards Corporation*, 370 US 451, 456 (1962) (holding that "the power of Congress to grant protection to interstate commerce against state regulation or taxation or to withhold it is so complete that its ideas of policy should prevail") (citations omitted).

36 See Michael G. Frey, "Unfairly Applying the Fair Use Doctrine: Princeton University Press v Michigan Document Services, 99 F3d 1381 (6th Cir 1996)," *University of Cincinnati Law Review* 66 (1998): 959, 1001; Frey asserts that "copyright protection exists primarily for the benefit of the public, not the benefit of individual authors. Copyright law does give authors a considerable benefit in terms of the monopolistic right to control their creations, but that right exists only to ensure the creation of new works. The fair use doctrine is an important safety valve that ensures that the benefit to individual authors does not outweigh the benefit to the public"; Marlin H. Smith ("The Limits of Copyright: Property, Parody; and the Public Domain," *Duke Law Journal* 42 [1993]: 1233, 1272) assets that "copyright law is better understood as that of a gatekeeper, controlling access to copyrighted works but guaranteeing, via fair use, some measure of availability to the public."

37 See Mark Gimbel ("Some Thoughts on the Implications of Trusted Systems for Intellectual Property Law," *Stanford Law Review* 50 [1998]: 1671, 1686), who notes that fair use can be "explained as a method of curing the market failure that results when high transaction costs discourage otherwise economically efficient uses of copyrighted material," and that "because technologies like trusted systems

promise to reduce the costs of licensing copyrighted works – thereby curing this market failure – some argue that the doctrine of fair use will for the most part be rendered unnecessary, obviating the need to regulate technologies that undermine it": Lydia Pallas Losen ("Redefining the Market Failure Approach in Fair Use in an Era of Copyright Permission System," *Journal of Intellectual Property Law* 5 [1997]: 1, 7) asserts that under a "narrowed market failure view of fair use. If a copyright owner can establish an efficient 'permission system' to collect less for a certain kind of use, then the copyright owner will be able to defeat a claim of fair use."

38 Stefik, "Letting Loose the Light," 244.

39 Efficient here both in the sense of cheap to track and in the sense of cheap to then discriminate in pricing; William W. Fisher III, "Property and Contract on the Internet," *Chicago-Kent Law Review* 74 (1998).

40 Julie E. Cohen, "A Right to Read Anonymously: A Closer Look at 'Copyright-Management' in Cyberspace," *Connecticut Law Review* 28 (1996): Reading anonymously is "so intimately connected with speech and freedom of thought that the First Amendment should be understood to guarantee such a right" (981, 982).

41 "The freedom to read anonymously is just as much a part of our tradition, and the choice of reading materials just as expressive of identity, as the decision to use or withhold one's name" (ibid., 1012).

42 See Lessig, "Translating Federalism," 125.

43 See *Ohmstead v United States* 277 US 438, 474 (1928) (Justice Louis Brandeis dissenting "Can it be that the Constitution affords no protection against such invasion of individual security?").

44 Peter Huber relies explicitly on the high costs of control in his rebuttal to Orwell's 1984; see *Orwell's Revenge: The 1984 Palimpset* (New York: Maxwell Macmillan International, 1994). But this is a weak basis on which to build liberty, especially as the cost of networked control drops, Frances Ciarncross (*The Death of Distance: How the Communications Revolution Will Change Our Lives* [Boston: Harvard Business School Press, 1997], 194–95) effectively challenges the idea as well.

45 Washington, *Writings of Thomas Jefferson*, 6: 180–81.

46 A founding work is David Lange, "Recognizing the Public Domain," *Law and Contemporary Problems* 44 (1981): 147. There are many important foundations, however, to this argument. See, for example, Benjamin Kaplan, *An Unhurried View of Copyright* (New York: Columbia University Press, 1967). Gordon ("Fair Use as Market Failure") argues that the courts should employ fair use to permit uncompensated transfers that the market is incapable of effectuating; see also Wendy J. Gordon, "On Owning Information: Intellectual Property and Restitutionary Impulse," *Virginia Law Review* 78 (1992): 149. In "Reality as Artifact: From Feist to Fair Use", *Law and Contemporary Problems* 555P9 (1992): 93–107. Gordon believes that, while imaginative works are creative, they may also comprise facts, which need to be widely available for public dissemination. Gordon's "Toward a Jurisprudence of Benefits: The Norms of Copyright and the Problem of Private Censorship" (*University of Chicago Law Review* 57 [1990]: 1009) is a discussion of the ability of copyright holders to deny access to critics and others:

see also Wendy Gordon, "An Inquiry into the Merits of Copyright: The Challenges of Consistency, Consent, and Encouragement Theory," *Stanford New Review* 41 (1989): 1343.

47 In addition to Boyle, I have learned most from Keith Aoki, Yochai Benkler, Julie Cohen, Niva Elkin-Koren, Peter Jaszi, Mark Lemley, Jessica Litman, Neil Netanel, Margaret Radin, and Pam Samuelson, but no doubt I have not read widely enough. See, for example. Keith Aoki, "Foreword to Innovation and the Information Environment: Interrogating the Entrepreneur," *Oregon Law Review* 75 (1996): 1; in "(Intellectual) Property and Sovereignty." Aoki discusses the challenges in the traditional concept of property that arise from the growth of digital information technology; in "Authors, Inventors, and Trademark Owners; Private Intellectual Property and the Public Domain" (*Columbia-VLA Journal of Law and the Arts* 18 [1993]: 1), he observes the shifting boundaries in intellectual property law between "public" and "private" realms of information and argues that trends to increase the number of exclusive rights for authors are converting the public domain into private intellectual property and constraining other types of socially valuable uses of expressive works that do not fit the "authorship" model underlying American copyright tradition; he also argues that recent expansion of trademark law has allowed trademark owners to obtain property rights in their trademarks that do not further the Lanham Act's goal of preventing consumer confusion. Benkler, "Free as Air to Common Use"; Yorhai Benkler, "Overcoming Agoraphohia: Building the Commons of the Digitally Networked Environment," *Harvard Journal of Law and Technology* 11 (1998): 287; Julie E. Cohen, "Copyright and the Jurisprudence of Self-Help," *Berkeley Technology Law Journal* 13 (1998): 1089; Julie E. Cohen, "Lochner in Cyberspace: The New Economic Orthodoxy of 'Rights Management,' " *Michigan Law Review* 97 (1998): 462; Julie E. Cohen, "Some Reflections on Copyright Management Systems and Laws Designed in Protect Them," *Berkeley Technology Law Journal* 12 (1997): 161, 181–82; Julie E. Cohen, "Reverse-Engineering and the Rise of Electronic Vigilantism: Intellectual Property Implications of 'Lock-Out' Programs," *Southern California Law Review* 68 (1995): 1091, Niva Elkin-Koren, "Contracts in Cyberspace: Rights Without Laws," *Chicago-Kent Law Review 73* (1998); Niva Elkin-Koren, "Copyright Policy and the Limits of Freedom of Contract," *Berkeley Technology Law Journal* 12 (1997): 93, 107–10 (criticizing the ProCD decision); Niva Elkin-Koren, "Cyberlaw and Social Change: A Democratic Approach to Copyright Law in Cyberspace," *Cardozo Arts and Entertainment Law Journal* 14 (1996): 215; in "Copyright Law and Social Dialogue on the Information Superhighway: The Case Against Copyright Liability of Bulletin Board Operators" (*Cardozo Arts and Entertainment Law Journal* 13 [1995]: 345, 390–99), Elkin-Koren analyzes the problems created by applying copyright law in a digitized environment. In "Goodbye to All That – A Reluctant (and Perhaps Premature) Adieu to a Constitutionally Grounded Discourse of Public Interest in Copyright Law" (*Vanderbilt Journal of Transnational Law* 29 [1996]: 595), Peter A. Jaszi advocates the development of new, policy-grounded arguments and constitutionally based reasoning to battle expansionist legislative and judicial tendencies in copyright to diminish public access to the "intellectual commons"; see also

Peter A. Jaszi, "On the Author Effect Contemporary Copyright and Collective Creativity," *Cardozo Arts and Entertainment Law Journal* 10 (1992): 293, 319–20; Peter A, Jaszi, "Toward a Theory of Copyright: The Metamorphoses of 'Authorship,'" *Duke Law Journal* 1991 (1991): 455. On the misuse of copyright, see Lemley, "Beyond Preemption"; Mark A. Lemley, "The Economics of Improvement in Intellectual Property Law," *Texas Law Review* 25 (1997): 989, 1048–68; in "Intellectual Property and Shrink-wrap Licenses" (*Southern California Law Review* 68 [1995]: 1239, 1239), Lemley notes that "software vendors are attempting en masse to 'opt out' of intellectual property law by drafting license provisions that compel their customers to adhere to more restrictive provisions than copyright . . . law would require," Jessica Litman ("The Tales That Article 2B Tells," *Berkeley Technology Law Journal* 13 [1998]: 931, 938) characterizes as "dubious" the notion that current law enables publishers to make a transaction into a license by so designating it. In her view, article 2B is "confusing and confused" about copyright and its relationship with that law, and would make new law. She believes that "whatever the outcome" of the debate over whether copyright makes sense in the digital environment (see "Reforming Information Law in Copyright's Image," *Dayton Law Review* 22 [1997], 587, 590), "copyright doctrine is ill-adapted to accommodate many of the important interests that inform our information policy. First Amendment, privacy, and distributional issues that copyright has treated only glancingly are central to any information policy." See also Jessica Litman, "Revising Copyright Law for the Information Age," *Oregon Law Review* 75 (1996): 19; and "The Exclusive Right to Read" (*Cardozo Arts and Entertainment Law Journal* 13 [1994]: 29, 48), in which Litman states that "much of the activity on the net takes place on the mistaken assumption that any material on the Internet is free from copyright unless expressly declared to be otherwise." In "Copyright as Myth" (*University of Pittsburgh Law Review* 53 [1991]: 235, 235–37), Litman provides a general overview of the issues of authorship and infringement in copyright law, indicating that debate continues regarding the definition of "authorship" (she defines "author" "in the copyright sense of anyone who creates copyrightable works, whether they be books, songs, sculptures, buildings, computer programs, paintings or films" [236, n.5]); she also discusses why copyright law is counterintuitive to the authorship process. See also "The Public Domain" (*Emory Law Journal* 39 [1990]: 965, 969), in which Litman recommends a broad definition of the public domain ("originality is a keystone of copyright law" [974]). Neil Weinstock Netanel, "Asserting Copyright's Democratic Principles in the Global Arena," *Vanderbilt Law Review* 51 (1998): 217, 232 n.48, 299 n.322; Neil Netanel, "Alienability Restrictions and the Enhancement of Author Autonomy in United States and Continental Copyright Law," *Cardozo Arts and Entertainment Law Journal* 12 (1994): 1, 42–43; in "[C]opyright and a Democratic Civil Society" (*Yale Law Journal* 106 (1996): 283, 288, 324–36), Netanel analyzes copyright law and policy in terms of its democracy-enhancing function: "Copyright is in essence a state measure that uses market institutions to enhance the democratic character of society." Margaret Jane Radin and Polk Wagner, "The Myth of Private Ordering: Rediscovering Legal Realism in Cyberspace," *Chicago–Kent Law Review* 73 (1998); Margaret Jane Radin, *Reinterpreting*

Property (Chicago: University of Chicago Press, 1993), 56–63. Pam Samuelson, "Encoding the Law into Digital Libraries," *Communications of the ACM* 41 (1999): 13, 13–14; Pamela Samuelson, foreword to "Symposium: Intellectual Property and Contract Law for the Information Age," *California Law Review* 87 (1998): 1; Pamela Samuelson observes in "Embedding Technical Self-Help in Licensed Software" (*Communications of the ACM* 40 [1997]: 13, 16) that "licensors of software or other information . . . will generally invoke self-help"; see also the criticism of the European database directive in J. H. Reichman and Pamela Samuelson, "Intellectual Property Rights in Data?," *Vanderbilt Law Review* 50 (1997): 51, 84–95; Samuelson, "The Copyright Grab," 134; Pamela Samuelson, "Fair Use for Computer Programs and Other Copyrightable Works in Digital Form: The Implications of Sony, Galonb and Sega," *Journal of Intellectual Property Law* 1 (1993): 49.

48 For a recent and compelling account of the general movement to propertize information, see Debora J. Halbert, *Intellectual Property in the Information Age: The Politics of Expanding Ownership Rights* (Westport, Conn.: Quorum, 1999). Seth Shulman's *Owning the Future* (Boston: Houghton Mifflin, 1999) gives the story its appropriate drama.

49 "We favor a move away from the author vision in two directions; first towards recognition of a limited number of new protections for cultural heritage, folkloric productions, and biological 'know-how.' Second, and in general, we favor an increased recognition and protection of the public domain by means of experience, 'fair use protection' company licensing, and narrower initial coverage of property rights in the first place"; Boyle, *Shamans, Software, and Spleens*, 169.

50 James Boyle, "A Politics of Intellectual Property: Environmentalism for the Net?," *Duke Law Journal* 47 (1997): 87.

3.5

Why software should not have owners,
by Richard Stallman

Digital information technology contributes to the world by making it easier to copy and modify information. Computers promise to make this easier for all of us.

Not everyone wants it to be easier. The system of copyright gives software programs "owners," most of whom aim to withhold software's potential benefit from the rest of the public. They would like to be the only ones who can copy and modify the software that we use.

The copyright system grew up with printing – a technology for mass production copying. Copyright fit in well with this technology because it restricted only the mass producers of copies. It did not take freedom away from readers of books. An ordinary reader, who did not own a printing press, could copy books only with pen and ink, and few readers were sued for that.

Digital technology is more flexible than the printing press: when information has digital form, you can easily copy it to share it with others. This very flexibility makes a bad fit with a system like copyright. That's the reason for the increasingly nasty and draconian measures now used to enforce software copyright. Consider these four practices of the Software Publishers Association (SPA):

- Massive propaganda saying it is wrong to disobey the owners to help your friend.
- Solicitation for stool pigeons to inform on their coworkers and colleagues.
- Raids (with police help) on offices and schools, in which people are told they must prove they are innocent of illegal copying.
- Prosecution (by the U.S. government, at the SPA's request) of people such as MIT's David LaMacchia,[1] not for copying software (he is not accused of copying any), but merely for leaving copying facilities unguarded and failing to censor their use.

Originally written in 1994, this version is part of *Free Software, Free Society: Selected Essays of Richard M. Stallman*, 2002, GNU Press (http://www.gnupress.org); ISBN 1-882114-98-1.

All four practices resemble those used in the former Soviet Union, where every copying machine had a guard to prevent forbidden copying, and where individuals had to copy information secretly and pass it from hand to hand as *samizdat*. There is of course a difference: the motive for information control in the Soviet Union was political; in the U.S. the motive is profit. But it is the actions that affect us, not the motive. Any attempt to block the sharing of information, no matter why, leads to the same methods and the same harshness.

Owners make several kinds of arguments for giving them the power to control how we use information:

Name calling

Owners use smear words such as "piracy" and "theft," as well as expert terminology such as "intellectual property" and "damage," to suggest a certain line of thinking to the public – a simplistic analogy between programs and physical objects.

Our ideas and intuitions about property for material objects are about whether it is right to take an object away from someone else. They don't directly apply to making a copy of something. But the owners ask us to apply them anyway.

Exaggeration

Owners say that they suffer "harm" or "economic loss" when users copy programs themselves. But the copying has no direct effect on the owner, and it harms no one. The owner can lose only if the person who made the copy would otherwise have paid for one from the owner.

A little thought shows that most such people would not have bought copies. Yet the owners compute their "losses" as if each and every one would have bought a copy. That is exaggeration – to put it kindly.

The law

Owners often describe the current state of the law, and the harsh penalties they can threaten us with. Implicit in this approach is the suggestion that today's law reflects an unquestionable view of morality – yet at the same time, we are urged to regard these penalties as facts of nature that can't be blamed on anyone.

This line of persuasion isn't designed to stand up to critical thinking; it's intended to reinforce a habitual mental pathway.

It's elementary that laws don't decide right and wrong. Every American should know that, forty years ago, it was against the law in many states for a black person to sit in the front of a bus; but only racists would say sitting there was wrong.

Natural rights

Authors often claim a special connection with programs they have written, and go on to assert that, as a result, their desires and interests concerning the program simply outweigh those of anyone else – or even those of the whole rest of the world. (Typically companies, not authors, hold the copyrights on software, but we are expected to ignore this discrepancy.)

To those who propose this as an ethical axiom – the author is more important than you – I can only say that I, a notable software author myself, call it bunk.

But people in general are only likely to feel any sympathy with the natural rights claims for two reasons.

One reason is an over-stretched analogy with material objects. When I cook spaghetti, I do object if someone else eats it, because then I cannot eat it. His action hurts me exactly as much as it benefits him; only one of us can eat the spaghetti, so the question is, which? The smallest distinction between us is enough to tip the ethical balance.

But whether you run or change a program I wrote affects you directly and me only indirectly. Whether you give a copy to your friend affects you and your friend much more than it affects me. I shouldn't have the power to tell you not to do these things. No one should.

The second reason is that people have been told that natural rights for authors is the accepted and unquestioned tradition of our society.

As a matter of history, the opposite is true. The idea of natural rights of authors was proposed and decisively rejected when the U.S. Constitution was drawn up. That's why the Constitution only permits a system of copyright and does not require one; that's why it says that copyright must be temporary. It also states that the purpose of copyright is to promote progress – not to reward authors. Copyright does reward authors somewhat, and publishers more, but that is intended as a means of modifying their behavior.

The real established tradition of our society is that copyright cuts into the natural rights of the public – and that this can only be justified for the public's sake.

Economics

The final argument made for having owners of software is that this leads to production of more software.

Unlike the others, this argument at least takes a legitimate approach to the subject. It is based on a valid goal – satisfying the users of software. And it is empirically clear that people will produce more of something if they are well paid for doing so.

But the economic argument has a flaw: it is based on the assumption that the difference is only a matter of how much money we have to pay. It assumes that "production of software" is what we want, whether the software has owners or not.

People readily accept this assumption because it accords with our experiences with material objects. Consider a sandwich, for instance. You might well be able to get an equivalent sandwich either free or for a price. If so, the amount you pay is the only difference. Whether or not you have to buy it, the sandwich has the same taste, the same nutritional value, and in either case you can only eat it once. Whether you get the sandwich from an owner or not cannot directly affect anything but the amount of money you have afterwards.

This is true for any kind of material object – whether or not it has an owner does not directly affect what it is, or what you can do with it if you acquire it.

But if a program has an owner, this very much affects what it is, and what you can do with a copy if you buy one. The difference is not just a matter of money. The system of owners of software encourages software owners to produce something – but not what society really needs. And it causes intangible ethical pollution that affects us all.

What does society need? It needs information that is truly available to its citizens – for example, programs that people can read, fix, adapt, and improve, not just operate. But what software owners typically deliver is a black box that we can't study or change.

Society also needs freedom. When a program has an owner, the users lose freedom to control part of their own lives.

And above all society needs to encourage the spirit of voluntary cooperation in its citizens. When software owners tell us that helping our neighbours in a natural way is "piracy," they pollute our society's civic spirit.

This is why we say that free software is a matter of freedom, not price.

The economic argument for owners is erroneous, but the economic issue is real. Some people write useful software for the pleasure of writing it or for admiration and love; but if we want more software than those people write, we need to raise funds.

For ten years now, free software developers have tried various methods of finding funds, with some success. There's no need to make anyone rich; the median U.S. family income, around $35k, proves to be enough incentive for many jobs that are less satisfying than programming.

For years, until a fellowship made it unnecessary, I made a living from custom enhancements of the free software I had written. Each enhancement was added to the standard released version and thus eventually became available to the general public. Clients paid me so that I would work on the enhancements they wanted, rather than on the features I would otherwise have considered highest priority.

The Free Software Foundation (FSF), a tax-exempt charity for free software development, raises funds by selling GNU CD-ROMs, T-shirts, manuals, and deluxe distributions, (all of which users are free to copy and change) as well as from donations. It now has a staff of five programmers, plus three employees who handle mail orders.

Some free software developers make money by selling support services. Cygnus Support,[2] with around 50 employees [when this article was written, in 1994], estimates that about 15 per cent of its staff activity is free software development – a respectable percentage for a software company.

A number of companies have funded the continued development of the free GNU complier for the language C. Meanwhile, the GNU compiler for the Ada language is being funded by the U.S. Air Force, which believes this is the most cost-effective way to get a high quality compiler [Air Force funding ended some time ago; the GNU Ada Compiler is now in service, and its maintenance is funded commercially].

All these examples are small; the free software movement is still small, and still young. But the example of listener-supported radio in the U.S. shows it's possible to support a large activity without forcing each user to pay.

As a computer user today, you may find yourself using a proprietary program. If your friend asks to make a copy, it would be wrong to refuse. Cooperation is more important than copyright. But underground, closet cooperation does not make for a good society. A person should aspire to live an upright life openly with pride, and this means saying "No" to proprietary software.

You deserve to be able to cooperate openly and freely with other people who use software. You deserve to be able to learn how the software works, and to teach your students with it. You deserve to be able to hire your favorite programmer to fix it when it breaks.

You deserve free software.

Notes

1 On January 27th, 1995, David LaMacchia's case was dismissed and has not yet been appealed.
2 Cygnus Support continued to be successful, but then it accepted outside investment, got greedy, and began developing non-free software. Then it was acquired by Red Hat, which has rereleased most of those programs as free software.

PART 4

Politics of new media technologies

In political science, politics is defined as the form of struggle that takes place in human societies over such things as resources, territory and power. More subtly, but still deriving from this originary dynamic, politics since the Enlightenment has also been about people, institutions and countries securing what are perceived to be their rights and legitimate interests. Struggles take place where these perceptions and interests clash; struggles take place when resources are scarce (or perceived to be); and struggles take place to secure the necessary power (military, ethical, economic) to achieve these political ends. Democracy, in its various philosophical interpretations and levels of organisational complexity, evolved as the mechanics with which to manage political power, and with such organisation comes the tendency towards systematisation and routine. However, widespread transformations of any kind in society tend to upset the political balances and delicate compromises that have been worked out over a period of time. A heightened form of politics comes to the fore during such times, and its realm extends to a wider section of society than is usual. New political actors are drawn in when change is seen to infringe upon their rights and interests. Others may be motivated to act when the force of transformation gives them little alternative. Others still, may help contribute to the new turbulent political landscape when they pursue opportunities created by deep-level change. Examples of such transformative times could be the economic crises of the 1930s or the 'cultural crises' of the 1960s.

Since the 1980s ICTs have swept the world as waves of change that have generated fresh political terrains and new dynamics of conflict. The digital has become political – precisely because the effects of computerisation have been felt in almost every register of life. ICTs have created a new space: the virtual space of the network. It is a space that is real, a 'real virtuality' in terms of the effects that it has on the physical world. You can, for example, earn your living in this virtual space, and millions do. You can shop in it, be entertained or informed in it. The virtual space of the network can shape your view of the world, and you can shape the views of others through your actions in it. Its constant turbulence is shaking the sociocultural and economic foundations of the pre-digital way of life. This means that it is also an inherently political realm. Moreover, the issues that have driven politics in the network society are the same ones that have driven politics for 200 years. Questions of governance, of citizenship, of access and equity, of democracy and of the nature of political representation in the age of information have all become salient and hotly disputed. New media technologies are creating new environments, new political fields of contestation where old political ques- tions are being fought anew. It is a field created so rapidly that the principles of cause and effect are not readily understood by the engineers, politicians, business leaders and the users who build it. And so it is here that theory has its use as a way to recognise the processes at work more clearly, and the following authors are valuable contributors to this understanding.

Andrew Barry's 'On interactivity' from his book *Political Machines*, assesses the political possibilities of new information technologies from the perspective of Foucault's concept of the 'disciplined subject', where societies are ordered through positive systems of power. Barry looks in particular at the idea of 'the revitalization of democracy in its various forms' through a greater understanding of science. In a novel approach, he discusses new media-based interactivity within science centres and museums of science as a means to a 'scientific and technological citizenship' where user/citizens are able to understand the world around them more clearly. It is a model, he argues, that has its flaws and its detractors, but it is also one that is applicable in a positive form to other vital social realms such as broadcasting, education and the workplace. The role of new media technologies in the building of a 'strong democracy' are sketched in three future scenarios in a sobering essay by Benjamin R. Barber. He terms these the *Pangloss*, the *Pandora* and the *Jeffersonian* scenarios. The first is that through a naive belief in neoliberal ideology we will leave our technological and democratic prospects in the hands for the 'free market', a recipe, he argues for our futures to be harnessed primarily to undemocratic corporate interests. Under the *Pandora* future, government will use ICTs to encroach on privacy, restrict free information flows and construct what could be termed a 'surveillance society'. Lastly, the *Jeffersonian* scenario is for Barber the optimal future for governance in a highly technologised society. Here, governments, business and citizens will use ICTs for the benefit of all, to promote democracy and strengthen civil society. Unfortunately, in Barber's analysis, this is the least likely scenario.

Cass Sunstein's essay 'Citizens' looks at the nature of freedom, choice, desires and preferences in the networked society. He makes the important point that the con- cepts of 'consumer' and 'citizen' should not be conflated, although they frequently are. The colossal 'freedom of choice' for consumers on the internet, then, is not the same as a political freedom of choice; indeed, consumer choice is a kind of 'unfreedom'. The domination of the internet and the network society more generally by commercial inter- ests feeds a kind of accelerating 'consumer treadmill' where consumption is an always unsatisfying and necessarily limited process – limited largely to the material. Authentic 'citizens of democratic polity' he concludes, 'may legitimately seek a communications market that departs from consumer choices, in favour of a system that promotes goals associated with both freedom and democracy'. This means that citizens in a networked society must be engaged, active, reflective, and able to function as a group which goes beyond the limited world of our 'options as individuals'.

The final extract in this chapter is from McKenzie Wark's *A Hacker Manifesto*. 'Abstraction class' paraphrases Marx in a manifesto that articulates the origins, aims and interests of the 'hacker class'. Hackers in Wark's conception are those tech-savvy users who, through their technical expertise ('their knowledge and their wits') are able to develop relatively autonomous political realms in cyberspace. 'To hack is to differ' is their maxim. Here, Wark encapsulates the convergence of the political and the digital. The manifesto is a conscious effort to 'use the system's' own tools – information technologies – to construct the new, 'in art, in science, in philosophy and in culture'. The realm of abstraction is for Wark the workshop for ideas because 'what makes life differ in one age after another is the application of new modes of abstraction', the 'virtual made actual'.

4.1

On interactivity,
by Andrew Barry

Technological citizenship

Much has been said in recent years about the declining rates of political participation to be found in Western liberal democracies, whether on the basis of measures of voting or the membership of political parties or civic associations. In this context, many intellectuals and politicians have called for a revival and a reworking of a classical ideal of citizenship; an idea which is taken to imply not just a set of political and social rights, but also a set of responsibilities and duties. According to political philosophers and sociologists to be a citizen today entails accepting a moral demand to be active in, and informed about, public life.[1] However, such a tough morality does not come naturally. Active, responsible and informed citizens have to be made. As David Burchell has argued, modern political philosophy, 'neglects the positive construction of the *persona* of the citizen, both as an historical process and a social fact'.[2]

In this chapter I argue that the relation between technology and contemporary forms of active and responsible citizenship has two dimensions. On the one hand, as I argue later in the chapter, interactive and networked technologies have come to be seen as a key resource in the making up of citizens. New technology is reckoned by many to play a critical part in the revitalisation of democracy, in its various forms. This is a period of a remarkable investment by many political and educational organisations in new technology. Interactive technology is expected to produce active citizens.[3] On the other hand, along with a reinvention of ideal of active political citizenship and the technological investment with which it has come to be associated, one can also talk about a moral preoccupation with the importance of *scientific and technological citizenship*. Today, the individual citizen is increasingly expected, and increasingly expects, to make his or her own judgements about scientific and technological matters. These expectations have come from a variety of directions and obey no simple logic. They are neither straightforwardly pro- nor anti-science. For politicians, business leaders and some educationalists, the problem is often diagnosed as one of the poor quality of science and maths education and a lack of flexibility in the workforce to adapt to new technological demands.[4] For many scientists there is a weakness in 'the public understanding of science'.[5] For a few, this weakness is compounded by the effects of Romantic, 'postmodern', 'relativist' and 'anti-scientific' currents in intellectual and political life.[6] For some consumer groups the problem may be with science itself, its forms of knowledge and organisation. Patients campaign for more access to medical records, or more choice concerning treatments. Pregnant mothers and their supporters argue for the importance of natural birth techniques. Others argue that the public would understand the virtues of organic farming not on the basis of a romantic attachment to nature, but on the basis of a scientific understanding of the risks of other methods. Still others call for a form of scientific citizenship which would be knowledgeable about the social relations of science and technology and the politics of expertise.[7] Such demands and concerns are not new, even if they now take a new and more urgent form. Writing in the late 1930s, the biologist and socialist, J. B. S. Haldane argued:

> I am convinced that is the duty of those scientists who have a gift for writing to make their subject intelligible to the ordinary man or woman. Without a much broader knowledge of science, democracy cannot be effective in an age when science affects all our lives continually.[8]

Today, few would believe that scientific writing, on its own, will be a sufficient instrument with which to produce the kind of citizen required to meet the political requirements of a modern technological democracy. Citizens and consumers have too many other demands on their time, and too many other readily available forms of self-improvement and entertainment, and above all too many other available media to gain all they need to know from books. In this multimedia context, the idea of 'interactive' technology has acquired particular importance in discussions of public knowledge in general, and public knowledge of science, in particular. There is no doubt, as Mark Poster notes, that the usage of the idea of interactivity can 'float and be applied in countless contexts having little to do with telecommunications'.[9] Yet in relation to discussions of scientific and technological citizenship, interactivity can have a remarkable significance, drawing together concerns both with, for example, public 'participation', 'active citizenship' and 'empowerment' and with more specific questions and anxieties about the proper way to bridge the gulf between popular culture and the esoteric worlds of technical expertise.[10] If the health of advanced industrial economies is to be measured, in part, in terms of their possession and acquisition of intellectual and scientific capital, then at least one of the functions of interactive techniques has been to improve and maintain this capital. Citizens, consumers, students and school children need to be actively engaged with science.

In exploring the contemporary politics of interactivity, this chapter focuses on the modern museum of science. To many this institution may seem somewhat marginal to the discussion of interactivity, which is primarily associated today with the development of digital technologies. However, I argue that an analysis of the museum of science may have some considerable significance for those concerned with understanding the wider phenomenon of interactivity. First, as we shall see, science museums have played a significant part in the history of interactive technique and the idea of interactivity. Second, and more importantly, an analysis of the museum of science is suggestive of the way in which interactivity is actually much more than a particular possibility inherent in the development of media. For the museum of science, putting the interactive model into practice promises to turn the unfocused visitor-consumer into the interested, engaged and informed technological citizen. Interactivity is more than a particular technological form. It provides what Deleuze calls a diagram for organising the relations between objects and persons.[11] Today, interactivity has come to be a dominant model of how objects can be used to produce subjects. In an interactive model, subjects are not disciplined, they are *allowed*.

The second subsidiary theme of the chapter concerns what might call the historical geography of interactivity in science museums. This takes us from the Exploratorium in San Francisco to the National Museum of Science and Industry in London and the Cité des Sciences et de l'Industrie at la Villette in Paris.[12] My focus here is less on the details of interactive exhibits, or the abstract concept of interactivity, than on the ways in which the concern with interactivity circulates across different museums, and how it becomes associated with quite distinct and local preoccupations, political rationalities and institutional forms.[13] There are continual movements of persons and devices between American and European museums. Here, the movement of the idea and the techniques of interactivity between institutions and countries tells us something about the complexity of its invention. The 'invention' of interactivity was not a sudden discovery, but was rather a history of episodes, in which the techniques acquired ever-new forms and resonances.[14] The story also provides an indication of the shape of the kinds of global ideoscapes and technoscapes suggested by Arjun Appadurai's theory of global culture discussed in chapter two. In this case, the idea and the techniques of interactivity link together diverse projects in the public display of science and technology across national boundaries forming an international technological zone. Interest in interactives is, to use Will Straw's terms, a global *scene*.[15] Yet, at the same time, there is a marked disjuncture, to use Appadurai's term, between the technological zones of European integration discussed in earlier chapters and the absence of an account of this technological formation in the major European science museums.[16] There is no *European* museum of science.

One way of understanding how a connection came to be forged between interactivity, government and the agency and body of the museum visitor might be in terms of the place of interactivity in cybernetics and communications theory. Historically, the idea of interactivity is one of a number of terms (including noise, feedback and network) which have acquired particular significance since the development of communications theory, cybernetics and related fields in the 1940s with the work of, amongst others, Norbert Wiener. In the cybernetic account there is no essential distinction between the capacities of the human and the non-human actor. Both the human and the machine act as sources and receivers of information, thereby functioning as part of an interacting system. As Peter Galison reminds us, 'according to the cyberneticist, the world is nothing more than the internal relations of these incoming and outgoing messages'.[17] Certainly, within the contemporary science museum, the technology of interactivity can be intended, if not necessarily to obliterate, at least to reconfigure the distinction between the human visitor and the non-human exhibit.

Cybernetics does figure in this story. But I focus on a different theme. One which connects to a rather more long-standing concern with the body as a source of experimental knowledge and with what we might call, following Foucault, the *political anatomy* of the museum visitor.[18] As Simon Schaffer notes, in the eighteenth and early nineteenth centuries the body of the natural philosopher, or of his audience, frequently functioned as an essential part of the experimental apparatus. The eighteenth-century Parisian lecturer Jean Antoine Nollet, for example, 'described "beatifying electricity", when sparks were drawn from victims' hair'.[19] In 1800 the English chemist Humphry Davy reported on his experiments with the inhalation of gas. Davy 'lost all connection with external things . . . I existed in a world of newly connected and newly modified ideas. I theorised – I imagined that I made discoveries.'[20]

Since the late nineteenth century, however, the significance of scientist's body to experiment has changed. The body of the practising scientist has become disciplined; capable of performing meticulous practical tasks and making exact observations but no longer serving as an experimental instrument in itself. The process of science education is, at least in part, a matter of turning the untutored body of the student into that of a reliable technician. As John Law observes, the discipline of the scientist's body can play an important role in laboratory work.[21] Experimental events are no longer *experienced* by the scientist; they are *recorded* by the scientist's instruments. By contrast, the relatively undisciplined body of the visitor has an increasingly important part to play both in the contemporary science museum and what is often called 'the science centre'.[22] Today, the visitor to the museum or the science centre is often encouraged to interact or to 'play' with an exhibit. In effect, the visitor is expected to make scientific principles visible to themselves through the use of touch, smell, hearing or the sense of physical effects on their own bodies.[23] In a manner foreign to the practice of contemporary experimental science, the body is itself a source of knowledge.[24] As we shall see, interactivity is expected to turn the visitor into an experimental self. Self-experimentation becomes part of the solution to the anxiety of government.

Spirit and economy

In the first annual A. W. Franks lecture given at the British Museum in London in 1997, the former chair of the London stock exchange, and the then chair of the National Art Collections Fund, Sir Nicholas Goodison, defended the importance of objects. Quoting Phillipe de Montebello, Director of the Metropolitan Museum in New York, Goodison urged his audience not to take 'a headlong plunge into the still somewhat murky waters of the new technologies'. The interactive touchscreens which have become an increasingly ubiquitous feature of many contemporary museums were to be shunned. The desire of the public to engage with exhibits hands-on was, he thought, problematic. For Goodison, objects 'should be allowed to speak for themselves and not be debased'. 'The object is at the hub of a museum's purpose . . . it is not the role of the museum to ape Madame Tussaud's or Disneyland'. Rather it has a spiritual purpose: to 'inspire those who are receptive to inspiration'.[25]

But Goodison was not simply a cultural conservative. An equally powerful theme in his lecture was a concern that museums should conceive of themselves as businesses. At one level, there was a need to develop 'clear objectives, identify long-term liabilities, capital needs . . . develop robust management, measurements of success and on-going monitoring of standards'. Evidently museums needed to become further embedded in what Michael Power has termed the audit society.[26] At another level, there was a need for a coherent national framework both for management and for funding agreements. Even university-funded museums might want to come under the same organisational umbrella as those that were under the control of the then Department of National Heritage. Indeed, recognising them both as a spiritual resource *and as a business could be*, Goodison reckoned, an appropriate agenda for the New Labour government – whose election he warmly welcomed. He hoped that the arts ministers of the new government could develop a bold approach towards museums – and develop a new relationship between the *spiritual* and the *economic* which Goodison saw in the vision of Prime Minister Tony Blair.[27]

Goodison's attacks against interactivity and his proposals for museum management are perhaps an indication of what might be at stake in the museum world today – not just in Britain. They might be contrasted with a statement put out in a different setting – the web site of the British Interactives Group (BiG) – the organisation for individuals involved in all aspects of *hands-on* exhibitions and activities. At the time of Goodison's speech the BiG web site listed more than twenty projects related to interactivity in the UK receiving funding of no less than £500 million from the National Lottery. These included the new Wellcome gallery at the Science Museum; what is said to be the world's first geological visitor centre The Dynamic Earth, in Edinburgh and the Newcastle International Centre for Life which is said to incorporate a huge structure modelled on the DNA helix. In addition, Bristol 2000 would involve a complex which will include amongst other things Science world (a hands-on presentation of science and technology) and an 'electronic zoo' called Widescreen world.[28] Goodison drew a line between interactivity and the business of museums. Elsewhere, as he recognised, this line was blurred. Goodison's remarks provoked a lively response from interactives designers. One questioned Goodison's distinction between interactives and art. Clear rather than murky water was an appropriate image: 'Like some paintings and sculptures, the best interactive exhibits are, literally, wonderful and making them is an art. Try cupping your hands to divert a real tornado of water vapours, eight feet high, or touch the image of your own hand, out in the air in front of a real image mirror.'[29]

In Britain the debate on 'interactivity' intensified in the context of huge sums of money made available through the National Lottery.[30] But the debate is more than of local interest. For it can also be understood, in part, in relation to earlier changes in the public function of the museum. The modern science museum originally developed in the nineteenth century as a place where the successes of the imperial state could be displayed and where 'European productive prowess was typically explained as a justification for empire'.[31] But it was also intended to be a liberal space within which a bourgeois public would participate, and be seen to participate, in their own cultural and moral improvement. Thus, the population would be managed, as Tony Bennett argues, 'by providing it with the resources and contexts in which it might become self-educating and self-regulating'.[32] As an institution of government, the museum would act not so much through controlling and disciplining the public, but by enlisting its active support for liberal values and objectives. 'Museums and expositions, in drawing on . . . techniques and rhetorics of display and pedagogic relations . . . provided a context in which working-and middle-class publics could be brought together and the former – having been tutored into forms of behaviour to suit them for the occasion – could be exposed to the improving influence of the latter'.[33] The complex of museums developed at South Kensington in the 1850s became the paradigm of this liberal exhibitionary strategy.

In recent years, however, the liberal conception of culture as a means of individual improvement has had to run alongside – if not compete with – neo-liberal notions of culture as a consumer product.[34] The traditional museum has been accused of being too paternalist, too dominated by the concerns of curators and the fetishism of the artefact, and too dependent upon public subsidy.[35] What is said to be required is a new recognition of the competitive character of the visitor business in addition to the older preoccupations with scholarship and public education. The museum is but a 'part of the leisure and tourist industries'.[36] For Neil Cossons, the director of the London Science Museum in the late 1980s and 1990s, this was a challenge that should be welcomed for, with the decline of state funding, 'spending power, and therefore choice, [would be put] into the hands of the people'. The implications for the museums he reckoned were clear: 'The battlefield will be the marketplace and the casualties will be those museums that fail to adapt'.[37] Such rhetoric created enemies. One former curator resented the accusation of being called a dinosaur.[38]

Seen in this context, 'interactivity' was to have a double function. First, it is one of a range of a range of technical methods – along with cost control, visitor research, quality assurance, marketing and customer relations – which would enable the museum to forge a more 'economic' relation both with its visitors, and with private industry.[39] At the level of the institution, the museum was increasingly expected to respond to the public's demands rather than simply tell the public what it needs to know – the public needed to understand science but, before this is possible, the museum must first understand what the public wants.[40] At the level of the gallery, museum staff aimed to design exhibits which enable visitors to make choices and to experience a gallery 'in their own way'.[41] And at the level of the individual display, the museum sought to develop and employ techniques which encourage greater dialogue with the visitor. As an influential Management Plan for London's Science Museum noted:

> Passive and poorly interpreted attractions will suffer at the expense of those that develop live demonstrations, provide participation, interactive displays, and give a quality of personal rather than institutional service to their visitors. Informality and friendliness will be valuable attractions.[42]

For one commentator interactive media had a particular role to play in such a reorientation:

> . . . for interactive media the combination of: 1. multiplexing as a delivery mode; 2. interactivity as an intrinsically engaging form of media; 3. niche marketing as an advertising strategy; 4. the affluent status of museum visitors as a demographic group; 5. museums' status as pillars of respectability on scientific, environmental

and heritage issues . . . will greatly increase the attractiveness of museums to sponsors.[43]

Second, the technology of interactivity had a function in the context of broader changes in political thinking on both the left and the right. Contemporary political thinking is sceptical of the political and economic competence of the state and, in its stead, relies on the self-governing capacities of the individual, the family, the enterprise or the community. As Nikolas Rose observes, the subject of what he calls 'advanced' liberal forms of government is given unprecedented responsibility for governing his or her own affairs. For advanced liberalism, the task of the public authorities is not to direct or provide for the citizen but to establish the conditions within which the citizen could become an active and responsible agent in his or her own government.[44] Seen in this context, interactive devices had a function, for they might foster agency, experimentation and enterprise, thus enhancing the self-governing capacities of the citizen. Interactivity promised, in other words, to turn the museum visitor into a more active self.[45]

Empowerment

The association of the idea and techniques of interactivity with a broader conception of the public function of the science museum was not new. In 1969, the nuclear physicist Frank Oppenheimer, who had been blacklisted from practising as a scientist by the House Un-American Activities Committee, established the Exploratorium in San Francisco as an alternative to the traditional science museum. For Oppenheimer, existing museums in the United States often glorified the achievements of earlier scientists at the expense of enabling visitors to engage in a process of discovery themselves. The radical message of the Exploratorium was one of *democratic empowerment*.[46] The public would be empowered through being able to interact with objects as an experimental scientist does in the natural world of the laboratory, an idea which had been suggested to him following earlier visits to the Children's gallery at the Science Museum and the Palais de la Découverte in Paris.[47] According to Hilde Hein 'interactive pedagogic technique contains a key to empowerment that could transform education on a broad scale and make an avenue of general self-determination'.[48] In short, visitors would be participants rather than mere observers. Increasingly concerned about the growing interest in mysticism, drugs and Eastern religions in the younger generation, Oppenheimer himself expressed the intellectual and political aspirations of the Exploratorium in these terms:

> The whole point of the Exploratorium is to make it possible for people to believe that they can understand the world around them. I think a lot of people have given up trying to comprehend things, and *when they give up with the physical world they give up with the social and political world as well*.[49]

If the idea of interaction was central to what the Exploratorium was trying to do, how was it possible to realise this in practice? What was an interactive technique and how could interactivity *empower*? In the early years, the Exploratorium's attempts to develop participatory and interactive exhibits were, no doubt, rudimentary. The Exploratorium staff had, themselves, to learn how to embody Oppenheimer's radical philosophy in a technical form. However, the centre was able draw on and translate other models of interactivity. One was a temporary exhibition of 'Cybernetic Serendipity' which had originally been shown at the Institute of Contemporary Arts (ICA) in London from August to October 1968 and which was designed to explore the relations between creativity and 'cybernetic' technologies such as computers, robots and mechanical feedback systems. For Oppenheimer and the Exploratorium the origins of the 'Cybernetic Serendipity' as an art exhibition accorded with the centre's modernist philosophy. First, neither Oppenheimer nor the exhibition organisers perceived a fundamental distinction between art and science. For Oppenheimer, science had an 'aesthetic dimension' and art and science were united in the 'human quest for understanding'.[50] According to the exhibition organisers, 'at no point was it clear to any of the visitors walking around the exhibition, which of the various drawings, objects and machines were made by artists and which made by engineers; or, whether the photographic blow-ups of texts mounted on the walls were the works of poets or scientists'.[51] Blurring the boundaries of art and science was an important part of the Exploratorium's pedagogic strategy for by doing so it was hoped that the centre's visitor might begin to understand that science was a *creative* activity.

In terms of the Exploratorium philosophy, a second positive feature of the ICA exhibition was that it engaged with science at the level of material practice rather than merely at the level of metaphorical association. Visitors could have a practical as well as visual experience of technology. The instructions to one of exhibits of 'Cybernetic Serendipity', for example, invited the museum visitor to interact with a machine by turning knobs that adjusted the phase and frequency of two wave oscillations relative to one another in order to produce a variety of patterns.[52] Thus, the relationship between scientific or mathematical truth and art would, through a process of interaction, be revealed to the uninitiated. This philosophy still persists. Addressing what he perceived to be the 'crisis in science education' the director of the Exploratorium, Dr Goéry Délacôte has created a 'Center for Public Exhibition' which 'provides informal science education through interactive exhibits which address and explore the relationship between science, art and human perception'.[53]

A further intellectual rationale for the idea of the interactive exhibit in the Exploratorium was found in the work of the psychologist, Richard Gregory. In his Royal Institution Christmas lectures of 1967–1968, Gregory had expounded a theory which held that visual perception entailed a complex integration of the perceiver's interpretative dispositions with external stimuli. According to Gregory, 'perception is not a matter of sensory information giving perception and guiding behaviour directly, but rather the perceptual system is a "look up" system; in which sensory information is used to build gradually, and to select from, an internal repertoire of "perceptual hypotheses" '.[54] Translating this into practical terms, the Exploratorium 'let the visitor be the laboratory subjects of their own perceptual experiments'.[55] The intended effect of this pedagogic strategy was not just to teach perceptual theory, but to encourage the visitor to experience the process of discovery and thus to become an experimenter.

The extraordinary enthusiasm for interactivity, which had been initiated by the

Exploratorium in the late 1960s and subsequently spread across the United States, finally arrived in Europe in the mid-1980s with the opening of Launch Pad gallery at the London Science Museum, the Cité des Sciences et de l'Industrie in Paris and Richard Gregory's own Exploratory in Bristol. One key figure in this movement was Gillian Thomas, who set up the Cité des Enfants at La Villette, subsequently became the head of education at the Science Museum and then moved to lead the Bristol 2000 project. For Thomas, particular historical objects such as a lunar-landing vehicle could have an iconic value – as signifiers of technological progress in particular fields – but were of secondary importance to the development of interactives. In galleries such as the Earth Gallery of the Natural History Museum (1996) and the Materials Gallery (1997) at the Science Museum, individual iconic objects form a part of a display which is substantially interactive. Hands-on experiments communicate scientific truths. Iconic objects merely signify the importance and beauty of science. Background information is largely provided through interactive touchscreen computer terminals.

Certainly, by the early 1990s the growth of interactive science exhibits in Britain had been phenomenal.[56] Indeed, a veritable interactives movement had emerged with the formation of associations such as BiG and the European Collaborative for Science, Industry and Technology Exhibitions (ECSITE). Curators, educationalists and museum managers began to share their ideas about the function and design of interactives and encourage the use of interactives in exhibition spaces in which they had previously not been found, such as art galleries. Crudely, two tendencies in this movement might be identified. On the one hand, at least one strand of the interactives movement extolled the virtues of the kind of experimental culture fostered by the Exploratorium. The Exploratorium's own three-volume guide to the development of interactives is called the 'cookbook' – stressing the informality of interactives design. The first BiG workshop for interactive fabricators held at the former home of the Royal Greenwich Observatory at Herstmonceux castle had at least some Californian resonances: 'If you've done hands-on and brains-on but want to try souls-on (what-ever that may or may not be) this is the forum for you.' 'Mind, body and soul: the holistic approach to hands-on learning.' On the other hand, in conjunction with the use of new media technologies, interactives design has become highly professionalised and extraordinarily sophisticated and correspondingly expensive. Indeed, the Science Museum considered selling its professional services in interactives design to many of the other museums and centres in receipt of funding who do not have any well-developed expertise in this area. Interactivity may become an industry and a commodity. One of the ways that the Science Museum distinguishes itself as a national museum from other well-funded science centres is as a centre of excellence in interactive-exhibit design.

If the Exploratorium provided a model for the interactives movement in Britain, it would be a mistake to imagine that interactivity in Britain was simply a copy of the American original. As sociologists of technology have been at pains to argue, the process whereby a technology is 'transferred' from one place to another should be thought of as a form of translation or reinterpretation rather than merely a form of diffusion.[57] In the UK, the radical concerns of the American centre with the issue of empowerment and freedom were marginalised and, with exceptions, Oppenheimer's interests in the links between science and art were ignored. Some existing boundaries needed to be maintained. Instead, interactivity came to operate in relation to the failure of the traditional science museum to address a rather more mundane set of concerns with the public understanding of science and the attractiveness of the museum to visitors.[58]

Criticism of the traditional science museum was most forcefully made by Richard Gregory, founder of the Bristol Exploratory and former advisor to the Exploratorium. For Gregory, 'looking at the traditional museums of science we find remarkably little science'.[59] For Gregory, the essential feature of science was experimentation, so that in order to enable the public to get an 'intuitive feel for . . . the principles of science' hands-on interactive experiences were, he believed, critical. 'I suggest', wrote Gregory, 'that the major aim of interactive science centres, after stimulating interest and curiosity, should be setting up hand-waving explanations giving useful intuitive accounts'.[60] There was a particular need for such interest and curiosity. For the public were thought to be ambivalent about the authority of science and, at the same time, were said to be uninformed.[61] The promotion of the public understanding of science was, in this context, a necessary but insufficient solution.[62]

The new interactive science centres were certainly popular. 'Science centres attract visitors like magnets' noted the education officer at the Science Museum responsible for Launch Pad.[63] Interactive exhibits, whether located within science centres or in more traditional object-centred exhibitionary spaces were also consistently rated highly by the public according to visitor research. According to the Science Museum's own internal audit, Launch Pad received 714 visitors per square metre of gallery space per year, while the entire museum received only 44 visitors per square metre per year.[64] This popularity has proved both a benefit and problem for the development of interactive exhibitions. Certainly the fact that interactives are popular is of considerable commercial and political significance in a period when the museum or the science centre is increasingly understood as one part of a broader leisure industry and when the traditional curatorial concern with collection has been down played. Accusations that interactive science centres are merely expensive playgrounds which convey little of the tedious and difficult reality of science can be met with the response that this is what the public wants.[65] If interactive galleries enable visitors to have fun and to enjoy some kind of experience of science then, in this view, that is sufficient justification for their development. In a period when visitor numbers are taken to be one of the key performance indicators used in museums, and an important source of revenue, then the case for increasing the space given to interactive exhibits within the museum can appear unanswerable.[66]

However, the recognition that visitors came to interactive science centres and exhibitions to enjoy themselves created a problem for proponents of interactivity.[67] In the view of their designers, interactive exhibits were always expected to be as much instruments of informal education as a means of entertainment. The museum visitor was conceived of as an active learner and not just as a consumer. In this context, critics pointed to the lack of historical or industrial contextualisation of many interactive exhibits and the frequent absence of any explanation of what scientific principles were supposed to be revealed through the process of interaction. Some exhibits, it was said, can be interpreted in ways which lead museum visitors to *false* conclusions.[68] Indeed, it was unclear whether any of the scientific principles that many interactives were meant to demonstrate would be grasped by any except those already possessing a good scientific education.[69] Moreover, some questioned whether many interactive devices are really interactive. Many so-called interactive touch screen computers, for example, simply allowed the visitor to select from a predetermined set of options. Far from providing the possibilities for experimentation such interactive devices merely serve to create the illusion of choice.[70] Indeed, interactivity may, in practice, be associated with what Slavoj Zizek has called *interpassivity*. The user of the interactive device allows the machine to be active on the user's behalf, thereby *displacing* any creative activity of his or her own. The activity of the user is projected into the machine, but the machine's 'activity' is largely predictable.[71] We can contrast this with the possibility of a more creative relation to museum exhibitions (or to works of art) in general. In such a relation, the museum visitor may not be visibly 'active' at all, but will be open to the imaginary experience which allows the museum to act on her behalf. This is a different kind of pleasure to the pleasure of interacting with a quasi-interactive device; it is 'a pleasure in anticipating that the anticipation that expectations will be simply be met will be confounded'. This is a 'creative passivity'.[72]

There have been many different responses to such criticisms. At the London Science Museum large numbers of human 'explainers' are employed to make sure that the interactive exhibits do the job they are intended to do. New galleries such as Health Matters and the temporary exhibition space, Science Box, incorporated increasingly sophisticated interactive exhibits as a matter of course. On the other hand, one new gallery came to be marked by the *absence* of any interactives. The new gallery devoted to the remarkable scientific-instrument collection of King George III, for example, was accompanied by an exquisitely produced, well-researched book, but did not incorporate any interactives. Senior museum managers determined that interactives would be inappropriate.[73] In this way the purity of the original objects would be preserved. The lesson is a familiar one. The body is reckoned to be the site of education and popular entertainment. But, as Bourdieu reminds us, serious forms of aesthetic contemplation and historical appreciation are only thought to be possible at a distance.[74] The historical object is thus fetishised. Ironically, George III's instruments were, in their day, interactive, and it may have been particularly instructive to make a working model for visitors to use. Interactivity is not a new development in the history of science and technology, but has been *made* new. What is involved here is not so much the invention of a tradition, but a denial of the connections that can and should be made between the past and the present.

But along with the remarkable emphasis on interactivity in galleries of *contemporary* science, what is perhaps striking is the diversity of forms new galleries came to take. Internally, the museum has come to as something like a television station producing *different* programmes for *different* audiences – a post-Fordist industrial organisation to use the terminology of contemporary sociology.[75] Different galleries take different forms depending on their intended audience, their subject matter, the availability of commercial sponsorship and the philosophy and experience of their designers. There is more emphasis on tailoring interactives to particular age ranges so that it is possible to act on the specific technical competencies and interests of the young visitor. In these circumstances, gallery designers increasingly draw on the diverse insights of visitor research, ergonomics, sociology, developmental psychology and educational theory to ensure that the new interactive galleries prove to be educational as well as entertaining *and* meet their *specific objectives*.[76] This has implications for the relation between the museum and its visitors. To an extent unparalleled in the past, the museum visitor has become the object of investigation and an element of the museum's internal audit. If interactive technologies are expected to enhance the agency of the visitor and to channel it in the most productive direction, then the specific dynamic of this agency must itself be known. The visitor, it seems, has been increasingly called on to interact with exhibits and respond to the growing number of explainers, actors and researchers who also inhabit the museum. Constant *feedback* is a requirement of the new regime.[77]

A cyborg regime

In what follows I want to look at a museum where 'interactivity' has a rather different set of resonances. At La Cité des Sciences et de l'Industrie at La Villette in Paris, 'interactivity' functions not just in relation to notions of the visitor as active consumer and learner, but in terms of a project which centres around a particular vision of the relation between humans and machines. Opened in 1986, La Villette was one of a number of other major construction projects – including the Bastille opera house and the Beaubourg – which dominated Parisian cultural policy in the 1970s and 1980s. Whereas in the UK, the imperatives of cultural policy became increasingly understood in terms of notions of consumer demand and commercial viability, the ostensible objective of the developments in Paris was to broaden public participation in culture. As Nathalie Heinich has noted, one goal of the Beaubourg project was to 'democratise culture' and to somehow 'reconcile the imperatives of mass consumption with "higher" cultural production'.[78] Likewise, a key aim of the development of the site at La Villette was to enable a larger public to recognise the value and experience the excitement of science. Thus, the public would come to place as much value in science and technology as the French State itself.[79]

In practice, the techniques used at La Villette to encourage public interest in science have obeyed no simple logic and are, no doubt, contradictory. On the one hand, the Cité tries to go to meet the wider public's taste not just through *vulgarisation*, but, by blurring the traditional boundaries between education and popular culture. Echoing the philosophy of many late nineteenth-century exhibitions, science is presented not just as knowledge but also as spectacle and entertainment:

> Above all the Cité des Sciences et de l'Industrie is a place to learn and a place to have fun.

> La Villette: a new way of seeing, listening, learning of amazement and emotion! A place for creativity and leisure, for discovery and play.[80]

On the other hand, La Villette is not entirely without its own marks of cultural capital. In the park outside the Cité, there are a number of 'deconstructionist' architectural follies designed by Bernard Tschumi,[81] an experimental postmodern garden, a research centre for the history of science and technology, as well the new national conservatory of music – 'a complex conceived as a stimulating environment and meeting place for the arts, sciences and music'.[82] Even in the Cité itself there is a multimedia library, an international conference centre and associated information services. In addition, mirroring the philosophy of the Exploratorium, there is the 'Experimental gallery' which exhibits 'initiatives in art'.

> . . . the Experimental gallery exhibits artwork closely related to the fields of science, technology and industry. Though these works are neither illustrative nor educational in nature, they do represent a certain poetry, myth, humour and even criticism. The artists do not share the same views on the world as do scientists but instead provide an answer to these views.[83]

At first sight, La Villette's gestures towards art and its flirtations with postmodernism appear to mirror the Beaubourg's enthusiasm for technology. Since its opening, for example, the Beaubourg has been associated with Pierre Boulez's Institut de Recherche et de Coordination Acoustique/Musique (IRCAM), a centre which carries out research in avant-garde computer music.[84] And in 1984 to 1985 the Beaubourg supported experiments in collective computer writing in an exhibit entitled 'Les Immatériaux' which provided a vehicle for the philosopher, Jean-François Lyotard, to speculate about the impossibility of consensus through communication.[85]

Yet despite the apparent parallels between the cultural strategies of the two institutions their broader ideological resonances are quite different. In the case of the Beaubourg, the centre's close relation to technology serves to legitimise its identity as an innovative cultural institution – reinforcing the image given to it by Richard Rogers's bold architectural design. By comparison, in the case of the Cité, 'art' will always remain at the margins of an establishment which is dominated by a vision of the information age, and which tries too hard to be futuristic. Ironically, it is the Cité which appears to be the more conventional of the two institutions: its high-tech structure immediately conjuring up not so much an image of innovation and creativity, but a history of so many earlier exhibitions and philosophies in which progress has been equated with technological change.

Although the Cité's relation to the future is only too familiar, its representation of technology is nonetheless distinctive. Whereas the museums of the nineteenth and early twentieth centuries articulated the evolutionary metaphors of biology and political economy, the Cité's taxonomies draw on the new ahistorical sciences of communications theory, cybernetics, psychology and ecology.[86] Exhibit areas are devoted to whole series of topics concerned with the bodily and perceptual capacities of humans: sound, vision, light games, the representation of space, expression and behaviour. Moreover, although the Cité does possess the shiny rockets and cars to be found in all traditional science museums, its dominant images are those associated, not so much with hardware, but with language, software and the metaphors of the 'information society'. This is a museum of information, networks, environment, multimedia, interfaces and participation.[87]

In practice, these ideas are manifested in a number of different ways. At the most basic level, the Cité is full of 'interactive exhibits and audiovisual presentations', 'computer-based displays and games', 'participative, hands-on displays' and 'state-of-the-art museum technology'. Each of these devices has, no doubt, a specific didactic function and entertainment value. But collectively, the museum's interactive media also have a metonymic effect. As one curator put it to me, alluding to McLuhan, 'the medium *is* the message'. At La Villette, the future *is* interactive. Visitors to the museum do not purchase a ticket, but a machine readable smart card on which is written the demand 'Découvrez!'.[88]

However, interactive technologies do not simply function as rhetorical tropes. They also serve to organise the internal space of the museum. As Roger Silverstone has argued, the visitor's experience of a museum may be understood as a narrative in space, the structure of which is governed, but not determined, by the spatial organisation of the museum itself. This idea, derived from the work of Michel de Certeau, 'encourages us . . . to begin to analyse the rhetorical and narrative strategies which are present both in an exhibition's layout and in the routes which individuals construct through it'.[89] In the case of the Cité, the internal space of the museum apparently takes a quite conventional form: the visitor is guided around a three-dimensional space divided into exhibitions, shops, galleries and cafés. However, the existence of 'interactive' devices and technologies creates discontinuities in this space, puncturing the visitor's route and establishing a further 'fourth' audiovisual dimension within which the visitor is encouraged to place herself, to participate and to interact. Thus, the visitor is not simply an observer of the museum's machines – she is positioned within them. In the 'Sound' exhibit area, for example, a computer game called a 'voice-actuated note-gobbler' serves to display the tone of a person's voice. The 'Light games' area includes a section devoted to the explanation of interference which brings together a number of 'hands-on' displays. In the 'Aeronautics' area some of the most popular exhibits are flight simulators. In the 'Environment' area computer based interactive multimedia allow the visitor to explore topics such as greenery, air and trees. Interaction is compulsory and compulsive.[90]

Just outside of the Cité, the position of the museum visitor in the museum's exhibitionary strategy is dramatically symbolised by a huge 3-D Omnimax cinema – La Géode – in which 'visual effects combine with sound effects to transport the spectators into the midst of the action surrounding them'.[91] Reflecting on the significance of La Géode, Paul Virilio reminds us that 'the fusion/confusion of camera, projection system and auditorium in the Imax/Omnimax process, is part of a long tradition of "mobile framing" in cinema, dating from the invention of the tracking shot in 1898'.[92] Placing the Omnimax in relation to the early history of cinema is certainly appropriate. Like the cinema of the 1890s and 1900s, contemporary Imax/Omnimax cinema is less concerned with narrative than with exhibition, spectacle and affect.[93] However, the economic conditions of Imax and early cinema are quite different. Whereas small-scale production companies played an important role in the development of early cinema, the relative scarcity of Imax/Omnimax auditoria and the expense of film production has meant that the development of Imax/Omnimax depends on corporate sponsorship.[94] In la Géode, one popular programme is a film of the Space Shuttle produced by NASA and the Lockheed Corporation. The Space Shuttle is a particularly appropriate subject at the Cité for its design is based on the view that it *matters* that research in space depends on the involvement of humans and does not just rely on the operation of remote controlled instruments. In the Shuttle, humans are 'explorers' pushing back the final frontier of space; they have the *Right Stuff*. However, equally significantly, the physical and perceptual capacities of their own bodies are the objects of the Shuttle scientists' experiments. Thus, at least some of the experiments performed in the Shuttle bear some comparison to those that might be found in the main body of the museum.

In the Cité, the idea that science and technology reconfigure the boundaries between humans and non-humans is a pervasive one – represented not just in the ubiquity of 'interactive' techniques but in the vocabulary and taxonomy of the museum's exhibits. The Earth is understood as a 'machine' and as a 'spaceship'. Computers can 'talk'.[95] 'Animal and vegetable kingdoms come to life in the form of automatons.' Robots and humans live in a 'cybernetic zoo'. And marriage is presented in terms of notions of 'trade' and 'system'. The contrast between La Villette, on the one hand, and the Exploratorium and the Science Museum, on the other, is considerable. For whereas all three institutions use a mixture of mechanical, made-up and computer-based interactives, it is only La Villette which fully embraces the vision of an interactive information society. For the other two institutions, however, interactivity does not primarily connote information technology, but rather a more wide-ranging attempt to reinvent the contemporary museum

Have there been explicit contestations of the interactive model? At one level, a series of questions has properly been asked about the use and effectiveness of interactives, not least by museum professionals and interactive designers themselves. Experimentation in interactives design was, after all, a central feature of the Exploratorium philosophy. Do they possibly convey the scientific principles that they are intended to? Are they really cost effective given the wear and tear to which they may be subjected? How do visitors use them? Can they be brought together with objects from the museum's collections? However, the force of such questioning has not been any decline in interest in interactives. On the contrary, criticism has provoked professionals to improve the design of interactive devices, tailoring their design more closely to the needs, capacities and behaviour of *real* museum visitors, and integrating them more carefully with the more traditional text- and object-based exhibits. In brief, the notion of interactivity has come to be the centre of a rapidly expanding cycle of intellectual, financial and psychological investments in the public presentation of science and technology.

At another level, a few historians and sociologists of science have proposed a very different model of the future of the museum of science. For many proponents of interactivity, museum collections are reckoned to have primarily an iconic value. In comparison to the cluttered display cabinets of an earlier period in the history of museums, there are relatively few historical objects in the interactive museum of science. In the model proposed by some historians of science, however, museum collections acquire new significance for they are illustrative of the critical importance of technical devices in scientific practice.[96] The task of the museum curator, in this view, is not to design ever-more-sophisticated interactives, but to forge a new political rhetoric of display. The purpose of such a rhetoric would not necessarily be to encourage the visitor to experiment or interact with custom-made interactive devices. Rather it would be to try to use the particular advantages of the museum as a medium to tell stories about the complexity and technicality of scientific practice, and the radical differences between science as it is encountered in textbooks, school experiments, political arena and exhibitions and science as it encountered in the laboratory and the field.[97] Rather than excite interaction, such an approach might encourage visitors to map some of the paths which lead between the messy imprecision and uncertainty of technical scientific work and the critical importance of notions of scientific precision and certainty in public political and cultural life. Such an approach is certainly not the only one available for the contemporary museum of science. Yet, in its difference, it brings into focus the remarkable preoccupation with the virtues of the interactive model today.

Political anatomy

Is the science centre and the museum of science an isolated case, only of interest to specialists in the history and sociology of museums? I do not think so. Although science centres and science museums were one of the first institutions to develop an explicit programme of interactive technological development, the interactive model can be, and has been, generalised to other sites and situations: to education and broadcasting, marketing and the workplace. Today, the promise of interactivity, is at the centre of of a whole series of attempts to reinvent educational, political and broadcasting institutions.[98] We can now speak of the importance of interactive devices and methods in the classroom, in marketing and in the mass media.[99] At the same time, in the field of party politics and public service, an array of new technical methods such as focus-group research and electronic democracy also take some elements of the interactive model, in so far as they emphasise the importance of *working with* rather than directing the political imagination of ordinary citizens. In this model of political life, intensive interaction with 'the public' in carefully managed environments is expected both to maximise and intensify feedback between government and the governed and to minimise the possibilities for unexpected political controversies and conflicts at a later date.[100]

In his discussion of 'docile bodies' in *Discipline and Punish*, Foucault notes the importance of what he terms 'body-object articulation' for the exercise of disciplinary power. 'Discipline defines each of the relations that the body must have with the object that it manipulates'.[101] Reflecting on an eighteenth-century set of instructions for handling a rifle, he speaks of the way in which the body and the rifle are brought into one functioning arrangement: 'over the whole surface of contact between the body and the object it handles, power is introduced, fastening one to another'. In this way, Foucault argues, the body is reconstituted as a 'body-weapon, body-tool, body-machine complex'.[102] Discipline operates by fixing the relations between body and tool to form a unified apparatus.

In comparison to the instruments and codes of discipline, the various techniques of interactivity imply a much less rigid articulation of bodies and objects, coupled with a liberal sense of the limits of permissable control. There is a degree of play and flexibility between the interactive device and the user's body. Above all, the use of interactives is not intended to regiment the body, but to turn it into a source of pleasure and experiment. 'Present-day hands-on interactive science centres are delightful, full of the fun of surprises, and discovering new phenomena and seeing how things work'.[103] Whereas discipline is exhaustive in its application, interactivity is specific, instantaneous and intensive. Whereas disciplinary technology manipulates and manages the body in detail, interactive technology is intended to channel and excite the curiousity of the body and its senses; resulting in anticipated effects on the intellectual productivity, questioning and creativity of those who interact. Whereas discipline is direct and authorative, interactivity is intended to turn the user (visitor, school child, citizen or consumer) into a more creative, participative or active subject *without* the imposition of a direct form of control or the judgement of an expert authority.[104] Discipline implies normalisation; the injunction is 'You must!' Interactivity, by contrast, is associated with the expectation of activity; the injunction is, 'You may!'[105] We may draw up an ideal–typical set of contrasts:

Discipline[106]	Interactivity
The time-table: 'Precision and application are, with regularity, the fundamental virtues of disciplinary time'	**Flexible time:** interactivity depends on the choice of the user
The correlation of the body and the gesture: 'a well-disciplined body forms the operational context of the slightest gesture'	**An orientation of creative capacity:** Interactivity does not depend on discipline but on the potential of the undisciplined body and the unfocused mind. 'For the child, or the aware but not especially knowledgeable adult, failed predictions can signal the need for further experiment or to see the phenomenon in a fresh way'[107]
Body–object articulation: through rules and codes. The constitution of **'a body–weapon, body–tool, body–machine complex'** which persists over time.	**Body–object articulation:** through guidance rather than rules. The constitution of a **brief 'body–machine interaction'.**
Exhaustive use: 'Discipline . . . arranges a positive economy; it poses the principle of a theoretically ever-growing use of time, ever more available moments and, from each moment, ever more useful forces'	**Intensive use:** the value of brief interactions must be maximised. Exhaustive use is likely to be impossible
The authority of the expert: the scientist who lectures and who acts as an authority	**The concealment of expertise:** the authority of expertise is partially hidden in order to maximise the possibilities for interaction. The imagination and expertise of the ordinary citizen is worked with rather than contradicted by the voice of authority.
Injunctions: **Learn! You must!**	Injunctions: **Discover! You may!**

In studying the relations between technology and government there is the temptation to take one of two approaches. One temptation is to write the history of technology as simply an adjunct to the history of political doctrines or ideas. Such an approach would focus our attention on the texts of political theorists, intellectuals and politicians. It would concern itself with the great statements of liberalism and socialism, republicanism, communitarianism and conservatism concerning the conduct of government. A second temptation would be to associate grand transformations in politics and government with significant developments in the history of technology. Seen in this context, writers such as Jean-François Lyotard and Mark Poster, at particular moments in their writing, have placed the emergence of new information sciences and technologies at the centre of their analysis of the political present. For Lyotard, 'the postmodern condition' was intimately associated with the emergence of the new cybernetic and information sciences.[108] For Poster, the present era is marked by a movement from the mode of production to the mode of information.[109]

One of the virtues of focusing on the topic of interactivity is that it displaces both 'political ideas' and information technology from the centre of our analyses. On the one hand, interactivity is both much less and yet, in a certain sense, much more than media and information technology.[110] It is a diagram for the exercise of power which will have the use of new media and information technologies. In this way, interactivity provides the model for a whole series of specific elaborations, innovations and investments across a range of media and institutions. On the other hand, a focus on interactivity cuts across the conventional terms of political theory, with all its endless preoccupation with the differences between liberalism, neo-liberalism and social democracy, pluralism, authoritarianism and conservatism. As we have seen, in order to account for the significance of interactivity in different locations one must examine how the idea and the technology becomes associated with particular political strategies and ideas in specific circumstances. Through the use of interactive devices, political doctrine can be rendered into technical form. Yet interactivity is also both much less and much more than simply a political idea or doctrine. It is much less in so far as interactivity is not, in general, the subject of any political manifesto, nor is it the object of political controversy. Explicit attacks on the idea of interactivity are rare. The public intervention of the Director of the British Museum was exceptional in this respect. Yet it is political in the sense that it has become a model for the exercise of political power which does not take a disciplinary form. Although the interactive model is not, as we have seen, a recent invention, it has acquired a remarkable political currency today.[111] Politics does not circulate just through the flow of ideologies or rationalities of government, but through diagrams, instruments and practices.

Notes

1 For different accounts see Mouffe 1992, Mulgan 1994a, chapter 3, Giddens 1998. The moralism of some recent talk of citizenship is suggested by Geoff Mulgan's claim that the idea of citizenship implies a 'tough ethics' (1994, p. 68). Anthony Giddens speaks of the association of such a tough ethics and the political project of the 'third way' associated with British Prime Minister, Tony Blair.

According to Giddens: 'One might suggest as a prime moto for the new politics, *no rights without responsibilities*' (1998, p. 65, emphasis in the original).

2 Burchell 1995, p.556. On this point see also Cruikshank 1996, 1999, Donald 1999.

3 According to Philip Gould, advisor to British Prime Minister, Tony Blair, on 'public opinion', the Internet should be used prevent parliament appearing 'impotent and irrelevant' and to 'ensure the people's voice should always be heard', *Financial Times*, 15 October 1999, p. 2.

4 Since the early 1990s, the European Commission has funded periodic investigations into the state of scientific literacy in Europe. Such studies have demonstrated that 'scientific literacy in Europe is far from satisfactory and that a relation exists between an understanding [of science] and a responsible acceptance or rejection of new technologies' (Fasella 1997, p. 166).

5 Irwin and Wynne 1996.

6 This anxiety took many different forms, reflecting differences in national intellectual political cultures and preoccupations. In the United States it was manifested in the so-called 'Science Wars'. On the 'Science Wars' and their ramifications elsewhere see *Social Text* 1996, Ross 1996, Latour 1999a, Hacking 1999.

7 Alan Irwin (1995) develops the notion of scientific citizenship along these lines. For an indication of how such debates have emerged in the realm of parliamentary politics see House of Lords (2000).

8 Quoted in Irwin 1995, p. 11.

9 Poster 1995, p. 33.

10 On the notion of the 'boundary object' which forms a bridge between different worlds, see Star and Grieserner 1989.

11 Deleuze 1988, p. 40.

12 Throughout this chapter I refer to the National Museum of Science Museum (NMSI) as the Science Museum.

13 Note Appadurai's injunction: 'It is only through the analysis of . . . trajectories that we can interpret the human transactions and injunctions that enliven things' (Appadurai 1986, p. 5). Although there are some specific designs of interactive exhibits shared between different museums, here I am primarily concerned with the circulation of the frame within which these diverse interactive exhibits are inscribed.

14 Cf. Foucault 1977, p. 138.

15 Straw 1991.

16 Bruno Latour and Mickes Coutouzis (1993) describe the failure of the *Eurometrics* project which was intended to involve the various national science museums in Europe in a joint venture to represent the process of technical harmonisation. In the case of the Expo '92 exhibition studied by Penelope Harvey, different national pavilions exhibited different responses to the question of whether the importance of the nation-state could be assumed or not. The European Community was 'present as a classic example of the western egalitarian nation-state' (Harvey 1996, p. 76).

17 Galison 1994, pp. 255–256.

18 Foucault 1977, 138, see also Schaffer 1992b, p. 329.
19 Schaffer 1992b, p. 333.
20 Ibid., p. 359.
21 Law 1986, p. 21.
22 Unlike the traditional science museum, the typical science centre does not house an historical collection but is likely to rely heavily on the use of interactive exhibits. For a discussion of the difference see Durant (1992).
23 Durant 1992, p. 8.
24 Gregory 1989, p. 4.
25 In the version [obtained from the British Museum press office somebody had pencilled '?!' next to this statement.
26 Power 1997.
27 The British Prime Minister's christian education at Oxford has often been remarked on by political commentators.
28 http://www.exploratory.org.uk/big/handbook/lot.proj.html. The Science Museum received £23 million from the heritage fund out of £44 million total costs, the Dynamic Earth centre received £15 million from the heritage fund; the Newcastle Centre and Bristol 2000 each received £27 million.
29 R. Johnson, letter to the *Guardian*, 27 May 1997.
30 The weekly UK National Lottery was established during the last years of the Conservative Government in the mid-1990s. Funds deriving from the lottery are given to five good causes, primarily for capital grants. Public museums have been major recipients of lottery funding.
31 Bennett et al. 1993, p. 59. For a discussion of the history of the science museum in the eighteenth century see Hooper-Greenhill (1992). According to Schaffer the public presentation of science sometimes involved an extraordinary level of public debate: natural philosophers competed for patronage and audiences and "critics sought to subvert the status of the lecturer's enterprise" (Schaffer 1993, p. 490).
32 Bennett 1995, p. 40.
33 Ibid., p. 86.
34 Silverstone 1992, p. 41.
35 See for example the article by the Science Museum director Dr Neil Cossons in the *Listener* (1987).
36 Kirby 1988, p. 91.
37 Cossons 1987, p. 18.
38 'The inference in the article that the staff in the national museums are a load of dinosaurs with uncaring attitudes to the public was not well received' (letter to the author 30 June 1987).
39 A combination of increasing attention to marketing and the development of a public controversy about imposing museum entry charges has given the Science Museum a higher public profile (cf. Cossons 1991, p. 185). However, its activities probably draw much less public comment than other museums of comparable size. As one museum curator noted: "what is done by the National Gallery, the V&A, the Tate etc is always subject to both media hype *and* informed comment, from layman and specialist alike. Alas the same cannot be said of the Science

Museum" (letter to the author 18 June 1987). The silence of the media and the public in relation to the politics of the Science Museum appears to be inversely related to the noise generated by Museum visitors. According to one Museum souvenir guide, "[The Science Museum] is somewhere where people feel free, and often excited; where they talk loudly (sometimes too loudly) and even laugh. It is different from most museums" (van Riemsdijk 1980, p. 1).

40 Here, of course, one must not imagine that 'the public' has any homogeneity or unity independently of the way that is constituted by the science museum. Recall Raymond Williams's dictum, 'there are no masses, only ways of seeing people as masses' (Williams 1989, p. 11).

41 Macdonald and Silverstone 1990, p. 184. According to one recent commentator: "Museums are . . . inherently interactive multimedia. The visitor is in control of the paths along which they navigate through the artifacts, images, sounds and texts and they are under no obligation to follow the linear structure imposed by the curator" (Bearman 1993, p. 183).

42 Science Museum, 1986.

43 Nash 1992, p. 184.

44 Rose 1996b, Rose 1999, p. 139.

45 Cf. Strathern 1992a, pp. 41–43, Macdonald 1993.

46 On empowerment see Cruikshank 1996. The theme of the relation between political and scientific empowerment has been taken up by more recent US writers and science. See, for example, Richard Sclove's claim: 'If it is vital that citizens be empowered to help shape legislative or electoral agendas, it is likewise vital that they have extensive opportunity to participate in technological research and design' (Sclove 1995, p. 181).

47 According to Hein there were two important influences on Oppenheimer's thinking. One was the London Science Museum Children's Gallery (1936–1994), which contained exhibits which could be operated by the child. The other was the Palais de la Découverte, which unlike traditional science museums did not concern itself primarily with the preservation of artefacts. Created in 1937, the Palais described itself as 'a scientific cultural centre' in which a large number of scientific experiments were (and still are) demonstrated to visitors (Hudson 1987, p. 103). According to its founder, Jean Pettin, one of the objectives of the Palais was to realise the potential for scientific research which he hoped might be found in the population at large. For Pettin, those young people who hadn't been favoured by a good education, but who had a particular aptitude for research and who had enough enthusiasm and energy to make it their vocation should be recognised and encouraged by the National Research Service (Maury 1994, p. 24).

48 Hein 1990, p. xvi.

49 Ibid., p. xv, my emphasis.

50 Ibid., p.xvi.

51 Reichardt 1971, p. 11.

52 Hein 1990, p. 38.

53 Délacôte 1992.

54 Gregory 1970, p. 174.

55 Hein 1990, p. 72.
56 Stevenson 1994, p. 30.
57 Callon et al. 1986, de Laet and Mol 2000.
58 On the public understanding of science see Wynne 1992, Irwin and Wynne 1996, Michael 1996a.
59 Gregory 1989, p. 7.
60 Ibid., p. 5.
61 Wynne 1992, p. 281.
62 The idea that there was a crisis in the public understanding of science had become a political problem in Britain following the publication of a Royal Society report on the matter in 1985. There followed a substantial research programme on the problem and the development of a variety of initiatives (such as 'National science week') to solve it. Despite these initiatives university science departments continued to close and student interest in the natural sciences (in comparison to the social sciences and humanities) continued to decline.
63 Stevenson 1987, p. 18.
64 Thomas n.d., p. 3. For an overview of contemporary museum visitor studies see Bicknell and Farmelo 1993.
65 One widely cited example of such an accusation is Shortland 1987. One feature of this denigration of computer-based interactive museum exhibits is their association with interactive computer games. As Leslie Haddon observes 'moral panics about games, including fears of addiction, the "effects" of desensitisation and of escapism have spanned a range of political campaigns, media attention and academic, mainly psychological analysis' (Haddon 1993, p. 124).
66 Cf. Thomas n.d.
67 Gregory 1989, p. 2.
68 One member of the Science Museum education staff remembered the example of an interactive where a light signal was interpreted by many visitors as the cause rather than the effect of the phenomenon that the interactive was meant to demonstrate. Another suggested that many scientific principles which are supposed to be revealed by interactives would only be comprehensible by A-level students and above (Interviews conducted at the Science Museum, London, June 1995).
69 Macdonald 1992, p. 408.
70 Strathern 1992a, p. 42. Allucquére Rosanne Stone outlines the terms of a debate concerning what is *really* interactive which occured between programmers and managers in a research laboratory developing interactive game software. 'There are five corollaries of Lippman's definition [of interactivity]. One is interruptibility, which means that each participant must be able to interrupt the other, mutually and simultaneously. The second is graceful degradation, which means that unanswerable questions must be handled in a way which doesn't halt the conversation . . . the third is limited look-ahead, which means that because both parties can be interrupted there is a limit to how much of the shape of the conversation can be anticipated by either party. The fourth is no default, which means that the conversation must not have a preplanned path, it must truly develop in an interaction. The fifth is that participants must have the impression of an infinite database . . . Interactivity implied two conscious agencies in

conversation . . . [by contrast] to the Ashibe management . . . interactivity meant taking turns, not interruption; it meant that the user pushed a button and the machine did something as a result' (Stone 1995, p. 182).

71   Zizek 1997, p. 111. Zizek poses the provocative question 'What if the "subjective" gesture, the gesture constitutive of subjectivity, is not that of autonomously "doing something" but, rather, that of the primordial substitution, of withdrawing and letting another do it for me, in my place?' (pp. 118–119). See also Zizek 1998.

72   Born 2000. A creative passivity is one that implies the possibility of learning from the other.

73   In the Science Museum there was considerable disagreement about whether the juxtaposition of historical artefacts and interactives should be considered a problem or not, Proponents of interactivity noted that the Museum had a long-standing interest in interactivity from the opening of the *Children's Gallery* (1936) onwards, and moreover disputed the rival claims to have established the interactive model made on behalf of both the Exploratorium or the Palais de la Découverte (cf. Woolgar 1976). Many others thought that integration of interactives with historical objects could be a problem as it raised questions, for example, about how to define the boundaries between objects with which the public could and could not interact. More generally, the development of interactivity in the museum not only raised questions about the function of interactive devices but also about the function of traditional objects. On these points my thanks to Sharon Macdonald, Stephen Johnston and Gillian Thomas.

74   Bourdieu 1984.

75   On post-Fordism see Amin 1994.

76   In Lash and Utty's (1994) terms the museum began to be engaged in a process of reflexive modernisation. In this process, the museum visitor was not necessarily conceptualised as an individual consumer. Many visitors came as part of family groups or in school parties and visitor research and exhibition design has to take this into account. In addition, the museum was aware that many of its adult visitors were male and middle class and, in this context, issues of class and gender have become a feature of exhibition design. A detailed examination of the ways in which different designs of interactive exhibits addressed specific kinds of museum visitor is beyond the scope of this chapter.

77   But see Macdonald 1997 for a discussion of the difficult position of an anthropologist working in the museum. A concern with feedback is not just a feature of the contemporary museum. Witness the increasing emphasis on feedback in the operations of public service broadcasting and the universities.

78   Heinich 1988, pp. 199–200.

79   The post-war French State has, at least at the level of political rhetoric, tended to place great stress on the importance of science and technology for the modernisation of France. By contrast, in the UK, interest in interactivity amongst scientists and museum staff developed at the height of what was perceived to be government hostility towards science in the mid-1980s.

80   Cité, n.d.

81   Derrida 1986.

82 Cité, n.d. The juxtaposition of scientific exhibitions and innovative architecture was not new in Paris – see Stamper 1989.

83 Cité, 1988, p. 30.

84 Born 1995.

85 Poster 1990, p. 114.

86 Cf. Jordonova 1989, p. 23.

87 Cité 1995, p. 23.

88 Slavoj Zizek argues that in comparison to repressive political regimes, a characteristic feature of contemporary liberal democratic societies is the demand to enjoy. Thou shall not is displaced by 'You may!' Zizek 1999.

89 Silverstone 1988, p. 235.

90 Donna Haraway notes the disjuncture that must be experienced by urban American children visiting the American Museum of National History in New York, 'What is the experience of New York streetwise kids wired to Walkman radios and passing the Friday afternoon cocktail bat by the lion diorama? These are the kids who came to the museum to see the high-tech Nature-Max films. But soon, for those not physically wired into the communication system of the late nineteenth century, another time begins to form' (Haraway 1989, p. 29). La Villette by contrast was built during the period which saw the introduction of the Walkman into urban culture. Its interactive exhibits are, like the Walkman, compulsive.

91 Cité 1988, p. 54.

92 Virilio 1990, p. 173.

93 Elsaesser 1990.

94 Wollen 1993.

95 As Cornelius Castoriadis notes: 'Ordinary mortals are ensnared together with Nobel laureates in the coils of a new mythology ("machines which think", or "thought as a machine")' (1984, p. 230).

96 On the technicality of scientific practice see, for example, Latour and Woolgat 1986, Gooding, Pinch and Schaffer 1989, Lynch 1993. 'Many of our former collection displays were uninspired, unimaginative and unchallenging . . . [but] collections are the foundations of all great museums' and they should continue to have a central place in museum display (Bennett 1998, p. 174).

97 Bennett 1998 describes one innovative attempt to do this in the Whipple Museum of the History of Science in Cambridge. For accounts of the need to represent controversy in science museums and the difficulties of doing so, see Levidow and Young 1984; Macdonald and Silverstone 1992, M. Ross 1995 and Schaffer 1997.

98 'The new [interactive information services] represent a genuine opportunity for the competitiveness of the European economy and the diffusion of European culture, and an opportunity to take full advantage of the diversity of European society' M Monti, Member of the Commission, Debates of the European Parliament, 4–500/260, 16 May 1997.

99 On the importance of interactives in the mass media see, for example, Birt 1999, p. 5.

100 For one fantastic account of the potential for virtual democracy Budge 1996. For

more nuanced analyses of the limitations as well as the advantages of new media in particular political contexts see Tsagarousianou et al. 1998.

101 Foucault 1977, pp. 152–153.
102 Ibid., p. 153.
103 Gregory 1989, p. 1.
104 According to Oppenheimer, 'We do not want people to leave with the implied feeling: "Isn't somebody else clever." Our exhibits are honest and simple . . .'.
105 Zizek 1999.
106 Foucault 1977, pp. 149–156.
107 Gregory 1989, p. 6.
108 Lyotard 1984, p. 3.
109 Poster 1990.
110 Cf. Foucault 1977, pp. 224–225 quoted in Deleuze 1988, p. 40. New media and information technologies have an enormous empirical importance, and a specificity in comparison to other media such as photography and film, but it is unclear why we would should characterise our era in terms of the presence of such technologies. Interactivity is not the same as its specific technical manifestations.
111 Mulgan 1994b.

4.2

Pangloss, Pandora or Jefferson? Three scenarios for the future of technology and strong democracy,
by Benjamin R. Barber

Modernity may be defined politically by the institutions of democracy, and socially and culturally by the civilization of technology. The relationship between democracy and technology remains ambiguous, however. Proponents of classical participatory democracy such as Jean Jacques Rousseau have generally understood the progress of science to be corrosive to the intimacy and equality of political relations. Proponents of the liberal open society such as Sir Karl Popper and Bertrand Russell, however, have posited a close connection between the spirit of science and the success of liberal democratic institutions.

About the future role of democracy in society we cannot be certain. Because it is a fragile form of social organization, its prospects are clouded. But we do know, however we organize our political world, that we shall live in a society dominated by technology. Indeed, the theme of technology and society has become sufficiently popular to make it a favorite both with academics and after dinner speakers.

Notwithstanding it being in vogue, the relationship between technology and democracy is a matter of genuine urgency for modern men and women. Will technology nourish or undermine democratic institutions? Is technological growth likely to support or corrupt freedom? Are we finally to be mastered by the tools with which we aspire to master the world? The scientistic wisdom suggests that science and technology, by opening up society and creating a market of ideas, foster more open politics; the Soviet experience with copying machines and computers is cited as an example. Yet technology coexisted with tyrannical government in Nazi Germany, and was made to expedite the liquidation of the Jews in a fashion that suggests its utility in rendering dictatorship more efficient. And the inversion of control that attends technocratic forms of society is well enough known to cause comment by the Prince of Wales: Prince Charles used his keynote address at the 350th anniversary of Harvard University to caution against the domination of society by technology, issuing a call to his listeners to restore "moral control over the things they make."

Moreover, such generalizations as we can hazard about the connections between technology and society must remain provisional in the face of the extraordinary rate of change typical of the evolution of modern science and technology. As Arthur Schlesinger, Jr., has noticed in his The Cycles of American History, if we assume roughly 800 lifetimes separate us from the beginning of human life, there has been more change in the last two lifetimes than in the 798 that preceded them. Henry Adams had already observed at the beginning of this century that between the years 1800 and 1900, "measured by any standard known to science – by horsepower, calories, volts, mass in any shape – the tension and vibration and volume and so-called progression of society were fully a thousand times greater." Whilst for thousands of generations life for a cohort of grandchildren roughly resembled life for their grandparents, in our century there is enough change in a decade to confuse people in the fifteen years it takes to grow up.

The world's population took 10,000 years to reach a billion, around 1800. The second billion had arrived by 1900, the third by 1940, the fourth by 1960. Movable type appeared only four centuries ago, the steam engine in the eighteenth century, the telegraph in the nineteenth, and wireless at the beginning of the twentieth. The internal combustion engine, rocketry, and the typewriter came of age between the two World Wars, and television, microchips, and lasers are still more recent. The first computer built after the war filled a large room and performed less complex calculations for its ardent cybernetic attendants than a handheld instrument performs for students today.

The overall impact of these stunning developments over the last half millennium has been to shrink both time and space. Aristotle once observed that the ideal size for a democratic polity could be measured by the amount of land a man could traverse in a day – assuring that all citizens could attend a popular assembly. By this standard, Marshall McLuhan's global village is a reality that is confirmed anew each day by advances in satellite and laser optic communication and computer information systems and the spread of the internet. Technology shrinks the world, foreshortening space and conquering time. News that once took months or years to cross an ocean now flashes around the globe in seconds, and no people are more remote from the political present than the distance from a transistor radio or a short wave telephone. Orbiting satellites leave "footprints" that encompass the globe, overstepping national boundaries and treating national sovereignty like some charming vestige of a decrepit stone wall. The Vatican has embraced the innovations: indulgences are now granted via television to pious viewers hundreds of miles away. And even Jihadic warriors against modern technology use the worldwide web to get out their Luddite message.

We stand today on the threshold of a new generation of technology as potentially important to society as the printing press or the internal combustion engine. This technology is defined by computer chips, video equipment, electromagnetic tape, lasers, fiber optics, satellites, low-frequency transmission and, more significantly, by the revolution in information and communications made possible by combining these several low-price, high-speed, high-volume innovations. The possibilities for the mastery of time and space, and of knowledge and its transmission, offered by this complex, integrated technology seem almost limitless.

Can democracy, a form of government born in the ancient world and designed to bring small numbers of individuals with consensual interests together into a self-governing community where they might govern themselves directly, survive the conditions of modern mass society? Does technology help replicate the ancient conditions? Or does it underscore the distinctiveness of the modern condition? In 1752, Rousseau argued that the development of the arts and sciences had had a corrupting effect on politics and morals; has modern technology corrupted or improved our polity?

We know how profoundly simple innovations have affected social and political history in the past. Electric fences brought to an end two millennia of common grazing in Switzerland and altered the communal character of Swiss liberty; gunpowder revolutionized and ultimately democratized warfare, which was freed from the special skills of a warrior caste; the printing press destroyed both ecclesiastic and worldly priesthoods based on privileged knowledge and so, in undermining hierarchy, created the conditions for the Protestant Reformation and the rise of the democratic state; and, as George Ball said a decade ago in supporting the opening of a Fiat plant in the USSR, "the automobile is an ideology on four wheels."

Yet this is not to say that technology is wholly determining, that it overrides the plans, ideas, and institutions of man and writes its own history independent of human intentions. Where technology takes our political and social institutions will depend, in part, on where we take technology. Science and its products remain tools, and although the parable of the tools that come to enslave the tool-makers is an ancient one, it is not necessarily the only description of the modern technological dilemma. Rather, we must see technological determinism as one among a number of possible scenarios that depend at least in part on the choices we make about technology's use. If it enslaves us we will have chosen to act (or not act) in a fashion that permits our enslavement. I certainly do not share the neo-Luddite posture which makes the success of our free institutions depend on the suppression of technology. For better or worse, technology is with us; our fate will depend on how we use or abuse it. As with fire, gunpowder, and now atomic energy, all modern technology consists of discoveries that cannot be undiscovered, gifts of the gods that cannot be returned or exchanged. There is no way back to innocence for Prometheus; we are destined to learn to live with the booty of his visionary theft – or to die with it.

There are, in fact, at least three prospects for the future of technology and democracy – three scenarios of their relationship – that are within the realm of technological possibility. I will call them, rather fancifully, the Pangloss scenario, which is rooted in complacency and is simply a projection of current attitudes and trends; the Pandora scenario, which looks at the worst possible case in terms of the inherent dangers of technological determinism; and the Jeffersonian scenario, which seeks out the affirmative uses of the new technology in the nurturing of modern democratic life. In terms of the psychological moods they evoke, the three may be described as the posture of complacency, the posture of caution, and the posture of hope. We can aspire to hope and we should cultivate caution, but it is, of course, complacency that is most likely to attend and determine our actual future.

The Pangloss scenario

Anyone who reads good-time pop-futurology knows the penchant of the future mongers for Panglossian parody. Their view of the future is always relentlessly upbeat and ahistorical, mindlessly naive about power and corruption as conditioners of all human politics. Both former Speaker Newt Gingrich and Vice President Al Gore are techno-zealots who seem to believe that computers for the poor and hard-wired schools will

solve real social problems – that the technological present and the future it will naturally produce are wholly benevolent and without costs. Without either having consciously to plan to utilize technology to improve our lives, or having to worry about
the insidious consequences of such usage, we can rely on market forces to realize the
perfect technological society. The invisible hand governs this scenario, carrying with
it the presumption that market incentives such as profitability and consumer interest
will take technology in socially useful directions without planning of any kind.

Now it is certainly true that market forces push the new technologies in directions
that serve corporate efficiency, media communications, and consumer entertainment,
but it is not clear that they do anything for electoral efficiency, civic communication,
or political education. The untoward fate of Warner-Amex's now nearly ancient
"Qube" system – an innovation in interactive television that first promised interactive
communication with the screen via a five-position module – offers a vivid illustration.
Warner-Amex introduced the device into its Columbus, Ohio, cable system back in
the 1980s but on a purely commercial basis. Its primary use was for quick question-
answer polls, for so-called gong entertainment shows which permitted viewers to
"gong" acts they did not like off the air; and for video shipping, banking, and home
surveillance. Although Warner-Amex originally planned to introduce Qube into all of
the major cities they were cabling in the 1980s, lack of consumer interest led them to
cancel the project. The possibilities of the interactive use of Qube for electronic town
meetings, voter education, and elections were never considered, and apparently will
not be. With deregulation, the giveaway of digitalized broadcast spectra, and the
privatizing Federal Communications Act of 1996, commerce has trumped civics and
education. As private uses of the new technologies multiply, public uses vanish. Thus,
although several Western nations have developed videotex services aimed at public
information and the public weal, the USA continues to develop them exclusively for
commercial (primarily corporate) purposes. Video teleconferences are regular
features of corporate communications, but are only rarely resorted to in the civic
realm (for example, the Los Angeles Televote conducted in 1982 or Minnesota
E-Democracy, a popular civic web site in the 1990s). The privatization of the satellite
business and its attendant modes of world communication have also thrust this
important sector of the new technology into private hands. Recent failures in NASA's
space program point in the same direction, have also promoted pri-vate-sector
development, and what was once a public research venture is rapidly becoming the
shuttle payload business. What Bob Dole called the "giveaway" of the century, placed
digitalized spectra in the hands of private broadcasters for free!

Despite the absence of explicit political applications, the new technologies have
had a certain market impact on political culture and economic and social structure.
With the multiplication of communication spectra and the lowering of costs of
hardware over the last two decades, traditional views of the airwaves as limited
and therefore subject to private or (in the European case) public monopoly have
been challenged. Spectrum scarcity meant government ownership in Europe and
heavy government regulation in the USA. Spectrum abundance supposedly lessens
the dangers of private monopoly and thus the need for public monopoly. A 1979
Supreme Court decision in the USA ruled that spectrum abundance had antiquated
certain aspects of traditional Federal Communications regulations (the Federal

Communications Act of 1934) rooted in the First Amendment – equal time, for example, or the "Fairness Doctrine," which has recently been abandoned. A new doctrine to protect freedom of information and privacy in the cable/satellite/laser age has yet to be developed. Combine the possibilities of over 200 discrete cable spectra, low frequency and satellite broadcasting, and laser and fibre-optic technologies with the vertical integration of the new global communications monopolies like Murdoch's News Corporation, Disney's ABC, and Time-Warner's CNN, and the hold of government broadcast corporations on the airwaves is patently loosened.

For a while in the USA it appeared as though new cable networks like Ted Turner's and superstations that utilized satellite broadcast capabilities would offer a major challenge to the monopoly-like networks, and create a genuinely competitive market. Increasingly, the problem faced by democracies seemed no longer to be Big Brother (George Orwell imagined two-way television surveillance in Nineteen Eighty-Four) but a host of complacent little cousins – a plethora of broadcasting sources that would inundate the public in programming and divide the population into a series of discrete markets, each one the particular target of new "narrowcasting" strategies. In a 1982 essay, I warned against the fragmenting effect this might have on the integral American nation which heretofore had been protected from regional parochialisms by the national hearthside of network television. At the same time, I suggested that the new technological diversity might, for the first time, allow information and communication sovereignty to pass from the hands of the producers with monopolies over limited spectra to consumers who, because they now had literally hundreds of choices, could assume genuine responsibilities for what they saw and listened to. Indeed, the new plenitude appeared to challenge national sovereignty too, for anyone with a satellite dish was now able to tune into broadcasts from around the world. Armed with a VCR, a cable hookup, a satellite dish, and a television set, consumers could construct a world of entertainment and information geared to their own tastes, their own schedules, and their own needs. To this degree, the new technologies, by favoring decentralization, the multiplication of choice, and consumer sovereignty, did inadvertently benefit democratic political culture.

But in the last few years, other less benevolent market forces have conspired to work against these developments. The theoretical availability of multiple spectra has not been matched by real program or information diversification, or by any real increase in the power of the consumer over programming. This is due in part to the uncompetitive character of the real markets in hardware, software, and programming, and a surge of corporate takeovers that has shrunk this market still more. A limited number of programming and software giants have emerged from the sorting out process as monopolistic purveyors of information, news, and entertainment. Despite the fact that outlets for their product have multiplied, there has been little real substantive diversification. Thus, despite the presence of hundreds of television channels, cable stations have remained content to mimic the networks, or run movies, or develop "narrowcast" programming aimed at special audiences (religious, Spanish-speaking, sports, etc.) in search of certain profits. Although consumers are freed from traditional time constraints by video recorders and can watch live, record programs to watch at a time of their choice, or rent or buy video cassettes or laser discs, the actual content available is pretty much identical with what was available on the networks ten years ago. Moreover, the development of programming remains in the hands of the same few production companies that have always controlled films and entertainment. Indeed, such independence as the networks possessed is being eroded by their corporate takeover and subordination to global companies that also own newspapers, magazines, publishing houses, film studios, sports teams, and theme parks. Murdoch, Disney, and Turner each own baseball teams and networks on which to show games. And each has gone global, competing for spectators in Teheran and Beijing as well as New York and London.

Elsewhere in the world, television companies (mostly national) take their cue from the English-speaking networks in the USA and the UK. Reruns of old suspense and comedy programs lead the schedule on most such networks (including those in countries with radical ideologies). Contradictions abound – The Cosby Show (about an average American black family) was the most watched program in pre-liberated South Africa; Dallas (about the sexual and business escapades of the rich and meretricious in Texas) is popular in the Third World; accented mini-series from the BBC and Thames Television continue to draw a rapt American viewing audience that cannot get enough of the Royal Family it abandoned two hundred years ago; and violent, racist films like Rambo are regularly shown in Asia (where Rambo's Asian enemies are made to seem Arab in the overdub) and, on easily available black market cassettes, in Russia, Pakistan, and Indonesia. No wonder Thomas L. McPhail entitled his book on international broadcasting Electronic Colonialism.

In fact, for all of its technological potential for diversification, the domination of these new technologies by the market (or by the corporate monopolies that the market conceals) assures that to a growing degree, the profit-making entertainment industry in the Anglo-American world will control what is seen, felt, and thought around the globe (the primary concern of my book Jihad versus McWorld). It is hardly surprising that nations elsewhere are demanding a new information order. Though this demand is often construed in the West (to a degree correctly) as resulting from the tyrannical impulse to control information, it must also be viewed as a desperate reaction to the market tyranny already being exercised over world communication by Anglo-American programming and software monopolies.

None of this denies the potential of the new technology for efficient planning and information enhancement. Teleconferencing, videotex, and the interactive possibilities of this technology are being systematically exploited in the commercial world by corporations bent on enhancing efficiency through enhancing information and communication. But this has meant that a technology whose cheapness and universality promises a new communicative egalitarianism is, in fact, replicating in the domain of information the inequality that otherwise characterizes market relations in the West. Increasingly a gap can be described between information-rich and information-poor segments of Western nations – the former, technologically literate and able to utilize the new technologies to gain mastery over their commercial and political environments; the latter, technologically illiterate and thrown more and more to the periphery of a society where power and status are dependent on information and communication.

I do not mean to suggest here a conscious attempt at control or at the sustaining of nonegalitarianism on the part of those who are major players in the "free" market – although the evidence presented here would not be inconsistent with such an interpretation. I do mean to say that even at its most innocent, the market is likely to have an impact on free and developing societies in ways unforeseen by the happy futurologists; that, at best, the market will do nothing for uses of the new technology that do not have obvious commercial or entertainment or corporate payoffs, and, at worst, will enhance uses that undermine equality and, freedom. Nor has anything happened in the decade since I first advanced this skeptical thesis to suggest my pessimism was misplaced.

The Pandora scenario

Pangloss is a peril to every society, but the greater danger to democracy comes from Pandora's scenario, which envisions what might happen if a government consciously set out to utilize the new technologies for purposes of standardization, control, or repression. Clearly the new technology, which facilitates centralization of control over information and communication, enables government to retain files and "keep tabs" on all computer and telephonic communications, and makes new kinds of surveillance possible, can be a powerful weapon in the hands of a controlling political or economic elite, Brute tyrants must control, by brute force, which requires constant physical control over subjects; subtle tyrants possess their subjects' hearts and minds through the control of education, information, and communication and, thereby, turn subjects into allies in the enterprise of servitude. The new technologies enhance this subtle form of control and give government instruments of indirect surveillance and control unlike any known to traditional dictators.

Nor need abuses be planned by elites conspiring to repress. The citizens of Sweden recently learned that a number of young men had been the unknowing subjects of a twenty year longitudinal surveillance that, in the name of a social scientific project, "keeps tabs" on their economic, social, personal, and sexual lives – without their knowledge (let alone permission). Credit and insurance organizations in the USA and Europe are assembling mammoth information files on clients, files that are for the most part held and used at the company's own discretion without any government regulation. The Qube system offered a surveillance mode that transmitted electronic reports to a central office on the comings and goings of all residents; what and when they watched television, when lights went on and off, and so forth. Warner-Amex corporate officers "promised discretion" – a guarantee somewhat less ironclad than the Bill of Rights. Computer banking, increasingly common throughout Europe and the USA, leaves a permanent trail of files on financial transactions that permit those with access to learn the details of an individual's financial life.

Clearly the costs to privacy of the efficient operation of this new technology can be very high; neither can the individual be secured by traditional print media protections. The Fairness Doctrine, as developed by the Federal Communications Act of 1934, was not adapted to the new technology and has thus been laid aside. A number of commentators, including John Wicklein, Ithiel de Sola Pool, and David Burnham (erstwhile communications specialist for The New York Times), have decried the dangers to privacy and the individual posed by technological innovations. Fred Friendly, onetime head of CBS news, called for an "electronic bill of rights." Twenty years after his appeal, no such bill is in sight. On the contrary, privacy issues seem to have been privatized, left to the whims of bankers, merchandisers, and other commercial users of the new technology.

Moreover, despite the diversification of communications and information channels made possible by the new technologies, control and ownership of the corporations that manufacture hardware and software and create news, information, and entertainment programming remain in the hands of a few super-corporations that exercise an effective monopoly or, as in France (and despite the recent accrediting of a private television network), of a government monopoly. Between them, the conglomerates that now control hardware, software, programming, and financing control a preponderance of what is made and produced in the communications/information field. These media giants make nonsense of the theoretical diversification of the technology. While minor players like Apple can still play the game, the large corporations generally let them take the risks and then buy out or imitate the successes, or are taken over by them. The individual entrepreneur may still make a profit on his risk-taking, but the public is deprived of genuine competition or a real market choice. This is the essence of the U.S. government's current antitrust suit against Microsoft.

The entertainment business provides a powerful lesson. As the television industry takes over the film industry and the film industry takes over Broadway and the West End, the English-speaking theater ceases to exist as a cultural artifact and becomes another small cog in the great profit-making entertainment machine of the major media corporations. Shown on the hundreds of cable networks nowadays are mostly network reruns, third-rate movies never released to the theater chains, and sporting events. Innovation is commercially unviable and little supported. The "cultural" channels have mostly gone under for lack of funding, the public access channels are underutilized and unwatched (cable franchisers are often asked to put aside a channel for public access by the licensing municipality, but are never required to put aside funds to train people in the use of television, or to make available directorial and production support for groups wishing to avail themselves of public air time). Thus, no one watches. That's the market, say the cable companies (as if they would offer amateur underfunded programming of that kind to their paying viewers). The UK's Channel 4 is ingeniously financed and has developed some new programming, but it also specializes in upscale American prime-time programming (Hill Street Blues, St. Elsewhere, and Cheers, for example).

If then we measure power by the potential for monopoly and control over information and communication, it is evident that the new technology can become a dangerous facilitator of tyranny. Even in the absence of conscious government abuse, this potential can constrict our freedom, encroach on our privacy, and damage our political equality. There is no tyranny more dangerous than an invisible and benign tyranny, one in which subjects are complicit in their victimization, and in which enslavement is a product of circumstance rather than intention. Technology need not inevitably corrupt democracy, but its potential for benign dominion cannot be ignored.

The Jeffersonian scenario

Despite the potential of the telecommunications market for inequality and of the technology it supports for abuse, the new technologies, in themselves, can also offer powerful assistance to the life of democracy. A free society is free only to the degree that its citizens are informed and that communication among them is open and informed. Although among the three scenarios sketched here, the Jeffersonian is the least probable and, given current trends, unlikely to become more probable, it remains both technologically feasible and politically attractive. As Nicholas Johnson, former chairman of the Federal Communications Commission (FCC) noted some time ago, "the ultimate promise of the new technology is the rebuilding of community." In this sense, a guarded optimism is possible about technology and democracy, but only if citizen groups and governments take action in adapting the new technology to their needs.

At the outset, I noted that democracy is a form of government that depends on information and communication. It is obvious then that new technologies of information and communications can be nurturing to democracy. They can challenge passivity, they can enhance information equality, they can overcome sectarianism and prejudice, and they can facilitate participation in deliberative political processes.

Traditional media emphasize active programming and passive spectatorship. The new technology's interactive capability permits viewers to become active both as choosers of what they watch and respondents to programming (via interactive television, information network hookups, and public access cable channels). The old picture of passive television viewers glued to their sets for seven docile hours of complacent viewing can now be challenged by active users of a complex computer/telephone/video set-up, who utilize the system to enhance their public and private lives. Linked together horizontally by a point-to-point medium like the internet, citizens can subvert political hierarchy and nurture an unmediated civic communication.

The educational potential of computer information networks and interactive television is very great and, when appropriately subsidized, allows equal access to information by all citizens. Computer terminals equipped with user-friendly programs and manned by user-friendly technicians, if housed at public libraries, town halls, and other public places, could place the world-wide-web's enormous banks of information available through computer networks at the disposal of the general public. Governments could offer their own networks providing information on employment, housing, zoning regulation, small business laws, and other matters of public concern. Private networks might be persuaded to offer service to public terminals at cost as a pro bonum return on the profits their use of public airwaves and wire make possible. Anyone can create a website and initiate communication.

The possibilities of using the interactive capabilities of recent television and internet technology for civic education has been underexplored. Networks run instant telephone polls on controversial debates ("are you for or against a nuclear freeze?") after half an hour of opinionated sparring by warring "experts," but have not tried to structure several programs over time aimed at actually informing opinion and giving issues full deliberation. Yet the technology is there to do so. The few times that it has been used, it has achieved unusual successes. The experiment with a civic network that began as a senior citizen and shut-in network in Reading, Pennsylvania; the "televote" experiments in New Zealand, Hawaii, and Los Angeles; and the League of Women Voters' three state teleconferences in New York – New Jersey – Connecticut are but three examples of the technology's civic possibilities. More recently, "Project Vote Smart" has opened a much used internet voter information site.

A third use of the new technology has been implicit in electronic communications from the start of the radio and television era: the overcoming of regional parochialism, local prejudice, and national chauvinism. Technology has made the metaphor of the global village an electronic reality. Satellite "footprints" know no borders and individuals or communities with a satellite dish (and perhaps a descrambler) can tune in on the world. The world-wide-web, unlike the World Series, is actually world wide. It makes closed societies difficult to maintain, and information blackouts a contradiction in terms.

In order to be something more than the government of mass prejudice, democracy must escape the tyranny of opinion. Television often merely reinforces opinion and prejudice, but its global character and capacity for interactive communication also enable it to overcome them and sustain rational discourse and citizen education. It can, to be sure, permit instant plebiscites of the most dangerous kind where unthinking prejudices are numerically recorded to establish the momentary shape of mass prejudice on an issue (these plebiscitary dangers have been noted by various liberal critics of the new technology who, however, seem Luddite in their prejudice against alternatives uses). But it also permits ongoing communication and deliberation among individuals and (via electronic town meetings) communities that can inform and improve democracy.

Imagine a situation in which the state of California wishes to offer a referendum to its citizens on a law banning Sunday retail commerce. Normally, the private sector would go to work on voters, plying them with expensive advertisements portraying the loss to the economy of Sunday closings, and church and the retail industry would indulge in a war of publicists. Voters, having passively received this bounty of misinformation, would eventually be constrained to vote their prejudices (religion versus convenience) and the matter would be "democratically" resolved. Yet with the assistance of the new technologies a very different scenario can be imagined. Every township and municipality in California might, for example, call a town meeting to discuss an issue initially. The state might fund a neutral documentary maker to produce a one hour special on the issue, which might be shown on television prior to a debate by proponents of each side. A second set of town meetings would follow this, including a video hookup (teleconference) of urban and rural meetings to let different parts of the state understand how the issue was being discussed elsewhere. This could be followed by a final debate on television coupled with an interactive hookup permitting home viewers to pose questions to the "experts." Such a multiple-phase process involving information, adversarial debate, and the direct engagement by citizens within their local communities, and among the communities and the experts would offer genuine civic education. More public-regarding ways of looking at problems could emerge, and the final decision on the referendum would be both informed and more public-minded. The cumulative effect on the political competence of the electorate of a series of such procedures, replicated on different issues over several years, would be immense. The state of Oregon used a people's parliament method to develop a state health plan in the early 1990s: today we can technologically enhance that method with the internet.

The institutional tools necessary to realize this scenario are not beyond our reach. A "Civic Communicative Co-operative" in the USA would permit an independent public corporation to oversee civic uses of the new media, and perhaps establish a model program channel. Local municipalities responsible for franchising cable operators could insist on institutional networks, public access channels with personnel and technical support, and public information terminals as a condition of a cable franchise or a network license (most municipalities focus on the number and entertainment quality of program channels and rarely raise issues of civic education and information).

It is then the will and not the way that is missing at present. Certainly Thomas Jefferson would not be disappointed to learn that technology has made possible a quality and degree of communication among citizens and between citizens and bureaucrats, experts, and their information banks he could not have dreamed of. It was always Jefferson's belief that the inadequacies of democracy were best remedied by more democracy: that civic incompetence was not a reason to disempower citizens, but empowerment a remedy to redress incompetence.

Which democracy? Progress for whom?

The new technologies – not only television, including cable networks, but also computers and the internet – can potentially enhance lateral communication among citizens, can open access to information by all, and can furnish citizens with communication links across distances that once precluded direct democracy. Yet there is a formidable obstacle in the way of implementation of these technologies: unless we are clear about what democracy means to us, and what kind of democracy we envision, technology is as likely to stunt as to enhance the civic polity. Is it representative democracy, plebiscitary democracy, or deliberative democracy for which we seek technological implementation? The differences between the three are not only theoretically crucial, but have radically different entailments with respect to technology.

Do we aspire to further the representative system, a democracy rooted in the election of accountable deputies who do all the real work of governing? Most advocates of this form of indirect democracy are properly suspicious of the new technologies and their penchant for immediacy, directness, lateral communication, and undeliberativeness. Or is it plebiscitary majoritarianism we seek, a democracy that embodies majority opinions assembled from the unconsidered prejudices of private persons voting private interests? New technology can be a dangerously facile instrument of such unchecked majoritarianism: the net affords politicians an instrument for perpetual polling that can aggravate the focus group mentality that many rue as Dick Morris's political legacy. Will any politicians ever again gather the courage to lead in the face of a technology that makes following so easy?

Yet if we are in search of what I have called "strong democracy," a democracy that reflects the careful and prudent judgment of citizens who participate in deliberative, selfgoverning communities, we will need to tease out of the technology other capabilities. If democracy is to be understood as deliberative and participatory activity on the part of responsible citizens, it will have to resist the innovative forms of demagoguery that accompany innovative technology and that are too often overlooked by enthusiasts, and listen carefully to those like Theodore Becker and James Fishkin, who have tried to incorporate deliberative constraints into their direct democratic uses of the technologies.[1] In other words, it turns out there is no simple or general answer to the question "Is the technology democratizing?" until we have made clear what sort of democracy we intend. Home voting via interactive television might further privatize politics and replace deliberative debate in public with the unconsidered instant expression of private prejudices, turning what ought to be public decisions into private consumerlike choices; but deliberative television polling of the kind envisioned by James Fishkin can offset such dangers, while the use of the internet for deliberation across communities can actually render decision making less parochial.[2] In politics, fast is often bad, slow sometimes good.

Strong democracy calls not only for votes but for good reasons; not only for an opinion but for a rational argument on its behalf. Those who once preferred open to secret ballots, who preferred open debate about well-grounded viewpoints to closed votes aggregating personal interests, will today prefer technologies that permit frank interactive debate with real identities revealed to technologies that allow game playing and privately registered, unsupported opinions.

Traditional proponents of Madisonian representative democracy are likely to find much of the new interactive technology intimidating, since it threatens to overwhelm what they regard as a pristine system assuring government by expert politicians with a free-for-all among "ignorant" masses who swamp the polity with their endless demands and overheated prejudices. Such critics already complain that traditional broadcast television is destructive of party identity and party discipline, and they will properly worry about technologies that further erode the boundaries between the governors and the governed. Plebiscitary democrats will be mindlessly enthralled by interactive instant polling and imagine a time when private consumers make precedent-shattering public choices with no more serious thought than they give to which button to hit when they are surfing a hundred-channel cable system. "Let's see," mutters the glib new net surfer, "do I want to play checkers or outlaw abortion? Do I prefer Sylvester Stallone to Bill Clinton? Shall we download the 'Playmate of the Month' or vote to expand NATO to the Russian border? Time for a mock battle with Darth Vader on my Star Wars simulation. . . . Or should I just declare war for real on Libya?" Deliberative democrats can only shudder at such prospects, insisting that they do more to destroy than to enhance democracy. Deliberation, on the other hand, does require intervention, education, facilitation, and mediation – all anathema to devotees of an anarchic and wholly user-controlled net whose whole point is to circumvent facilitation, editing, and other "top-down" forms of intervention.

Technology can then help democracy, but only if programmed to do so and only in terms of the paradigms and political theories that inform the program. Left to the market, it is likely only to reproduce the vices of politics as usual. How different is the anonymous flaming that typifies certain kinds of internet chatter from the anonymous vilification that characterizes talk radio and scream television? Will the newer technologies be any less likely to debase the political currency, any less likely to foster sound-bite decision making rather than sound political judgment?

By the same token, if those who deploy the technologies consciously seek a more participatory, deliberative form of strong democracy and a newly robust civil society, they can also find in telecommunications innovation an extraordinarily effective ally. The trouble with the zealots of technology as an instrument of democratic liberation is not that they misconceive technology but that they fail to understand democracy. They insist that market-generated technology can, all by itself and in the complete absence of common human willing and political cooperation, produce liberty, social responsibility, and citizenship. The viruses that eat up our computer programs, like sarin in the Tokyo subway, are but obvious symbols of technology's ever-present dark side, the monster who lurks in Dr. Frankenstein's miraculous creation.

With participatory interaction comes the peril of political and economic surveil-lance.[3] With interactive personal preference modules comes the risk of majoritarian tyranny. With digital reasoning comes the danger that adversarial modes of thought will inundate consensus and obliterate common ground. Computer literacy cannot finally exist independently of lifelong educational literacy. The age of information can reinforce extant inequalities, we have noted, making the resource- and income-poor the information-poor as well.[4] The irony is that those who might most benefit from the net's democratic and informational potential are least likely to have access to it, the tools to gain access, or the educational background to take advantage of the tools. Those with access, on the other hand, tend to be those already empowered in the system by education, income, and literacy.

And how easily liberating technologies become tools of repression. As consumers tell shopping networks what they want to buy and tell banks how to dispense their cash and tell pollsters what they think about abortion, those receiving the information gain access to an extensive computer bank of knowledge about the private habits, attitudes, and behaviors of consumers and citizens. This information may in turn be used to reshape those habits and attitudes in ways that favor producers and sellers working the marketplace or the political arena. Moreover, the current antiregulatory fever has assured that the new data banks being compiled from interaction and surveillance are subject neither to government scrutiny nor to limitation or control – a sunset provision, for example, that would periodically destroy all stored information.[5] The model of Channel One, an invidious classroom network founded by Chris Whittle's Whittle Communications (and now owned by the K-III Corporation), which extorts classroom advertising time from needy schools in return for des-perately wanted hardware, suggests that the public is likely to be served by the new technologies only in as far as someone can make serious money off it.[6]

It may be a cause of satisfaction, as Walter Wriston insists, that nowadays it is the citizen who is watching Big Brother and not the other way around. But if Big Brother is no longer watching you, nor is he watching those who are watching you, and even adversaries of regulation may find reason to be disturbed by that omission. If the classical liberal question used to be, who will police the police? the pertinent liberal question in today's McWorld ought to be, who will watch those who are watching the watchers? Who will prevent the media from controlling their clients and consumers? Who will act in lieu of a government that has demurred from representing the public's

interests? These are issues for democratic deliberation and decision, not for technological resolution. For technology remains a tool allied to particular conceptions
of democracy; if we know what kind of democracy we want, it can enhance civic
communication and expand citizen literacy. Left to markets, (and that is where it is
presently being left), it is likely to augment McWorld's least worthy imperatives,
including surveillance over and manipulation of opinion, and the cultivation of
artificial needs rooted in lifestyle "choices" unconnected to real economic, civic, or
spiritual needs.

If democracy is to benefit from technology then, we must start not with technology but with politics. Having a voice, demanding a voice, in the making of
science and technology policy is the first step citizens can take in assuring a democratic technology.[7] The new technology is still only an instrument of communication, and it cannot determine what we will say or to whom we will say it. There is a
story about the wireless pioneer Guglielmo Marconi who, when told by his associates that his new wireless technology meant he could now "talk to Florida," asked,
presciently, "And do we have anything to say to Florida?" Enthusiasts exalt over the
fact that on the net we can talk to strangers throughout the world. But many of
today's problems arise from the fact that we no longer know how to talk to our
husbands and wives, our neighbors and fellow citizens, let alone strangers. Will our
blockages and incivilities locally be overcome by the miracles of long-distance computer communication? Will virtual community heal the ruptures of real communities? Will we do on our keyboards what we have notably failed to do face to
face?

If in the coming millennium – a millennium in which technology is likely to
dominate our lives as never before – we want democracy to be served, then the
bittersweet fruits of science will have to be subordinated to our democratic ends and
made to serve as a facilitator rather than a corruptor of our precious democracy. And
whether this happens will depend not on the quality and character of our technology
but on the quality of our political institutions and the character of our citizens.

Notes

1   See Theodore Becker, "Televote: Interactive, Participatory Polling" in Becker and
     R. A. Couto, Teaching Democracy by Being Democratic (Westport, CT: Praeger,
     1996).
2   James Fishkin has devised a deliberative technique that brings citizens together
     for several days and permits them to interact with one another and with experts,
     so that their views are not merely registered but pondered and modified. In 1993,
     Channel Four in the United Kingdom broadcast an exemplary weekend of
     Fishkin's project; a similar broadcast was shown on public television during the
     1996 American presidential elections. For details, see Fishkin's Democracy and
     Deliberation (New Haven: Yale University Press, 1991).
3   Precisely because it is interactive, new telecommunications technology "learns"
     about its users as its users learn about it. A system that "knows" what you buy,
     how you pay for it, what your consumer and political preferences are, and even
     (in programs providing home security) when you leave and when you come

home, and which then stores and disseminates such information in the absence of any regulatory safeguards, is hardly a system political skeptics should trust.

4   Robert Reich has drawn an American portrait in which privileged information/ communication workers increasingly withdraw public support from the larger society as they move to insular suburbs, with private recreational, schooling, security, and sanitation services for their own walled communities, which the public at large can no longer afford. Their withdrawal (Reich labels it the politics of secession) leaves the poor poorer, the public sector broke, and society ever more riven by economic disparities that technology reinforces. Robert Reich, "The New Community" in The Work of Nations (New York: Knopf, 1991), chap. 23.

5   An early and prophetic book about the problems of electronic surveillance is John Wicklein's Electronic Nightmare: The Home Communications Set and Your Freedom (Boston: Beacon Press, 1981).

6   Channel One currently is in about twelve thousand junior high and high schools. It loans free televisions, VCRs, and a satellite dish to schools (usually needy ones) willing to dish up two minutes of soft news, three minutes of commercials, and nine minutes of infotainment to its students during regular school hours. Channel One sells spots for up to $195,000 for a thirty-second ad, and has attracted many of the corporations on McWorld's frontier, including Pepsi and Reebok. In 1994, Chris Whittle sold the network for nearly $240 million to K-III, an "educational" publisher.

7   This suggests that science and technology policy need themselves to be subjected to democratic scrutiny. Technology should not try to produce an appropriate democracy; democracy should try to produce an appropriate technology. Experts in technology are not experts in the appropriate public uses of technology. Richard Sclove's project on community science boards speaks to these issues: Democracy and Technology (Cambridge, MA: MIT Press, 1995).

4.3

Citizens,
by Cass Sunstein

The authors of the American Constitution met behind closed doors in Philadelphia during the summer of 1787. When they completed their labors, the American public was, naturally enough, exceedingly curious about what they had done. A large crowd gathered around what is now known as Convention Hall. One of its members asked Benjamin Franklin, as he emerged from the building, "What have you given us?" Franklin's answer was hopeful, or perhaps a challenge: "A republic, if you can keep it." In fact we should see Franklin's remark as a reminder of a continuing obligation. The text of any founding document is likely to be far less important, in maintaining a republic, than the actions and commitments of the nation's citizenry over time.

This suggestion raises questions of its own. What is the relationship between our choices and our freedom? Between citizens and consumers? And how do the answers relate to the question whether, and how, government should deal with people's emerging power to filter speech content?

In this chapter my basic claim is that we should evaluate new communications technologies, including the Internet, by asking how they affect us as citizens, not mostly, and certainly not only, by asking how they affect us as consumers. A central question is whether emerging social practices, including consumption patterns, are promoting or compromising our own highest aspirations. More particularly I make two suggestions, designed to undermine, from a new direction, the idea that consumer sovereignty is the appropriate goal for communications policy.

The first suggestion is that people's preferences do not come from nature or from the sky. They are a product, at least in part, of social circumstances, including existing institutions, available options, and past choices. Prominent among the circumstances that create preferences are markets themselves. "Free marketeers have little to cheer about if all they can claim is that the market is efficient at filling desires that the market itself creates."[1] Unrestricted consumer choices are important, sometimes very important. But they do not exhaust the idea of freedom, and they should not be equated with it.

The second suggestion has to do with the fact that in their capacity as citizens, people often seek policies and goals that diverge from the choices they make in their capacity as consumers. If citizens do this, there is no legitimate objection from the standpoint of freedom – at least if citizens are not using the law to disfavor any particular point of view or otherwise violating rights. Often citizens attempt to promote their highest aspirations through democratic institutions. If the result is to produce a communications market that is different from what individual consumers would seek – if as citizens we produce a market, for example, that promotes exposure to serious issues and a range of shared experiences – freedom will be promoted, not undermined.

The two points are best taken together. Citizens are often aware that their private choices, under a system of limitless options, may lead in unfortunate directions, both for them as individuals and for society at large. They might believe, for example, that their own choices, with respect to television and the Internet, do not promote their own well-being, or that of society as a whole. They might attempt to restructure alternatives and institutions so as to improve the situation.

At the same time, I suggest that even insofar as we are consumers, new purchasing opportunities, made ever more available through the Internet, are far less wonderful than we like to think. The reason is that these opportunities are accelerating the "consumption treadmill," in which we buy more and better goods not because they make us happier or better off but because they help us keep up with others. As citizens, we might well seek to slow down this treadmill, so as to ensure that social resources are devoted, not to keeping up with one another, but to goods and services that really improve our lives.

Choices and circumstances: the formation and deformation of preferences

Many people seem to think that freedom consists in respect for consumption choices, whatever their origins and content. Indeed, this thought appears to underlie enthusiasm for the principle of consumer sovereignty itself. On this view, the central goal of a well-functioning system of free expression is to ensure unrestricted choice. A similar conception of freedom underlies many of the celebrations of emerging communications markets.

It is true that a free society is generally respectful of people's choices. But freedom imposes certain preconditions, ensuring not just respect for choices and the satisfaction of preferences, whatever they happen to be, but also the free formation of desires and beliefs. Most preferences and beliefs do not preexist social institutions; they are formed and shaped by existing arrangements. Much of the time, people develop tastes for what they are used to seeing and experiencing. If you are used to seeing stories about the local sports team, your interest in the local sports team is likely to increase. If news programming deals with a certain topic – say, welfare reform or a current threat of war – your taste for that topic is likely to be strengthened. And when people are deprived of opportunities, they are likely to adapt and to develop preferences and tastes for what little they have. We are entitled to say that the deprivation of opportunities is a deprivation of freedom – even if people have adapted to it and do not want anything more.

Similar points hold for the world of communications. If people are deprived of access to competing views on public issues, and if as a result they lack a taste for those views, they lack freedom, whatever the nature of their preferences and choices. If people are exposed mostly to sensationalistic coverage of the lives of movie stars, or only to sports, or only to left-of-center views, and never to international issues, their preferences will develop accordingly. There is, in an important respect, a problem from the standpoint of freedom itself. This is so even if people are voluntarily choosing the limited fare.

The general idea here – that preferences and beliefs are a product of existing institutions and practices and that the result can be a form of unfreedom, one of the most serious of all – is hardly new. It is a longstanding theme in political and legal thought. Thus Tocqueville wrote of the effects of the institution of slavery on the desires of many slaves themselves: "Plunged in this abyss of wretchedness, the Negro hardly notices his ill fortune; he was reduced to slavery by violence, and the habit of servitude has given him the thoughts and ambitions of a slave; he admires his tyrants even more than he hates them and finds his joy and pride in servile imitation of his oppressors."[2] In the same vein, John Dewey wrote that "social conditions may restrict, distort, and almost prevent the development of individuality." He insisted that we should therefore "take an active interest in the working of social institutions that have a bearing, positive or negative, upon the growth of individuals." For Dewey, a just society "is as much interested in the positive construction of favorable institutions, legal, political, and economic, as it is in the work of removing abuses and overt oppressions."[3] More recently, Robert Frank and Philip Cook have urged that in the communications market, existing "financial incentives strongly favor sensational, lurid and formulaic offerings" and that the resulting structure of rewards is "especially troubling in light of evidence that, beginning in infancy and continuing through life, the things we see and read profoundly alter the kinds of people we become."[4]

Every tyrant knows that it is important, and sometimes possible, not only to constrain people's actions but also to manipulate their desires, partly by making people fearful, partly by putting certain options in an unfavorable light, partly by limiting information. And nontyrannical governments are hardly neutral with respect to preferences and desires. They hope to have citizens who are active rather than passive, curious rather than indifferent, engaged rather than inert. Indeed, the basic institutions of private property and freedom of contract – fundamental to free societies and indeed to freedom of speech – have important effects on the development of preferences themselves. Thus both private property and freedom of contract have long been defended, not on the ground that they are neutral with respect to preferences, but on the ground that they help to form good preferences – by producing an entrepreneurial spirit and by encouraging people to see one another, not as potential enemies, or as members of different ethnic groups, but as potential trading partners.[5] The right to free speech is itself best seen as part of the project of helping to produce an engaged, self-governing citizenry.

Limited options: of foxes and sour grapes

When government imposes restrictions on people's opportunities and information, it is likely to undermine freedom not merely by affecting their choices but also by affecting their preferences and desires. Of course this is what concerned Tocqueville and Dewey, and in unfree nations, we can find numerous examples in the area of communications and media policy, as official censorship prevents people from learning about a variety of ideas and possibilities. This was common practice in communist nations, and both China and Singapore have sought to reduce general access to the Internet, partly in an effort to shape both preferences and beliefs. When information is unavailable and when opportunities are shut off, and known to be shut off, people may not end up not wanting them at all.

The social theorist Jon Elster illustrates the point through the old tale of the fox and the sour grapes.[6] The fox does not want the grapes, because he believes them to be sour, but the fox believes them to be sour because they are unavailable, and he adjusts his attitude toward the grapes in a way that takes account of their unavailability. The fox cannot have the grapes, and so he concludes that they are sour and that he doesn't want them. Elster says, quite rightly, that the unavailability of the grapes cannot be justified by reference to the preferences of the fox, when the unavailability of the grapes is the very *reason* for the preferences of the fox.

Elster's suggestion is that citizens who have been deprived of options may not want the things of which they have been deprived; and the deprivation cannot be justified by reference to the fact that citizens are not asking for these things, when they are not asking *because* they have been deprived of them. In the area of communications and media policy, it follows that a system of few or dramatically limited options – including, for example, an official government news program and nothing else – cannot reasonably be defended, even if there is little or no public demand for further options. The absence of the demand is likely to be a product of the deprivation. It does not justify the deprivation. This point holds with respect to television stations and the Internet as with everything else.

Thus far I have been making arguments for a range of opportunities, even in societies in which people, lacking such opportunities, are not asking for more. Of course the issue is very different in the communications universe that is the main topic of this book – one in which people have countless possibilities from which to choose. But here too social circumstances, including markets, affect preferences, not only the other way around. From the standpoint of citizenship, and freedom as well, problems also emerge when people are choosing alternatives that sharply limit their own horizons.

Preferences are a product not only of the number of options but also of what markets accentuate and of past choices, and those choices can impose constraints of their own. Suppose, for example, that one person's choices have been limited to sports, and lead him to learn little about political issues; that another person focuses only on national issues, because she has no interest in what happens outside American borders; and that still another restricts himself to material that reaffirms his own political convictions. In different ways, each of these person's choices constrains both citizenship and freedom, simply because it dramatically narrows their field of interests and concerns. This is not a claim that people should be required to see things that do not interest them; it is a more mundane point about how any existing market, and our own choices, can limit or expand our freedom.

Indeed people are often aware of this fact, and make choices so as to promote wider understanding and better formation of their own preferences. Sometimes we select radio and television programs and Websites from which we will learn something, even if the programs and the sites we choose are more demanding and less fun than the alternatives. And we may even lament the very choices that we make, on the ground that what we have done, as consumers, does not serve our long-term interests. Whether or not people actually lament their choices, they sometimes have good reason to do so, and they know this without saying so.

These points underlie some of the most important functions of public forums and of general interest intermediaries. Both of these produce unanticipated exposures that help promote the free formation of preferences, even in a world of numerous options. In this sense, they are continuous with the educational system. Indeed they provide a kind of continuing education for adults, something that a free society cannot do without. It does not matter whether the government is directly responsible for the institutions that perform this role. What matters is that they exist.

Democratic institutions and consumer sovereignty

None of these points means that some abstraction called "government" should feel free to move preferences and beliefs in what it considers to be desirable directions. The central question is whether citizens in a democratic system, aware of the points made thus far, might want to make choices that diverge from those that they make in their capacity as private consumers. Sometimes this does appear to be their desire. What I am suggesting is that when this is the case, there is, in general, no legitimate objection if government responds. The public's effort to counteract the adverse effects of consumer choices should not be disparaged as a form of government meddling or unacceptable paternalism, at least if the government is democratic and reacting to the reflective judgments of the citizenry.

What we think and what we want often depends on the social role in which we find ourselves, and the role of citizen is very different from the role of consumer. Citizens do not think and act as consumers. Indeed, most citizens have no difficulty in distinguishing between the two. Frequently a nation's political choices could not be understood if viewed only as a process of implementing people's desires in their capacity as consumers. For example, some people support efforts to promote serious coverage of public issues on television, even though their own consumption patterns favor situation comedies; they seek stringent laws protecting the environment or endangered species, even though they do not use the public parks or derive material benefits from protection of such species; they approve of laws calling for social secur-ity and welfare even though they do not save or give to the poor; they support antidis-crimination laws even though their own behavior is hardly race- or gender-neutral. The choices people make as political participants seem systematically different from those they make as consumers.

Why is this? Is it a puzzle or a paradox? The most basic answer is that people's behavior as citizens reflects a variety of distinctive influences. In their role as citizens, people might seek to implement their highest aspirations in political behavior when they do not do so in private consumption. They might aspire to communications system of a particular kind, one that promotes democratic goals, and they might try to promote that aspiration through law. Acting in the fashion of Ulysses anticipating the Sirens, people might "precommit" themselves, in democratic processes, to a course of action that they consider to be in the general interest. And in their capacity as citizens, they might attempt to satisfy altruistic or other-regarding desires, which diverge from the self-interested preferences often characteristic of the behavior of consumers in markets. In fact social and cultural norms often incline people to express aspirational or altruistic goals more often in political behavior than in markets. Of course selfish behavior is common in politics; but such norms often press people, in their capacity as citizens, in the direction of a concern for others or for the public interest.

Indeed, the deliberative aspects of politics, bringing additional information and perspectives to bear, often affects people's judgments as these are expressed through governmental processes. A principal function of a democratic system is to ensure that through representative or participatory processes, new or submerged voices, or novel depictions of where interests lie and what they in fact are, are heard and understood. If representatives or citizens are able to participate in a collective discussion of broad-casting or the appropriate nature of the Internet, they can generate a far fuller and richer picture of the central social goals, and of how they might be served, than can be provided through individual decisions as registered in the market. It should hardly be surprising if preferences, values, and perceptions of what matters, to individuals and to societies, are changed as a result of that process.

Unanimity and majority rule

Arguments based on citizens' collective desires are irresistible if the measure at issue is adopted unanimously – if all citizens are for it. But more serious difficulties are produced if (as is usual) the law imposes on a minority what it regards as a burden rather than a benefit. Suppose, for example, that a majority wants to require free television time for candidates or to have three hours of educational programming for children each week – but that a minority objects, contending that it is indifferent to speech by candidates, and that it does not care if there is more educational program-ming for children. Or suppose that in response to the danger of group polarization, a majority wants to require that Websites that propound one political view must pro-vide links to Websites promoting another view. It might be thought that those who perceive a need to bind themselves to a duty, or a course of action of some kind, should not be permitted to do so if the consequence is to bind others who perceive no such need.

Any interference with the preferences of the minority is indeed unfortunate. But in general, it is difficult to see what argument there might be for an across-the-board rule against the modest kind of democratic action that I will be defending here. If the majority is prohibited from promoting its aspirations or vindicating its considered judgments through legislation, people will be less able to engage in democratic self-government. The choice is between the considered judgments of the majority and the preferences of the minority. I am not suggesting, of course, that the minority should be foreclosed where its rights are genuinely at risk. As we shall see in chapter 8, the remedies that I will suggest do not fall in that category.

Unhappy sovereigns: the consumption treadmill

Throughout the discussion I have assumed that insofar as people are indeed acting as consumers, new communications technologies are an unambiguous boon. This is a widespread assumption, and it is easy to see why. If you want to buy anything at all, it has become much easier to do so. If you'd like a Toyota Camry, or a Ford Taurus, or a sports utility vehicle, many sites are available; wallets and watches and wristbands are easily found on-line; shirts and sweaters can be purchased in seconds. Nor is convenience the only point. As a result of the Internet, ordinary people have a much greater range of choices, and competitive pressures are, in a sense, far more intense for producers. Just to take one example, priceline.com allows you to "Name Your Own Price" for airline tickets, hotel rooms, groceries, new cars, mortgages, rental cars, sporting goods, strollers, swings, televisions, exercise equipment, and much more.

Indeed the growth of options for consumers has been a prime engine behind the growth of the Internet.

Insofar as the number of .coms is growing, it might seem clear that consumers, as consumers, are far better off as a result. But there is a problem: Extensive evidence shows that *our experience of many goods and services is largely a product of what other people have, and when there is a general improvement in everyone's consumer goods, people's well-being is increased little or not at all.*[7] Notwithstanding the evidence on its behalf, this might seem to be a positively weird suggestion. Isn't it obvious that better consumer goods are good for consumers? Actually it isn't so obvious. The reason is that people evaluate many goods by seeing how they compare to goods generally. If consumer goods as a whole are (say) 20 percent better, people are not going to be 20 percent happier, and they may not be happier at all.

To see the point, imagine that your current computer is the average computer from ten years ago. Chances are good that ten years ago, that computer was entirely fine, for you as for most other people. Chances are also good that if there had been no advances in computers, and if each of us had the same computer, in terms of quality, as we had ten years ago, little would be amiss. But in light of the massive improvement in computers in the last decade, you would undoubtedly be disappointed by continuing to own a computer from ten years before. Partly this is because it would seem hopelessly slow and infuriatingly inefficient, since the frame of reference has been set by much more advanced computers. Partly this is because your decade-old computer will not be able to interact well with modern ones, and it will place you at a serious disadvantage in dealing with others, not least in the marketplace.

This point need not depend on a claim that people are envious of their neighbors (though sometimes they are), or that people care a great deal about their status and on how they are doing in comparison with others (though status is indeed important). For many goods, the key point, developed by the economist Robert Frank, is that the frame of reference is set socially, not individually.[8] Our experience of what we have is determined by that frame of reference. What the Internet is doing is to alter the frame of reference, and by a large degree. This is not an unmixed blessing for consumers, even if it is a terrific development for many sellers.

To evaluate the Internet's ambiguous effects on consumers, it is necessary only to see a simple point: When millions of consumers simultaneously find themselves with improved opportunities to find goods, they are likely to find themselves of a kind of "treadmill" in which each is continually trying to purchase more and better, simply in order to keep up with others and with the ever-shifting frame of reference. Indeed, what is truc for computers is all the more true for countless other goods, including most of the vast array of products available on the Internet, such as sports utility vehicles, CD players, and televisions. Computers are evaluated socially, to be sure, but at least it can be said that fast and efficient ones might genuinely improve our lives, not least by enabling us to improve the operation of our democracy. But for many consumer goods, where the frame of reference is also provided socially, what really matters is how they compare to what other people have, and not how good they are in absolute terms. What would be a wonderful car or television, in one time and place, will seem ridiculously primitive in another.

In sum, the problem with the consumption treadmill, moving ever faster as a result of the Internet, is that despite growing expenditures, and improved goods, the shift in the frame of reference means that consumers are unlikely to be much happier or better off. Even if the Internet is making it far easier for consumers to get better goods, or the same goods at a better price, there is every reason to doubt that this is producing as much of an improvement in life, even for consumers, as we like to think.

This argument should not be misunderstood. Some "goods" actually do improve people's well-being, independently of shifts in the frame of reference. Robert Frank argues that these goods tend to involve "inconspicuous consumption," from which people receive benefits apart from what other people have or do.[9] When people have more leisure time, or when they have a chance to exercise and keep in shape, or when they are able to spend more time with family and friends, their lives are likely to be better, whatever other people are doing. But when what matters is the frame set for social comparison, a society focused on better consumer goods will face a serious problem: People will channel far too many resources into the consumption "treadmill," and far too few into goods that are not subject to the treadmill effect, or that would otherwise be far better for society (such as improved protection against crime or environmental pollution, or assistance for poor people).

For present purposes my conclusions are simple. New technologies unquestionably make purchases easier and more convenient for consumers. To this extent, they do help. But they help far less than we usually think, because they accelerate the consumption treadmill without making life much better for consumers of most goods. If citizens are reflective about their practices and their lives, they are entirely aware of this fact. As citizens, we might well choose to slow down the treadmill, or to ensure that resources that now keep it moving will be devoted to better uses. And insofar as citizens are attempting to accomplish that worthy goal, the idea of liberty should hardly stand in the way.

Democracy and preferences

When people's preferences are a product of excessively limited options, there is a problem from the standpoint of freedom, and we do freedom a grave disservice by insisting on respect for preferences. When options are plentiful, things are much better. But there is also a problem, from the standpoint of freedom, when people's past choices lead to the development of preferences that limit their own horizons and their capacity for citizenship.

My central claim here has been that the citizens of a democratic polity may legitimately seek a communications market that departs from consumer choices, in favor of a system that promotes goals associated with both freedom and democracy. Measures that promote these goals might be favored by a large majority of citizens even if, in their capacity as consumers, they would choose a different course. Consumers are not citizens and it is a large error to conflate the two. One reason for the disparity is that the process of democratic choice often elicits people's aspirations. When we are thinking about what we as a nation should do – rather than what each of us as consumers should buy – we are often led to think of our larger, long-term goals. We may therefore seek to promote a high-quality communications market even if, as consumers, we seek "infotainment." Within the democratic process, we are also able to act as a group, and not limited to our options as individuals. Acting as a group, we are thus in a position to solve various obstacles to dealing properly with issues that we cannot, without great difficulty, solve on our own.

These points obviously bear on a number of questions outside of the area of communications, such as environmental protection and antidiscrimination law. In many contexts, people, acting in their capacity as citizens, favor measures that diverge from the choices they make in their capacity as consumers. Of course it is important to impose constraints, usually in the form of rights, on what political majorities may do under this rationale. But if I am correct, one thing is clear: A system of limitless individual choices, with respect to communications, is not necessarily in the interest of citizenship and self-government. Democratic efforts to reduce the resulting problems ought not to be rejected in freedom's name.

Notes

1 Robert H. Frank and Philip J. Cook, *The Winner-Take-All Society* 201 (1995).
2 Alexis de Tocqueville, *Democracy in America* 317 (1987).
3 John Dewey, *The Future of Liberalism, in Dewey and His Critics* 695, 697 (Sidney Morgenbesser ed. 1977).
4 See Frank and Cook. *Winner-Take-All Society* 19.
5 See Albert Hirschmann, *The Passions and the Interests* (1967).
6 See Jon Elster, *Sour Grapes* (1983).
7 See Robert Frank, *Luxury Fever* (1998) for a good discussion.
8 See id.
9 See id.

4.4

Abstraction/class,
by McKenzie Wark

Abstraction

A double spooks the world, the double of abstraction. The fortunes of states and armies, companies and communities depend on it. All contending classes, be they ruling or ruled; revere it – yet fear it. Ours is a world that ventures blindly into the new with its fingers crossed.

All classes fear this relentless abstraction of the world, on which their fortunes yet depend. All classes but one: the hacker class. We are the hackers of abstraction. We produce new concepts, new perceptions, new sensations, hacked out of raw data. Whatever code we hack, be it programming language, poetic language, math or music, curves or colorings, we are the abstracters of new worlds. Whether we come to represent ourselves as researchers or authors, artists or biologists, chemists or musicians, philosophers or programmers, each of these subjectivities is but a fragment of a class still becoming, bit by bit, aware of itself as such.

And yet we don't quite know who we are. That is why this book seeks to make manifest our origins, our purpose and our interests. A hacker manifesto: Not the only manifesto, as it is in the nature of the hacker to differ from others, to differ even from oneself, over time. To hack is to differ. A hacker manifesto cannot claim to represent what refuses representation.

Hackers create the possibility of new things entering the world. Not always great things, or even good things, but new things. In art, in science, in philosophy and culture, in any production of knowledge where data can be gathered, where information can be extracted from it, and where in that information new possibilities for the world produced, there are hackers hacking the new out of the old. While we create these new worlds, we do not possess them. That which we create is mortgaged to others, and to the interests of others, to states and corporations who monopolize the means for making worlds we alone discover. We do not own what we produce – it owns us.

Hackers use their knowledge and their wits to maintain their autonomy. Some take the money and run. (We must live with our compromises.) Some refuse to compromise. (We live as best we can.) All too often those of us who take one of these paths resent those who take the other. One lot resents the prosperity it lacks, the other resents the liberty it lacks to hack away at the world freely. What eludes the hacker class is a more abstract expression of our interests as a class, and of how this interest may meet those of others in the world.

Hackers are not joiners. We're not often willing to submerge our singularity. What the times call for is a collective hack that realizes a class interest based on an alignment of differences rather than a coercive unity. Hackers are a class, but an abstract class. A class that makes abstractions, and a class made abstract. To abstract hackers as a class is to abstract the very concept of class itself. The slogan of the hacker class is not the workers of the world united, but the workings of the world untied.

Everywhere abstraction reigns, abstraction made concrete. Everywhere abstraction's straight lines and pure curves order matters along complex but efficient vectors. But where education teaches what one may produce with an abstraction, the knowledge most useful for the hacker class is of how abstractions are themselves produced. Deleuze: "Abstractions explain nothing, they themselves have to be explained."[1]

Abstraction may be discovered or produced, may be material or immaterial, but abstraction is what every hack produces and affirms. To abstract is to construct a plane upon which otherwise different and unrelated matters may be brought into many possible relations. To abstract is to express the virtuality of nature, to make known some instance of its possibilities, to actualize a relation out of infinite relationality, to manifest the manifold.

History is the production of abstraction and the abstraction of production. What makes life differ in one age after the next is the application of new modes of abstraction to the task of wresting freedom from necessity. History is the virtual made actual, one hack after another. History is the cumulative qualitative differentiation of nature as it is hacked.

Out of the abstraction of nature comes its productivity, and the production of a surplus over and above the necessities of survival. Out of this expanding surplus over necessity comes an expanding capacity to hack, again and again, producing further abstractions, further productivity, further release from necessity – at least in potential. But the hacking of nature, the production of surplus, does not make us free. Again and again, a ruling class arises that controls the surplus over bare necessity and enforces new necessities on those peoples who produce this very means of escaping necessity.

What makes our times different is the appearance on the horizon of possibility of a new world, long imagined – a world free from necessity. The production of abstraction has reached the threshold where it can break the shackles holding hacking fast to outdated and regressive class interests, once and for all. Debord: "The world already possesses the dream of a time whose consciousness it must now possess in order to actually live it."[2]

Invention is the mother of necessity. While all states depend on abstraction for the production of their wealth and power, the ruling class of any given state has an uneasy relationship to the production of abstraction in new forms. The ruling class seeks always to control innovation and turn it to its own ends, depriving the hacker of control of her or his creation, and thereby denying the world as a whole the right to manage its own development.

Class

A class arises – the working class – able to question the necessity of private property. A party arises, within the worker's movement, claiming to answer to working class desires – the communists. As Marx writes, "in all these movements they bring to the front, as the leading question in each, the property question, no matter what its degree of development at the time." This was the answer communists proposed to the property question: "centralize all instruments of production in the hands of the state."[3] Making property a state monopoly only produced a new ruling class, and a new and more brutal class struggle. But is that our final answer? Perhaps the course of the class struggle is not yet over. Perhaps there is another class that can open the property question in a new way – and in keeping the question open end once and for all the monopoly of the ruling classes on the ends of history.

There is a class dynamic driving each stage of the development of this vectoral world in which we now find ourselves. The vectoral class is driving this world to the brink of disaster, but it also opens up the world to the resources for overcoming its own destructive tendencies. In the three successive phases of commodification, quite different ruling classes arise, usurping different forms of private property. Each ruling class in turn drives the world towards ever more abstract ends.

First arises a pastoralist class. They disperse the great mass of peasants who traditionally worked the land under the thumb of feudal lords. The pastoralists supplant the feudal lords, releasing the productivity of nature that they claim as their private property. It is this privatization of property – a legal hack – that creates the conditions for every other hack by which the land is made to yield a surplus. A vectoral world rises on the shoulders of the agricultural hack.

As new forms of abstraction make it possible to produce a surplus from the land with fewer and fewer farmers, pastoralists turn them off their land, depriving them of their livelihood. Dispossessed farmers seek work and a new home in cities. Here capital puts them to work in its factories. Farmers become workers. Capital as property gives rise to a class of capitalists who own the means of production, and a class of workers, dispossessed of it – and by it. Whether as workers or farmers, the direct producers find themselves dispossessed not only of their land, but of the greater part of the surplus they produce, which accumulates to the pastoralists in the form of rent as the return on land, and to capitalists in the form of profit as the return on capital.

Dispossessed farmers become workers, only to be dispossessed again. Having lost their agriculture, they lose in turn their human culture. Capital produces in its factories not just the necessities of existence, but a way of life it expects its workers to consume. Commodified life dispossess the worker of the information traditionally passed on outside the realm of private property as culture, as the gift of one generation to the next, and replaces it with information in commodified form.

Information, like land or capital, becomes a form of property monopolized by a class, a class of vectoralists, so named because they control the vectors along which information is abstracted, just as capitalists control the material means with which goods are produced, and pastoralists the land with which food is produced. This information, once the collective property of the productive classes – the working and farming classes considered together – becomes the property of yet another appropriating class.

As peasants become farmers through the appropriation of their land, they still retain some autonomy over the disposition of their working time. Workers, even though they do not own capital, and must work according to the clock and its merciless time, could at least struggle to reduce the working day and release free time from labor. Information circulated within working class culture as a public property belonging to all. But when information in turn becomes a form of private property, workers are dispossessed of it, and must buy their own culture back from its owners, the vectoralist class. The farmer becomes a worker, and the worker, a slave. The whole world becomes subject to the extraction of a surplus from the producing classes that is controlled by the ruling classes, who use it merely to reproduce and expand this matrix of exploitation. Time itself becomes a commodified experience.

The producing classes – farmers, workers, hackers – struggle against the expropriating classes – pastoralists, capitalists, vectoralists – but these successive ruling classes struggle also amongst themselves. Capitalists try to break the pastoral monopoly on land and subordinate the produce of the land to industrial production. Vectoralists try to break capital's monopoly on the production process, and subordinate the production of goods to the circulation of information: "The privileged realm of electronic space controls the physical logistics of manufacture, since the release of raw materials and manufactured goods requires electronic consent and direction."[4]

That the vectoralist class has replaced capital as the dominant exploiting class can be seen in the form that the leading corporations take. These firms divest themselves of their productive capacity, as this is no longer a source of power. They rely on a competing mass of capitalist contractors for the manufacture of their products. Their power lies in monopolizing intellectual property – patents, copyrights and trademarks – and the means of reproducing their value – the vectors of communication. The privatization of information becomes the dominant, rather than a subsidiary, aspect of commodified life. "There is a certain logic to this progression: first, a select group of manufacturers transcend their connection to earthbound products, then, with marketing elevated as the pinnacle of their business, they attempt to alter marketing's social status as a commercial interruption and replace it with seamless integration."[5] With the rise of the vectoral class, the vectoral world is complete.

As private property advances from land to capital to information, property itself becomes more abstract. Capital as property frees land from its spatial fixity. Information as property frees capital from its fixity in a particular object. This abstraction of property makes property itself something amenable to accelerated innovation – and conflict. Class conflict fragments, but creeps into any and every relation that becomes a relation of property. The property question, the basis of class, becomes the question asked everywhere, of everything. If "class" appears absent to the apologists of our time, it is not because it has become just another in a series of antagonisms and articulations, but on the contrary because it has become the structuring principle of the vectoral plane which organizes the play of identities as differences.

The hacker class, producer of new abstractions, becomes more important to each successive ruling class, as each depends more and more on information as a resource. Land cannot be reproduced at will. Good land lends itself to scarcity, and the abstraction of private property is almost enough on its own to protect the rents of the pastoral class. Capital's profits rest on mechanically reproducible means of production, its factories and inventories. The capitalist firm sometimes needs the hacker to refine and advance the tools and techniques of productions to stay abreast of the competition. Information is the most easily reproducible object ever captured in the abstraction of property. Nothing protects the vectoralist business from its competitors other than its capacity to qualitatively transform the information it possesses and extract new value from it. The services of the hacker class become indispensable to an economy that is itself more and more dispensable – an economy of property and scarcity.

As the means of production become more abstract, so too does the property form. Property has to expand to contain more and more complex forms of difference, and reduce it to equivalence. To render land equivalent, it is enough to draw up its boundaries, and create a means of assigning it as an object to a subject. Complexities will arise, naturally, from this unnatural imposition on the surface of the world, although the principle is a simple abstraction. But for something to be represented as intellectual property, it is not enough for it to be in a different location. It must be qualitatively different. That difference, which makes a copyright or a patent possible, is the work of the hacker class. The hacker class makes what Bateson calls "the difference that makes the difference."[6] The difference that drives the abstraction of the world, but which also drives the accumulation of class power in the hands of the vectoral class.

The hacker class arises out of the transformation of information into property, in the form of intellectual property. This legal hack makes of the hack a property producing process, and thus a class producing process. The hack produces the class force capable of asking – and answering – the property question, the hacker class. The hacker class is the class with the capacity to create not only new kinds of object and subject in the world, not only new kinds of property form in which they may be represented, but new kinds of relation, with unforseen properties, which question the property form itself. The hacker class realizes itself as a class when it hacks the abstraction of property and overcomes the limitations of existing forms of property.

The hacker class may be flattered by the attention lavished upon it by capitalists compared to pastoralists, and vectoralists compared to capitalists. Hackers tend to ally at each turn with the more abstract form of property and commodity relation. But hackers soon feel the restrictive grip of each ruling class, as it secures its dominance over its predecessor and rival, and can renege on the dispensations it extended to hackers as a class. The vectoralist class, in particular, will go out of its way to court and coopt the productivity of hackers, but only because of its attenuated dependence on new abstraction as the engine of competition among vectoral interests. When the vectoralist act in concert as a class it is to subject hacking to the prerogatives of its class power.

The vectoral world is dynamic. It puts new abstractions to work, producing new freedoms from necessity. The direction this struggle takes is not given in the course of things, but is determined by the struggle between classes. All classes enter into relations of conflict, collusion and compromise. Their relations are not necessarily dialectical. Classes may form alliances of mutual interest against other classes, or may arrive at a "historic compromise," for a time. Yet despite pauses and setbacks, the class struggle drives history into abstraction and abstraction into history.

Notes

1   Gilles Deleuze, *Negotiations* (New York: Columbia University Press, 1995), p. 145. Throughout *A Hacker Manifesto*, certain protocols of reading are applied to the various textual archives on which it draws, and which call for some explanation. It is not so much a "symptomatic" reading as a homeopathic one, turning texts against their own limitations, imposed on them by their conditions of production. For instance, there is an industry in the making, within the education business, around the name of Deleuze, from which he may have to be rescued. His is a philosophy not restricted to what is, but open to what could be. In *Negotiations*, he can be found producing concepts to open up the political and cultural terrain, and providing lines along which to escape from state, market, party and other traps of identity and representation. His tastes were aristocratic – limited to the educational culture of his place and time – and his work lends itself to the trap of purely formal elaboration of the kind desired by the Anglo-American educational market particularly. One does better to take Deleuze from behind and give him mutant offspring by immaculate conception. Which was, after all, Deleuze's own procedure. He can be turned away from his own sedentary habits.

2   Guy Debord, *Society of the Spectacle* (Detroit: Black and Red, 1983), 164. This classic work in the crypto-Marxist tradition sets the standard for a critical thought in action. Debord's text is so designed that attempts to modify its theses inevitably moderate them, and thus reveal the modifier's complicity with the "spectacular society" that Debord so (anti)spectacularly condemns. It is a work that can only be honored by a complete reimagining of its theses on a more abstract basis, a procedure Debord himself applied to Marx, and which forms the basis of the crypto-Marxist procedure.

3   Karl Marx and Friedrich Engels, "Manifesto of the Communist Party," in *The Revolutions of 1848: Political Writings*, vol. 1, ed. David Fernbach (Harmondsworth: Penguin, 1978), pp. 98, 86. Karatani would see the property question coming from Marx, but the state ownership answer as belonging to Engels, and a distortion of Marx's whole trajectory. See Kolin Karatani, *Transcritique: On Kant and Marx* (Cambridge MA: MIT Press, 2003). *A Hacker Manifesto* is clearly neither an orthodox Marxist tract nor a post-Marxist repudiation, but rather a crypto-Marxist reimagining of the materialist method for practicing theory within history. From Marx one might take the attempt to discover abstraction at work in the world, as an historical process, rather than as merely a convenient category in thought with which to create a new intellectual product. Crypto-Marxist thought might hew close to the multiplicity of the time of everyday life,

which calls for a reinvention of theory in every moment, in fidelity to the moment, rather than a repetition of a representation of a past orthodoxy, or a self-serving "critique" of that representation in the interests of making Marx safe for the educational process and its measured, repetitive time.

4   Critical Art Ensemble, *The Electronic Disturbance* (New York: Autonomedia, 1994), pp. 16–17. See also Critical Art Ensemble, *The Molecular Invasion* (New York: Autonomedia, 2002). This group discover, through their always-inventive practice, just what needs to be thought at the nexus of information and property, and provide useful tools for beginning just such a project. Their work is particularly illuminating in regard to the commodification of genetic information – a frontline activity for the development of the vectoral class. All that is required is a deepening of the practice of thinking abstractly. Together with groups, networks and collaborations such as Adilkno, Ctheory, EDT, Institute for Applied Autonomy, I/O/D, Luther Blissett Project, Mongrel, Nettime, Oekonux, Old Boys' Network, Openflows, Public Netbase, subRosa, Rhizome, ®™ark, Sarai, The Thing, VNS Matrix and The Yes Men, Critical Art Ensemble form a movement of sorts, where art, politics and theory converge in a mutual critique of each other. These groups have only a "family resemblance" to each other. Each shares a characteristic with at least one other, but not necessarily the same characteristic. *A Hacker Manifesto* is among other things an attempt to abstract from the practices and concepts they produce. See also Josephine Bosma et al., *Readme! Filtered by Nettime* (New York: Autonomedia, 1999).

5   Naomi Klein, *No Logo* (London: Harper Collins, 2000), p. 35. See also Naómi Klein, *Fences and Windows* (New York: Picador, 2002). This exemplary work of journalism discovers the nexus between the brand and logo as emblems of the hollowing out of the capitalist economy in the overdeveloped world, and the relegation of the great bulk of capitalist production to the sweatshops of the underdeveloped world. We see clearly here that capital has been superseded as an historical formation in all but name. Klein stops short at the description of the symptoms, however. She does not offer quite the right diagnosis. But then that isn't the task she sets herself. There can be no one book, no master thinker for these times. What is called for is a practice of combining heterogeneous modes of perception, thought and feeling, different styles of researching and writing, different kinds of connection to different readers, proliferation of information across different media, all practiced within a gift economy, expressing and elaborating differences, rather than broadcasting a dogma, a slogan, a critique or line. The division of genres and types of writing, like all aspects of the intellectual division of labor, are antithetical to the autonomous development of the hacker class as class, and work only to reinforce the subordination of knowledge to property by the vectoral class.

6   Gregory Bateson, *Steps Towards an Ecology of Mind* (New York: Ballantine, 1972). Bateson grasped the link between information and nature on an abstract level, even as he shrank from examining the historical forces that forged just this link: And yet he is a pioneer in hacker thought and action in his disregard for the property rules of academic fields. He skips gaily from biology to anthropology to epistemology, seeing in the divisions between fields, even between statements, an

ideological construction of the world as fit only for zoning and development in the interests of property. At the moment when the foundations of the ideology of the vectoral class were in formation, in information science, computer science, cybernetics, and when information was being discovered as the new essence of social and even natural phenomena, Bateson alone grasped the critical use of these nascent concepts.

PART 5

Time and space in the age of information

A governing trope to describe the effects of the ICT revolution and the dynamics of neoliberal globalisation which gave it its political and economic momentum is that of 'time–space compression'. David Harvey coined it in his 1989 book *The Condition of Postmodernity*, and deployed it to characterise what he saw as a defining feature of an evolving post-Fordist, postmodernity (pp. 240–242). Time–space compression, for Harvey, was the effect of a rigid social and economic system of industrialisation made (or forced to become) 'flexible'. This occurred through the dismantling of post-war Fordism beginning in the 1970s. Capitalism was then able to be true to its 'essence' and expand, relatively uncontrolled, to every corner of the earth in its historical project of globalisation. The effect was a rapid process of time–space compression where the world increasingly became (and continues to become) a smaller place, with social and cultural relations accelerating in synchrony with a fast-moving contemporary postmodernity.

Around the same time, Anthony Giddens, in *The Consequences of Modernity*, was developing a similar theory which was rooted more in sociology than Harvey's political economy. Giddens termed it 'time–space distantiation' (1990). Essentially, for Giddens, the concept means a *separation* – or what he called the 'disembedding' – of time and space from localised *place* and its local contexts of interaction. Through the communicative dynamism of modernity, social relations are stretched across time and space and social action is increasingly conducted beyond one's immediate physical presence (in space or place). For Giddens, these processes – made possible through advances in communications technologies – serve to 'empty out' localised space to create a one-world globalisation, a globalised space or 'a single world where none existed previously' (1990:27).

In media theory, and in the social sciences more generally, these authors, with their accounts of transformations in time and space through the increasingly complex and comprehensive processes of modernity and industrialism, have been influential. We choose not to reprint them here, however. This is because they are not about media theory per se, and also because they are widely available either in their original form or in the various readers in which extracts have been reproduced (e.g. Cassell, 1993; Lechner and Boli, 2000). They nonetheless are recommended texts for anyone wishing to investigate more deeply the issues of time and space and how our experience of them can be transformed through technological innovation. They also provide an excellent context through which the following texts may be explored.

James Carey begins this final part by providing an historical context. The revolutionary new innovation of the 19th century, he argues, was the telegraph, a technology that 'ushered in the modern phase of history and determined, even to this day, the major lines of development of American communications'. Most important for Carey was that the telegraph 'marked the decisive separation of "transportation" and "communication", terms that hitherto had been synonymous. He argues that the 'media' of communication was transformed through this single technology. Not only did it infinitely accelerate the process of 'time–space compression' – which corresponded exactly with needs of an emerging industrialisation – but also 'reworked the nature of written language [telegraph meaning "to write at a distance"] and . . . the nature of awareness itself'. For Carey the telegraph was thus *ideological* in its import. It served to 'naturalize' the spread of capitalism and of modernity and functioned to internalise the 'rhetoric of the technological sublime' that underscored them both. Moreover, the spread of the telegraph, he argues, worked to rationalise the use of language into a mode more aligned to business and to science, 'disembedding' at the same time – to use Giddens's term – the subtleties and variation of regional, local and colloquial forms of language use.

The social, economic and cultural effects of the telegraph are considered in the extract from Jeremy Stein. The full essay focuses on the Canadian town of Cornwall, Ontario, from the time of the introduction of the telegraph in the 1860s. Here we reprint the preface to this discussion which is a useful observation on the various contemporary theories of 'time–space compression'. The fundamental question Stein asks is whether our experience of space and time is *revolutionised* by powerful new media technologies in the ways that theorists such as Harvey and Giddens would argue, or is the process more evolutionary? Like Carey's work, Stein's concentration on the historical context and the telegraphic media has powerful implications for contemporary theories of new media.

Nicola Green brings us up to the present with her essay 'On the move: technology, mobility, and the mediation of social time and space', which looks at the experience of time and space through the use of that most ubiquitous of new media technologies, the mobile phone. Green's work is important because it recognizes a unique convergence of technology use within time and space. For Green, the act of being 'mobile' and communicating across time and space represents a qualitatively different experience from that of other media technologies such as the telegraph, or television or the internet, where users are required, usually, to be fixed in space. Using qualitative data gathered from the experience of users themselves, she asks the crucial question: what does it mean to be mobile in a mobile world?

And it is from the relatively 'fixed' position of the online user that Lee and Liebenau, in the next extract, consider the temporality of the internet. What time is it on the internet, when the local times of users would span every time zone in the world? On the internet, they observe '9PM is no longer different from 8:17PM'. Instead of being unthinkingly dependent on the clock for our understanding of time, the notion of temporal 'duration', or our experience of the 'passing' of time or the 'time it takes' for a particular task, takes on a new significance. They argue that the 'fiction' of real time is revealed through such a perspective, and that instead the internet generates its own times through the activities of its users. With such a potential for an awareness of duration, the 'fact' that it is 12:16PM or whatever, becomes increasingly less relevant on the internet and the inherently asynchronous 'lags' and 'cycles' and 'rhythms' of the network space become more pronounced.

In the last extract from Thomas Hylland Eriksen's *Tyranny of the Moment: Fast and Slow Time in the Age of Information* the focus on temporality shifts from the times of the internet to the speed of everyday life. Again, through new media innovation, we are forced to think beyond the metering of the clock to consider the force and origin of contemporary social acceleration or the effects on our temporal awareness by information technologies. 'Speed is contagious', argues Eriksen, a pandemic spread by connection on connection in the digital network. The 'carrier' is new media technologies that saturate time and space with an increasingly accelerated panoply of signs and symbols. These are rendered in the form of *Information* that acts as the guide with which we increasingly orient ourselves in the world. But the constant blizzard of informationalised signs and symbols tends to confuse and bewilder, forcing us to fall back on an easily cognated and narrowly focused perception of the world. Social acceleration, Eriksen argues, means that in more and more realms of life, 'context and understanding' are diminished. Acceleration becomes a central technological process in almost wholly technologised world. The 'tyranny' of the moment for Eriksen is the tyranny of the present, a constant now where the past and the future recede and our ability to reflect and project is correspondingly reduced.

References

Cassell, P. (1993) *The Giddens Reader*, Stanford, CA: Stanford University Press.
Giddens, A. (1990) *The Consequences of Modernity*, Cambridge: Polity Press.
Harvey, D. (1989) *The Condition of Postmodernity*, Oxford: Blackwell.
Lechner, F. J. and Boli, J. (eds) (2000) *The Globalization Reader*, Oxford: Blackwell.

5.1

Technology and ideology: the case of the telegraph,
by James Carey

In one of the most famous paragraphs of our most famous autobiography, Henry Adams located the precise moment when "eighteenth-century troglodytic Boston" joined industrial America: "the opening of the Boston and Albany Railroad; the appearance of the first Cunard Steamers in the bay; and the telegraphic messages which carried from Baltimore to Washington the news that Henry Clay and James K. Polk were nominated for the presidency. This was May, 1844" (Adams, 1931: 5).

Adams signaled the absorption of genteel New England into industrial America by three improvements in transportation and communication. Yet for all the significance attached to the telegraph in that famous passage, it remains a product of one of the least studied technologies, certainly the least studied communications technology. The effect of the telegraph on modern life and its role as a model for future developments in communications have scarcely been explored. The first twenty-three volumes of *Technology and Culture* are virtually without reference to the telegraph. Robert L. Thompson's *Wiring a Continent*, the principal history of the telegraph, is now more than forty years old, takes the story only to 1866, and focuses almost exclusively on the formation of Western Union (Thompson, 1947).

I take the neglect of the telegraph to be unfortunate for a number of reasons. First, the telegraph was dominated by the first great industrial monopoly – Western Union, the first communications empire and the prototype of the many industrial empires that were to follow. The telegraph, in conjunction with the railroad, provided the setting in which modern techniques for the management of complex enterprises were first worked out, though for the telegraph in what was eventually monopolistic circumstances.[1] Although the telegraph did not provide the site for the first of the titanic nineteenth-century patent struggles (that prize probably goes to Elias Howe's sewing machine) it led to one of the most significant of them in the rewriting of American law, particularly in the great "telegraph war" between Jay Gould and the Vanderbilt interests for control of the Edison patents for the quadraplex telegraph system, the innovation that Gould rightly prized as the "nerve of industry."[2]

Second, the telegraph was the first product – really the foundation – of the electrical goods industry and thus the first of the science- and engineering-based industries. David Noble's *American by Design: Science, Technology and the Rise of*

Corporate Capitalism (1977) implies throughout a sharp distinction between forms of engineering, such as civil engineering, grounded in a handicraft and guild tradition, and chemical engineering and electrical engineering, which were science-based from the outset. Much that is distinctive about the telegraph, from the organization of the industry to the rhetoric that rationalized it, derives from the particular nature of the engineering it brought into being. More to the point, the telegraph was the first electrical engineering technology and therefore the first to focus on the central problem in modern engineering: the economy of a signal.[3]

Third, the telegraph brought about changes in the nature of language, of ordinary knowledge, of the very structures of awareness. Although in its early days the telegraph was used as a toy – as was the computer, which it prefigured – for playing long-distance chess, its implications for human knowledge were the subject of extended, often euphoric, and often pessimistic debate. Adams saw the telegraph as a demonic device dissipating the energy of history and displacing the Virgin with the Dynamo, whereas Thoreau saw it as an agent of trivialization. An even larger group saw the telegraph as an agency of benign improvement – spiritual, moral, economic, and political. Now that thought could travel by "the singing wire," a new form of reporting and a new form of knowledge were envisioned that would replace traditional literature with a new and active form of scientific knowledge.

Fourth, and partly for the foregoing reasons, the telegraph was a watershed in communication, as I hope to show later. Now, it is easy to overemphasize the revolutionary consequences of the telegraph. It is not an infrequent experience to be driving along an interstate highway and to become aware that the highway is paralleled by a river, a canal, a railroad track, or telegraph and telephone wires. In that instant one may realize that each of these improvements in transportation and communications merely worked a modification on what preceded it. The telegraph twisted and altered but did not displace patterns of connection formed by natural geography: by the river and primitive foot and horse paths and later by the wooden turnpike and canal.

But the innovation of the telegraph can stand metaphorically for all the innovations that ushered in the modern phase of history and determined, even to this day, the major lines of development of American communications. The most important fact about the telegraph is at once the most obvious and innocent: It permitted for the first time the effective separation of communication from transportation. This fact was immediately recognized, but its significance has been rarely investigated. The telegraph not only allowed messages to be separated from the physical movement of objects; it also allowed communication to control physical processes actively. The early use of the telegraph in railroad signaling is an example: telegraph messages could control the physical switching of rolling stock, thereby multiplying the purposes and effectiveness of communication. The separation of communication from transportation has been exploited in most subsequent developments in communication down to computer control systems.

When the telegraph reached the West Coast eight years in advance of a transcontinental railroad, the identity of communication and transportation was ended in both fact and symbol. Before the telegraph, "communication" was used to describe transportation as well as message transmittal for the simple reason that the movement of messages was dependent on their being carried on foot or horseback or by rail. The telegraph, by ending the identity, allowed symbols to move independently of and faster than transportation. To put it in a slightly different way, the telegraph freed communication from the constraints of geography. The telegraph, then, not only altered the relation between communication and transportation; it also changed the fundamental ways in which communication was thought about. It provided a model for thinking about communication – a model I have called a transmission model – and displaced older religious views of communication even as the new technology was mediated through religious language. And it opened up new ways of thinking about communication within both the formal practice of theory and the practical consciousness of everyday life. In this sense the telegraph was not only a new tool of commerce but also a thing to think with, an agency for the alteration of ideas.

II

A thorough treatment of the consequences of the telegraph would attempt to demonstrate how this instrument altered the spatial and temporal boundaries of human interaction, brought into existence new forms of language as well as new conceptual systems, and brought about new structures of social relations, particularly by fostering a national commercial middle class. These consequences were also displacements: older forms of language and writing declined, traditional social interactions waned, and the pattern of city-state capitalism that dominated the first half of the nineteenth century was broken up (Carey and Sims, 1976: 219–41). I intend now to concentrate on the relationship between the telegraph and ideas, between, broadly, the telegraph and ideology. I hope also to insinuate throughout some observations on the broader matters noted earlier.

There are three relationships between the telegraph and ideology. Two of them have received some attention, and I will mention them only in passing in order to concentrate on a relationship that has not as yet been investigated.

The first is the relationship between the telegraph and monopoly capitalism, the principal subject of Thompson's *Wiring a Continent*. That is, the telegraph was a new and distinctively different force of production that demanded a new body of law, economic theory, political arrangements, management techniques, organizational structures, and scientific rationales with which to justify and make effective the development of a privately owned and controlled monopolistic corporation. This problem can be looked at as one of the relationships among a force of production, the organizational forms and administrative techniques that realize it, and the explanatory and justifying ideology that guides and legitimates its institutionalization. Unfortunately, even in this context the telegraph has not been investigated adequately, partly because of the tendency to eschew historical investigations and to treat forces of production, *tout court*, as all-encompassing rather than to investigate the particular consequences and ideological implications of particular technologies. Technology as such is too abstract a category to support any precise analysis; therefore, changes in technology go unanalyzed except for classifying them within various stages of capitalist development.

Before the telegraph, business relations were personal; that is, they were mediated through face-to-face relations, by personal correspondence, by contacts among people who, by and large, knew one another as actual persons. The overall coordination of these atomic relations and transactions was provided by the "invisible hand" of the market.

With the telegraph and, of course, the railroads and improvements in other techniques of transport and communication, the volume and speed of transactions demanded a new form of organization of essentially impersonal relations – that is, relations not among known persons but among buyers and sellers whose only relation was mediated through an organization and a structure of management. "The visible hand of management replaced the invisible hand of market forces where and when new technology and expanded markets permitted a historically unprecedented high volume and speed of materials through the processes of production and distribution" (Chandler, 1977: 12). Through the telegraph and railroad the social relations among large numbers of anonymous buyers and sellers were coordinated. But these new and unprecedented relations of communication and contact had themselves to be explained, justified, and made effective. What we innocently describe as theory, law, common sense, religion were means by which these new relations were carried through to explicit consciousness and "naturalized" – made to seem merely of the order of things.

The second connection between ideology and the telegraph resides in the popular imagery, largely religious, that accompanied the latter's introduction. This aspect of the problem has been rather more thoroughly investigated, at least in a general way, within American studies and particularly within what is called the "myth and symbol" school. The telegraph, widely hailed at the time of its introduction as the "noiseless tenant of the wilderness," was clothed in the language of religious aspiration and secular millenarianism, a language Leo Marx names the "rhetoric of the technological sublime." John Quirk and I, thinking more directly of the telegraph and subsequent developments, have called this same language the "rhetoric of the electrical sublime."

There were other technological marvels of the mid-nineteenth century, but the inscrutable nature of the telegraph made it seem more extraordinary than, and qualitatively different from, other inventions. The key to the mystery was, of course, electricity – a force of great potency and yet invisible. It was this invisibility that made electricity and the telegraph powerful impetuses to idealist thought both in religious and philosophical terms. It presented the mystery of the mind–body dualism and located vital energy in the realm of the mind, in the nonmaterial world. Electricity was, in standard terms of the day, "shadowy, mysterious, impalpable. It lives in the skies and seems to connect the spiritual and material" (Czitrom, 1982: 9).[4]

Electricity, the Reverend Ezra S. Gannett told his Boston congregation, was both the "swift winged messenger of destruction" and the "vital energy of material creation. The invisible, imponderable substance, force, whatever it be – we do not even certainly know what it is which we are dealing with . . . is brought under our control, to do our errands, nay, like a very slave" (Czitrom, 1982: 19). Another preacher of the era, Gardner Spring, exclaimed that we were on the "border of a spiritual harvest because thought now travels by steam and magnetic wires" (Miller, 1965: 48). This new technology enters American discussions not as mundane fact but as divinely inspired for the purposes of spreading the Christian message farther and faster, eclipsing time and transcending space, saving the heathen, bringing closer and making more probable the day of salvation.

There were dissenters, of course, but the general uniformity of reaction to the telegraph demonstrated how it was able to fuse the opposite poles of the electrical sublime: the desire for peace, harmony, and self-sufficiency with the wish for power, profit, and productivity. The presumed "annihilation of time and space" heralded by the telegraph promised to bind the country together just as the portents of the Civil War were threatening to tear it apart. Here the organic metaphors, so easily attributed to German philosophy, floated into American thought as means to describe how the telegraph would change life. As early as 1838, Morse anticipated twentieth-century notions of the "global village." It would not be long, he wrote, "ere the whole surface of this country would be channeled for those nerves which are to diffuse with the speed of thought, a knowledge of all that is occurring throughout the land; making in fact one neighborhood of the whole country" (Czitrom, 1982: 11–12).

And finally, a piece of doggerel typical of the era, entitled "To Professor Morse, In Pleasant Memory of Oct. 9, 1856, at the Albion," expresses the mixture of science, commerce, politics, and pious religious unity that surfaced in popular consciousness with the telegraph:

> A good and generous spirit ruled the hour;
>   Old jealousies were drowned in brotherhood;
> Philanthropy rejoiced that Skill and Power,
>   Servants to Science, compass all men's good;
>   And over all Religion's banner stood,
> Upheld by thee, true patriarch of the plan
> Which in two hemispheres was schemed to shower
> Mercies from God on universal man.
>   Yes, this electric chain from East to West
> More than mere metal, more than mammon can,
>   Binds us together – kinsmen, in the best,
> As most affectionate and frankest bond;
> Brethren as one; and looking far beyond
>   The world in an Electric Union blest!
>   (Martin F. Typper, in *Prime*, 1875: 648).

One finds in this rhetoric of the electrical sublime a central tenet of middle-class ideology: that "communication, exchange, motion brings humanity, enlightenment, progress and that isolation and disconnection are evidence of barbarism and merely obstacles to be overcome" (Schivelbusch, 1978: 40). The eighteenth-century ideal of universalism – the Kingdom of God and the Brotherhood of Man – included a belief in a universal Human Nature. People were people – everywhere the same. Communication was the engine that powered this ideal. Each improvement in communication, by ending isolation, by linking people everywhere, was heralded as realizing the Universal Brotherhood of Universal Man.

The argument is not an abstract one. Charles F. Briggs and Augustus Maverick, writing in 1858, made the equation precise:

It has been the result of the great discoveries of the past century, to effect a revolution in political and social life, by establishing a more intimate connection between nations, with race and race. It has been found that the old system of exclusion and insulation are stagnation and death. National health can only be maintained by the free and unobstructed interchange of each with all. How potent a power, then, is the telegraph destined to become in the civilization of the world! This binds together by a vital cord all the nations of the earth. It is impossible that old prejudices and hostilities should longer exist, while such an instrument has been created for an exchange of thought between all the nations of the earth (Briggs and Maverick, 1858: 21–22).

In another work of the era, Sir William P. Andrews, justifying the Euphrates Valley Railroad connecting India to Africa, quotes an anonymous writer who got the whole matter rather more correctly:

Nor can it for a moment be doubted that a line of electric telegraphs between Europe and India must be a successful commercial enterprise, putting altogether out of sight the important moral effects which such a means of rapid communication must of necessity bring about. It may, on the contrary, be doubted whether any more efficient means could be adopted to develop the resources of India, and to consolidate British power and strengthen British rule in that country, than by the formation of the proposed system of railways in central Asia and the carrying out of the proposed telegraph communication with Europe.
(Andrews, 1857: 141)

An essentially religious view of communication – or one cloaked, at least, in religious metaphors – is as a mediator – a progressively vanishing mediator – between middle-class aspiration and capitalist and, increasingly, imperial development.[5] Max Weber's tour de force retains its original significance in this context; for Weber's archetype of the formation of the Protestant ethic, Benjamin Franklin, reappears in the mid-nineteenth century as the first electrician, the first to release this new force of moral and social progress. But what needs to be more closely investigated is the relationship between a later stage of economic development, new forms of electrical technology, and a transposed body of religious belief. This is particularly true because, from the telegraph forward, technological development came to be housed in professional engineering societies, universities, and research laboratories. As technological development became more systematic, so did the development of justifying ideologies become more consciously planned and directed by these same groups.

III

In the balance of this chapter I wish to concentrate on the effect of the telegraph on ordinary ideas: the coordinates of thought, the natural attitude, practical consciousness, or, less grandly, common sense. As I have intimated, I think the best way to grasp the effects of the telegraph or any other technology is not through a frontal assault but, rather, through the detailed investigation in a couple of sites where those effects can be most clearly observed.

Let me suggest some of the sites for those investigations – investigations to be later integrated and referred for elucidation to some general theoretical notions. First, much additional work needs to be done on the effects of the telegraph on language and journalism. The telegraph reworked the nature of written language and finally the nature of awareness itself. There is an old saw, one I have repeated myself, that the telegraph, by creating the wire services, led to a fundamental change in news. It snapped the tradition of partisan journalism by forcing the wire services to generate "objective" news, news that could be used by papers of any political stripe (Carey, 1969: 23–38). Yet the issue is deeper than that. The wire services demanded a form of language stripped of the local, the regional; and colloquial. They demanded something closer to a "scientific" language, a language of strict denotation in which the connotative features of utterance were under rigid control. If the same story were to be understood in the same way from Maine to California, language had to be flattened out and standardized. The telegraph, therefore, led to the disappearance of forms of speech and styles of journalism and story telling – the tall story, the hoax, much humor, irony, and satire – that depended on a more traditional use of the symbolic, a use I earlier called the fiduciary.[6] The origins of objectivity may be sought, therefore, in the necessity of stretching language in space over the long lines of Western Union. That is, the telegraph changed the forms of social relations mediated by language. Just as the long lines displaced a personal relation mediated by speech and correspondence in the conduct of trade and substituted the mechanical coordination of buyer and seller, so the language of the telegraph displaced a fiduciary relationship between writer and reader with a coordinated one.

Similarly, the telegraph eliminated the correspondent who provided letters that announced an event, described it in detail, and analyzed its substance, and replaced him with the stringer who supplied the bare facts. As words were expensive on the telegraph, it separated the observer from the writer. Not only did writing for the telegraph have to be condensed to save money – telegraphic, in other words – but also from the marginal notes and anecdotes of the stringer the story had to be reconstituted at the end of the telegraphic line, a process that reaches high art with the news magazines, the story divorced from the story teller.

But as every constraint is also an opportunity, the telegraph altered literary style. In a well-known story, "cablese" influenced Hemingway's style, helping him to pare his prose to the bone, dispossessed of every adornment. Most correspondents chafed under its restrictiveness, but not Hemingway. "I had to quit being a correspondent," he told Lincoln Steffens later. "I was getting too fascinated by the lingo of the cable."[7] But the lingo of the cable provided the underlying structure for one of the most influential literary styles of the twentieth century.

There were other effects – some obvious, some subtle. If the telegraph made prose lean and unadorned and led to a journalism without the luxury of detail and analysis, it also brought an overwhelming crush of such prose to the newsroom. In the face of what was a real glut of occurrences, news judgment had to be routinized and the organization of the newsroom made factory-like. The reporter who produced the new prose moved into prominence in journalism by displacing the editor as the archetype of the journalist. The spareness of the prose and the sheer volume of it allowed news – indeed, forced news – to be treated like a commodity: something that could be transported, measured, reduced, and timed. In the wake of the telegraph, news was subject to all the procedures developed for handling agricultural commodities. It was subject to "rates, contracts, franchising, discounts and thefts.[8]

A second site for the investigation of the telegraph is the domain of empire. Again, it is best not to assault the problem as an overarching theory of imperialism but, rather, to examine specific cases and specific connections: the role of the telegraph in coordinating military, particularly naval, operations; the transition from colonialism, where power and authority rested with the domestic governor, to imperialism, where power and authority were reabsorbed by the imperial capital; the new forms of political correspondence that came about when the war correspondent was obliged to use the telegraph; and the rise of the first forms of international business that could be called multinational.

While the growth of empire and imperialism have been explained by virtually every possible factor, little attention has been paid to telegraphy in generating the ground conditions for the urban imperialism of the mid-nineteenth century and the international imperialism later in the century.[9] It is probably no accident that the words "empire" and "imperialism" entered the language in 1870, soon after the laying of the transatlantic cable. Although colonies could be held together with printing, correspondence, and sail, the hold, as the American experience shows, was always tenuous over great distance. Moreover, in colonial arrangements the margin had as much power as the center. Until the transatlantic cable, it was difficult to determine whether British colonial policy was being set in London or by colonial governors in the field – out of contact and out of control. It was the cable and telegraph, backed, of course, by sea power, that turned colonialism into imperialism: a system in which the center of an empire could dictate rather than merely respond to the margin.[10]

The critical change lay in the ability to secure investments. There was no heavy overseas investment until the control made possible by the cable. The innovation of the telegraph created, if not the absolute impetus for imperial expansion, then at least the wherewithal to make the expansion theoretically tenable. But it also created a tension between the capability to expand and the capacity to rule.

With the development of the railroad, steam power, the telegraph and cable, a coherent empire emerged based on a coherent system of communication. In that system the railroad may be taken as the overland extension of the steamer or vice versa, and the telegraph and cable stood as the coordinating, regulating device governing both.[11]

Although the newspaper and imperial offices are among the best sites at which to look for the effects of the telegraph, there are humbler locations of equal interest. It surely is more than an accident that many of the great nineteenth-century commercial empires were founded in the humble circumstances of the telegraph operator's shack. The case of Richard B. Sears of North Redwood, Minnesota, is instructive. One must not forget that Edison and Carnegie began the same way and that the genius of Jay Gould lay in his integration of the telegraph with the railroad. The significance of the telegraph in this regard is that it led to the selective control and transmission of information. The telegraph operator was able to monopolize knowledge, if only for a few moments, along a route; and this brought a selective advantage in trading and speculation. But it was this same control of information that gave the telegraph a central importance in the development of modern gambling and of the business of credit. Finally, it was central to the late nineteenth-century explosion in forms of merchandising, such as the mail-order house.[12]

In the balance of this essay I want to cut across some of these developments and describe how the telegraph altered the ways in which time and space were understood in ordinary human affairs and, in particular, to examine a changed form in which time entered practical consciousness. To demonstrate these changes I wish to concentrate on the developments of commodity markets and on the institutionalization of standard time. But first let me reiterate the basic argument.

The simplest and most important point about the telegraph is that it marked the decisive separation of "transportation" and "communication." Until the telegraph these words were synonymous. The telegraph ended that identity and allowed symbols to move independently of geography and independently of and faster than transport. I say decisive separation because there were premonitions earlier of what was to come, and there was, after all, pre-electric telegraphy – line-of-sight signaling devices.

Virtually any American city of any vintage has a telegraph hill or a beacon hill reminding us of such devices. They relied on shutters, flaps, disks, or arms operating as for semaphoric signaling at sea. They were optical rather than "writing at a distance" systems and the forerunners of microwave networks, which rely on relay stations on geographic high points for aerial transmissions.

Line-of-sight telegraphy came into practical use at the end of the eighteenth century. Its principal architect was a Frenchman, Claud Chappe, who persuaded the Committee of Public Instruction in post-Revolutionary France to approve a trial. Joseph Lakanal, one of its members, reported back to the committee on the outcome: "What brilliant destiny do science and the arts not reserve for a republic which by its immense population and the genius of its inhabitants, is called to become the nation to instruct Europe" (Wilson, 1976: 122).

The National Convention approved the adoption of the telegraph as a national utility and instructed the Committee of Public Safety to map routes. The major impetus to its development in France was the same as the one that led to the wave of canal and railroad building in America. The pre-electric telegraph would provide an answer to Montesquieu and other political theorists who thought France or the United States too big to be a republic. But even more, it provided a means whereby the departments that had replaced the provinces after the Revolution could be tied to and coordinated with the central authority (Wilson, 1976: 123).

The pre-electric telegraph was also a subject of experimentation in America. In 1800, a line-of-sight system was opened between Martha's Vineyard and Boston (Wilson, 1976: 210). Between 1807 and 1812, plans were laid for a telegraph to stretch from Maine to New Orleans. The first practical use of line-of-sight telegraphy was for the transmission of news of arriving ships, a practice begun long before 1837 (Thompson, 1947: 11). But even before line-of-sight devices had been developed, alterations in shipping patterns had led to the separation of information from cargo, and that had important consequences for international trade. I shall say more on this later.

Despite these reservations and qualifications, the telegraph provided the decisive and cumulative break of the identity of communication and transportation. The great theoretical significance of the technology lay not merely in the separation but also in the use of the telegraph as both a model of and a mechanism for control of the physical movement of things, specifically for the railroad. That is the fundamental discovery: not only can information move independently of and faster than physical entities, but it also can be a simulation of and control mechanism for what has been left behind. The discovery was first exploited in railroad dispatching in England in 1844 and in the United States in 1849. It was of particular use on the long stretches of single-track road in the American West, where accidents were a serious problem. Before the use of the telegraph to control switching, the Boston and Worcester Railroad, for one example, kept horses every five miles along the line, and they raced up and down the track so that their riders could warn engineers of impending collisions (Thompson, 1947: 205–206). By moving information faster than the rolling stock, the telegraph allowed for centralized control along many miles of track. Indeed, the operation of the telegraph in conjunction with the railroad allowed for an integrated system of transport and communication. The same principle realized in these mundane circumstances governs the development of all modern processes in electrical transmission and control from guided gun sights to simple servo mechanisms that open doors. The relationship of the telegraph and the railroad illustrates the basic notion of systems theory and the catch phrase that the "system is the solution," in that the integrated switched system is more important than any of its components.

The telegraph permitted the development, in the favorite metaphor of the day, of a thoroughly encephalated social nervous system in which signaling was divorced from musculature. It was the telegraph and the railroad – the actual, painful construction of an integrated system – that provided the entrance gate for the organic metaphors that dominated nineteenth-century thought. Although German romanticism and idealism had their place, it is less to the world of ideas and more to the world of actual practice that we need to look when trying to figure out why the nineteenth century was obsessed with organicism.

The effect of the telegraph on ideology, on ordinary ideas, can be shown more graphically with two other examples drawn from the commodities markets and the development of standard time. The telegraph, like most innovations in communication down through the computer, had its first and most profound impact on the conduct of commerce, government, and the military. It was, in short, a producer good before it was a consumer good. The telegraph, as I said earlier, was used in its early months for the long-distance playing of chess. Its commercial significance was slow to be realized. But once that significance was determined, it was used to reorganize commerce; and from the patterns of usage in commerce came many of the telegraph's most profound consequences for ordinary thought. Among its first effects was the reorganization of commodity markets.

It was the normal expectation of early nineteenth century Americans that the price of a commodity would diverge from city to city so that the cost of wheat, corn, or whatever would be radically different in, say, Pittsburgh, Cincinnati, and St. Louis. This belief reflected the fact that before the telegraph, markets were independent of one another, or, more accurately, that the effect of one market on another was so gradually manifested as to be virtually unnoticed. In short, the prices of commodities were largely determined by local conditions of supply and demand. One of the leading historians of the markets has commented, "To be sure in all articles of trade the conditions at all sources of supply had their ultimate effect on distant values and yet even in these the communication was so slow that the conditions might change entirely before their effect could be felt" (Emery, 1896: 106).

Under such circumstances, the principal method of trading is called arbitrage: buying cheap and selling dear by moving goods around in space. That is, if prices are higher in St. Louis than in Cincinnati, it makes sense to buy in Cincinnati and resell in St. Louis, as long as the price differential is greater than the cost of transportation between the two cities. If arbitrage is widely practiced between cities, prices should settle into an equilibrium whereby the difference in price is held to the difference in transportation cost. This result is, in turn, based on the assumption of classical economics of perfect information – that all buyers and sellers are aware of the options available in all relevant markets – a situation rarely approached in practice before the telegraph.

Throughout the United States, price divergence between markets declined during the nineteenth century. Arthur H. Cole computed the average annual and monthly price disparity for uniform groups of commodities during the period 1816–1842, that is, up to the eve of the telegraph. Over that period the average annual price disparity fell from 9.3 to 4.8; and the average monthly disparity, from 15.4 to 4.8 (Cole, 1938: 94–96, 103). The decline itself is testimony to improvements in communication brought about by canal and turnpike building. The steepness of the decline is probably masked somewhat because Cole grouped the prices for the periods 1816–1830 and 1830–1842, whereas it was late in the canal era and the beginnings of large-scale railroad building that the sharpest declines were felt.

Looked at from one side, the decline represents the gradual increase in the effective size of the market. Looked at from the other side, it represents a decline in spatially based speculative opportunities – opportunities, that is, to turn trade into profit by moving goods between distinct markets. In a sense the railroad and canal regionalized markets; the telegraph nationalized them.

The effect of the telegraph is a simple one: it evens out markets in space. The telegraph puts everyone in the same place for purposes of trade; it makes geography irrelevant. The telegraph brings the conditions of supply and demand in all markets to bear on the determination of a price. Except for the marginal exception here and there, it eliminates opportunities for arbitrage by realizing the classical assumption of perfect information.

But the significance of the telegraph does not lie solely in the decline of arbitrage; rather, the telegraph shifts speculation into another dimension. It shifts speculation from space to time, from arbitrage to futures. After the telegraph, commodity trading moved from trading between places to trading between times. The arbitrager trades Cincinnati for St. Louis; the futures trader sells August against October, this year against next. To put the matter somewhat differently, as the telegraph closed down spatial uncertainty in prices it opened up, because of improvements in communication, the uncertainty of time. It was not, then, mere historic accident that the Chicago Commodity Exchange, to this day the principal American futures market, opened in 1848, the same year the telegraph reached that city. In a certain sense the telegraph invented the future as a new zone of uncertainty and a new region of practical action.

Let me make a retreat from that conclusion about the effects of the telegraph on time because I have overdrawn the case. First, the opportunities for arbitrage are never completely eliminated. There are always imperfections in market information, even on the floor of a stock exchange: buyers and sellers who do not know of one another and the prices at which the others are willing to trade. We know this as well from ordinary experience at auctions, where someone always knows a buyer who will pay more than the auctioned price. Second, there was a hiatus between arbitrage and the futures market when time contracts dominated, and this was a development of some importance. An approximation of futures trading occurred as early as 1733, when the East India Company initiated the practice of trading warrants. The function of a warrant was to transfer ownership of goods without consummating their physical transfer. The warrant did not represent, as such, particular warehoused goods; they were merely endorsed from person to person. The use of warrants or time contracts evolved rapidly in the United States in the trading of agricultural staples. They evolved to meet new conditions of effective market size and, as importantly, their evolution was unrestrained by historic practice.

The critical condition governing the development of time contracts was also the separation of communication from transport. Increasingly, news of crop conditions reached the market before the commodity itself. For example, warrant trading advanced when cotton was shipped to England by sail while passengers and information moved by steamer. Based on news of the crop and on samples of the commodity, time contracts or "to-arrive" contracts were executed. These were used principally for transatlantic sales, but after the Mississippi Valley opened up to agricultural trade, they were widely used in Chicago in the 1840s (Baer and Woodruff, 1935: 3–5).

The telegraph started to change the use of time contracts, as well as arbitrage. By widely transmitting knowledge of prices and crop conditions, it drew markets and prices together. We do not have good before-and-after measures, but we do have evidence, cited earlier, for the long-run decline in price disparities among markets. Moreover, we have measures from Cincinnati in particular. In the 1820s Cincinnati lagged two years behind Eastern markets. That meant that it took two years for disturbances in the Eastern market structure to affect Cincinnati prices. By 1840 the lag was down to four months; and by 1857 – and probably much earlier – the effect of Eastern markets on Cincinnati was instantaneous. But once space was, in the phrase of the day, annihilated, once everyone was in the same place for purposes of trade, time as a new region of experience, uncertainty, speculation, and exploration was opened up to the forces of commerce.

A back-door example of this inversion of space and time can be drawn from a later episode involving the effect of the telephone on the New York Stock Exchange. By 1894 the telephone had made information time identical in major cities. Buyers and sellers, wherever they were, knew current prices as quickly as traders did on the floor of the exchange. The information gap, then, between New York and Boston had been eliminated and business gravitated from New York to Boston brokerage firms. The New York exchange countered this movement by creating a thirty-second time advantage that ensured New York's superiority to Boston. The exchange ruled that telephones would not be allowed on the floor. Price information had to be relayed by messenger to an area off the floor of the exchange that had been set aside for tele-phones. This move destroyed the temporal identity of markets, and a thirty-second monopoly of knowledge was created that drew business back to New York (Emery, 1896: 139).

This movement of commodities out of space and into time had three other con-sequences of great importance in examining the effect of the telegraph. First, futures trading required the decontexualization of markets; or, to put it in a slightly different way, markets were made relatively unresponsive to local conditions of supply and demand. The telegraph removed markets from the particular context in which they were historically located and concentrated on them forces emanating from any place and any time. This was a redefinition from physical or geographic markets to spiritual ones. In a sense they were made more mysterious; they became everywhere markets and everytime markets and thus less apprehensible at the very moment they became more powerful.

Second, not only were distant and amorphous forces brought to bear on markets, but the commodity was sundered from its representations; that is, the development of futures trading depended on the ability to trade or circulate negotiable instruments independently of the actual physical movement of goods. The representation of the commodity became the warehouse receipts from grain elevators along the railroad line. These instruments were then traded independently of any movement of the actual goods. The buyer of such receipts never expected to take delivery; the seller of such receipts never expected to make delivery. There is the old joke, which is also a cautionary tale, of the futures trader who forgot what he was up to and ended up with forty tons of wheat on his suburban lawn; but it is merely a joke and a tale. The futures trader often sells before he buys, or buys and sells simultaneously. But the buying and selling is not of goods but of receipts. What is being traded is not money for commodities but time against price. In short, the warehouse receipt, which stands as a representation of the product, has no intrinsic relation to the real product.

But in order to trade receipts rather than goods, a third change was necessary. In futures trading products are not bought or sold by inspection of the actual product or a sample thereof. Rather, they are sold through a grading system. In order to lend itself to futures trading, a product has to be mixed, standardized, diluted in order to be reduced to a specific, though abstract, grade. With the coming of the telegraph, products could no longer be shipped in separate units as numerous as there were owners of grain. "The high volume sales required impersonalized standards. Buyers were no longer able personally to check every lot" (Chandler, 1977: 211). Con-sequently, not all products are traded on the futures market because some resist the attempt to reduce them to standardized categories of quality.

The development of the futures markets, in summary, depended on a number of specific changes in markets and the commodity system. It required that information move independently of and faster than products. It required that prices be made uniform in space and that markets be decontextualized. It required, as well, that com-modities be separated from the receipts that represent them and that commodities be reduced to uniform grades.

These were, it should be quickly added, the conditions that underlay Marx's analysis of the commodity fetish. That concept, now used widely and often indiscriminately, was developed in the *Grundrisse* and *Das Kapital* during the late 1850s, when futures trading became the dominant arena for the establishment of agricultural values. In particular, Marx made the key elements in the commodity fetish the decontextualization of markets, the separation of use value from exchange value brought about by the decline in the representative function of the warehouse receipt, and the abstraction of the product out of real conditions of production by a grading system. In the *Grundrisse* he comments, "This locational movement – the bringing of the product to market which is a necessary condition of its circulation, except when the point of production is itself a market – could more precisely be regarded as the transformation of the product into a commodity" (Marx, 1973: 534).

Marx's reference is to what Walter Benjamin (1968) would later call the "loss of aura" in his parallel analysis of the effect of mechanical reproduction on the work of art. After the object is abstracted out of the real conditions of its production and use and is transported to distant markets, standardized and graded, and represented by fully contingent symbols, it is made available as a commodity. Its status as a commodity represents the sundering of a real, direct relationship between buyer and seller, separates use value from exchange value, deprives objects of any uniqueness (which must then be returned to the object via advertising), and, most important, masks to the buyer the real conditions of production. Further, the process of divorcing the receipt from the product can be thought of as part of a general social process initiated by the use of money and widely written about in contemporary semiotics; the progressive divorce of the signifier from the signified, a process in which the world of signifiers progressively overwhelms and moves independently of real material objects.

To summarize, the growth of communications in the nineteenth century had the practical effect of diminishing space as a differentiating criterion in human affairs. What Harold Innis called the "penetrative powers of the price system" was, in effect, the spread of a uniform price system throughout space so that for purposes of trade everyone was in the same place. The telegraph was the critical instrument in this spread. In commerce this meant the decontextualization of markets so that prices no longer depended on local factors of supply and demand but responded to national and international forces. The spread of the price system was part of the attempt to colonize space. The correlative to the penetration of the price system was what the composer Igor Stravinsky called the "statisticalization of mind": the transformation of the entire mental world into quantity, and the distribution of quantities in space so that the relationship between things and people becomes solely one of numbers. Statistics widens the market for everything and makes it more uniform and interdependent. The telegraph worked this same effect on the practical consciousness of time through the construction of standard time zones.

IV

Our sense of time and our activities in time are coordinated through a grid of time zones, a grid so fixed in our consciousness that it seems to be the natural form of time, at least until we change back and forth between standard and daylight saving time. But standard time in the United States is a relatively recent invention. It was introduced on November 18, 1883.

Until that date virtually every American community established its own time by marking that point when the sun reached its zenith as noon. It could be determined astronomically with exactitude; but any village could do it, for all practical purposes, by observing the shortest shadow on a sundial. Official local time in a community could be fixed, as since time immemorial, by a church or later by a courthouse, a jeweler, or later still the railroad stationmaster; and a bell or whistle could be rung or set off so that the local burghers could set their timepieces. In Kansas City a ball was dropped from the highest building at noon and was visible for miles around, a practice still carried out at the annual New Year's Eve festivities in New York City's Times Square (Corliss, 1952).

Not every town kept its own time; many set their clocks in accord with the county seat or some other nearby town of commercial or political importance. When the vast proportion of American habitats were, in Robert Wiebe's (1967) phrase, "island communities" with little intercourse with one another, the distinctiveness of local time caused little confusion and worry. But as the tentacles of commerce and politics spread out from the capitals, temporal chaos came with them. The chaos was sheerly physical. With every degree of longitude one moved westward, the sun reached its zenith four minutes later. That meant that when it was noon in Boston it was 11:48 a.m. in Albany; when it was noon in Atlanta it was 11:36 a.m. in New Orleans. Put differently, noon came a minute later for every quarter degree of longitude one moved westward, and this was a shorter distance as one moved north: in general thirteen miles equaled one minute of time.

The setting of clocks to astronomically local time or, at best, to county seat time led to a proliferation of time zones. Before standard time Michigan had twenty-seven time zones; Indiana, twenty-three; Wisconsin, thirty-nine; Illinois, twenty-seven. The clocks in New York, Boston, and Philadelphia, cities today on identical time, were several minutes apart (Corliss, 1952: 3). When it was 12:00 in Washington, D.C., it was 11:30 in Atlanta, 12:09 in Philadelphia, 12:12 in New York, 12:24 in Boston, and 12:41 in Eastport, Maine.

As the railroads spread across the continent, the variety of local times caused enormous confusion with scheduling, brought accidents as trains on different clocks collided, and led to much passenger irritation, as no one could easily figure when a train would arrive at another town. The railroads used fifty-eight local times keyed to the largest cities. Moreover, each railroad keyed its clocks to the time of a different city. The Pennsylvania Railroad keyed its time to that of Philadelphia, but Philadelphia's clocks were twelve minutes behind New York's and five minutes ahead of Baltimore's. The New York Central stuck to New York City time. The Baltimore and Ohio keyed its time to three cities: Baltimore; Columbus, Ohio; and Vincennes, Indiana (Bartky and Harrison, 1979: 46–53).

The solution, which was to establish standard time zones, had long attracted the interest of scholars. The pressure to establish such zones was felt more strongly in North America, which averaged eight hours of daylight from Newfoundland to western Alaska. Although standard time was established earlier in Europe, the practical pressure there was less. There is only a half-hour variance in sun time across

England; and France, while larger, could be run on Paris time. But England, for purposes of empire, had long been interested in standard time. The control of time allows for the coordination of activity and, therefore, effective social control. In navigation, time was early fixed on English ships according to the clock of the Greenwich observatory; and no matter where a ship might be in the Atlantic, its chronometer always registered Greenwich time. Similarly, Irish time was regulated by a clock set each morning at Big Ben, carried by rail to Holyhead, ferried across the Irish sea to Kingstown (now Dun Laoghaire), and then carried again by rail to Dublin, where Irish clocks were coordinated with English time (Schivelbusch, 1978: 39).

And so it was no surprise when in 1870 a New Yorker, Charles Dowd, proposed a system of standard time zones that fixed Greenwich as zero degrees longitude and laid out the zones around the world with centers 15 degrees east and west from Greenwich. As 15 degrees equals one hour, the world was laid out in twenty-four zones one hour apart.

Dowd's plan was a wonderful example of crackpot realism. The lines were laid out with geometric exactness and ignored geography, topography, region, trade, or natural affinity. Maine and Florida were put in separate time zones. It is a wonderful example of the maxim that the grid is the geometry of empire. Dowd recommended the plan to the railroads, which adopted it provisionally and created an index out of it so that the traveler could convert railroad time to local time by adding or subtracting so many minutes to or from the railroad schedule.

For thirteen years the Dowd system was debated but never officially adopted by the General Time Convention. The railroads tried during that period to get Congress to adopt it as a uniform time system, but Congress would not and for an obvious reason: standard time offended people with deeply held religious sentiments. It violated the actual physical working of the natural order and denied the presence of a divinely ordained nature. But even here religious language was a vanishing mediator for political sentiments; standard time was widely known as Vanderbilt's time, and protest against it was part of the populist protest against the banks, the telegraph, and the railroad.

In 1881, the Philadelphia General Time Convention turned the problem over to William Frederick Allen, a young civil engineer; two years later he returned a plan. It was based on Dowd's scheme but with a crucial difference: it allowed for the adjustment of time zones for purposes of economy and ecology. In his scheme time boundaries could be shifted up to 100 miles away from the geometric lines in order to minimize disruption. Most important, he recommended that the railroads abandon the practice of providing a minute index and that they simply adopt standard time for regulating their schedules and allow communities and institutions to adjust to the new time in any manner they chose.

In the Allen plan the United States was divided into four time zones, with centers on the 75th, 90th, 105th, and 120th meridians: Philadelphia, St. Louis, Denver, and Reno were the approximate centers. The zones extended seven and a half degrees to either side of the center line. November 18, 1883, was selected as the date for the changeover from local to standard time, and an ambitious "educational" campaign was mounted to help citizens adjust to the new system. On that date Chicago, the railroad hub, was tied by telegraph to an observatory in Allegheny, Pennsylvania.

When it reached one o'clock over the center of the Eastern time zone, the clocks were stopped at noon in Chicago and held for nine minutes and thirty-two seconds until the sun centered on the 90th meridian. Then they were started again, with the railroad system now integrated and coordinated through time.

The changeover was greeted by mass meetings, anger, and religious protest but to no avail. Railroad time had become standard time. It was not made official U.S. time until the emergency of World War I. But within a few months after the establishment of railroad time, the avalanche of switches to it by local communities was well under way. Strangely enough, the United States never did go to 24-hour time and thus retained some connection between the diurnal cycle of human activity and the cycle of the planets.

The boundaries of the time zones have been repeatedly adjusted since that time. In general they have been made to follow state borders, but there are a number of exceptions. The western edge of the Eastern time zone was once in eastern Ohio, but now it forms a jagged line along the Illinois–Indiana border. Boise, Idaho, was moved from Pacific to Mountain time, and recently twelve thousand square miles of Arizona was similarly moved. The reasons for such changes tell us much about America's purposes. One gets the distinct feeling, for example, that the television networks would prefer a country with three time zones: east, central, and west.

Standard time zones were established because in the eyes of some they were necessary. They were established, to return to the point of this chapter, because of the technological power of the telegraph. Time was sent via the telegraph wire; but today, thanks to technical improvements, it is sent via radio waves from the Naval observatory in Maryland. The telegraph could send time faster than a railroad car could move; and therefore it facilitated the temporal coordination and integration of the entire system. Once that was possible, the new definitions of time could be used by industry and government to control and coordinate activity across the country, infiltrate into the practical consciousness of ordinary men and women, and uproot older notions of rhythm and temporality.

The development of standard time zones served to overlay the world with a grid of time in the same way the surveyor's map laid a grid of space on old cities, the new territories of the West, or the seas. The time grid could then be used to control and coordinate activities within the grid of space.

V

When the ecological niche of space was filled, filled as an arena of commerce and control, attention was shifted to filling time, now defined as an aspect of space, a continuation of space in another dimension. As the spatial frontier was closed, time became the new frontier. Let me mention, in closing, two other dimensions of the temporal frontier.

An additional time zone to be penetrated once space was exhausted was sacred time, in particular the sabbath. The greatest invention of the ancient Hebrews was the idea of the sabbath, though I am using this word in a fully secular sense: the invention of a region free from control of the state and commerce where another dimension of life could be experienced and where altered forms of social relationship could occur.

As such, the sabbath has always been a major resistance to state and market power. For purposes of communication, the effective penetration of the sabbath came in the 1880s with the invention of the Sunday newspaper. It was Hearst with his New York Sunday *World* who popularized the idea of Sunday newspaper reading and created, in fact, a market where none had existed before – a sabbath market. Since then the penetration of the sabbath has been one of the "frontiers" of commercial activity. Finally, when the frontier in space was officially closed in 1890, the "new frontier" became the night, and since then there has been a continuous spreading upward of commercial activity. Murray Melbin (1987) has attempted to characterize "night as a frontier." In terms of communication the steady expansion of commercial broadcasting into the night is one of the best examples. There were no 24-hour radio stations in Boston, for example, from 1918 through 1954; now half of the stations in Boston operate all night. Television has slowly expanded into the night at one end and at the other initiated operations earlier and earlier. Now, indeed, there are 24-hour television stations in major markets.

The notion of night as frontier, a new frontier of time that opens once space is filled, is a metaphor, but it is more than that. Melbin details some of the features common to the spatial and temporal frontiers: they both advance in stages; the population is more sparsely settled and homogeneous; there is solitude, an absence of social constraints, and less persecution; settlements are isolated; government is decentralized; lawlessness and violence as well as friendliness and helpfulness increase; new behavioral styles emerge. That is, the same dialectic between centralization and decentralization occurs on the temporal frontier as on the spatial frontier. On the one hand, communication is even more privatized at night. On the other hand, social constraints on communication are relaxed because the invasive hand of authority loosened.

The penetration of time, the use of time as a mechanism of control, the opening of time to commerce and politics has been radically extended by advances in computer technology. Time has been redefined as an ecological niche to be filled down to the microsecond, nanosecond, and picosecond – down to a level at which time can be pictured but not experienced. This process and the parallel reconstruction of practical consciousness and practical activity begins in those capacities of the telegraph which prefigure the computer. The telegraph constructed a simulacrum of complex systems, provided an analogue model of the railroad and a digital model of language. It coordinated and controlled activity in space, often behind the backs of those subject to it.

E. P. Thompson finds it ominous that the young Henry Ford should have created a watch with two dials: one for local time and another for railroad time. "Attention to time in labour depends in large degree upon the need for the synchronization of labour" (Thompson, 1967: 70). Modern conceptions of time have rooted into our consciousness so deeply that the scene of the worker receiving a watch at his retirement is grotesque and comic. He receives a watch when the need to tell time is ended. He receives a watch as a tribute to his learning the hardest lesson of the working man – to tell time.

As the watch coordinated the industrial factory; the telegraph via the grid of time coordinated the industrial nation. Today, computer time, computer space, and computer memory, notions we dimly understand, are reworking practical consciousness coordinating and controlling life in what we glibly call the postindustrial society. Indeed, the microcomputer is replacing the watch as the favored gift for the middle class retiree. In that new but unchanging custom we see the deeper relationship between technology and ideology.

Notes

1 See Chandler (1977), esp. Part II.
2 Among the most readable, accessible sources on the patent struggles is Josephson (1959).
3 See Wiener (1948: 38–44).
4 Whereas I have commented on the essentially religious metaphors that greeted the telegraph in the essays cited, Czitrom (1982) brings this material together in a systematic way.
5 By a vanishing mediator – a concept borrowed from Fredric Jameson – I mean a notion that serves as a bearer of change but that can disappear once that change is ratified in the reality of institutions. See Jameson (1974: 111–149).
6 See chapter 1. On changes in styles of journalism, see Sims (1979).
7 Steffens (1958: 834). For a memoir that discusses the art and adversity of writing for the cable, see Shirer (1976: 282 ff.).
8 The quotation is from an as yet unpublished manuscript by Douglas Birkhead of the University of Utah. Birkhead develops these themes in some detail.
9 On urban imperialism, see Schlesinger (1933) and Pred (1973).
10 Among the few studies on the telegraph and empire, the most distinguished is Fortner (1978); see also Field (1978: 644–68).
11 In making these remarks I am much indebted to the work of Fortner and Field.
12 On these matters there are useful suggestions in Boorstin (1973).

5.2

Reflections on time, time–space compression and technology in the nineteenth century,
by Jeremy Stein

Introduction

Social scientists have long been aware of the significance of developments in transport and communication for the reorientation of temporal and spatial relationships between places (Janelle, 1968; Falk and Abler, 1980). The concepts 'time–space convergence' and 'time–space compression' were developed by geographers to describe the cumulative effects of historical improvements in the speed of movement of goods, services and information. The former concept refers to the increased velocity of circulation of goods, people and information, and the consequent reduction in relative distances between places. The latter concept describes the sense of shock and disorientation such experiences produce (Harvey, 1989, 1990). As Harvey describes it, time–space compression refers to:

> processes that so revolutionise the objective qualities of space and time that we are forced to alter, sometimes in quite radical ways, how we represent the world to ourselves. I use the word 'compression' because a strong case can be made that the history of capitalism has been characterised by speed-up in the pace of life, while so overcoming spatial barriers that the world sometimes seems to collapse inwards upon us.
>
> (Harvey, 1989: 240)

Harvey's discussion of time–space compression relates mainly to contemporary capitalism. He views new ways of experiencing time and space as coinciding with intense periods of technological change, a consequence of capitalism's need to speed up the circulation of capital and information. Other writers emphasise how new communications technologies shape contemporary economic, social and political processes. These writers point to the increasing speed, volume and significance of capital and information flows in recent times (Castells, 1989; Leyshon, 1995). Enabled by instantaneous communication between places, organisations are increasingly able to integrate and co-ordinate their activities on a global basis, captured by the term 'globalisation'. At their most extreme, writers suggest that an era of ceaseless global flows of money, capital and information heralds the end of geography (O'Brien, 1991). However, as Thrift and others argue, flows of capital and information rarely lack a geography of their own, and because communities of experts are required to interpret their significance, this often reinforces traditional national, institutional and urban geographies (Thrift, 1995, 1996; Michie, 1997).

The main aim of this chapter is to show that contemporary notions and experiences of time–space compression were prefigured in the nineteenth century. In the next section, I will briefly summarise these experiences and their significance. I suggest that these accounts of changing experiences of time and space may need revision in at least two ways. First, interpretations of time–space compression typically rely on accounts of privileged social observers, and are thereby elitist. Is it right to assume that the experiences of time and space documented by privileged travellers were equally felt by the general population, or that the rapidity of change was the same for everyone? Second, changing experiences of time and space are often assumed to result from the advent of new technologies. This is a form of technological determinism. The danger here is to assume and to exaggerate the consequences of technology. Are new technologies always faster and more efficient than earlier ones? Moreover, do interpretations of time–space compression that see it resulting from improvements in technology risk ignoring the social processes in which technology is embedded? After reviewing historical accounts of time–space compression, I will draw on my own research on a nineteenth-century Canadian textile town to develop a more nuanced interpretation of the historical experiences of time and space.

A shrinking world

As Harvey and other writers have suggested, experiences of time–space compression are not limited to the contemporary period. Giddens' interpretation of modernity, for example, emphasises the role of technology and institutions associated with it (state agencies, businesses, news media) in extending economic, social and political influence over time and space during the nineteenth and twentieth centuries (Giddens, 1990). Berman stresses the unifying role of technology, defining nineteenth-century modernity as the shared experience of unity and disunity (Berman, 1991). For several writers the period between 1880 and the end of the First World War witnessed an intense phase of time–space compression. Marvin describes how the introduction of electrification at the end of the nineteenth century led to intense cultural anxiety concerning the effects of these technologies on Victorian and Edwardian societies, governed by strict systems of hierarchy and social etiquette (Marvin, 1988). Kern demonstrates how during this period a set of new technologies, including the telephone and the wireless telegraph, generated intense feelings of simultaneity coincident with novel ways of thinking about time and space in areas of social thought as diverse as physics and psychology, contemporary art and music (Kern, 1983).

The rapid introduction of a set of new technologies at the end of the nineteenth century no doubt contributed to intense feelings of simultaneity during this period. However, this does not mean that a revolution occurred in the experience of time and space. It is more appropriate to see these changes in the context of on-going processes of change occurring from at least the late eighteenth century. In the next few paragraphs I will summarise the most salient aspects of these changes and their consequences. Before doing so it is worth noting that authors such as Kern have been criticised for other reasons: for their overreliance on elite sources, such as the electrical trade literature that not surprisingly glorifies technological advances; and for their technological determinism. Kern, for example, argues that, because of its immediacy and democratic qualities, technologies such as the telephone invaded privacy, result- ing in nervous dispositions and undermining social and spatial barriers. Critics question whether the consequences of technology are inevitable or predictable, and whether the characteristics of a technology can automatically be assumed to be impressed on to its users (Fischer, 1985, 1992; Marx, 1997a, 1997b).

Without doubt, the cumulative effects of technological change, especially over the past century and a half in the field of transport and communication, have been impressive. This was particularly the case in Europe and North America during the nineteenth century when the introduction of railway, telegraph and steamship ser- vices radically reoriented geographic and temporal relationships. 'The annihilation of space and time' was a common mid-nineteenth century phrase used to describe the experience and significance of these changes. Karl Marx, writing in the 1850s, used similar terminology to describe the significance of improved transport and communi- cations for the circulation and reproduction of capital. In the *Grundrisse* he wrote that 'while capital must on one side strive to tear down every spatial barrier to intercourse . . . it strives on the other side to annihilate this space with time, i.e. to reduce to a minimum the time spent in motion from one place to another' (Marx, 1973: 539).

Developments in transport and communications in Britain during the eighteenth and nineteenth centuries had profound consequences for the economy, society and culture. The railway's impact, for example, was noticeable by the 1830s and 1840s, most significantly in the increased speed of the trains with consequent dramatic reductions in travel times between places (Perkin, 1970; Thrift, 1990a: 463). The effect was to shrink national space. The 'annihilation of space and time' was a com- mon term used to characterise the experience of railway travel in the mid-nineteenth century. The metaphor of 'annihilation' evoked the sudden impact and violence of the railway as it overturned existing notions of time and distance. On the one hand, the railway opened up new spaces and made them much more accessible. On the other, the railway seemingly destroyed space and diminished the uniqueness of individual places (Schivelbusch, 1977: 41). The uniqueness of place was further eroded by the introduction of uniform railroad time. Growth of the railway network, the consequent complexity of railway scheduling and the wish to avoid accidents, gradually made the existence of multiple local times untenable, and led railway com- panies to introduce 'standard time' along their routes (Bartky, 1989; Kern, 1983; Stephens, 1989; Thrift, 1981).

The railway was intimately associated with developments in communications technology, particularly the electric telegraph and the telephone. These technologies inaugurated simultaneous communication and a phase of 'time–space convergence' (Janelle, 1968; Falk and Abler, 1980; Harvey, 1989, 1990). Railway companies required first class communications and from an early phase in railway development the telegraph was used as a safety device and as a means of traffic control. The Great Western Railway used the telegraph experimentally in 1839. It was used throughout on the Norfolk Railway in 1844 and during the same period on the South Eastern Railway. The telegraph, and later the telephone, was an important means of internal communication allowing railway companies to better manage their staff and complex operations. Telephone systems allowed the central office of a railway company to be in constant and immediate communication with every signal box, station, yard, office or other point in its organisation. The railway companies were also quick to take advantage of teleprinters and exchange switching technology, giving them greater flexibility and capacity to handle information (Ellis, 1959; Parris, 1965; Kieve, 1973).

Elsewhere, authors have speculated on the cultural and ideological consequences of new communications technologies. Carey, for example, argues that the introduction of the telegraph in America had profound ideological significance. The telegraph in America was dominated by Western Union, the first great industrial monopoly, which established the principles upon which modern businesses were managed. Carey suggests that the telegraph had a set of ideological consequences. Culturally, it brought changes in language, knowledge and awareness, leading, for example, to 'scientific' newspaper reporting, with news stripped of its local and regional context. By separating communication from transportation it changed the ways in which communication was thought about, for example, contributing to organic and systematic modes of thinking. Politically, it made the idea of 'empire' practically possible by allowing distant colonies to be controlled from the centre. Economically, it evened out commodity markets, diminished the significance of local conditions of supply and demand, made geography seemingly irrelevant, and shifted speculation from space to time, making possible the emergence of a futures market (Carey, 1983). Cronon usefully extends this argument and the metaphor of 'annihilating space' to the Chicago grain and meat-packing industries. He demonstrates how, in conjunction with the railway and the introduction of grain elevators and new technology in the abattoirs, the telegraph speeded up the delivery of goods to urban markets. The result was regional integration of the wheat and meat markets and the emergence of standard abstract product qualities, for example, September wheat, that could be easily traded on Chicago's stock market (Cronon, 1992).

As this last example suggests, it was a combination of technologies that gave nineteenth-century commentators the sense of a shrinking world. Hobsbawm describes, for example, how in the middle decades of the nineteenth century the world was unified by a combination of land and subterranean telegraphs, the construction of trans-continental railroads, steamship services and the completion of major construction projects such as the Suez canal (opened in 1869) (Hobsbawm, 1975: 49–67). It was these tremendous mid-century improvements in transport and communications that enabled Jules Verne to envisage his fictional character, Phileas Fogg, circumnavigating the globe in eighty days (a feat that would have taken eleven months in 1848) and for the results of the 1871 Derby to be transmitted from London to Calcutta in five minutes (Hobsbawm, 1975: 52–3). Improved communications in the nineteenth century were accompanied by greater global interdependency. The upside to this was the creation of a genuinely world market and significant reductions in the speed of movement of goods, people and information. The downside was the increased uncertainty of events and the threat of global slumps. The acceleration in the speed of communications intensified the contrast between those areas of the globe having access to improved technology and those that did not: 'in widening the gap between the places accessible to the new technology and the rest, it intensified the relative backwardness of those parts of the world where horse, ox, mule, human bearer or boat still set the speed of transport' (Hobsbawm, 1975: 60). Greater global inter-dependency, a consequence of improved communications, increased the frequency of contact and the apparent contrast between technologically advanced and techno-logically backward regions of the globe, contributing to emerging nineteenth century ideologies of Western dominance (Headrick, 1981; Adas, 1989).

To summarise, time–space compression was apparent in Britain from at least the late eighteenth century. By the mid-nineteenth century, with the coming of the rail-way to Europe and North America, it was commonly experienced, and its effects were increasingly global. However the changes described above took place over several decades so that it would be wrong to view experiences of time–space compression in any one period as being revolutionary. It is also questionable how widely felt these experiences were. Writers, such as Schivelbusch, typically dwell on the dramatic epi-sodes of technological change such as the coming of the railway (Schivelbusch, 1977). We learn that contemporaries' reflections on these events were captured by the metaphor of 'annihilation': symbolising, on the one hand, technological and societal progress, and on the other, the downside of rapid social and technological transform-ation. However Schivelbusch does not indicate how widespread these reflections were, whether they varied along gender and class lines, and whether the ideology of progress was espoused by specific social groups.

Advances in transport and communication were not limited to communications between places. This was equally a feature within cities. Beginning in the early nineteenth century European and North American cities constructed an infra-structure of pipes and wires for the systematic centralised distribution of fuel, light, power and information (Tarr and Dupuy, 1988). These early 'networked' or 'wired' cities may be regarded as forerunners of today's electronic or informational cities (Castells, 1989; Stein, 1996, 1999). Improved intra-urban communication is typically not discussed in academic treatments of time–space compression, and is generally under-researched and poorly understood. Moreover, detailed studies of the diffusion of new communications technologies often challenge exaggerated accounts of the effects of these technologies. During the nineteenth century, for example, the major-ity of telegraphic and telephonic communication remained local (Stein, 1999: 47–51). Similarly, Fischer's study of the diffusion of the motor car and the telephone in early-twentieth-century America shows that far from undermining localism, these technologies sustained it, by extending the volume of local and extra-local contacts (Fischer, 1992: 193–221).

5.3

On the move: technology, mobility, and the mediation of social time and space, by Nicola Green

The spaces and experiences of modern social life

One of the most significant developments of modernization across the 20th century has been the construction of the modern urban metropolis. In the modern city, the construction of urban spaces transforms previously continuous geographical locations into a series of fleeting places, images, and encounters in crowds (Simmel, 1997). The construction of modern urban space (including telecommunications infrastructures), by concentrating population and allowing for dense copresent but ever-changing interactions amongst centralized infrastructures, has contributed to a changing experience of time-bound social relationships. These have shifted from those of durable copresent interactions to fragmented and disconnected spatial and temporal connections. The spaces of the city separate "the private" from "the public," and institute locations (geographically defined spaces) and places (subjectively, socially, culturally, and geographically defined spaces) that have little connection with each other. Public social life therefore becomes an experience of discontinuity, where activities became compartmentalized in a series of fleeting encounters and impressions of little duration (Simmel, 1997; Frisby, 1985). Private social life, by contrast, becomes that of copresence, continuity, and proximity, instituting a divide between geographically defined public and private spaces.

Social and organizational activities in the newly emerging city required new forms of coordination, and technologies to manage it. Travel was one such set of technologies, as people became newly mobile and needed to coordinate times to meet or organize activities (Lash & Urry, 1994). The coordination of copresent activities via the technologies of travel required greater attention or orientation to (and discipline by) "clock time" as the prevailing organization of temporally based activities, including attention to measurable, calculable, and linear units of standardized time. The development of new production processes in industrialization and the role of clock time in new forms of work organization all helped institute new forms of time, centered around changes in interval, sequencing, and duration. The main thrust of these arguments is the move toward measurable, calculable units of clock time, standardized and shifting toward ever shorter time periods (Lash & Urry, 1994).

Lash and Urry (1994, p. 229) argue that the ascendence of clock time is attributable to such interacting changes as

> the disembedding of time from social activities as it becomes significantly stripped of meaning; the breakdown of time into a larger number of small units; the emergence of the disciplinary power of time; the increasing timetabling and hence mathematization of social life; and the emergence of a synchronized measure of life first across national territories and later across the globe with the development of Greenwich and "world time."

Simmel (1997) implies that the public life of the city in this case becomes an aggregation of privatized and individualized activities and agendas, bearing little relation to others. This particular development is detailed in du Gay et al. (1997) in their research on the Sony Walkman. In the case of the Walkman, private, subjective, and emotional geographies are mapped on to the public spaces of the city, transforming public space into a continuation of private, subjective experiences, rather than a collective of shared experiences. Cooper et al. (forthcoming, p. 4) suggest that "it is worth considering whether the increasing development and use of mobile technologies represents a kind of accentuation of the fragmented and individualized experience of modernity. Whereas it could be argued that the development of new tools and technologies are driving these changes, they reflect changing social notions of time more generally across the twentieth century."

As Lash and Urry (1994) note, it is not only the individual moving through city streets who experiences the changed times and spaces of modern urban life, but also the car, train, and bus travelers, who "transcend" what was formally understood as the "tyranny" of distance. Raymond Williams (1974, p. 26) identifies "mobile privatisation" as the contemporary experience of car travel:

> at most active social levels people are increasingly living as private small-family units, or . . . as private and deliberately self-enclosed individuals, while at the same time there is a quite unprecedented mobility of such restricted privacies . . . what is experienced inside them . . . is movement, choice of direction, the pursuit of self-determined private purposes. All the other shells are moving, in comparable ways but for their own different private ends. They are not so much other people, in any full sense, but other units which signal and are signalled to, so that private mobilities can proceed safely and relatively unhindered.

The increase in mobility, the development of temporal coordination, and the emergence of technologies designed to address the problem of "distance" in the city contributed to changing relations of physical presence and absence in newly formed urban spaces, and a changing subjective understanding of what Giddens (1990) calls "presence-availability." This includes both distance and proximity as related to physical copresence, as well as presence and availability as newly mediated via emerging technologies. The central argument is that throughout the 20th century, changes in physical proximity and distance – including the effects of technologies designed to address time and distance, as well as a shifting consciousness of temporality – have "dislocated," "disembedded," and "disembodied" individuals from local, collective and copresent understandings of, and activities in, time, by "stretching" social relations.

However, if we turn to examine specific contemporary communications and information technologies, and the social relations that attend them, the general and universalizing arguments around changes in "presence availability" begin to look more problematic.

Spatial mobility, time, and telecommunications technologies

Marshall McLuhan (1964, p. 271) wrote, "The telephone is an irresistible intruder in time and space." Historical analyses have indicated that changes in temporal organization across the 20th century have involved changing relationships between natural, social, clock, and subjective time, as well as changes in space, mobility, and the boundaries of the public and private in the construction of the modern city. Other recent research has traced the specific transformations that have taken place with the introduction of different kinds of telecommunications and new information technologies. Social investigations of the "tele-presence" that the telegraph (Standage, 1998), the telephone (Fischer, 1988), and more recently the Internet (Boden & Molotch, 1994) have made possible have pointed to the central role these technologies have played in changing relationships across geographical space and time. Indeed, technologies such as the telephone are specifically spatial: Their sole function is to support social communication at a distance, and their ability to collapse distance has made possible many spatial features of contemporary urban life. The office towers of late modernity, for example, could not exist without the telecommunications technologies to coordinate their internal spaces (Pool, 1977; Townsend, 2001).

It is a well-established premise in social thought that the dominant technologies of a particular historical period define temporal organization and cultural understandings of it. Recent investigations of capital, industrial, and labor times (Thompson, 1967; Thrift, 1996; Rifkin, 1987; Adam, 1990), or "internet time" (Lee & Liebenau, 2000), are cases in point. According to some researchers (Ling & Yttri, 1999), mobile devices again reconfigure the spaces of urban social life. If mobile devices are "space-adjusting technologies" that provide resources for understanding a sense of place and relationship in both professional and private life, as Frissen (1995) suggests, then the changing times that attend changing spaces are also at issue. In research on the social aspects of mobile technologies thus far, for example, the notion of time flexibility has been a recurring theme, as has the "compression" of activities and relationships into more periods of shorter duration of communication (Townsend, 2001). There also seems to be an unprecedented level of simultaneous copresent and tele-present interaction made possible through mobile technologies (Cooper et al., forthcoming).

These concerns about duration, interval, and sequencing, as well as issues of presence, absence, and availability, are sometimes explained via analytical projects that concentrate on the specific changing temporal organization of new information and communication technologies (see, e.g., Lee & Liebenau, 2000). These projects describe changes in the context of spatial proximity and distance, such that changing activities are said to intensify to the extent that the subjective experience of time is "fast" or "speeding" (an intensification of more and different activities of a shorter duration) (Virilio, 2000; Townsend, 2001). The decentralization of communication creates new webs of potential interaction between atomized individuals, which on the one hand increases the communication activities carried out, while at the same time fragmenting that communication into more numerous communications of shorter duration. According to Townsend (2001, p. 4), this is "dramatically speeding the metabolism of urban systems, increasing capacity and efficiency. The 'realtime city,' in which system conditions can be monitored and reacted to instantaneously, has arrived." Some theorists, such as Virilio (2000), therefore note the ways that the "speed" of electronic communications involves an immediacy of action such that movement in physical space becomes no longer even necessary. Lash and Urry (1994) also cite Nowotny (1994), who argues that the immediacy presented by new technologies of information and communication result in an experience of "instant-aneous time." As Adam (1990, p. 140) notes, if all multiple activities in time are experienced as "instant" in this way, the future conflates with the present, concentrat-ing and intensifying social action, entailing panic about and distrust of "the future" (Adam, 1990, p. 140).

For those who accept that the experience of time is "intensifying," "speeding up," or becoming "instantaneous," this type of change is attributable to a number of different factors. Harvey (1990), for example, attributes the "space–time compres-sion" just outlined to the acceleration of the activities of capital over the 20th century, in which time and space both become abstractions and cease to have meaning or value in themselves; their meaning and value are instead determined by the circulation of capital, especially in commodification and representation. Giddens's (1990) view largely echoes Harvey's, but also considers how time and space "distanciate" as well as "compress." Although time–space compression (or "convergence" in Giddens's argument) describes shrinking distance in time (the span of time it takes to move from one location to another), "time–space distanciation" describes "the processes by which societies are 'stretched' over shorter or longer spans of time and space" (Lash & Urry, 1994). The structuring of time–space distanciation relies on such social relations as "presence-availability" – the organization of presence, absence proximity and availability, and the degree of copresent activities in relation to "tele-present" activities. It also relies on mediating technologies, such as information and communi-cations technologies, and the control and storage capacity of them. These relations are interlinked, such that the relation of time and space may be routinized in different ways depending on forms of urban structure, the interaction of different transportation and communication technologies, the role of the state and surveillance of populations (Green, 2001), and the commodification of time in labor, industry, leisure, and consumption.

As Lash and Urry (1994) note, however, Giddens's and Harvey's theories rely on a largely generalized and universalized approach to "western societies" that tend to ignore the role of the specific and the local, and how changing times become routinised in mundane and habitual daily life. Several points in Thrift's (1996, pp. 1468–1469) critique of theories of new information and communication technol-ogies are salient here: Thrift argues that these theories tend to argue from extremes; that the technologies are assumed to replace the ones that had gone before; that the technologies are described as seamless systems without interruptions or limits, presented as coherent and consistent, without difference or locality; that the technologies are assumed to be likely to spread everywhere, quickly; that they are "rarely seen as a linked repertoire of practices"; that they are positioned in opposition to a distanced and controlled nature; and that they are mainly comprised of representation, rather than technical repertoires in use.

Doreen Massey (1993, pp. 61–62) adds that "power-geometries" are also crucial in the construction of space–time relations, and can be drawn out by asking *whose* mobility, *whose* times and spaces are under discussion:

> For different social groups and different individuals are placed in very distinct ways in relation to the flows and interconnections. This point concerns not merely the issue of who moves and who doesn't . . . it is also about power relation *to* the flows and the movement. Different social groups have distinct relationships to this anyway – differentiated mobility: some are more in charge of it than others; some initiate flows and movement, others don't; some are more on the receiving end of it than others; some are effectively imprisoned by it. . . . This is, in other words, a highly complex social differentiation. There is the dimension of the degree of movement and communication, but also dimensions of control and initiation.

Massey argues coherently for analytical sensitivity to both geographical space and social and cultural locality in considering the relations of space–time. She argues for attention to the complex relations between space, locality, time, social organization, and culture, so that the heterogeneous effects of changing social institutions alongside changing technologies can be understood and "mapped." This argument emerges from a concern to (re)introduce notions that describe social and cultural difference, such as gender, ethnicity, and sexuality, to analyses of time and space. As an illustration, one story that we were told in the course of fieldwork pertained to the case of India, and was related by an educational anthropologist. After traveling several days to reach a small village in northern India, she spent time in the village looking at educational systems. While there, she came across the one person in the village who owned a mobile phone. This individual had made a business out of calling friends and relatives of villagers elsewhere (in the absence of any fixed line services), taking on the role once held by village letter writers. The notion of "changing mobile temporalities" has very different origins, and very different implications for these villagers, than they do for the "flexible schedulers" (like myself) in the West.

In summary then, sociologists have identified a number of overlapping times that both reflect and contribute to social organization, including various "natural" times and cycles such as diurnal, lunar and seasonal times, the calendar, clock, universal/standardized, and regional times that emerged with the development of the modern city, as well as the locally organized and lived times of the public and the private (such as "on time" and "off time") (Adam, 1990; Lash & Urry, 1994). They have also traced how various technologies have historically mediated these rhythms, and how technologies can have multiple temporal effects. As Massey (1992) and Thrift (1996) suggest, setting out the connections between presence, absence, proximity, distance, and "time–space adjusting technologies" entails attention to local and situated temporal organization, as well as global and extended times. It therefore entails empirical research as well as theoretical pronouncements. While social activities mediated by mobile technologies potentially encourage fragmentation and the individualization of the experience of time, extending time–space "compression," "convergence," and "distanciation," and the speed and intensity of modern, Western life, locally shared rhythms and the social activities of lived times must also be accounted for. The emerging mobile times in their local and situated, as well as "global" incidence, can be usefully accessed via ethnographic materials.

The next section therefore outlines the relations we have encountered in our ethnography of mobile phones. They demonstrate emerging "mobile times" that must (increasingly) be considered in any theoretical discussion of temporal organization in contemporary Western societies.

Mobile temporality

I suggest in the discussion that follows that we might differentiate three sets of rhythms salient to "mobile time." It is the specific character of these rhythms that are important in the emerging organization of mobile times: the rhythms of mobile use; the rhythms of integrating mobile use into everyday life; and the rhythms of relation between use in everyday life and institutional social change. Rhythms of mobile use relate to the time taken interacting with a mobile device, and refers primarily to the duration and sequencing of interaction between an individual and that device (in this case, a mobile phone). Rhythms of mobile use in everyday life refer to the local temporalities associated with social and cultural relationships in which specific device use is embedded. Rhythms of institutional change refer to the historical and infrastructural elements that enable mobile use, including such dimensions as the institutionalization of travel, cycles of technological development, or the time taken to establish and maintain network technologies.

Lee and Liebenau (2000, pp. 50–51) suggest, in a study of the times of Internet use, that analytical attention should focus on the multiple "actors" of Internet systems – "the users (and uses), the publishers (and their servers), and the powers (including economic powers and regulatory or governance authorities)." If we are to account for potential social change brought about by mobile technologies, issues of access to and control over the temporal rhythms of mobility should also be addressed. Lee and Liebenau (2000) identify six dimensions of focus, including duration, temporal location, sequence, deadlines, cycles, and rhythms. I would add that these dimensions might also include the cultural and political dimensions of mobile use in everyday life. Our ethnography has been carried out over the past 2 years, and has involved fieldwork with groups such as those mobile in their working life, students, teenagers and their parents, as well as observation in main streets, in malls, on trains, and at train stations. Drawing on this research, I would like to illustrate such an analysis.

Rhythms of device use

The first dimension of analysis pertinent to the temporal organization of mobile devices is that of the temporal rhythms of the use of devices and their applications.

Most obvious here are the changing durations of device use for users. On the one hand, there is some evidence that mobile phones presently encourage short conversations, and introduce new opportunities for more conversation unavailable before. According to one teenager:

> It gets really confusing if you're talking to more than one person at a time. Cause if you forget what you said . . . Or you start writing to one person . . . Say like you're talking to one person and they're friends with one person that you're not . . . It gets into a big mess! And then someone phones you and when you're on the phone you can hear the beep as the message comes in. And you're like "I have to go. My bath's run." And you really just want to check your message. (A)

Ling and Yttri (1999) describe this as "micro coordination" and suggest that temporalities change as individuals engage in a kind of instant coordination when mobile, which could contribute to a subjective sense of speed, the intensification of tasks, and the fragmentation of communication. Teenagers use mobile phones in the same ways as adults for these coordinating activities:

> Just like cause I always ring my mum to tell her whether I'm walking home or whether I want her to pick me up. Just like pick up times and stuff and whether I'm staying late cause sometimes I help out and I teach. And also I use it at break times, and when I'm at work as well. (J1)

The use of short text messaging (SMS), especially among young people, might also support these arguments. Language in which words and phrases are abbreviated might contribute to interactions of much shorter duration than previously available, adding to a subjective sense of temporal fragmentation. Teenagers describe their use of language in these circumstances:

> You know, instead of "you are" you just put "u r," or "2" instead of "to." (G)
>   With abbreviations it's more like a colloquial thing. As in who you're in with . . . It's the way you guys speak together anyway. (A)
>   Like if you were talking to your Mum, you wouldn't write "CU." You'd have to write "See you." But if you're talking to your friends then you write "cul8r," because they understand it as well, they're like the same sort of . . . they understand the phones more than the parents do. (J)

The relatively short duration taken to read the messages is also involved. One mobile phone professional commented:

> I use it at work . . . but then when I message, it's to my friends, especially if I'm on the train or something . . . mostly its just one-liners . . . like a competition about who can come up with the best one-liner. (M)

At the same time, however, many teenagers reported that they spend many hours a day (and night), sometimes hours at a time, short text messaging among their peers. These long durations act to consolidate their peer relationships, differentiate them from family or household relations, and contribute to a growing sense of both independence (from family) and collectivity (among peers).

I'm just text messaging all the time . . . like the longest time I spent was about three hours. (G)

It's a bit like text messages, they're addictive. (A)

I can't sleep so I have to send a message to people. And then I get moody if they don't reply. I've got ones that are recorded at like three o'clock in the morning. (J)

Text messages are things that you store . . . they're kind of memories you want to keep. It would be really cool to have like a memory card for each person so I can put all their text messages in there so I can retrieve them one at a time when I want them. (L)

Different forms of communication or device use also take on different meanings depending on the context of the communication in shifting peer relationships.

I'd much rather phone someone, but you don't, because . . . you say things that you really want to say to them in text messages. (J)

Yeah, there are some things that you don't really want to say to someone's face or on the phone to them. You just send a text. (A)

Yesterday a friend of mine was asking me if I still had feelings for his brother. And it's like the minute he asked the question I knew it was going to be one of those text messages that keeps going to go on and on and on. (A)

[Dumping people by text message] That is the worst way. That is like a bitchy thing to do. (J)

It's worse than being a coward. Its worst when calling someone when you know they're a thousand miles away and going "oh yeah, by the way, you're dumped." It's terrible. (A)

This is supported by impressions from some of the parents:

I suspect, I may be totally wrong on this one, but I think what is happening is that kids will sometimes say things in a message that they won't, like the heart sign and things like that. You don't go like "I Love you." She had this boyfriend in Liverpool . . . I suspect a lot of the messages were more like greeting cards, or soppy . . . I think if you want to say something like "Pick me up at the station," I'm not sure you would really message that, would you? It is something you need to get an answer to straight away.

Other features of device interaction reinforce this, such as time spent adjusting and sharing mobile phone address book entries (on a "who's got whose number" basis), or spending time showing friends messages that have been sent and received.

People will always just look at your phone . . . (A)
    . . . and read your messages. (J)
    But everyone does it. But the thing is it's like someone's diary. (J)
    Yeah, I think its personal. I don't read anyone's messages. (A)
    Only unless they show you. If they say "oh, look at this," then I'll look at it. (J)
    It's the way you interact with each person individually, I think. So it reflects with the way you use their phones as well. . . . Even when they give you text messages to read I think that's boring when I don't know who's sent it. So, if it's a sweet message, I don't get it because I don't know the other person so it's just wasted on you. But if it's a funny one you go "ha ha! That was funny, who sent it?" (A)

As these examples show, the duration spent in interaction with the device, with other people, acts to both functionally and symbolically cement the durability of social relationships in local communities. In this case, the duration of "clock time" becomes a less salient feature of ongoing interaction with significant others through the device, than subjective time. The act of using the device, and the time spent doing so, might in this way contribute to a sense of social memory among groups. As Connerton (1989) notes, the minutiae of bodily habits with objects reinforce social and cultural memory. He argues that the use of artifacts literally "incorporates" those memories and relationships in the habits of the body. Time spent using devices makes relationships durable and ongoing, rather than "fragmented."

The durations and sequencing of device use also have durable meanings for organizations such as device manufacturers. Certainly, device manufacturers study the "usability" of their devices in terms of the actions of the body and the duration of time taken to complete specific tasks. This temporal measurement contributes to the design of devices, and these times become durable, literally "objectified" in the devices themselves (such as measurements of the time taken to write text messages on a mobile device, leading to the development of predictive text software).

The results from teens just cited indicate that in the case of design, the measure of duration of activity as a measure of significance for the "usability" of devices may not be as salient as previously thought. Located practical action also has bearing on the duration and sequencing of functions: In many settings for example, we observed pedestrians on main streets or in malls coming to a standstill in order to use some of the functions on their mobile. They were compelled to become immobile to use their mobile device.

Moreover, our interviews with sales and marketing personnel in network operator organizations indicated that network operators record times and intensities of network activities both for billing purposes, and thereafter use the information to build a picture of their consumers. If duration is significant in local ways, network activity, the mathematization of categorization of users into high-use/high-value, low-use/low-value groups as an indicator of consumer practices, might belie changing social patterns of communication and changing patterns of sociality. Perhaps what is more salient is the relationship being maintained through those time-bound activities.

Rhythms of everyday life

These aspects of device use are integrated into emerging patterns of organizing mobile communications and relations in everyday life. One aspect of temporal location significant for users (and for service providers) is the "anytime, anywhere" availability provided by mobile devices, which integrates microcoordination and device use discussed earlier with the rhythms of work, family, and leisure times (Green & Harvey, 1999). For users, the always-availability implied by mobile time and space affects the sequencing of life tasks, deadlines organized around work and home activities, the cycles of work, leisure, and family life, and the rhythms of diurnal, lunar, seasonal, and calendar change – all of which have social implications. The case of Catherine, a sales representative whose work communications are primarily conducted via her mobile phone, is illustrative.

> My mobile is my life . . . well, my car and my mobile. I live in the car. I'll use the mobile for work calls at home in the morning, and then when I'm driving as well, to report back to the office about visits, or to make queries on orders, or whatever . . . I use it to call friends when I'm on the road, but mostly when I'm stuck in traffic jams. If someone rings I'll take the call . . . but mostly, if I'm stuck, I'll ring my Mum. My Mum and I talk quite a lot most days.

Although Catherine's life remains, at least in part, structured through formal or clock time (for example, she regulates work time into compartments of daily and weekly duration), decentralization of both her work and home life prompts flexibility and individualized scheduling. The mobile phone interrupts the time-based coordination of communication and information activities required for scheduling from fixed locations. Individuals may thus organize their activities around flexible compartments of time, rather than compartments of time associated with particular geographical spaces.

At a mundane level, there has been significant research on the "always-availability" of mobile temporality (Green, 2001; Green & Harvey, 1999; Brown et al., 2001.) – to be always and at every time "on call" – and its potential to transform the ways that individuals organize their activities in time and the ways they arrange their "schedules." A kind of spatial and temporal "boundary rearrangement" becomes possible, and has begun to appear in our research. This involves both the case of "public" activities and responsibilities (as in the case of work) that become embedded in the temporal rhythms of the home, as well as "private" relationships becoming integrated into the public sphere in mobile relations.

In the former case, research has tended to concentrate on how mobile teleworkers organize their work and home life, and Ellen Ullman's (1997, p. 136) work echoes the findings of our own research:

> It's not surprising to me . . . [m]y work hours have leaked into all parts of the day and week. Eight in the morning, ten at night, Saturday at noon, Sundays: I am never not working. Even when I'm not actually doing something that could be called work, I might get started at any minute. So everything is an interruption . . . everything must be refused because it is possible that from one moment to the

next I will get back to something. . . . The building I live in . . . is full of little one- and two-person companies. . . . In the afternoons, I see us virtuals emerge blinking into the sunlight. In the dead hours after 3 p.m., we haunt cafés and local restaurants. We run into each other at the FedEx drop-box or the copy shop. They, like me, have a freshly laundered look, just come out of pajamas or sweat pants, just showered and dressed.

It is this time-based (rather than space-based) organization of activities that defines "accessibility," a redefinition of "public" and "private" time into "on time" and "off time." Laurier (1999) suggests that using the technology to its full potential can, precisely, help individuals to control time, and thus to control the organizational relationships of which they are a part. The decentralization of work activities, and the practices of "assembling the mobile office" on the part of "nomadic workers," entail the simultaneous management of private activities, as when mobile teleworkers coordinate their work life from/at home (Steward, 2000). "Public" work activities are drawn into "private" spaces, with a variety of effects on an individual's home and family life. Nevertheless, while this temporal boundary rescheduling might positively produce spatial and temporal flexibility for users, this is not necessarily the case (Steward, 2000).

Some research, including our own, has indicated that mobile teleworking can have negative effects for workers and families when they have been compelled, rather than chosen, to work in this manner. Hill, Hawkins, and Miller (1996), for example, investigated the domestic effects of mobile telework. In a quantitative and qualitative survey, the private contexts of mobile use for telework were examined, and teleworkers reported that the flexibility to be permanently available for work impacted on their personal and domestic life such that they had *less* time for their home and family. The advantages of mobility and "telepresence" were, for those surveyed, sometimes offset by the drawbacks of permanent availability for work. Debbie, a student who is also a mother, and works for a charity, says:

> I always try to turn my mobile off on the train. I mean, its like, if you don't then there's always something . . . always someone trying to get hold of you. . . . I mean apart from it being really boring having to listen to other people's conversations . . . and I *like* having that journey, it's time to myself, on the train. If you're going to places, on your way to places, then people can't get hold of you if you don't want them to.

These effects were also strongly influenced by their degree of choice in "becoming mobile." Mobility was perceived negatively when individuals had not chosen to undertake their work via mobile and telepresent means, but were required to do so by their employer. It seems that mobile teleworking and the temporal rhythms as well as geographical locations involved have different effects for users depending on their levels of access to and control over mobile work activities and their status as mobile teleworkers.

Such issues of access and control of mobile activities draw attention to the differential effects of mobile technologies for different users. If we are to consider Massey's

(1993) notion of power geometries, we need to ask who has access, who has control of time, and who doesn't, in emerging mobile temporalities. This is also at issue in instances where the temporalities of private relations are potentially shifted via mobile technologies into public life.

We have encountered numerous instances in our research where the use of mobiles in public space has been employed to maintain "private," family, or community relations. Young people, especially young women, will use devices to maintain relationships with significant others both while traveling alone (to avoid encounters with strangers) and at specific times (such as late night, or "when it's dark"). Their marginalization in public space, at specific times, leads to their increased use to the device to maintain contact with significant others. The mobile therefore has different uses and effects for these groups than for others.

> It's a security thing, kind of. (S)
> Yeah, whenever I'm walking somewhere and I'm really scared I have like 999 [the UK emergency number] dialed already. I just have my finger on the button. (L)
> When I used to finish work and I'd be walking to Claire's house or something, . . . I'd always phone Paul so I could speak to him while I'm walking so I'm not quite so scared. (S)
> I mean a lot of parents buy their phones for their daughters anyway . . . or maybe sons, 'cause they want to know where they are, keep in contact and they can ring whenever. (P)

This theme of mobile technologies creating the subjective experience of being "in touch" or connected when alone at specific times is beginning to loom large, and also indicates that a gender analysis is crucial in the experience of everyday rhythms of mobile temporality.

At the same time, relationships between teens and parents can also become fraught with anxiety when mobility becomes mapped on to the teenager's struggles over autonomy, and this often has specific temporal aspects (such as curfews). Teenagers who buy pagers to stay in contact with their friends (at any time) become frustrated when parents use those technologies to contact the teenager and monitor their activity in space and time:

> My mum used to be like that, and hates them, but she always wanted to know where I was, so . . . that's what I don't like. Everyone knows where you are all the time, that's why I don't like them. (D)
> You don't tell them where you are! (G)
> I'll be out, and I'll go to my friend's house . . . until really late, and mum would get worried, and I won't phone home . . . and so they're all getting all stressed, and "you're not going anywhere again," and with the phone they can just say "oh, what time are you coming home, are you all right, blah blah." (G)
> Sometimes they [ask where I am]. If I say "I'm going there," they'll think I'm still there, and stuff like that. . . . Or I won't say, I'll say "I'm just out with one of my friends." (H)

> If you say you're at a friend's house then they know you're there, they think its better . . . because they can try and call you on the house phone 'cos that's where you're supposed to be, so they'll try and call there, 'cos then they know where you are. (G)
>
> You just lie. It's just lying. (H)

For parents then, mobile technologies may assist in the temporal ordering and regulation of individual and family activities. Parents have also, however, talked about disruptions to the temporal rhythms of domestic life caused by mobile phones in our research. Some are convinced that teenagers who call their children in the early hours of the morning would not do so on a fixed-line phone for fear of disrupting the temporal rhythms of the household. There might also be differences in the social implications of "always-availability" on the part of parents. When we consider that women have demonstrably invested more time in the maintenance of familial and intimate relationships via telecommunications devices (Rakow, 1992; Rakow & Navarro, 1993), it would seem that being "always available" for home as well as work activities via mobile devices may have significantly different effects for women and men. One mother says:

> I like to feel, not that I can instantly get hold of her, but that she can get hold of me. . . . But having said that I think I get more calls like can I go and pick her up, "I've just missed the last bus." In that sense I think it creates more work for parents.

In summary then, the personalization of mobile device – their attachment to an individual person/body and their temporal rhythms, rather than to specific locations, the personalized nature of the technologies and the attendant atomization of communications – can then potentially fragment both "public" and "private" communication activities, collapsing each into the other. Being available, being connected may be seen as a strategic form of social behavior that enables participation in a preferred and familiar social space no matter what the immediate surroundings may be. At the same time, when all social activities become coordinated through the same device, what time is on and off, and when, for what, becomes a primary site of negotiating social relationships and conflicting roles in everyday life. The issues of who has access to and control of mobile devices (or not), and when, seem the central issues in the local organization of mobile temporality.

The relations of everyday life just described should be seen in the context of the temporal rhythms that regulate and inform the practices of network operators, service providers, and governmental and regulatory authorities. On the one hand, there are the specific temporal cycles of the present cellular (and potential satellite) infrastructures. Cellular networks go through regular cycles of call loads, regular times when the network is "busy." Furthermore, the temporal location of the cellular infrastructure in any particular place will also affect who can call whom, where, and when. Long-term cycles of infrastructural development, including decisions about where to locate physical cell sites (masts/antennae), how many, and when, go through regular cycles of strategic planning and development, which depend on the different contingencies of the network operators' schedules. The rhythms of the technical infrastructure do not depend only on technology development, however. They are also determined by the monthly, quarterly, and yearly rhythms of the financial calendar, and how particular organizations organize strategic analysis, market development, and the (sometimes overlapping, sometimes contradictory) programs of business planning and management. While linked to longer term technical and social change (discussed later), these temporal aspects of mobile organization affect how mobility takes place in everyday life for users (who gets to connect and when), and also determine the daily, monthly, and yearly scheduling and deadlines within operator organizations.

Rhythms of institutional change

The temporal locations, the deadlines, cycles, and sequences of the technical infrastructure, and the organizational temporalities related to its planning and development draw attention to the time scales involved in the relationship between technical development in industry organizations and government and policymaking processes.

Although ostensibly in competition, industry actors often coordinate their interaction with public authorities in time, affecting both the nature of technical infrastructures and the networks and services available to consumers. The process of formulating network standards and the governmental regulation of business activity and auctions of network bands are examples of standards setting, regulation, and policymaking processes that are situated in time. The yearly schedules of when governments meet and policy is set, the regular cycles of civil service regulation, and the product and service development attendant upon them in corporate organizations all have impact on the technical and economic times of mobile development.

Certainly for industry players, time is money, in this sense. Or perhaps, as Barbara Adam suggests, money is time (1990, p. 114). One thing that is certain in the mobile industry, as elsewhere, is that time itself has become a commodity – hence the value of mobile devices and services in markets. Once time becomes a commodified resource (we can "save" and "invest" time, for example), it becomes not only disembedded from related value, but disembodied from any specific activities in daily life. It is only in this culturally specific connection between time and money, for example, that cultural perceptions of "wasting" time, of "dead time," become influential. Perry et al. (2001) have suggested, for example, that mobile devices act as "Lazarus" devices – devices that "resurrect" mobile time that would have previously been considered "dead," "economically unproductive" (such as time taken to travel from one place to another). This implies that an emerging mobile temporality is "Lazarus time," productive time that has been resurrected from unproductive "dead time" via the use of mobile technologies. The implication that time is money is relevant not only for those in the mobile business, therefore, but also for the mobile temporalities of users. According to Townsend (2001),

> time becomes a commodity to buy, sell, and trade over the phone. The old schedule of minutes, hours, days, and weeks becomes shattered into a constant stream of negotiations, reconfigurations, and rescheduling. One can be interrupted or interrupt friends and colleagues at any time. Individuals live in this

phonespace – they can never let it go, because it is their primary link to the temporally, spatially fragmented network of friends and colleagues they have constructed for themselves. It has become their new umbilical cord. (p. 70)

"Institutional change" in the form of mobile temporality, therefore, is not only related to the governance of social institutions or the dominance of corporate business, and the "convergence" or "distanciation" to the infrastructural elements of whole societies (although the importance of these elements has, I hope, become apparent). Nor does it only lie in changing technical infrastructures and the social implications they might have for changing temporality when mobile. Nor is social change simply related to the changing daily activities of individuals as they reschedule and become flexible. To consider the implications of mobile temporality for social practices, understandings, and organization of time is also crucially to consider questions of value. Who gains what through mobile temporalities? Where, and under what local and collective conditions?

Conclusions

Many sociological arguments have been made for new temporal formations through the use of new and mobile information and communication technologies – the "timeless time" of Castells (1996, p. 433), Nowotny's (1994) "instantaneous time," Virilio's "speed" (2000), and Giddens's "time–space distanciation" and "convergence" (1990). The logic of these arguments would suggest that a reconfiguration of space and time is taking place, a rearrangement that entails the individualization and fragmentation of availability, duration, cycles, and rhythms, such that the forms and purposes of the communication and the social relationships mediated and maintained through them are reconfigured.

Certainly, arguments about mobile work, flexible scheduling, changes in the duration and cycles of activities, proximity, distance, and presence might suggest that widespread social and cultural change in the practice and understanding of temporality is occurring. While the "speed" of modern urban life and potential fragmentation in social relationships via temporal changes can certainly be noted, mobile technologies also introduce opportunities for new continuities across space and time, previously disjoined through centralization. The ethnographic data presented here have been one means to address these new temporal continuities.

Furthermore, I have argued here that if attention is paid to local and situated times, to the rhythms of daily life as well as the cycles of social organization between groups of social actors detailed in analyses such as those of Giddens and Harvey, many temporalities (the social practices and understandings that form them, the activities and relationships they mediate and maintain) can be demonstrated to be relatively enduring. At least some of the relationships that comprise mobile temporalities – including those of organization and regulation – are not dissimilar (or have not changed) from well-established temporal patterns in the production and reproduction of technical and social infrastructure. What is at issue is how different temporal rhythms intersect in new ways as they are configured in different locations, and in everyday, situated action.

If we can think of social "space–time" as the network of relationships within which individuals and groups operate in everyday life, social time is comprised of the social (rather than geographical) proximity of those relationships, as they are shaped by resources, location, value, and knowledge. The simultaneity of copresence and telepresence becomes the mechanism for connection with others. The device and its functionalities can stand in for, but can also create, a community or network. On the one hand, social space and time are "extended," and on the other, they remain locally continuous. Communities are being formed in highly contradictory ways, which reflect new disjunctures, as well as new continuities, in the relationship between space, time, and location.

What seems most at issue is not only the fact or extent of temporal change in the face of mobile technologies, but also the situated, differential effects of those changes for different individuals and social groups. These are not only descriptive questions (what has changed and how?) but also qualitative questions (with what consequences, for whom?). When the value of (mobile) time is taken into account, these questions become more pressing. The connection between mobile space and time, as articulated in multiple, heterogeneous places and rhythms, is not constant and does not have equal effects for all. Access to and control of time and mobility are always shaped by the context of situated social practice, as collectively created and maintained by a number of different individuals and social groups. In asking who benefits from these heterogeneous causes and effects, we are asking questions about the power geometries of mobile time.

References

Adam, Barbara. 1990. *Time and social theory*. Cambridge: Polity Press, Blackwell.

Boden, Deirdre, and Molotch, Harvey L. 1994. The compulsion of proximity. In *NowHere: Space, time and modernity*, eds. Roger Friedland and Deidre Boden, pp. 257–286. Berkeley, University of California Press.

Brown, Barry, Green, Nicola, and Harper, Richard, eds. 2001. *Wireless world: Social and interactional implications of wireless technology*. London: Springer Verlag.

Castells, Manuel. 1996. *The rise of the network society*. Cambridge, MA: Blackwell.

Connerton, Paul. 1989. *How societies remember*. Cambridge: Cambridge University Press.

Cooper, Geoff, Green, Nicola, Harper, Richard, and Murtagh, Ged. Forthcoming. Mobile society? Technology, distance and presence. In *Virtual society? Get real!*, ed. Steve Woolgar. Cambridge: Cambridge University Press.

Du Gay, Paul, Hall, Stuart, Janes, L., Mackay, H., Negus, Keith, and Tudor, A. 1997. *Doing cultural studies: The story of the Sony Walkman*. London: Sage.

Fischer, Claude. 1988. *America calling: A social history of the telephone to 1940*. Berkeley: University of California Press.

Frisby, David. 1985. *Fragments of modernity*. Cambridge: Polity.

Frissen, Valerie. 1995. Gender is calling: Some reflections on past, present and future uses of the telephone. In *The gender-technology relation*, eds. Keith Grint and Rosalind Gill, pp. 79–94. London: Taylor & Francis.

Giddens, Anthony, 1990. *The consequences of modernity*. Cambridge: Polity.

Green, Nicola. 2001. Who's watching whom? Monitoring and accountability in mobile relations. In *Wireless world: Social and interactional implications of wireless technology*, eds. Barry Brown, Nicola Green, and Richard Harper, pp. 32–45. London: Springer Verlag.

Green, Sarah, and Harvey, Penny. 1999. *Scaling place and networks: An ethnography of ICT "innovation" in Manchester.*" Internet and Ethnography Conference, Hull, December.

Harvey, David. 1990. *The condition of postmodernity: An enquiry into the conditions of cultural change.* Oxford: Blackwell.

Hill, E. Jeffrey, Hawkins, Alan J., and Miller, Brent C. 1996. Work and family in the virtual office: Perceived influences of mobile telework. *Family Relations* 45: 293–301.

Lash, Scott, and Urry, John. 1994. *Economies of signs and space.* London: Sage.

Laurier, Eric. 1999. *Converzations in the corridor (M4): Assembling the mobile office.* BSA Conference Proceedings, Glasgow.

Lee, Heejin, and Liebenau, Jonathan. 2000. Time and the Internet at the turn of the millennium. *Time and Society* 9(1):43–56.

Ling, Richard, and Yttri, Birgitte. 1999. *"Nobody sits at home and waits for the telephone to ring": Micro and hyper-coordination through the use of the mobile telephone.* Perpetual Contact Workshop, Rutgers University, New Brunswick, NJ, December.

Massey, Doreen. 1992. Politics and space/time. *New Left Review* 196:65–84.

Massey, Doreen. 1993. Power-geometry and a progressive sense of place. In *Mapping the futures, local cultures, global change,* eds. J. Bird, B. Curtis, T. Putnam, G. Robertson, and L. Tickner, pp. 59–69. London: Routledge.

McLuhan, Marshall. 1964. *Understanding media: The extensions of man.* London: Routledge and Kegan Paul.

Nowotny, H. 1994. *Time. The modern and postmodern experience.* Cambridge: Polity.

Perry, Mark, O'Hara, Kenton, Sellen, Abigail, Brown, Barry, and Harper, Richard. 2001. Dealing with mobility: Understanding access anytime, anywhere. *Transactions on Computer Human Interaction* 8(4):323–347.

Pool, Ithiel del Sola, ed. 1977. *The social uses of the telephone.* Cambridge, MA: MIT Press.

Rakow, Lana F. 1992. *Gender on the line: Women, the telephone and community life.* Urbana: University of Illinois Press.

Rakow, Lana, and Navarro, Vija. 1993. Remote mothering and the parallel shift: Women meet the cellular telephone. *Critical Studies in Mass Communication* 10:144–157.

Rifkin, J. 1987. *Time wars: The primary conflict in human history.* New York: Henry Holt.

Simmel, Georg. 1997. The metropolis and mental life. In *Simmel on culture,* eds. David Frisby and Mike Featherstone, pp. 174–185. London: Sage.

Standage, Tim. 1998. *The Victorian Internet.* London: Weidenfeld and Nicolson.

Steward, Barbara. 2000. Changing times: The meaning, measurement and use of time in teleworking. *Time and Society* 9(1): 57–74.

Thompson, E. P. 1967. Time, work discipline and industrial capitalism. *Past and Present* 38:56–97.

Thrift, Nigel. 1996. New urban eras and old technological fears: Reconfiguring the good will of electronicthings. *Urban Studies* 33(8):1463–1493.

Townsend, Anthony. 2001. Mobile communications in the twenty-first century city. In *Wireless world: Social and interactional implications of wireless technology,* eds. Barry Brown, Nicola Green, and Richard Harper, pp. 62–77. London: Springer Verlag.

Traweek, Sharon. 1988. *Beamtimes and lifetimes: The world of high energy physicists.* Cambridge, MA: Harvard University Press.

Ullman, Ellen. 1997. *Close to the machine: Technophilia and its discontents.* San Francisco: City Lights Books.

Virilio, Paul. 2000. *Polar inertia* (trans. Patrick Camiller). London: Sage.

Williams, Raymond. 1974. *Television: Technology and cultural form.* London: Fontana.

5.4

Time and the internet,
by Heejin Lee and Jonathan Liebenau

3 Time and computers

There is not much research that addresses time and computers substantially. However, the topic is already attracting the attention of researchers from various academic disciplines. Negroponte (1995) mentions the impact of electronic mail on work time. Electronic mail changes the rhythm of work and play:

> Nine-to-five, five days a week, and two weeks off a year starts to evaporate as the dominant beat to business life. Professional and personal messages start to commingle: Sunday is not so different from Monday. (p. 193)

Electronic mail also can make people less sensitive to international time-zone differences (Failla and Bagnara, 1992: 672). Negroponte gives another example (p. 49). The 'nine o'clock news' has a special meaning in everyday life over almost all the world. Some people are keen to arrive home by then, especially when a big issue is in the news. The time of 9 p.m. functions as a reference time for them in organizing their day. Cable TV news networks such as CNN cause the time 9 p.m. increasingly to lose its meaning as a temporal reference point because they repeat updated news every 15 or 30 minutes. The Internet can accelerate this trend. On the Internet, one can retrieve and watch news when one wants, not when it is delivered by broadcasting companies. Once this practice is generalized among the population, 9 p.m. is no longer different from 8:17 p.m. Then the lifestyle which employs it as one of its important temporal anchors (e.g. 9 a.m. for starting work, noon or 1 p.m. for lunch, and 5 p.m. for calling it a day) will be transformed. In these ways both the seven-day week and the currently patterned day are weakened by the Internet.

According to Failla and Bagnara (1992), information technology causes profound changes in the time-frame patterns of the decision-making process. It also eliminates rigidity in work rhythms, giving flexibility. The organization of work is becoming less and less rigid in terms of time-patterns. This is especially true of professional work performed in offices with information technology support. The application of information technologies to knowledge-based activities

... generates work methods that cut across the 'traditional' sequence of events, changing the durations customarily regarded as 'appropriate' and reducing the need to 'program' activities, and hence to resort to rigid timetables. The effect of these changes is to disrupt the traditional work rhythms. In this sense, information technologies help to eliminate or diminish the importance of time-frames generally accepted as appropriate for performing a given activity.

(Failla and Bagnara, 1992: 678)

The impacts of information technology on time assume different patterns depending on the stages in the development of information technology. Failla and Bagnara classify its development into three stages: the automation of routine activities, decision support technologies, and virtual reality technologies. Each stage has a different meaning in terms of time.

In the automation of routine activities at the early stages of computerization, there still remains the same high degree of rigidity in work rhythms. Such high rigidity characterized the mechanical technologies of the first industrial revolution. In this phase users complain that computers dictate the rhythm of work. They are required to adapt to machine time. Some attitudes of resistance to computers can be attributed to the disorientating effect of the 'new' rigid time-frames imposed by the technology. The next stage is characterized by the proliferation of direct users of information technology generated by the advent of the personal computer. This phase sees the development of information technology for individual decision-making such as spreadsheets, databases and packages for statistical analysis. Although these technologies for decision support systems result in changes in decision-making processes, the most significant transformation is their disruptive effect on rigid time-frames. Due to the decentralization of processing capacity through the personal computer and the subsequent development of specific applications to support individualized decision-making, a new relationship with technology has been generated. The relationship is no longer subject to the time constraints of centralized systems. When the technology evolves from supporting individual decision-making, to aiding organizational decision-making such as group decision support systems (GDSS) or computer supported cooperative work (CSCW), bigger impacts on time are expected. At present, information technology is experiencing another phase of development which is likely to have a qualitative impact on time. The new technologies make it possible to project a virtual reality environment, and help us to simulate the consequences *in advance*. The decision-making process has always been based on *past* experiences. With this technology, however, we can gain experience of scenarios or events that have never been encountered in real life. Virtual reality technology therefore allows 'future' or unexperienced experiences to be experienced. We can reconstruct the experience needed to generate alternatives with the help of information technology. It allows simulation of the future and thereby modifies the time-frames which are no longer relegated to repetitions of the past with little variation.

There are empirical studies on time and information technology in organizations. Barley (1988) investigated the impacts of computer-based radiology equipment on temporality and social relations in hospital radiology departments. He found a dichotomy in ways of organizing time: monochronic and polychronic ways (Hall, 1959, 1966, 1983). In the former, people do one thing at a time; in the latter, several things are done at once. Barley found that the new computer-based equipment increased the monochronicity of radiologists' work by restructuring the duration, sequence, temporal location and rate of recurrence of events. It in turn enhanced the symmetry of temporal organization between radiologists' and technicians' work. Furthermore the increased symmetry contributed to decreased conflict between radiologists and technicians.

Lee (1997, 1999) further developed the points made by Barley. He suggested six dimensions of temporality in business processes: duration, temporal location, sequence, deadline, cycle and rhythm. They were used to describe and analyse temporal changes in the work under study. In his case study, information technology transformed temporal profiles of work and also created a temporal symmetry between work groups interacting with each other. Unlike in Barley's study, however, the main direction of change was polychronic.

4 Temporal dimensions of the Internet and corporate intranets

We can simplify the features of the Internet and other networks such as internal corporate networks that can be analysed for a new temporal view. These features can be described in terms of the users (and uses), the publishers (and their servers), and the powers (including economic powers and regulatory or governance authorities).

Users have the opportunity to alter their temporal perceptions by virtue of having access at any time. That access gives the illusion of being instantaneous. Users are assumed to have short attention spans, and this has influenced the design of much material. The experience of television holds strong sway over the style of presentation.

Internet servers are (supposed to be) always switched on. Their constant presence means that all materials are always available, and in aggregate the Internet is as accessible in the middle of the night as at the height of the working day. The burden of costs is shifted from consumers to publishers, the owners of infrastructure, and those who attempt to govern the Internet. This current state is not symmetrical with the distribution of powers, which is more difficult to assess, since they are spread among suppliers of hardware and software, other standards setters, and a small number of companies, including the largest Internet service providers and search engines.

We can apply the analytical dimensions of temporality to the Internet and other networks to discern a structure in the confusing variety of features. This then provides us with the opportunity to differentiate researchable features, some of which lend themselves to measurement or direct comparison across situations where different users or distinct uses can be assessed.

Duration

The notion that the Internet provides instantaneous access to a world of information is a useful fiction. There are, however, two ways in which we might regard the concept of duration as applying: in the ways in which users typically go about locating and browsing materials, and in the real experience of viewing identified sites. It would be better to recognize that there are lag times in accessing and downloading sought-after material and that this often causes frustration and sometimes expense. In that sense we can regard the experience of using the Internet as one of pseudo-instantaneous access.

The style of web surfing that is currently common is another sense in which duration plays a role. As we have learned from our behaviour with television, the shortening of attention spans and the preference for short bursts of superficial material have altered the way we regard material on the Internet. We are unlikely to feel the same need to sustain our attention for long periods, as we do when we read a book.

Temporal location

The Internet is 'always on'. We can access it at any time and real business can be transacted independently of any cycle or working period. This is not a unique feature of the Internet but since it is the case with all users, unlike, say, automatic trading systems, it stands out as a distinct shift. Increasingly, dedicated networks are also being used independently of their location and corporate intranets have been especially useful for geographically dispersed companies as well as temporally dispersed users. This has been interpreted by some to mean that employees will face 24-hour demands to work, but this is not yet discernible as a real trend.

Sequence

One of the most vexing problems of the early days of the world wide web was the confusion of sequencing which users experienced. The concept of 'navigation aids' was the means to address this problem of users feeling lost, and other common features include files which show the 'history' of a search. However, the fundamental problem of sequence appears mainly because of the facility of 'hypertext', which was designed to provide an alternative to linear reading. This loss of linearity is both a physical and a temporal change because, although searching is still temporally linear in a concrete sense, it loses that feeling of continuity for users much of the time.

Deadlines

Deadlines are a constant, static presence in our working lives. Usually dictated by procedure and governed by traditional practice, they solidify our schedules. We can observe, however, that Internet applications shift the concept and allow us, at least, to renegotiate our structure of deadlines. It is largely the features described above, the differences in duration, temporal location and sequence, which provide the opportunity to place deadlines at different positions in the course of a task. This was studied in detail in the case of temporal shifts at the Korean electronic trading system, KTNET (Lee, 1999) where daily routines were radically shifted by the changes in deadlines that were applied to business procedures.

Cycles

Interaction among collaborators is traditionally cycled by a combination of day/week/ month/year demarcations and task cycles. As duration, sequence and deadlines shift, new cycles are allowed to appear in using networks. These can be constantly renegotiated as befits the task, and there are possibilities of charting and managing numerous simultaneously operating cycles.

There are also cases where the concept of cycle is radically altered, as when global organizations engage in the continuous production of products such as software. Some developers have structured production such that procedures are smoothly handed over from workers in Hong Kong at the end of their working day to their colleagues in London, who then hand over to colleagues in California. This allows for almost constant work on a single product, uninterrupted by normal daily work cycles (Gorton and Motwani, 1996).

Rhythms

The rhythms which guide us, the alternations between work and play and the ways in which we split the day, set up patterns which inculcate themselves into our lives. Such rhythms of 'busy-ness' also shift when we use electronic media to take advantage of the opportunity to condense or disperse our working effort. Since different people are 'busy' at different times, the collaborative character of electronic work can be controlled by each individual. E-mail provides a similar opportunity because it allows us to change our working rhythms. We can accumulate messages, or even messages of one particular type, and become 'busy' with them at a chosen time.

References

Adam, B. (1994) 'Perceptions of Time', in T. Ingold (ed.) *Companion Encyclopedia of Anthropology: Humanity, Culture and Social Life*, pp. 503–26. London: Routledge.
Barley, S. R. (1988) 'On Technology, Time, and Social Order: Technologically Induced Change in the Temporal Organization of Radiological Work', in F.A. Dubinskas (ed.) *Making Time: Ethnographies of High-Technology Organizations*, pp. 123–69. Philadelphia, PA: Temple University Press.
Blyton, P., Hassard, J., Hill, S. and Starkey, K. (1989) *Time, Work and Organization*. London: Routledge.
Bohannan, P. (1967) 'Concepts of Time among the Tive of Nigeria', in J. Middleton (ed.) *Myth and Cosmos*, pp. 315–30. New York: Natural History Press.
Bolter, J. D. (1984) *Turing's Man: Western Culture in the Computer Age*. London: Duckworth.
Boorstin, D. J. (1983) *The Discoverers*. New York: Random House.
Castells, M. (1996) *The Rise of the Network Society*. Oxford: Blackwell.
Coveney, P. and Highfield, R. (1990) *The Arrow of Time: A Voyage Through Science To Solve Time's Greatest Mystery*. New York: Fawcett Columbine.
Durkheim, E. (1965) *The Elementary Forms of the Religious Life*. New York: The Free Press.
Evans-Pritchard, E. E. (1940) *The Nuer: A Description of the Modes of Livelihood and Political Institutions of a Nilotic People*. London: Oxford University Press.

Failla, A. and Bagnara, S. (1992) 'Information Technology, Decision, Time', *Social Science Information* 31(4): 669–81.

Gorton, I. and Motwani, S. (1996) 'Issues in Co-operative Software Engineering Using Globally Distributed Teams', *Information and Software Technology* 38: 647–55.

Hall, E. T. (1959) *The Silent Language*. Garden City, NY: Doubleday.

Hall, E. T. (1966) *The Hidden Dimension*. New York: Anchor Press.

Hall, E. T. (1983) *The Dance of Life: The Other Dimension of Time*. Garden City, NY: Anchor Press/Doubleday.

Hallowell, A. I. (1955) 'Temporal Orientation in Western Civilization and in a Pre-literate Society', in A. I. Hallowell (ed.) *Culture and Experience*, pp. 216–35. Philadelphia: University of Pennsylvania Press.

Hassard, J. (1989) 'Time and Industrial Sociology', in P. Blyton, J. Hassard, S. Hill and K. Starkey (eds) *Time, Work and Organization*, pp. 13–34. London: Routledge.

Hassard, J. (ed.) (1990) *The Sociology of Time*. Basingstoke: Macmillan.

Hassard, J. (1996) 'Images of Time in Work and Organization', in S. R. Clegg, C. Hardy and W. R. Nord (eds) *Handbook of Organization Studies*, pp. 581–98. London: Sage.

Landes, D. (1983) *Revolution in Time: Clocks and the Making of the Modern World*. Cambridge, MA: Harvard University Press.

Lee, H. (1997) 'Temporal Implications of Electronically Mediated Business Procedures on Organisational Work: EDI Applications in Trade', unpublished doctoral dissertation, London School of Economics and Political Science.

Lee, H. (1999) 'Time and Information Technology: Monochronicity, Polychronicity and Temporal Symmetry', *European Journal of Information Systems* 8(1): 16–26.

Macey, S. L. (1980) *Clocks and the Cosmos: Time in Western Life and Thought*. Hamden, CT: Archon Books.

Moore, W. (1963) *Man, Time and Society*. New York: John Wiley.

Mumford, L. (1934) *Technics and Civilization*. New York: Harcourt, Brace & Co.

Negroponte, N. (1995) *Being Digital*. London: Hodder & Stoughton.

Pocock, D. F. (1967) 'The Anthropology of Time Reckoning', in J. Middleton (ed.) *Myth and Cosmos*, pp. 303–14. New York: Natural History Press.

Pronovost, G. (1989) 'The Sociology of Time', *Current Sociology* 37(3).

Rifkin, J. (1987) *Time Wars: The Primary Conflict in Human History*. New York: Henry Holt & Co.

Thompson, E. P. (1967) 'Time, Work-Discipline, and Industrial Capitalism', *Past and Present* 38: 56–97.

Whitrow, G. J. (1988) *Time in History: Views of Time from Prehistory to the Present Day*. Oxford: Oxford University Press.

Zerubavel, E. (1977) 'The French Republican Calendar: A Case Study in the Sociology of Time', *American Sociological Review* 42: 868–77.

Zerubavel, E. (1979) *Patterns of Time in Hospital Life*. Chicago and London: The University of Chicago Press.

Zerubavel, E. (1982) 'The Standardization of Time: A Sociohistorical Perspective', *American Journal of Sociology* 88(1): 1–23.

5.5

Speed is contagious,
by Thomas Hylland Eriksen

This holds true in the media, as elsewhere. The fastest media, at the moment television and Internet newspapers, are being imitated by the printed media. The articles become shorter and shorter, with clearer 'messages' and less analysis. Dedicated news channels on radio, for their part, boast that they update their news every hour, while the WAP format epitomises everything that is fast in contemporary mass communication. WAP phones and similar devices have a 'screen' which is about twice as large as the display of an ordinary mobile phone, as well as direct access to limited sectors of the Internet. One can, for example, check the stock exchange rates, the evening's cinema programme, the news headlines and the e-mail on a WAP telephone, and the superbrief news items are updated virtually continuously. In the bad old days, one had to wait until the TV news in the early evening for an update.

It is not unlikely that this kind of technology will become widespread. In a situation with an information surplus, everyone has 10 seconds to spare, but very few have a whole minute. This gives a competitive edge to the fastest and most compact media. A general rule of the information revolution is that in a 'free and fair' competition between a slow and a fast version of 'the same thing', the fast version wins. The question is what gets lost on the way. The short answer to this question is *context* and *understanding*; the longer one involves *credibility*. It is hard enough to edit a credible daily newspaper, which, among other things, attracts readers through being first with the latest. But, as a senior editor of a major broadsheet mentioned to me during a fast and fragmentary conversation on a streetcorner: just imagine being managing editor for the WAP edition of a newspaper, which demands continuous updating! One would scarcely have the time to type the news before it was published and therefore in need of revision. This situation is just around the corner as I write this.

Ramonet claims that during the last 30 years, more information has been produced than during the previous 5,000 years! He illustrates the point with an example: 'A single copy of the Sunday edition of the *New York Times* contains more information than a cultivated person in the eighteenth century would consume during a lifetime.'

I have no way of knowing whether performances of Beethoven's sixth symphony, the idyllic *Pastoral* symphony, are much faster today than the performances of 200 years ago. But as already mentioned, plays have accelerated very noticeably during the twentieth century. A political scientist recently studied the development of the annual financial debate in the Norwegian parliament, comparing the speed of speech in selected years from 1945 to 1995. He shows that the members of parliament spoke at an average velocity of 584 phonemes per minute in 1945. In 1980, the number of sounds had risen to 772, and in 1995 it had reached 863. In other words, the average politician spoke 50 per cent faster in 1995 than his or her predecessors did in the mid-1940s.

Or one could put it like this: it is as if one lives in an old, venerable but slightly dilapidated house and decides to refurbish the bathroom. Having finally done this, a poorer but hopefully happier person following a budgetary deficit worthy of the United Nations, one discovers for the first time that the kitchen is really quite run-down. So one begins to tear out the old kitchen fittings, and soon enters a new frustrating round of phone calls to plumbers and masons. Then one is bound to discover, almost immediately, how old and worn the hall is, and really, wouldn't it be a terrific idea to give the living room a coat of paint and a new floor? Speed is contagious in an analogous way.

If one gets used to speed in some areas, the desire for speed will tend to spread to new domains. Five minutes spent waiting for the bus lasts longer the faster the airport express train takes you from the terminal to the bus stop. As computer networks have become faster, many of us have grown accustomed to an Internet connection where waiting time is in principle, and often in practice, minimal. Still, we will not rest content until the web pages are accessed the very same moment we press the button. Two seconds of waiting time today is as unacceptable as 10 seconds would have been a couple of years ago.

This principle has a general validity. If the plane from Oslo to Copenhagen takes 40 minutes, 15 minutes' delay makes a lot of difference. If, on the other hand, one chooses to take the boat, which takes an evening and a night to cross the Skagerrak, 15 minutes lost or saved makes little difference, since the rhythm of the boat militates against petty time-saving schemes. Other activities can wait. Fast time, in other words, is contagious both between persons and between life domains.

Gains and losses tend to equal each other out

In 1965, the engineer Gordon Moore spelled out the principle that has come to be known as 'Moore's Law'. It states that the capacity (read: speed) of microprocessors is doubled every 18 months. (Recently, it has been supplemented by 'Gilder's Law', which states that the transmission speed – bandwidth – on the Net is doubled every year.) So far, Moore has been right. However, a computer scientist at my university supplemented Moore with 'Knut's Law'. It states that Moore's law is correct, but that computer software doubles in complexity and size every 16 months. According to Knut, then, the daily chores performed by any computer nowadays take *longer* than before.

Knut is obviously a witty man, and he exaggerates. (Actually his law reminds me of a newspaper story from a few years back, on the assumed health benefits of jogging.

It noted that people who jog do live longer than others – on average, exactly as much longer as the time they spend jogging.) But in a general sense, Knut is right. Allow me to illustrate with a few examples from my own computer world, which is called Macintosh. The first version of the word processor MacWrite, launched in 1984, took a little more than 50 Kb of disk space (disks back then, remember, took all of 400 Kb). The program I am using to write this book, WriteNow 4 (that is, the 1994 version), takes 348 Kb of disk space. The latest version of the world's most popular word processor, which is Microsoft Word, requires 5.1 Mb, in other words well over 5,000 Kb. And for the program to function properly, a heap of additions are needed. Some of them are shared with the sister programs Excel and PowerPoint. Altogether, Microsoft's office package requires more than 100 Mb, and most people install all programs.

In the old days, that is a little over a dozen years ago, the total capacity of an ordinary hard disk was 20 Mb. We felt we had a lot of space back then, we who had grown up with computers without hard disks! We might have a word processor such as MacWrite (50 Kb), a presentation program like More (384 Kb in the last and best version) and a spreadsheet such as CricketGraph (200 Kb) at our disposal, and were able to perform the same tasks that an average user of Microsoft Word now needs more than 100 Mb of disk space to perform. Naturally, he or she also needs a much faster computer than we could even dream of at the time.

So the software has been improved? That depends on what one is after. Personally I prefer the simple and stable programs. They are easy to learn and straightforward to relate to, and although I write hundreds of pages every year, I never seem to need more than what humble WriteNow is able to offer. Yes, Word does make it possible to make tables of contents and fancy templates, and to run a number of functions automatically through macros; but in my experience, it is easier to tailor documents to one's special needs as one goes along. The simpler a computer program is, the less time and energy is spent on relating to the actual technology and trying to read the thoughts of the programmers, and more concentration can be expended on the task at hand. The larger and more complex a program is, the greater the risk of crashes and breakdowns. Irritating macro viruses have in recent years become widespread among computer users, but only among Word users.

This is to do with too much complexity of the wrong kind. Increased speed does not even necessarily make us more efficient – a point to which I shall return later. The magazine *WIRED* ran a story a few years ago about the new CEO of mighty Sun Microsystems, and how he wanted to improve the efficiency of his staff. He came up with several ideas, but one in particular took the computer addicts on the staff by surprise. Now, many of the employees routinely made transparencies for use in external and internal presentations of what they were up to. As an aid, they had loads of templates, illustrations, suggestions and previously used presentations lying around on the shared hard disks of the company. While working on a particular presentation, people would browse these files to look for ideas, suitable templates, etc. The CEO found out that there were altogether 12.9 gigabytes of PowerPoint stuff on the servers. He deleted everything. From now on, the staff had to make their own presentations from scratch. And indeed, they now worked more efficiently, and spent less time on each transparency than before.

Technological change leads to unpredicted side-effects

All technology has unintended consequences, and whenever one gets more of a particular kind of technology, the result is not necessarily 'more of the same'. It could just as well be 'something entirely different'. One telling example is the transition from single-channel (or, at any rate, two- or three-channel) television to multi-channel television operated by a remote control. In most European countries, this change has taken place since around 1980. National television is a fantastic tool for propaganda – or, put differently, it can create a very powerful, shared national identity. It communicates directly, simultaneously and emotionally to literates as well as illiterates. It synchronises large segments of the population, and presents a particular version of reality to all – from Leningrad to Vladivostok, or from Munich to Kiel. Research has indicated that the dialect variation in several European countries was reduced during the twentieth century thanks to national radio and television, where a few nationally acknowledged variants were dominant.

After a generation of single-channel television, satellite TV was introduced in remote Norway in 1983. To begin with, dedicated satellite channels such as Sky and Super were dominant, and the field was still so scantily populated that certain of Sky's video jockeys were able to achieve megastar status in some European countries, since a large percentage of the target group followed them. (Anyone remember Pat Sharp?) There were only a few alternatives. Eventually, TV viewers got access to new Norwegian channels (around five or six at the latest count), in addition to a growing selection of satellite channels. Not everyone has access to everything, and many of the channels operate on the basis of subscriptions. Nonetheless, media research shows that the old national monopoly, the Norwegian poor cousin of the BBC, has lost its grip on the population. The good old days when the majority of the population gathered around the screen when the evening news was on, are gone never to return. In other words: television (and radio) functioned in an immensely integrating manner, creating a shared field of discourse on a national level, so long as it was dominated by one or a few, often state-controlled channels. Then we got a little more of the same technology (more channels, and some more, and some more still), and suddenly television no longer creates integration, but fragmentation.

We have still only seen the beginning. Digital TV, which at the time of writing has graduated from the grapevine to the pipeline, entails that each household can in principle develop its own, unique pattern of viewing. I can watch jazz concerts and poetry recitals until I fall over, while my neighbour can concentrate his attention on classical Westerns, only interrupted by weather reports presented by young and beautiful women.

It is easy to find examples from cultural history to indicate that the introduction of new technology has led to consequences other than those anticipated. I have already suggested that some of the technologies of speed, intended to boost efficiency, may have grave side-effects – and that it cannot even be taken for granted that they do boost efficiency. This is going to be a major theme later, and I shall leave it for now. But take eyeglasses, for example. Although their exact origin is unknown, the first known reference to optical lenses is from Roger Bacon, writing in 1268. Spectacles made it possible for learned persons, monks and others, to continue reading for many years after their eyesight had begun to deteriorate. For several centuries, only convex glasses, to aid farsightedness (hyperopia), existed. This is the common form of eyesight deterioration among people above 40. The importance of this modest invention for the Renaissance and the beginning of the modern era should not be underestimated. The cumulative growth in knowledge was boosted enormously when members of the learned community of Europe could continue to expand their fields of learning throughout their lives.

Far-fetched example? Perhaps, but there are also excellent examples of wide-ranging unintended consequences of technological change to be found in mainstream cultural history. The clock, as noted earlier, was originally constructed to synchronise prayer times for monks working the fields during the day; today, it is a pillar of the modern way of life, and has become indispensable for industrial production, mass communication and large chunks of people's everyday life everywhere. When movable type was invented by Gutenberg, scarcely anyone thought that it would be decisive in the development of democracy and nationalism. And neither Gottlieb Daimler nor Henry Ford would have expected the car to lead to inner-city decay since it moved residential areas to the suburbs and shops to consumption reservations near major highways. On a minor note, it might be added that nobody would have thought, when commercial air traffic was introduced in a small way in the 1930s – as a luxurious treat for the wealthy and powerful – that intercontinental flights would be a backbone in the migration process from poor to rich countries.

New technology cannot be used for anything at all, but it is also never known how it will be used. Technological changes, no matter how dazzling, are always put to use by particular societies with particular needs. They also bring subtle, but often highly consequential side-effects with them. Writing, as mentioned in the previous chapter, impairs the faculty of memory.

Who would have believed, in the mid-1990s, that the most active users of mobile phones would be adolescents, and that they largely use them to send SMS messages in order to stay in touch with their friends hour by hour? (At the latest count, 9 billion SMS messages are sent annually in the world, a billion of them in Germany alone.) When personal computers were first marketed around 1980, reasonably well-informed journalists wrote in a deeply serious mode how they would be used to make shopping lists and inventories of the contents of the freezer. The new information technology that lurks in the background of this entire book, is still at a trial stage, and there is no way of knowing how it will be put to use in three, five or 20 years. It is nonetheless easy to see *some* consequences of information technology: it removes distance, shortens time and fills the gaps with cascades of information. Like the car and the jet plane, new information technology leads to acceleration and demands for further information, until time – seen as duration – approaches zero. But as complexity increases, so do the side-effects. Roads, for instance, have a curious tendency to be filled by cars, no matter how many lanes they have at their disposal. And a given computer network may function well for 1,000 users who run e-mail software and Netscape/Explorer, but badly for 10,000 users who are up to the same thing; just as it would function badly if the 1,000 users demanded transmissions of high-resolution video film in real time. Just as traffic jams occur worldwide in the rush hour, annoying delays and jams occur on the Net.

The proposed solutions are the same in both cases: we require more capacity and higher speed, as if that would solve anything in the long run. But let us not forget how happy we were when we finally got hard disks with a storage capacity of all of 20 Mb; at that time, we then had no idea that those devices would be ripe for the museum in less than four years.

The contagious nature of speed, and its intimate relationship to efficiency as a value in itself, is brought out clearly in a well-known story which exists in many versions. In the variant told by Heinrich Böll, a German tourist visits Spain and discovers, to his horror, a Spaniard dozing in the shade of a tree on the beach. The German approaches the man, a fisherman, and lectures him on the virtues of efficiency: 'If you had gone out fishing now instead of wasting your time, he explains, you might have caught three times as much fish and bought yourself a better boat.' Eventually, he fantasises, the Spaniard might employ others and build a factory. He could become a rich man! 'What for?', asks the Spaniard. 'Well', says the German, 'you could have gone into early retirement, living off the profits and spent your days dozing on the beach.' 'That', says the Spaniard before turning over, 'is exactly what I am doing.'

Something has run out of control. Time-saving technology has made time more scarce than ever. The wealth of available information has not made most of us more enlightened, but less enlightened. In the next chapter, I shall explain how this can be, and approach the question of what this 'something' is that seems to be out of control.

Biographical notes

Benjamin R. Barber is the Gershon and Carol Kekst Professor of Civil Society and Distinguished University Professor at the University of Maryland. Barber's 17 books include *Strong Democracy* (1984) reissued in 2004 in a twentieth anniversary edition; the recent international best-seller *Jihad vs. McWorld* and *Fear's Empire* (2003), also published in eight foreign editions. His collected American essays, *A Passion for Democracy*, were published by Princeton University Press in 1999, and his book *The Truth of Power* was published in 2001.

Andrew Barry teaches Geography at Oxford University where he is a Fellow of St Catherine's College. He is the author of *Political Machines: Governing a Technological Society* (Athlone, 2001) and co-editor of *The Technological Economy*' (Routledge, 2005) and *Foucault and Political Reason* (Chicago University Press, 1996).

James Boyle is William Neal Reynolds Professor of Law at Duke Law School and co-founder of the Center for the Study of the Public Domain. He is the author of *Shamans, Software and Spleens: Law and the Construction of the Information Society*. He writes widely on issues of intellectual property, internet regulation and legal theory. He is one of the founding Board Members of Creative Commons, which is working to facilitate the free availability of art, scholarship, and cultural materials by developing innovative, machine-readable licences that individuals and institutions can attach to their work, and of Science Commons, which aims to expand the Creative Commons mission into the realm of scientific and technical data. He is also a member of the academic advisory boards of the Electronic Privacy and Information Center, the Connexions open-source courseware project, and of Public Knowledge. He recently started writing as an online columnist for the *Financial Times*' New Economy Policy Forum.

James Carey was journalism and communications professor at Columbia University. Carey wrote several books and more than one-hundred articles and essays on mass communications and media. His best-known work is *Communication as Culture* (1989).

S.D. Noam Cook is a professor of philosophy at San Jose State University. His publications, research and consulting interests focus on social and technological change, particularly the roles of specialized knowledge, professional practice and values. Over the years, his work in applied philosophy has entailed involvement with several academic and professional fields, including education, social work, business, public policy, creative arts, and various areas of science and engineering. He has given invited presentations on his work for academic, industrial and governmental institutions in the US and abroad, including MIT, UCLA, Virginia Tech, Texas A&M, Leiden University in The Netherlands, the University of Westminster in London, MITRE Corporation, Xerox research centers in the US, UK and France, the national government of The Netherlands, and various US federal agencies. He holds B.A. and M.A. degrees in philosophy from San Francisco State University, and a Ph.D. in planning and social philosophy from M.I.T. After receiving his doctorate, he spent two years on the research staff of Harvard Business School doing research and curriculum development in the area of Business Ethics. He was for ten years a consulting researcher at Xerox PARC (Palo Alto Research Center). Since 1997 he has been a member of the San Francisco Symphony Chorus.

Ben Compaine is a researcher and writer on issues related to the economic, social and cultural policy implications of changing information technologies. He has been a consultant and director for research programs at MIT and Harvard University. From 1994 to 1997 he was the Bell Atlantic Professor of Telecommunications at Temple University. He is the author, co-author or editor of 10 books, including the award-winning *Who Owns The Media?* as well as *The Digital Divide: Facing a Crisis or Creating a Myth?* His articles have appeared in trade, popular, and scholarly journals, including *Telecommunications Policy*, *Foreign Policy*, *Reason*, and the *Journal of Communication*. A graduate of Dickinson College, he received his MBA from Harvard University and PhD from Temple University. He has been a consultant and invited speaker in Europe, South America, Asia, and Australia as well as in the United States and Canada. His website is www.compaine.com.

Thomas Hylland Eriksen is Professor of Social Anthropology at the University of Oslo and the Free University of Amsterdam. His main research has been concerned with ethnicity, cultural complexity and globalisation, and he has published widely in this field. His other work includes textbooks, essays and a novel. Some of his books are *Ethnicity and Nationalism* (1993), *Small Places, Large Issues* (1995), *A History of Anthropology* (2001), *Tyranny of the Moment* (2001) and *Engaging Anthropology* (2006).

Andrew Graham is the Master of Balliol College, Oxford, a Trustee of the Scott Trust (that oversees the *Guardian* and the *Observer*) and Chairman of the Advisory Board of the Oxford Internet Institute (which he largely created). He was Economic Adviser to the Prime Minister, 1967–69 and, 1974–76; and, from 1988–94, to the Leader of the Labour Party, John Smith. From 1998 to 2005, he was a non-executive director of Channel 4 Television. He is an expert on the principles underlying public service broadcasting. In 2003, Oxford University made him an Honorary Doctor of Civil Law. His partner, Peggotty, was until recently Dean of Social Sciences at the Open University. He is a passionate windsurfer.

Nicola Green is a Lecturer in the Department of Sociology, University of Surrey. Her research in recent years has focussed on how media, technology, culture, gender and embodiment intersect across a range of socio-technical practices. She is particularly interested in the development of methodological approaches aligned to feminist, poststructuralist and actor-network theory in the domain of media and technology relations. Her major research projects have included an ethnographic study of virtual reality technologies, a project on the social shaping of mobile multimedia and mobile personal communications, a fellowship in qualitative social research and technology design practice, and a study investigating notions of risk, trust, privacy and accountability in personal and location-based technologies. At present, she is engaged in projects related to the emergence and intensification of mobile personal data flows, and the transformation of interpersonal, collective and institutional memory in digital culture.

Ian Hunter is a research professor in the Centre for the History of European Discourses at the University of Queensland. He works in the history of political, philosophical and religious thought, with a particular focus on early modern Europe. Professor Hunter is the author of numerous works on these topics, including *Rival Enlightenments: Civil and Metaphysical Philosophy in Early Modern Germany* (Cambridge, 2001), and 'Christian Thomasius and the Desacralisation of Philosophy' (*Journal of the History of Ideas*, 2000). He has completed two collaborative works with David Saunders: a collection of papers on Natural Law and Civil Sovereignty, and a critical edition of the first English translation of Samuel Pufendorf's *De officio hominis et civis*, both of which were published in 2002. He has also just completed a book on the early enlightenment thinker Christian Thomasius, and is currently working on the theme of the 'persona' of the philosopher.

Kevin Kelly is Senior Maverick for *Wired* magazine, which he co-founded. Before that he was editor and publisher of the *Whole Earth Review*, and on the board of the WELL, a pioneering online community in the 1980s. He is the author of *New Rules for the New Economy* (1998) and *Out of Control* (1994). He currently publishes the popular COOL TOOLS on the web, and is writing a book about the long-term trends in technology called *What Technology Wants*. His homepage is www.kk.org.

Heejin Lee is a senior lecturer in the Department of Information Systems at the University of Melbourne. He completed his PhD on time and information technology at London School of Economics. He has published extensively on broadband Internet, standardisation, time and IT and IT/IS in developing countries. He is currently an Associate Editor of the *European Journal of Information Systems* and an editorial board member of *Information Technology for Development*.

Lawrence Lessig is a Professor of Law at Stanford Law School and founder of the school's Center for Internet and Society. He is the author of *Free Culture* (2004), *The Future of Ideas* (2001) and *Code and other Laws of Cyberspace* (1999). He chairs the Creative Commons project, and serves on the board of the Free Software Foundation, the Electronic Frontier Foundation, the Public Library of Science, and Public Knowledge.

Jonathan Liebenau teaches at the London School of Economics in the Department of Management and is an affiliate of the Columbia Institute for Tele-Information, Columbia University. He specialises in two areas: fundamental concepts of information, and the problems and prospects of information and communication technology in economic development. He has previously worked in academic administration, technology policy, and the economic history of science-based industry, all positions in which he has emphasised the use of information in organisations. He is the author or editor of several books and over 70 other major publications and has provided consultancy services to leading companies and strategic government agencies, including BT, IBM, Nortel, EDS, Lloyd Thompson, the UK Department of Trade and Industry and the Home Office.

Jessica Litman teaches copyright law, Internet law, and trademarks and unfair competition law at the University of Michigan Law School. She is the author of *Digital Copyright* (Prometheus 2001) and the co-author with Jane Ginsburg and Mary Lou Kevlin of *Trademarks and Unfair Competition: Cases and Materials* (Foundation 2001). Litman is a trustee of the Copyright Society of the USA, a member of the Intellectual Property and Internet Committee of the ACLU, and the chair-elect of the Association of American Law Schools Section on Intellectual Property Law. She has published many articles on intellectual property topics.

Lev Manovich (www.manovich.net) is the author of *Soft Cinema: Navigating the Database* (MIT Press, 2005), and *The Language of New Media* (MIT Press, 2001) which is hailed as 'the most suggestive and broad ranging media history since Marshall McLuhan.' He is a Professor of Visual Arts, University of California, San Diego (visarts.ucsd.edu) and a Director of The Lab for Cultural Analysis at California Institute for Telecommunications and Information Technology.

Michael Marien is founder and editor of *Future Survey*, a review of books, reports and articles published monthly by the World Future Society since 1979 (www.wfs.org).

Robert W. McChesney is Research Professor in the Institute of Communications Research (ICR) at the University of Illinois at Urbana-Champaign. McChesney is the President and co-founder of Free Press, a national media reform organisation (www.freepress.net). He has written or edited fourteen books, including: with John Nichols, *Tragedy and Farce: How the American Media Sell Wars, Spin Elections, and Destroy Democracy*; and *The Problem of the Media: U.S. Communication Politics in the 21st Century*, published in 2004. McChesney has also written some 150 journal articles and book chapters. His work has been translated into fourteen languages.

David E. Nye is the author of ten books on technology and culture, including *Electrifying America, American Technological Sublime*, and most recently, *Technology Matters: Questions to Live With*. In 2005 he received the Leonardo da Vinci Medal, the lifetime achievement award of the Society for the History of Technology.

Bruce M. Owen is the Morris M. Doyle Centennial Professor in Public Policy and Director of the Public Policy Program in the School of Humanities and Sciences,

Stanford University, Stanford, California. Mr. Owen is also the Gordon Cain Senior Fellow in Stanford's Institute for Economic Policy Research. He is the author or co-author of numerous articles and several books, including *Television Economics,* 1974, *Economics and Freedom of Expression,* 1975, *The Regulation Game,* 1978, and *The Political Economy of Deregulation,* 1983. He is co-author with Steven Wildman of *Video Economics,* published by Harvard University Press in 1992, with M. W. Franken a of *Electric Utility Mergers: Principles of Antitrust Analysis,* Praeger, 1994, and with several others of *Economics of a Disaster: The Exxon Valdez Oil Spill,* Praeger, 1995. His most recent book, *The Internet Challenge to Television,* was published by Harvard University Press in 1999.

Ithiel de Sola Pool was a pioneer media theorist. His book *Technologies of Freedom* (1983) is still a defining study of communications and human freedom, both a history of older systems of communication and a visionary account of the ways in which emerging digital technologies might transform social and political life.

Richard Stallman launched the development of the GNU operating system (see www.gnu.org) in 1984. The GNU does the technical jobs of any operating system, but its specific purpose is to give computer users the freedom to cooperate and to control the software they use. The GNU is free software: everyone has the freedom to copy it and redistribute it, as well as to make changes either large or small. The GNU/Linux system, basically the GNU operating system with Linux added, is used on tens of millions of computers today.

Kevin Robins is Professor of Sociology at City University, London. He has recently been involved in an EU Fifth Framework project, Changing City Spaces: New Challenges to Cultural Policy in Europe. He has also been working with the Council of Europe on questions of cultural diversity, and has recently published The Challenge of Transcultural Diversities (Council of Europe, 2006).

David Saunders is an Honorary Professor in the Centre for the History of European Discourses at the University of Queensland. His research concerns the historical relations of law, politics and religion. His publications in this field include Anti-lawyers: Religion and the Critics of Law and State (London and New York: Routledge, 1997). With Professor Ian Hunter, he has completed a re-edition of Andrew Tooke's 1691 The Whole Duty of Man According to the Law of Nature, the first English translation of Samuel Pufendorf's De officio hominis et civis of 1673 (Indianapolis: Liberty Fund, 2003). This volume also includes his translations of early eighteenth-century writings by Jean Barbeyrac, here appearing in English for the first time. Also with Ian Hunter, he has edited the recent collection of papers Natural Law and Civil Sovereignty: Moral Right and State Authority in Early Modern Political Thought (London and New York : Palgrave Macmillan, 2002).

Jeremy Stein is employed at the Business School at the University of Birmingham. He is Research fellow on the 'Dilemmas of a Maturing Technology', a project funded by the Leverhulme Trust. His research interests focus on technological and organisational innovation, corporate strategy and the history of technology.

Cass R. Sunstein teaches at the University of Chicago. His many books include

Infotopia: How Many Minds Produce Knowledge (2006), *Republic.com* (2001), and *Democracy and the Problem of Speech* (1993).

McKenzie Wark teaches media and cultural studies at the New School for Social Research and Eugene Lang College, in New York City. He is the author of *A Hacker Manifesto* (Harvard University Press, 2004) and many other works.

Frank Webster is Professor of Sociology, City University London. He was Professor of Sociology at Oxford Brookes University from 1990 to 1998, and Professor of Sociology at the University of Birmingham from 1999 to 2002. He has been Docent in the Department of Journalism and Mass Communications, University of Tampere, Finland since 1997. He is the author or editor of many articles and books. Recent publications include: *The Virtual University?*, with Kevin Robins (Oxford University Press, 2002), *The Intensification of Surveillance*, with Kirstie Ball (Pluto, 2003), *The Information Society Reader* (Routledge, 2004), *Theories of the Information Society* 3rd edition (Routledge, 2006), *Journalists under Fire: Information War and Journalistic Practices*, with Howard Tumber (Sage, 2006).

Dugald Williamson is an Associate Professor in the School of English, Communication and Theatre at the University of New England, Australia. He has published widely in media studies and is currently researching contemporary documentary and political communication.

Bibliography

Adam, B (1990) *Time and Social Theory*, Polity/Blackwell, Cambridge.

Adam, J A (1993) 'Virtual reality is for real', *IEEE Spectrum*, vol. 30, no. 10, pp. 22–9.

Adas, M (1989) *Machines as the Measure of Men: Science, Technology and Ideologies of Western Dominance*, Cornell University Press, Ithaca, New York.

Adler, P (ed.) (1992) *Technology and the Future of Work*, Oxford University Press, New York.

Albig, W (1939) *Public Opinion*, McGraw-Hill, New York.

American Geophysical Union v Texaco (2d Cir. 1995) 60 F.3d 913.

American Library Association (1995) *Information for a New Age: Redefining the Librarian, Library Instruction Round Table*, Libraries Unlimited, Englewood, Colorado.

Amin, A (1994) *Post-Fordism*, Basil Blackwell, Oxford.

Aoki, K (1993) 'Authors, inventors, and trademark owners: Private intellectual property and the public domain', *Columbia-VLA Journal of Law and the Arts*, vol. 18.

Aoki, K (1996) '(Intellectual) property and sovereignty: Notes toward a cultural geography of authorship', *Stanford Law Review*, vol. 48.

Aoki, K (1996) Foreword to 'Innovation and the information environment: Interrogating the entrepreneur', *Oregon Law Review*, vol. 75.

Appadurai, A (1986) *The Social Life of Things: Commodities in Cultural Perspective*, Cambridge University Press, New York.

Archer, P (1956) *The Queen's Courts*, Penguin, Harmondsworth.

Aronowitz, S & DiFazio, W (1994) *The Jobless Future: Sci-Tech and the Dogma of Work*, University of Minnesota Press, Minneapolis.

Arrow, K J (1962) 'Economic welfare and the allocation of resources for invention', in *The Rate and Direction of Inventive Activity: Economic and Social Factors*, conference of the Universities–National Bureau Committee for Economic Growth of the Social Science Research Council, Princeton University Press, Princeton, New Jersey.

Aukstakalnis, S & Blatner, D (1992) *Silicon Mirage: The Art and Science of Virtual Reality*, Peachpit, Berkeley, California.

Bagdikian, B H (1992) *The Media Monopoly*, 4th edn, Beacon, Boston, Massachusetts.

Ball, H (1944) *The Law of Copyright and Literary Property*, Bender, New York.

Bankes, S & Builder, C (1992) 'Seizing the moment: Harnessing the information society', *The Information Society*, vol. 8, no. 1, pp. 1–59.

Banta, M (1987) *Imaging American Women: Ideas and Ideals in Cultural History*, Columbia University Press, New York.

Barley, S R (1988) 'On technology, time, and social order: Technologically induced change in the temporal organization of radiological work', in Dubinskas, F A (ed.) *Making Time: Ethnographies of High-Technology Organizations*, Temple University Press, Philadelphia, Pennsylvania, pp. 123–69.

Barnet, R J & Cavanagh, J (1994) *Global Dreams: Imperial Corporations and the New World Order*, Simon & Schuster, New York.

Barry, A, Osborne, T & Rose, N (1996) *Foucault and Political Reason: Liberalism, Neo-Liberalism and Rationalities of Government*, Chicago University Press, Chicago, Illinois.

Barry, J A (1991) *Technobabble*, MIT Press, Cambridge, Massachusetts.

Bartky, I R (1989) 'The adoption of standard time', *Technology and Culture*, vol. 30, pp. 25–56.

Bateson, G (1972) *Steps Towards An Ecology of Mind*, Ballantine, New York.

Bazelon, D (1979) 'The First Amendment and the new media', *Federal Communications Law Journal*, vol. 31, no. 2.

Bazelon, D (1982) 'The First Amendment's second chance', *Channels*, Feb.–Mar., pp. 16–17.

Bearman, D (1993) 'Interactivity in American museums', *Museums Management and Curatorship*, vol. 12, pp. 183–93.

Becker, J (1989) 'The concept of a university of the world', *The Information Society*, vol. 6, no. 3, pp. 83–92.

Becker, T (1996) 'Televote: Interactive, participatory polling', in Becker, T and Couto, R A (eds) *Teaching Democracy by Being Democratic*, Praeger, Westport, Connecticut.

Bell, D (1975) *The Cultural Contradictions of Capitalism*, Basic, New York.

Bell, D (1989) 'The third technological revolution and its possible socioeconomic consequences', *Dissent*, vol. 36, no. 2, pp. 164–76.

Bell, T W (1998) 'Fair use vs. fared use: The impact of automated rights management on copyright's fair use doctrine', *North Carolina Law Review*, vol. 76.

Belsie, L (1993) 'Smart cards connect customers', *Christian Science Monitor*, Aug. 13, p. 8.

Benkler, Y (1998) 'Overcoming agoraphobia: Building the commons of the digitally networked environment', *Harvard Journal of Law and Technology*, vol. 11.

Benkler, Y (1999) 'Free as the air to common use: First Amendment constraints on enclosure of the public domain', *NYU Law Review*, vol. 354.

Bennett, J (1992) 'The English quadrant in Europe: Instruments and the growth of consensus in practical astronomy', *Journal of the History of Astronomy*, vol. 23, no. 1, pp. 1–14.

Bennett, J (1998) 'Can science museums take history seriously?', in Macdonald, S (ed.) *The Politics of Display: Museums, Science, Culture*, Routledge, London.

Bennett, J, Brain, R, Bycroft, K, Schaffer, S, Sibum, H & Staley, R (1993) *Empires of Physics*, Whipple Museum of the History of Science, Cambridge.

Bennett, T (1995) *The Birth of the Museum: History, Theory, Politics*, Routledge, London.

Berman, M (1991) *All That is Solid Melts into Air: The Experience of Modernity*, Verso, London.

Bernays, L (1923) *Crystallizing Public Opinion*, Boni and Liveright, New York.

Bianculli, D (1992) *Teleliteracy: Taking Television Seriously*, Continuum, New York.

Bicknell, S & Farmelo, G (1993) *Museum Visitor Studies in the 1990s*, Science Museum, London.

Bikson, T K & Law, S A (1993) 'Electronic mail use at the World Bank: Messages from users', *The Information Society*, vol. 9, no. 2, pp. 89–124.

Birdsall, W F (1994) *The Myth of the Electronic Library: Librarianship and Social Change in America*, Greenwood, Westport, Connecticut.

Birkerts, S (1994) *The Gutenberg Elegies: The Fate of Reading in an Electronic Age*, Faber & Faber, New York.

Birt, J (1999) *The Prize and the Price: The Social, Political and Cultural Consequences of the Digital Age*, New Statesman Media Lecture, May, London.

Blackman, C & Schoof, H (1994) 'Competition and convergence', *Telecommunications Policy*, vol. 18, no. 8, pp. 571–667.

Boden, D & Molotch, H, L. (1994) 'The compulsion of proximity', in Friedland, R and Boden, D (eds) *NowHere: Space, Time and Modernity*, University of California Press, Berkeley, California, pp. 257–86.

Bogart, L (1995) *Commercial Culture: The Media System and the Public Interest*, Oxford University Press, New York.

Boorstin, D (1973) *The Americans: The Democratic Experience*, Random House, New York.

Bordwell, D & Thompson, K (1997) *Film Art: An Introduction*, 5th edn, McGraw-Hill, New York.

Borg, M (1990) 'An economic comparison of gambling behaviour in Atlantic City and Las Vegas', *Public Finance Quarterly*, vol. 18, no. 3, pp. 291–312.

Born, G (1995) *Rationalizing Culture: IRCalifM, Boulez and the Institutionalisation of the Musical Avant-Garde*, University of California Press, Berkeley, California.

Born, G (2000) 'Inside television: Television research and the sociology of culture', *Screen*, vol. 41, no. 4, pp. 68–96.

Bosma, J (1999) *Read Me! Filtered by Nettime: ASCII Culture and the Revenge of Knowledge*, Autonomedia, New York.

Boulding, K E & Senesh, L (1983) *The Optimum Utilisation of Knowledge: Making Knowledge Serve Human Betterment*, Westview, Boulder, Colorado.

Bourdieu, P (1984) *Distinction*, Routledge, London.

Boyle, J (1987) 'Thomas Hobbes and the invented tradition of positivism: Reflections on language, power, and essentialism', *University of Pennsylvania Law Review*, vol. 135.

Boyle, J (1996) *Shamans, Software and Spleens: Law and the Construction of the Information Society*, Harvard University Press, Cambridge, Massachusetts.

Boyle, J (1997) 'A politics of intellectual property: Environmentalism for the net?', *Duke Law Journal*, vol. 47.

Bradley, S P, Hausman, J A & Nolan, R L (1993) *Globalization, Technology, and Competition: The Fusion of Computers and Telecommunications in the 1990s*, Harvard Business School Press, Boston, Massachusetts.

Branscomb, A W (1994) *Who Owns Information? From Privacy to Public Access*, Basic, New York.

Breyer, S (1970) 'The uneasy case for copyright: A study of copyright in books, photocopies, and computer programs', *Harvard Law Review*, vol. 84, no. 2, pp. 281–351.

Bridges, W (1994) *Job Shift: How to Prosper in a Workplace Without Jobs*, Addison-Wesley, Reading, Massachusetts.

Brody, H (1993) 'Information highway: The home front', *Technology Review*, vol. 96, no. 6, pp. 30–40.

Brook, J & Boal, I A (1995) *Resisting the Virtual Life: The Culture and Politics of Information*, City Lights, San Francisco.

Brown, B, Green, N & Harper, R (2002) *Wireless World: Social and Interactional Aspects of the Mobile Age*, Springer, London.

Bruno, M (1987) 'Printing', in *McGraw-Hill Encyclopedia of Science and Technology*, vol. 14, McGraw-Hill, New York.

Budge, I. (1996) *The New Challenge of Direct Democracy*, Polity, Cambridge.

Burchell, D (1995) 'The attributes of citizens: Virtue, manners and the activity of citizenship', *Economy and Society*, vol. 24, no. 4, pp. 540–58.

Burke, J (1978) *Connections*, Little Brown, Boston, Massachusetts.

Burstein, D & Kline, D (1995) *Road Warriors: Dreams and Nightmares along the Information Highway*, Dutton/Penguin, New York.

Cairncross, F (1997) *The Death of Distance: How the Communications Revolution Will Change Our Lives*, Harvard Business School Press, Boston, Massachusetts.

Callon, M, Law, J & Rip, A (1986) *Mapping the Dynamics of Science and Technology*, Macmillan, London.

Carey, J (1983) 'Technology and ideology: The case of the telegraph', in Salzman, J (ed.) *Prospects: An Annual of American Cultural Studies*, Cambridge University Press, New York, pp. 303–25.

Cartwright, G F (1994) 'Virtual or real? The mind in cyberspace', *Futurist*, vol. 28, no. 2, pp. 22–6.

Casmir, F (1991) *Communication in Development*, Ablex, Norwood, New Jersey.

Castells, M (1989) *The Informational City: Economic Restructuring and Urban Development*, Blackwell, Oxford.

Castells, M (1996) *The Rise of the Network Society*, 2nd edn, Blackwell, Cambridge, Massachusetts.

Castoriadis, C (1984) *Crossroads in the Labyrinth*, MIT Press, Cambridge, Massachusetts.

Castoriadis, C (1984/85) 'Reflections on "rationality" and "development"', *Thesis Eleven*, no. 10/11.

Caudill, M (1992) *In Our Own Image: Building an Artificial Person*, Oxford University Press, New York.

Caufield, C (1990) *Multiple Exposures*, University of Chicago Press, Chicago, Illinois.

Chaffee, Z. (1945) 'Reflections on the law of copyright', *Columbia Law Review*, vol. 45.

Chandler, A (1977) *The Visible Hand: The Managerial Revolution in American Business*, Harvard University Press, Cambridge, Massachusetts.

Chaum, D (1992) 'Achieving electronic privacy', *Scientific American*, vol. 267, no. 2, pp. 96–101.

Childs, H L (1965) *Public Opinion: Nature, Formation and Role*, Van Nostrand, Princeton, New Jersey.

Cité des Sciences et de l'Industrie (1988) *Direction de la Communication et du Développement*, Cité des Sciences et de l'Industrie, Paris.

Cité des Sciences et de l'Industrie (1995) *Explora: Guide to the Permanent Exhibitions*, 6th edn, Direction de la Communication et de la Promotion, Paris.

Cité des Sciences et de l'Industrie (nd) 'Visitor information', Cité des Sciences et de l'Industrie, Paris.

Clinton, B (1997) speech to National Press Club, March 11.

Clinton, B & Gore, A (1997) *A Framework for Global Electronic Commerce*, White House, Washington, District Columbia.

Coates, J F (1994) 'The highly probably future: 83 assumptions about the year 2025', *Futurist*, vol. 28, no. 4.

Coates, J F (1995) 'Work and pay in the twenty-first century: An impending crisis', *Employment Relations Today*, vol. 22, no. 1, pp. 17–22.

Coates, J F & Jarratt, J (1994) 'White collar productivity: Key to future competitiveness', *The Future at Work*, vol. 9, Nov.

Coates, J F, Mahaffie, J B & Hines, A (1994) 'Technological forecasting: 1970–1993', *Technological Forecasting and Social Change*, vol. 47, no. 1, pp. 23–33.

Cohen, J E (1995) 'Reverse-engineering and the rise of electronic vigilantism: Intellectual property implications of "lock-out" programs', *Southern California Law Review*, vol. 68.

Cohen, J E (1996) 'A right to read anonymously: A closer look at "copyright management" in cyberspace', *Connecticut Law Review*, vol. 28.

Cohen, J E (1997) 'Some reflections on copyright management systems and laws designed to protect them', *Berkeley Technology Law Journal*, vol. 12.

Cohen, J E (1998) 'Copyright and the jurisprudence of self-help', *Berkeley Technology Law Journal*, vol. 13.

Cohen, J E (1998) 'Lochner in cyberspace: The new economic orthodoxy of "rights management" ', *Michigan Law Review*, vol. 97.

Committee on Obscenity and Film Censorship (1979) *Report*, Her Majesty's Stationery Office, London.

Compaine, B M & Gomery, D (2000) *Who Owns the Media? Competition and Concentration in the Mass Media*, 3rd edn, Erlbaum, Mahwah, New Jersey.

Computer Professionals for Social Responsibility (1993) *Serving the Community: A Public Interest Vision of the National Information Infrastructure*, Computer Professionals for Social Responsibility, Palo Alto, California.

Computer Software Rental Amendments Act 1990 (United States).

Connerton, P (1989) *How Societies Remember*, Cambridge University Press, Cambridge.

Connors, M (1993) *The Race to the Intelligent State: Towards the Global Information Economy of 2005*, Blackwell Business, Oxford.

Cook, P S, Gomery, D & Lichty, L W (1992) *The Future of News: Television, Newspapers, Wire Services, Newsmagazines*, Woodrow Wilson Center Press, Washington, District Columbia.

Cooper, G, Green, N, Harper, R & Murtagh, G (2002) *Mobile Society? Technology, Distance and Presence*, Cambridge University Press, Cambridge.

Corrigan, P & Sayer, D (1985) *The Great Arch: English State Formation as Cultural Revolution*, Blackwell, Oxford.

Cossons, N (1987) 'Adapt or die: Dangers of a dinosaur mentality', *Listener*, April, pp. 18–20.

Cossons, N (1991) 'Scholarship or self-indulgence', *RSA Journal*, vol. 139, Feb., pp. 184–91.

Crevier, D (1993) *AI: The Tumultuous History of the Search for Artificial Intelligence*, Basic, New York.

Critical Art Ensemble (1994) *The Electronic Disturbance*, Autonomedia, New York.

Critical Art Ensemble (2002) *The Molecular Invasion*, Autonomedia, New York.

Cronon, W (1992) *Nature's Metropolis: Chicago and the Great West*, Norton, New York.

Cruikshank, B (1996) 'Revolutions within: Self-government and self-esteem', in Barry, A, Osborne, T and Rose, N (eds) *Foucalt and Political Reason: Liberalism, Neo-Liberalism and Rationalities of Government*, Chicago University Press, Chicago, Illinois.

Cruikshank, B (1999) *The Will to Empower: Democratic Citizens and Other Subjects*, Cornell University Press, Ithaca, New York.

Cunningham, S & Porter, A L (1992) 'Communication networks: A dozen ways they'll change our lives', *Futurist*, vol. 26, no. 1, pp. 19–22.

Czitrom, D (1982) *Media and the American Mind: From Morse to McLuhan*, University of North Carolina Press, Chapel Hill, North Carolina.

Davies, D, Bathurst, D & Bathurst, R (1990) *The Telling Image: The Changing Balance between Pictures and Words in a Technological Age*, Oxford University Press, Oxford.

Davis, S & Botkin, J (1994) *The Monster Under the Bed: How Business Is Mastering the Opportunity of Knowledge for Profit*, Simon & Schuster, New York.

Day, J (1995) *The Vanishing Vision: The Inside Story of Public Television*, University of California Press, Berkeley, California.

de Laet, M & Mol, A (2000) 'The Zimbabwe bush pump: Mechanics of a fluid technology', *Social Studies of Science*, vol. 30, no. 2, pp. 225–63.

de Tocqueville, A (1945) *Democracy in America*, Knopf, New York.

Debord, G (1983) *Society of the Spectacle*, Black and Red, Detroit, Michigan.

Deleuze, G (1987) *Foucault*, Athlone, London.

Deleuze, G (1995) *Negotiations*, Columbia University Press, New York.

Deleuze, G & Guattari, F (1988) *A Thousand Plateaus: Capitalism and Schizophrenia*, Athlone, London.

Demsetz, H (1967) 'Toward a theory of property rights', *American Economics Review*, vol. 57.

Dent, H (1995) *Job Shock: Four New Principles Transforming Our Work and Business*, St Martin's, New York.

Department of the Interior (1986) *Aircraft Management Plan Environmental Assessment: Grand Canyon National Park*, DoI, Washington, District Columbia.

Derrida, J (1986) 'Point de folie: Maintenant l'architecture', *AA Files*, no. 12, pp. 65–75.

Dertouzos, M L (1991) 'Building the information marketplace', *Technology Review*, vol. 94, no. 1, pp. 28–40.

Dertouzos, M L (1991) 'Communications, computers and networks', *Scientific American*, vol. 265, pp. 62–9.

Desurvire, E (1992) 'Lightwave communications: The fifth generation', *Scientific American*, vol. 266, no. 1, pp. 114–21.

Dewey, J (1977) 'The future of liberalism', in Morgenbesser, S (ed.) *Dewey and His Critics: Essays from the Journal of Philosophy*, Journal of Philosophy, New York.

Diebold Institute for Public Policy Studies (1995) *Transportation Infrastructures: The Development of Intelligent Transportation Systems*, Praeger, Westport, Connecticut.

Donald, J (1999) *The City and the Modern Imagination*, Athlone, London.

Donaldson, M S & Lohr, K N (1994) *Health Data in the Information Age: Use, Disclosure, and Privacy*, National Academy Press, Washington, District Columbia.

Dordick, H S & Wang, G (1993) *The Information Society: A Retrospective View*, Sage, Newbury Park, California.

Dow, C M (1921) *Anthology and Bibliography of Niagara Falls*, State of New York, New York.

Drucker, P (1994) 'The age of social transformation', *Atlantic Monthly*, vol. 274, no. 5, pp. 53–80.

Drucker, P (1995) *Managing in a Time of Great Change*, Talley/Dutton, New York.

Du Gay, P, Hall, S, Janes, L, Mackay, H, Negus, K & Tudor, A (1997) *Doing Cultural Studies: The Story of the Sony Walkman*, Sage, London.

Dunn, S L (1994) 'The challenge of the nineties in US higher education: From Camelot to the 21st century', *Futures Research Quarterly*, vol. 10, no. 3, pp. 35–55.

Durant, J (1992) 'Introduction', in Durant, J (ed.) *Museums and the Public Understanding of Science*, Science Museum, London.

Durlach, N I & Mavor, A S (1995) *Virtual Reality: Scientific and Technological Challenges*, National Academy Press, Washington, District Columbia.

Dutton, W H (1992) 'The social impact of emerging telephone services', *Telecommunications Policy*, vol. 16, no. 5, pp. 377–87.

Dyson, E (1995) 'Friend and foe', *Wired*, vol. 3, no. 8.

Dyson, E (1995) 'Intellectual value', *Wired*, vol. 3, no. 7.

Dyson, E, Gilder, G, Keyworth, J & Toffler, A (1994) 'A Magna Carta for the knowledge age', *New Perspectives Quarterly*, vol. 11, no. 4, pp. 26–37.

Eames, C (1990) *A Computer Perspective: Background to the Computer Age*, Harvard University Press, Cambridge, Massachusetts.

Easterbrook, F H (1990) 'Intellectual property is still property', *Harvard Journal of Law and Public Policy*, vol. 13.

Effross, W A (1997) 'The legal architecture of virtual stores: World wide web sites and the uniform commercial code', *San Diego Law Review*, vol. 34.

Eldred v Reno (1999) DDC, filed Jan. 4.

Elkin-Koren, N (1995) 'Copyright law and social dialogue on the information superhighway:

The case against copyright liability of bulletin board operators', *Cardozo Arts and Entertainment Law Journal*, vol. 13.

Elkin-Koren, N (1996) 'Cyberlaw and social change: A democratic approach to copyright law in cyberspace', *Cardozo Arts and Entertainment Law Journal*, vol. 14.

Elkin-Koren, N (1996) 'Goodbye to all that: A reluctant (and perhaps premature) adieu to a constitutionally grounded discourse of public interest in copyright law', *Vanderbilt Journal of Transnational Law*, vol. 29.

Elkin-Koren, N (1997) 'Copyright policy and the limits of freedom of contract', *Berkeley Technology Law Journal*, vol. 12.

Elkin-Koren, N (1998) 'Contracts in cyberspace: Rights without laws', *Chicago-Kent Law Review*, vol. 73.

Elkin-Koren, N (2002) 'It's all about control', in Elkin-Koren, N. and Netanel, N. (eds) *The Commodification of Information*, Kluwer, The Hague.

Ellis, H (1959) *British Railway History: An Outline from the Accession of William IV to the Nationalisation of the Railways 1877–1947*, Allen & Unwin, London.

Ellul, J (1990) *The Technological Bluff*, William B Eerdmans, Grand Rapids, Minnesota.

Elsaesser, T (1990) *Early Cinema: Space, Frame, Narrative*, British Film Institute, London.

Elster, J (1983) *Sour Grapes: Studies in the Subversion of Rationality*, Cambridge University Press, Cambridge.

Engelberger, J F (1989) *Robotics in Service*, MIT Press, Cambridge, Massachusetts.

Estabrooks, M (1988) *Programmed Capitalism: A Computer-Mediated Global Society*, M E Sharpe, Armonk, New York.

Failla, A & Bagnara, S (1992) 'Information technology, decision, time', *Social Science Information*, vol. 31, no. 4, pp. 669–81.

Falk, T & Abler, R (1980) 'Intercommunications, distance and geographical theory', *Geografiska Annaler*, no. 62, pp. 59–67.

Fasella, F (1997) 'The role of the European Commission in supporting research', *European Review*, vol. 5, pp. 161–84.

Feigenbaum, E A (1989) 'Toward the library of the future', *Long Range Planning*, vol. 22, no. 1, pp. 118–23.

Feist Publications Inc. v Rural Telephone Service Co. (1991) 499 US 340, 346.

Ferris, C D (1980) quoted in *The Report*, Nov. 14, p. 11.

Field, J (1978) 'American imperialism: The worst chapter in almost any book', *American Historical Review*, vol. 83, no. 3, pp. 644–83.

Findlay, J (1986) *People of Chance: Gambling in American Society from Jamestown to Las Vegas*, Oxford University Press, New York.

Finley, M (1991) 'The best of all possible meetings', *Across the Board*, vol. 28, no. 9, pp. 40–5.

Fischer, C S (1985) 'Studying technology and social life', in Castells, M (ed.) *Technology, Space and Society*, vol. 28, Urban Affairs Annual Reviews, Sage, Beverly Hills, California, pp. 284–300.

Fischer, C, S. (1992) *America Calling: A Social History of the Telephone to 1940*, University of California Press, Berkeley, California.

Fischer, D H (1989) *Albion's Seed: Four British Folkways in America* , Oxford University Press, New York.

Fisher, W (1988) 'Reconstructing the fair use doctrine', *Harvard Law Review*, vol. 101.

Fisher, W (1998) 'Compulsory terms in internet-related contracts', *Chicago-Kent Law Review*, vol. 73.

Fisher, W (1998) 'Property and contract on the internet', *Chicago-Kent Law Review*, vol. 74.

Fisher, W (ed.) (1993) *American Legal Realism*, Oxford University Press, New York.

Fishkin, J (1991) *Democracy and Deliberation*, Yale University Press, New Haven, Connecticut.

Flaherty, D H (1989) *Protecting Privacy in Surveillance Societies: The Federal Republic of Germany, Sweden, France, Canada and the United States*, University of North Carolina Press, Chapel Hill, North Carolina.

Folsom v Marsh (1841) 9 Fed Cas. 342.

Forester, T (1992) 'Megatrends or megamistakes? What ever happened to the information society?', *The Information Society*, vol. 8, no. 3, pp. 133–46.

Forester, T & Morrison, P (1994) *Computer Ethics: Cautionary Tales and Ethical Dilemmas in Computing*, 2nd edn, MIT Press, Cambridge, Massachusetts.

Fortner, R (1978) *Messiahs and Monopolists: A Cultural History of Canadian Communication Systems, 1846–1914*, PhD dissertation, Institute of Communications Research, University of Illinois, Urbana, Illinois.

Foucault, M (1977) *Discipline and Punish: The Birth of the Prison*, Penguin, Harmondsworth.

Fowles, J (1992) *Why Viewers Watch: A Reappraisal of Television's Effects*, revised edn, Sage, Newbury Park, California.

Frank, R (1998) *Luxury Fever: Why Money Fails to Satisfy in an Era of Excess*, Free Press, New York.

Frank, R & Cook, P (1995) *The Winner Take All Society: How More and More Americans Compete for Ever Fewer and Bigger Prizes, Encouraging Economic Waste, Income Inequality, and an Impoverished Cultural Life*, Free Press, New York.

Franklin, B (1994) *Packaging Politics: Political Communications in Britain's Media Democracy*, Edward Arnold, London.

Frey, M G (1998) 'Unfairly applying the fair use doctrine: Princeton University Press v Michigan Document Services, 99 F3d 1381 (6th Cir 1996)', *University of Cincinnati Law Review*, vol. 66.

Fried, B H (1998) *The Progressive Assault on Laissez Faire: Robert Hale and the First Law and Economics Movement*, Harvard University Press, Cambridge, Massachusetts.

Frisby, D (1985) *Fragments of Modernity: Theories of Modernity in the Work of Simmel, Kracauer, and Benjamin*, Polity, Cambridge.

Frissen, V (1995) 'Gender is calling: Some reflections on past, present and future uses of the telephone', in Grint, K and Gill, R (eds) *The Gender–Technology Relation*, Taylor & Francis, London, pp. 79–94.

Froomkin, M (1998) 'Article 2B as legal software for electronic contracting: Operating system or Trojan horse?', *Berkeley Technology Law Journal*, vol. 13.

Galison, P (1994) 'The ontology of the enemy: Norbert Wiener and the cybernetic vision', *Critical Inquiry*, vol. 21, Autumn, pp. 228–66.

Gallucci, C (1994) 'How many votes did TV change?', *L'Espresso*, 11 Nov.

Ganley, G D (1992) *The Exploding Political Power of Personal Media*, Ablex, Norwood, New Jersey.

Garnham, N (1986) 'The media and the public sphere', in Golding, P, Murdock, G and Schlesinger, P (eds) *Communicating Politics: Mass Communications and the Political Process*, Leicester University Press, Leicester, pp. 37–53.

Gates, B (1995) *The Road Ahead*, Viking, New York.

Gavit, Bernard C (1932) *The Commerce Clause of the United States Constitution*, Principia, Bloomington, Indiana.

Gelernter, D (1992) *Mirror Worlds, or, The Day Software Puts the Universe in a Shoebox: How It Will Happen and What It Will Mean*, Oxford University Press, New York.

Geller, H (1998) 'Public interest regulation in the digital TV era', in Noll, R G and Price, M E (eds) *A Communications Cornucopia: Markle Foundation Essays on Information Policy*, Brookings Institution, Washington, District Columbia.

Gergen, K J (1991) *The Saturated Self: Dilemmas of Identity in Contemporary Life*, Basic, New York.

Gibbons v Ogden (1824) 22 US 1.

Gibbs, D (1993) 'Telematics and urban economic development policies: Time for caution?', *Telecommunications Policy*, vol. 17, no. 4, pp. 250–6.

Giddens, A (1981) *A Contemporary Critique of Historical Materialism: Power, Property and the State*, vol. 1, Macmillan, London.

Giddens, A (1990) *The Consequences of Modernity*, Polity, Cambridge.

Giddens, A (1998) *The Third Way: The Renewal of Social Democracy*, Polity, Cambridge.

Gilder, G (1989) *Microcosm: The Quantum Revolution in Economics and Technology*, Simon & Schuster, New York.

Gilder, G (1994) *Life After Television*, Whittle, Knoxville, Tennessee.

Gimbel, M (1998) 'Some thoughts on the implications of trusted systems for intellectual property law', *Stanford Law Review*, vol. 50.

Ginsburg, J C (1990) 'A tale of two copyrights: Literary property in revolutionary France and America', *Tulane Law Review*, vol. 64.

Ginsburg, J C (1997) 'Authors and users in copyright', *Journal of the Copyright Society of the USA*, vol. 45.

Ginsburg, J C (2000) 'From having copies to experiencing works: The development of an access right in US copyright law', in Hansen, H (ed.) *US Intellectual Property: Law and Policy*, Sweet & Maxwell, London.

Glastonbury, B & LaMendola, W (1992) *The Integrity of Intelligence: A Bill of Rights for the Information Age*, St Martin's, New York.

Gleick, J (1995) 'Making Microsoft safe for capitalism', *New York Times Magazine*, vol. 5, Nov., pp. 50–7.

Goldstein, P (1982) 'Derivative rights and derivative works in copyright', *Journal of the Copyright Society of the USA*, vol. 30.

Gonzalez-Manet, E (1992) *Informatics and Society: The New Challenges*, Ablex, Norwood, New Jersey.

Gordon, W (1982) 'Fair use as market failure: A structural and economic analysis of the Betamax case and its predecessors', *Columbia Law Review*, vol. 82.

Gordon, W (1989) 'An inquiry into the merits of copyright: The challenges of consistency, consent, and encouragement theory', *Stanford Law Review*, vol. 41.

Gordon, W (1990) 'Toward a jurisprudence of benefits: The norms of copyright and the problem of private censorship', *University of Chicago Law Review*, vol. 57.

Gordon, W (1992) 'On owning information: Intellectual property and restitutionary impulse', *Virginia Law Review*, vol. 78.

Gordon, W (1992) 'Reality as artifact: From Feist to fair use', *Law and Contemporary Problems*, vol. 55.

Gorton, I & Motwani, S (1996) 'Issues in co-operative software engineering using globally distributed teams', *Information and Software Technology*, vol. 38, pp. 647–55.

Gouldner, A (1976) *The Dialectic of Ideology and Technology*, Macmillan, London.

Green, N (2002) 'Who's watching whom? Monitoring and accountability in mobile relations', in Brown, B, Green, N and Harper, R (eds) *Wireless World: Social and Interactional Aspects of the Mobile Age*, Springer, London, pp. 32–45.

Green, S & Harvey, P (1999) *Scaling Place and Networks: An Ethnography of ICT 'Innovation' in Manchester*, paper presented to Internet and Ethnography conference, Hull, Dec. 13–14.

Haber, S (1964) *Efficiency and Uplift: Scientific Management in the Progressive Era, 1890–1920*, University of Chicago Press, Chicago, Illinois.

Habermas, J (1989) *The Structural Transformation of the Public Sphere: An Inquiry into a Category of Bourgeois Society*, Polity, Cambridge.

Hacking, I (1999) *The Social Construction of What?*, Harvard University Press, Cambridge, Massachusetts.

Haddon, L (1993) 'Interactive games', in Hayward, P and Wollen, T (eds) *Future Visions: New Technologies of the Screen*, British Film Institute, London, pp. 10–30.

Halal, W E (1993) 'The information technology revolution: Computer hardware, software, and services into the 21st century', *Technological Forecasting and Social Change*, vol. 44, no. 1, pp. 69–86.

Halal, W E & Liebowitz, J (1994) 'Telelearning: The multimedia revolution in education', *Futurist*, vol. 28, no. 6, pp. 21–6.

Halbert, D J (1999) *Intellectual Property in the Information Age: The Politics of Expanding Ownership Rights*, Quorum, Westport, Connecticut.

Hall, E T (1959) *The Silent Language*, Doubleday, New York.

Hall, E T (1966) *The Hidden Dimension*, Doubleday, New York.

Hall, E T (1983) *The Dance of Life: The Other Dimension of Time*, Doubleday, New York.

Hamelink, C J (1988) *The Technology Gamble: Informatics and Public Policy: A Study of Technology*, Ablex, Norwood, New Jersey.

Hamm, I & Harmgarth, F (1995) 'Responsibility of television: An introduction', in Bertelsmann Foundation and European Institute for the Media (eds) *Television Requires Responsibility: International Studies on the Structural Factors Ensuring Responsible Television*, vol. 2, Bertelsmann Foundation, Gütersloh.

Harasim, L (1993) *Global Networks: Computers and International Communication*, MIT Press, Cambridge, Massachusetts.

Haraway, D (1989) 'Teddy bear patriarchy: Taxidermy and the garden of Eden, New York City 1908–1936', in Haraway, D (ed.) *Primate Visions*, Verso, London.

Hart, R P (1994) *Seducing America: How Television Charms the Modern Voter*, Oxford University Press, New York.

Harvey, D (1990) 'Between space and time: Reflections on the geographical imagination', *Annals of the Association of American Geographers*, vol. 80, no. 3, pp. 418–34.

Harvey, D (1990) *The Condition of Postmodernity: An Enquiry into the Conditions of Cultural Change*, Blackwell, Oxford.

Harvey, P (1996) *Hybrids of Modernity: Anthropology, the Nation-State and the Universal Exhibition*, Routledge, London.

Hawaii Housing Authority v Midkiff (1984) 467 US229.

Haywood, T (1995) *Info-Rich/Info-Poor: Access and Exchange in the Global Information Society*, Bowker Saur, East Grinstead.

Headrick, D R (1981) *The Tools of Empire: Technology and European Imperialism in the Nineteenth Century*, Oxford University Press, New York.

Heaton, J A & Wilson, N L (1995) *Tuning in Trouble: Talk TV's Destructive Impact on Mental Health*, Jossey-Bass, San Francisco.

Heim, M (1993) *The Metaphysics of Virtual Reality*, Oxford University Press, New York.

Hein, H (1990) *The Exploratorium: The Museum as Laboratory*, Smithsonian Institution Press, Washington, District Columbia.

Heinich, N (1988) 'The Pompidou Centre and its public: The limits of a utopian site', in Lumley, R (ed.) *The Museum Time-Machine: Putting Cultures on Display*, Routledge, London.

Hill, C (1964) *Society and Puritanism in Pre-Revolutionary England*, Secker & Warburg, London.

Hill, E J, Hawkins, A J & Miller, B C (1996) 'Work and family in the virtual office: Perceived influences of mobile telework', *Family Relations*, vol. 45, pp. 293–301.

Hiltz, S R (1994) *The Virtual Classroom: Learning Without Limits via Computer Networks*, Ablex, Norwood, New Jersey.

Hines, A (1994) 'Jobs and infotech: Work in the information society', *Futurist*, vol. 28, no. 1, pp. 9–13.

Hirschman, A O (1967) *The Passions and the Interests: Political Arguments for Capitalism Before Its Triumph*, Princeton University Press, Princeton, NJ.

Hobbes, T (1976) *Leviathan*, accessed Feb. 13 2006 from http://etext.library.adelaide.edu.au/h/hobbes/thomas/h68l/.

Hobsbawm, E J (1975) *The Age of Capital 1848–75*, Weidenfeld & Nicolson, London.

Hooper-Greenhill, E (1992) *Museums and the Shaping of Knowledge*, Routledge, London.

Horner, V M (1991) 'Electronic links for learning', *Annals of the American Academy of Political and Social Science*, vol. 514 (special issue), pp. 1–174.

Horrocks, R J & Scarr, R W A (1993) *Future Trends in Telecommunications*, John Wiley, New York.

House of Commons (2000) *Science and Society*, Select Committee on Science and Technology, 3rd report, session 1999–2000, Her Majesty's Stationery Office, London.

Howard, A (1995) *The Changing Nature of Work*, Jossey-Bass, San Francisco.

Huber, P (1994) *Orwell's Revenge: The 1984 Palimpsest*, Free Press, New York.

Hudson, H E (1990) *Communication Satellites: Their Development and Impact*, Free Press, New York.

Hudson, K (1987) *Museums of Influence*, Cambridge University Press, Cambridge.

Hughes, J (1988) 'The philosophy of intellectual property', *Georgetown Law Journal*, vol. 77.

Hyde, H, M. (1964) *A History of Pornography*, Heinemann, London.

Ihde, D (1990) *Technology and the Life-World: From Garden to Earth*, Indiana University Press, Bloomington, Indiana.

'Intellectual property and contract law for the information age: The impact of Article 2B of the Uniform Commercial Code on the future of information and commerce' (1999) symposium, *California Law Review*, vol. 87.

Irwin, A (1995) *Citizen Science*, Routledge, London.

Irwin, A & Wynne, B (1996) *Misunderstanding Science: the Public Reconstruction of Science and Technology*, Cambridge University Press, Cambridge.

Iyengar, S (1991) *Is Anyone Responsible? How Television Frames Political Issues*, University of Chicago Press, Chicago, Illinois.

Jackson, C, Shooshan, H M & Wilson, J L (1982) *Newspapers and Videotex: How Free a Press?*, Modern Media Institute, St Petersburg, Florida.

Jameson, F (1974) 'The vanishing mediator', *Working Papers in Cultural Studies*, vol. 5, pp. 111–49, Centre for Contemporary Cultural Studies, Birmingham.

Janelle, D (1968) 'Central place development in a time-space framework', *Professional Geographer*, vol. 20, pp. 5–10.

Jaszi, P A (1991) 'Toward a theory of copyright: The metamorphoses of "authorship"', *Duke Law Journal*, vol. 1991, pp. 455–502

Jaszi, P A (1992) 'On the author effect: Contemporary copyright and collective creativity', *Cardozo Arts and Entertainment Law Journal*, vol. 10.

Jesitus, J (1991) 'Growing gambling Mecca reacts to dwindling supply of water', *Hotel and Motel Management*, vol. 206, Nov. 4.

Jones, M G (1995) *Electronic House Calls: 21st Century Options*, Consumer Interest Research Group, Washington, District Columbia.

Jones, S G (ed.) (1995) *Cybersociety: Computer Mediated Communication and Community*, Sage, Thousand Oaks, California.

Jordonova, L (1989) 'Objects of knowledge: An historical perspective on museums', in Vergo, P (ed.) *The New Museology*, Reaktion, London.

Josephson, M (1959) *Edison: A Biography*, Oxford University Press, New York.

Kahin, B & Abbate, J (eds) (1995) *Standards Policy for Information Infrastructure*, MIT Press, Cambridge, Massachusetts.

Kahin, B & Keller, J (1995) *Public Access to the Internet*, MIT Press, Cambridge, Massachusetts.

Kaniss, P (1995) *The Media and the Mayor's Race: The Failure of Urban Political Reporting*, Indiana University Press, Bloomington, Indiana.

Kaplan, B (1967) *An Unhurried View of Copyright*, Columbia University Press, New York.

Karatani, K (2003) *Transcritique: On Kant and Marx*, MIT Press, Cambridge, Massachusetts.

Karjala, D (1995) 'Copyright in electronic maps', *Jurimetrics Journal*, vol. 35.

Kegan, R (1994) *In Over Our Heads: The Mental Demands of Modern Life*, Harvard University Press, Cambridge, Massachusetts.

Kelly, K (1994) *Out of Control: The Rise of Neo-Biological Civilization*, Addison-Wesley, Reading, Massachusetts.

Kennedy, D (1979) 'The structure of Blackstone's commentaries', *Buffalo Law Review*, vol. 28, pp. 209–21.

Kennedy, J L & Morrow, T J (1994) *Electronic Job Search Revolution: Win with the New Technology that's Reshaping Today's Job Market*, John Wiley, New York.

Kern, S (1983) *The Culture of Time and Space 1880–1918*, Harvard University Press, Cambridge, Massachusetts.

Kernan, A (1990) *The Death of Literature*, Yale University Press, New Haven, Connecticut.

Kernochan, J M (1987) 'Imperatives for enforcing authors' rights', *Columbia-VLA Journal of Law and the Arts*, vol. 11.

Kernochan, J M (1989) 'The distribution right in the United States of America: Review and reflections', *Vanderbilt Law Review*, vol. 42.

Kewanee Oil Company v Bicron Corporation (1974) 416 US 470, 476.

Kieve, J (1973) *The Electric Telegraph: A Social and Economic History*, David & Charles, London.

Kimball, P (1994) *Downsizing the News: Network Cutbacks in the Nation's Capital*, Woodrow Wilson Center Press, Washington, District Columbia.

Kingston, J A (1989) 'Where information is all, pleas arise for less of it', *New York Times*, July 9.

Kirby, S (1988) 'Policy and politics: Charges, sponsorship and bias', in Lumley, R (ed.) *The Museum Time Machine*, Routledge/Comedia, London.

Klapp, O E (1986) *Overload and Boredom: Essays on the Quality of Life in the Information Society*, Greenwood, Westport, Connecticut.

Klein, N (2000) *No Logo*, HarperCollins, London.

Klein, N (2002) *Fences and Windows*, Picador, New York.

Kling, R (1994) 'Reading "all about" computerization: How genre conventions shape nonfiction social analysis', *The Information Society*, vol. 10, no. 3, pp. 147–72.

Kobrak, F & Luey, B (1992) *The Structure of International Publishing in the 1990s*, Transaction, New Brunswick, New Jersey.

Koch, T (1991) *Journalism for the 21st Century: Online Information, Electronic Databases, and the News*, Greenwood/Praeger, Westport, Connecticut.

Koelsch, F (1995) *The Infomedia Revolution: How It is Changing Our World and Your Life*, McGraw-Hill Ryerson, Toronto.

Kroes, R (1991) 'Flatness and depth', in Nye, D and Pedersen, C (eds) *Consumption and American Culture*, Free University Press, Amsterdam.

Kroker, A & Weinstein, M A (1994) *Data Trash: The Theory of the Virtual Class*, St Martin's, New York.

Kuhn, T (1962/1996) *The Structure of Scientific Revolutions*, University of Chicago Press, Chicago, Illinois.

Kurtzman, J (1993) *The Death of Money: How the Electronic Economy has Destabilized the World's Markets and Created Financial Chaos*, Simon & Schuster, New York.

Lalli, S (1991) 'Big projects boost Vegas', *Hotel and Motel Management*, vol. 206, Nov. 4.

Lande, N (1991) 'Toward the electronic book', *Publishers Weekly*, vol. 238, Sept. 20, pp. 28–30.

Landes, W M & Posner, R A (1989) 'An economic analysis of copyright law', *Journal of Legal Studies*, vol. 18.

Lange, B P & Woldt, R (1995) 'The results and main conclusions of the international comparisons', in Bertelsmann Foundation and European Institute for the Media (eds) *Television Requires Responsibility: International Studies on the Structural Factors Ensuring Responsible Television*, vol. 2, Bertelsmann Foundation, Gütersloh.

Lange, D (1981) 'Recognizing the public domain', *Law and Contemporary Problems*, vol. 44.

Lanham, R A (1993) *The Electronic Word: Democracy, Technology, and the Arts*, University of Chicago Press, Chicago, Illinois.

Las Vegas Chamber of Commerce (1993) 'Las Vegas perspective', *Las Vegas Review Journal*.

Lash, S & Urry, J (1994) *Economies of Signs and Space*, Sage, London.

Lasswell, H D (1941) *Democracy Through Public Opinion*, George Banta, Menasha, Wisconsin.

Lasswell, H D (1977) 'The vocation of propagandists', in Lasswell, H D (ed.) *On Political Sociology*, University of Chicago Press, Chicago, Illinois, pp. 234–5.

Latman, A (1963) 'Study # 14: Fair use 6–7', *Studies on Copyright*, vol. 778, pp. 784–5.

Latour, B (1999) *Pandora's Hope: Essays on the Reality of Science Studies*, Harvard University Press, Cambridge, Massachusetts.

Latour, B & Coutouzis, M (1993) *Should We Have Taken the Measure of Europe?*, Science Museum, London.

Latour, B & Woolgar, S (1986) *Laboratory Life: The Construction of Scientific Facts*, Princeton University Press, Princeton, New Jersey.

Laudon, K (1986) *Dossier Society: Value Choices in the Design of National Information Systems*, Columbia University Press, New York.

Laurier, E (1999) *Conversations in the Corridor (M4): Making Up the Mobile Office*, paper presented to British Sociological Association conference, Glasgow, April 6–9.

Law, J (1986) 'On power and its tactics: A view from the sociology of science', *Sociological Review*, vol. 34, no. 1, pp. 1–35.

Lee, H (1997) *Temporal Implications of Electronically Mediated Business Procedures on Organisational Work: EDI Applications in Trade*, PhD thesis, Department of Information Systems, London School of Economics and Political Science, London.

Lee, H (1999) 'Time and information technology: Monochronicity, polychronicity and temporal symmetry', *European Journal of Information Systems*, vol. 8, no. 1, pp. 16–26.

Lee, H & Liebenau, J (2000) 'Time and the internet at the turn of the millennium', *Time and Society*, vol. 9, no. 1, pp. 43–56.

Leebaert, D (ed.) (1991) *Technology 2001: The Future of Computing and Communications*, MIT Press, Cambridge, Massachusetts.

Leebaert, D (ed.) (1995) *The Future of Software*, MIT Press, Cambridge, Massachusetts.

Lemley, M A (1995) 'Intellectual property and shrink-wrap licenses', *Southern California Law Review*, vol. 68.

Lemley, M A (1997) 'The economics of improvement in intellectual property law', *Texas Law Review*, vol. 75.

Lemley, M A (1999) 'Beyond preemption: The federal law and policy of intellectual property licensing', *California Law Review*, vol. 87.

Lessig, L (1996) 'Translating federalism', *1995 Supreme Court Review*, vol. 125.

Lessig, L (1999) 'Pain in the OS', *Industry Standard*, Feb. 5.

Levidow, L & Young, R (1984) 'Exhibiting nuclear power: The science museum cover-up', *Radical Science*, vol. 14, pp. 53–79.

Levy, S (1994) 'E-money', *Wired*, vol. 2, no. 12, pp. 174–9.

Lewis, P H (1995) 'Security is lost in cyberspace', *New York Times*, Feb 22.

Leyshon, A (1995) 'Annihilating space? The speed-up of communications', in Allen, J and Hamnett, C (eds) *A Shrinking World? Global Unevenness and Inequality*, Open University Press, Milton Keynes.

Library of Congress Copyright Office (1961) *Report of the Register of Copyrights on the General Revision of the US Copyright Law*, vol. 6, Washington, District Columbia.

Ling, R & Yttri, B (2002) 'Hyper-coordination via mobile phones in Norway', in Katz, J A and Aakhus, M (eds) *Perpetual Contact Mobile Communication, Private Talk, Public Performance*, Cambridge University Press, Cambridge.

Linowes, D F (1989) *Privacy in America: Is Your Private Life in the Public Eye?*, University of Illinois Press, Urbana, Illinois.

Lippmann, W (1922) *Public Opinion*, Allen & Unwin, London.

Lippmann, W (1925) *The Phantom Public*, Harcourt, Brace, New York.

Litman, J (1990) 'The public domain', *Emory Law Journal*, vol. 39, pp. 977–92.

Litman, J (1991) 'Copyright as myth', *University of Pittsburgh Law Review*, vol. 53.

Litman, J (1992) 'Copyright and information policy', *Law & Contemporary Problems*, vol. 55.

Litman, J (1994) 'The exclusive right to read', *Cardozo Arts and Entertainment Law Journal*, vol. 13.

Litman, J (1996) 'Revising copyright law for the Information Age', *Oregon Law Review*, vol. 75.

Litman, J (1997) 'Reforming information law in copyright's image', *Dayton Law Review*, vol. 22.

Litman, J (1998) 'The tales that Article 2B tells', *Berkeley Technology Law Journal*, vol. 13.

Lloyd, P (ed.) (1994) *Groupware in the 21st Century: Computer Supported Cooperative Working Toward the Millennium*, Praeger, Westport, Connecticut.

Lochner v New York (1905) 198 US 45.

London v Biograph (1916) 231 F. 696.

Loren, L P (1997) 'Redefining the market failure approach to fair use in an era of copyright permission systems', *Journal of intellectual Property Law*, vol. 5.

Louw, E & Duffy, N (1992) *Managing Computer Viruses*, Oxford University Press, Oxford.

Lundberg, O (1991) 'The perils of being a visionary: One man's vision', *InterMedia*, vol. 19, no. 1, pp. 33–9.

Lyotard, J-F (1984) *The Postmodern Condition: A Report on Knowledge*, Manchester University Press, Manchester.

Macdonald, S (1992) 'Cultural imagining among museum visitors', *Museum Management and Curatorship*, vol. 11, no. 4, pp. 401–9.

Macdonald, S (1993) 'Un nouveau "corps des visiteurs": Musées et changements culturels', *Publics et Musées*, vol. 3, pp. 13–27.

Macdonald, S (1997) 'The museum as mirror: Ethnographic reflections', in James, A, Hockey, J and Dawson, A (eds) *After Writing Culture: Epistemology and Praxis in Contemporary Anthropology*, Routledge, London.

Macdonald, S & Silverstone, R (1990) 'Rewriting the museums' fictions: Taxonomies, stories and readers', *Cultural Studies*, vol. 4, no. 2, pp. 176–91.

Macdonald, S & Silverstone, R (1992) 'Science on display: The representation of scientific controversy in museum exhibitions', *Public Understanding of Science*, vol. 1, no. 1, pp. 69–87.

MacLachlan, S L (1993) 'Pagers' sophistication keeps sales growing', *Christian Science Monitor*, Aug. 7.

Madison, M J (1998) 'Legal war: Contract and copyright in the digital age', *Fordham Law Review*, vol. 67.

Maes, P (1995) 'Intelligent software', *Scientific American*, vol. 273, no. 3, pp. 84–6.

Makridakis, S (1995) 'The forthcoming information revolution: Its impact on society and firms', *Futures*, vol. 27, no. 8, pp. 799–821.

Marien, M (1984) 'Some questions for the Information Society', *The Information Society*, vol. 3, no. 2.

Markoff, J (1991) 'Is the electronic book closer than you think?', *New York Times*, Dec. 29.

Markoff, J (1995) 'Discovery of internet flaws is setback for on-line trade', *New York Times*, Oct. 11.

Martin, B (1992) 'Symbolic knowledge and market forces at the frontiers of postmodernism: Qualitative market researchers (Britain)', in Kellner, H and Berger, P (eds) *Hidden Technocrats: The New Class and New Capitalism*, Transaction, New Brunswick, New Jersey, pp. 111–56.

Marvin, C (1988) *When Old Technologies Were New: Thinking About Electric Communication in the Late Nineteenth Century*, Oxford University Press, New York.

Marx, G T (1994) 'New telecommunications technologies require new manners', *Telecommunications Policy*, vol. 18, no. 7, pp. 538–51.

Marx, K (1973) *Grundrisse: Foundations of the Critique of Political Economy*, Penguin, Harmondsworth.

Marx, K & Engels, F (1978) 'Manifesto of the Communist Party', in Fernbach, D (ed.) *The Revolutions of 1848: Political Writings*, Penguin, Harmondsworth.

Marx, L (1997) 'In the driving-seat? The nagging ambiguity in historians' attitudes to the rise of technology', *Times Literary Supplement*, Aug. 29, pp. 3–4.

Marx, L (1997) 'Technology: The emergence of a hazardous concept', *Social Research*, vol. 64, no. 3, pp. 965–88.

Maryland v Wirtz (1968) 392 US 183,201.

Mason, R O, Mason, F M & Culnan, M J (1995) *Ethics of Information Management*, Sage, Thousand Oaks, California.

Massey, D (1992) 'Politics and space/time', *New Left Review*, vol. 196, pp. 65–84.

Massey, D (1993) 'Power-geometry and a progressive sense of place', in Bird, J, Curtis, B, Putnam, T, Robertson, G and Tickner, L (eds) *Mapping the Futures: Local Cultures, Global Change*, Routledge, London, pp. 59–69.

Masuda, Y (1990) *Managing in the Information Society: Releasing Synergy Japanese Style*, Basil Blackwell, Oxford.

Mattelart, A (1991) *Advertising International: The Privatisation of Public Space*, Routledge, London.

Maury, J-P (1994) *Le Palais de la Découverte*, Gallimard, Paris.

Mayer-Kress, G & Barczys, C (1995) 'The global brain as an emergent structure from the worldwide computing network, and its implications for modeling', *The Information Society*, vol. 11, no. 1, pp. 1–28.

Mayo, J S (1990) 'The telecommunications revolution of the 1990s', *Vital Speeches of the Day*, vol. 57, no. 5, pp. 151–5.

Mayo, J S (1992) 'R&D in the third millennium: Requirements and challenges', *Vital Speeches of the Day*, vol. 59, no. 1, pp. 26–9.

McCain, N (1980) 'Field news service', *Boston Globe*, Aug. 31.

McCulloch v Maryland (1819) 17 US 316.

McKibben, B (1992) *The Age of Missing Information*, Random House, New York.

McLuhan, M (1964) *Understanding Media: The Extensions of Man* , Routledge, London.

McManis, C R (1999) 'The privatization (or "shrink-wrapping") of American copyright law', *California Law Review*, vol. 87.

McManus, J H (1994) *Market-Driven Journalism: Let the Citizen Beware?*, Sage, Thousand Oaks, California.

McNerney, W J & Bezold, C (1995) *Health Care Innovation: A Vision for the 21st Century*, Institute for Alternative Futures, Alexandria, Virginia.

Merges, R P, Lemley, M A & Menell, P S (1997) *Intellectual Property in the New Technological Age*, Aspen Law and Business, New York.

Michael, D N (1993) 'Governing by learning: Boundaries, myths and metaphors', *Futures*, vol. 25, no. 1, pp. 81–9.

Michael, M (1996) *Constructing Identities: The Social, the Nonhuman and Change*, Sage, London.

Michie, R C (1977) 'Friend or foe? Information technology and the London Stock Exchange since 1700', *Journal of Historical Geography*, vol. 23, no. 3, pp. 304–26.

Mill, J S (1975) *On Liberty*, W W Norton, New York.

Minoli, D (1995) *Video Dialtone Technology: Digital Video over ADSL, HFC, FTTC, and ATM*, McGraw-Hill, New York.

Minow, N N & LaMay, C L (1995) *Abandoned in the Wasteland: Children, Television, and the First Amendment*, Hill and Wang, New York.

Mitchell, W J (1992) *The Reconfigured Eye: Visual Truth in the Post-Photographic Era*, MIT Press, Cambridge, Massachusetts.

Mitchell, W J (1995) *City of Bits: Space, Place, and the Infobahn*, MIT Press, Cambridge, Massachusetts.

Mitroff, I I & Bennis, W (1989) *The Unreality Industry: The Deliberate Manufacturing of Falsehood and What It Is Doing to Our Lives*, Carol, New York.

Moore, R H (1995) 'Twenty-first century law to meet the challenge of twenty-first century organized crime', *Futures Research Quarterly*, vol. 11, no. 1, pp. 23–46.

Moore, R H. (1994) 'Wiseguys: Smarter criminals and smarter crime in the 21st century', *Futurist*, vol. 28, no. 5, pp. 33–7.

Morton, M (1991) *The Corporation of the 1990s: Information technology and Organizational Transformation*, Oxford University Press, New York.

Mouffe, C (1992) *Dimensions of Radical Democracy: Pluralism, Citizenship, Community*, Verso, London.

Mowshowitz, A (1994) 'Virtual organization: A vision of management in the information age', *The Information Society*, vol. 10, no. 4, pp. 267–88.

Mulgan, G (1994) 'Networks for an open society', *Demos*, vol. 4, pp. 2–6.

Mulgan, G (1994) *Politics in an Anti-Political Age*, Polity, Cambridge.

Mumford, L (1964) 'Authoritarian and democratic technics', *Technology and Culture*, vol. 5, no. 2.

Naisbitt, J (1982) *Megatrends: Ten New Directions Transforming Our Lives*, Warner, New York.

Nash, C (1992) 'Interactive media in museums: Looking backwards, forwards and sideways', *Museum Management and Curatorship*, vol. 11, no. 2, pp. 171–84.

National Park Service (1984) *Grand Canyon Natural and Cultural Resource Management Plan*, National Park Service, Washington District Columbia.

National Research Council: Computer Science and Telecoms Board (1994) *Information Technology in the Service Society: A Twenty-First Century Lever*, National Academy Press, Washington, District Columbia.

National Research Council: NRENAISSANCE Committee (1994) *Realizing the Information Future: The Internet and Beyond*, National Academy Press, Washington, District Columbia.

National Research Council: Office of International Affairs (1993) *Global Dimensions of*

Intellectual Property Rights in Science and Technology, National Academy Press, Washington, District Columbia.

National Research Council: System Security Study Committee (1991) *Computers at Risk: Safe Computing in the Information Age*, National Academy Press, Washington, District Columbia.

Negri, A (1989) *The Politics of Subversion: A Manifesto for the Twenty-First Century*, Polity, Cambridge.

Negroponte, N (1995) *Being Digital*, Hodder & Stoughton, London.

Netanel, N W (1994) 'Alienability restrictions and the enhancement of author autonomy in United States and continental copyright law', *Cardozo Arts and Entertainment Law Journal*, vol. 12.

Netanel, N W (1996) '[C]opyright and a democratic civil society', *Yale Law Journal*, vol. 106.

Netanel, N W (1998) 'Asserting copyright's democratic principles in the global arena', *Vanderbilt Law Review*, vol. 51.

Neuman, S B (1991) *Literacy in the Television Age: The Myth of the TV Effect*, Ablex, Norwood, New Jersey.

Newhall, B (1964) *The History of Photography from 1839 to the Present Day*, 4th edn, Museum of Modern Art, New York.

Nimmer, D, Brown, E & Frischling, G (1999) 'The metamorphosis of contract into expand', *California Law Review*, vol. 87.

Nowotny, H (1994) *Time: The Modern and Postmodern Experience*, Polity, Cambridge.

O'Brien, R (1991) *Global Financial Integration: The End of Geography*, Pinter, London.

O'Neil, J (1991) *Plato's Cave: Desire, Power, and the Specular Functions of the Media*, Ablex, Norwood, New Jersey.

O'Rourke M A (1997) 'Copyright preemption after the pro-CD Case: A market based approach', *Berkeley Technology Law Journal*, vol. 12.

Oamich, E J (1988) 'The right of personality: A common law basis for the protection of the moral rights of authors', *Georgia Law Review*, vol. 23.

Obscene Publications Act 1857 (United Kingdom).

Obscene Publications Act 1959 (United Kingdom).

Office of Technology Assessment (1985) *Federal Government Information Technology: Electronic Surveillance and Civil Liberties*, Government Printing Office, Washington, District Columbia.

Office of Technology Assessment (1986) *Electronic Record Systems and Individual Privacy*, Government Printing Office, Washington, District Columbia.

Office of Technology Assessment (1991) *Rural America at the Crossroads: Networking for the Future*, Government Printing Office, Washington, District Columbia.

Office of Technology Assessment (1993) *Adult Literacy and New Technologies: Tools for a Lifetime*, Government Printing Office, Washington, District Columbia.

Office of Technology Assessment (1994) *Electronic Enterprises: Looking to the Future*, Government Printing Office, Washington, District Columbia.

Office of Technology Assessment (1995) *Teachers and Technology: Making the Connection*, Government Printing Office, Washington, District Columbia.

Ogden, M R (1994) 'Politics in a parallel universe: Is there a future for cyberdemocracy?', *Futures*, vol. 26, no. 7, pp. 713–29.

Ohmae, K (1995) *The End of the Nation State: The Rise of Regional Economies*, Free Press, New York.

Olmstead v United States (1928) 277 US 438,474.

'One voice on Italy TV' (1995) *Free Press: Journal of the Campaign for Press and Broadcasting Freedom*, July/Aug., London.

Organization for Economic Cooperation and Development (1981) *Information Activities, Electronics and Telecommunications Technologies: Impact on Employment, Growth and Trade*, Organization for Economic Cooperation and Development, Paris.

Paley, W (1980) 'Press freedom: A continuing struggle', speech to Associated Press Broadcasters Convention, June 6, in *New York Times*, July 7, sec. B, p. 3.

Palmer, E L (1988) *Television and America's Children: A Crisis of Neglect*, Oxford University Press, New York.

Palmer, E L (1993) *Toward a Literate World: Television in Literacy Education – Lessons from the Arab Region*, Westview, Boulder, Colorado.

Papert, S (1993) *The Children's Machine: Rethinking School in the Age of the Computer*, Basic, New York.

Parker, R (1995) *Mixed Signals: The Prospects for Global Television*, Twentieth Century Fund Press, New York.

Parris, H (1965) *Government and the Railways in Nineteenth Century Britain*, Routledge and Kegan Paul, London.

Patterson, D A (1995) 'Microprocessors in 2020', *Scientific American*, vol. 273, no. 3, pp. 62–7.

Patterson, R (1992) 'Understanding fair use', *Law and Contemporary Problems*, vol. 55.

Pelton, J N (1989) 'Telepower: The emerging global brain', *Futurist*, vol. 23, no. 5, pp. 9–14.

Pensacola Telegraph Company v Western Union Telegraph Company (1877) 96 US 1, 9.

Penzias, A (1995) *Harmony: Business, Technology & Life After Paperwork*, Harper Business, New York.

Perelman, L J (1992) *School's Out: Hyperlearning, the New Technology, and the End of Education*, William Morrow, New York.

Perkin, H (1970) *The Age of the Railway*, Panther, London.

Perry, M, O'Hara, K, Sellen, A, Brown, B & Harper, R (2001) 'Dealing with mobility: Understanding access anytime, anywhere', *Transactions on Computer Human Interaction*, vol. 8, no. 4, pp. 323–47.

Philbrick, F (1938) 'Changing conceptions of property in law', *University of Pennsylvania Law Review*, vol. 691.

Piccone, P (1976) 'Paradoxes of reflexive sociology', *New German Critique*, no. 8, Spring.

Pickover, C A (ed.) (1995) *Future Health: Computers and Medicine in the Twenty-first Century*, St Martin's, New York.

Poems of Ralph Waldo Emerson (1904) *Collected Works*, vol. 9, Houghton Mifflin, Boston, Massachusetts.

Poletown Neighborhood Council v Detroit (1981) 304 N. W.2d 455, United States.

Pollack, A (1992) ' "Fifth generation" became Japan's lost generation', *New York Times*, June 5.

Pool, I de Sola (1977) *The Social Uses of the Telephone*, MIT Press, Cambridge, Massachusetts.

Pool, I de Sola (1978) 'From Gutenberg to electronics: Implications for the First Amendment', *Key Reporter*, vol. 43, no. 3.

Porat, M U & Rubin, M R (1977) *The Information Economy*, Government Printing Office, Washington, District Columbia.

Posner, R A (1988) *Law and Literature: A Misunderstood Relation*, Harvard University Press, Cambridge, Massachusetts.

Poster, M (1990) *The Mode of Information: Poststructuralism and Social Context*, Polity, Cambridge, Massachusetts.

Poster, M (1995) *The Second Media Age*, Polity, Cambridge, Massachusetts.

Postman, N (1992) *Technopoly: The Surrender of Culture to Technology*, Knopf, New York.

Powell, T R (1918) 'The Child Labor Law, the Tenth Amendment, and the Commerce Clause', *Southern Law Quarterly*, vol. 3.

Power, M (1997) *The Audit Society: Rituals of Verification*, Oxford University Press, Oxford.

Pred, A (1973) *Urban Growth and the Circulation of Information: The United States System of Cities, 1790–1840*, Harvard University Press, Cambridge, Massachusetts.

Price, D J de S (1975) *Science Since Babylon*, Yale University Press, New Haven, Connecticut.

Provenzo, E F (1991) *Video Kids: Making Sense of Nintendo*, Harvard University Press, Cambridge, Massachusetts.

R v Curl (1727) 93 E.R. 849.

R v Hicklin (1868) L.R. 3Q. B. 360.

R v Read (1708) 11 Mod. Rep. 142.

R v Sedley (1663) 1 Sid. 168.

Radin, M J (1993) *Reinterpreting Property*, University of Chicago Press, Chicago, Illinois.

Radin, M J & Wagner, P (1998) 'The myth of private ordering: Rediscovering legal realism in cyberspace', *Chicago-Kent Law Review*, vol. 73.

Raine, L P & Cilluffo, F J (eds) (1994) *Global Organized Crime: The New Empire of Evil*, Center for Strategic and International Studies, Washington, District Columbia.

Rakow, L F (1992) *Gender on the Line: Women, the Telephone and Community Life*, University of Illinois Press, Urbana, Illinois.

Rakow, L & Navarro, V (1993) 'Remote mothering and the parallel shift: Women meet the cellular telephone', *Critical Studies in Mass Communication*, vol. 10, no. 2, pp. 144–57.

Ramonet, I (1995) 'La pensée unique' (editorial), *Le Monde Diplomatique*, Jan.

Raphael, A (1990) 'What price democracy?', *Observer*, Oct. 14, pp. 7–47.

Record Rental Amendment of 1984 (codified as amended at 17 USCalif §§ 109, 115).

Reich, R. (1991) *The Work of Nations: Preparing Ourselves for 21st-century Capitalism*, Knopf, New York.

Reichardt, J (1971) *Cybernetics, Art and Ideas*, Studio Vista, London.

Reichman, J H & Samuelson, P (1997) 'Intellectual property rights in data', *Vanderbilt Law Review*, vol. 50.

Reidenberg, J R (1996) 'Governing networks and rule-making in cyberspace', *Emory Law Journal*, vol. 45.

Reynolds, R (1975) 'Our misplaced reliance on early obscenity cases', *American Bar Association Journal*, vol. 61, Feb., pp. 220–2.

Rheingold, H (1993) *The Virtual Community: Homesteading on the Electronic Frontier*, Addison-Wesley, Reading, Massachusetts.

Rice, P O & Robillard, J A (1991) *The Future of Serials: Proceedings of the North American Serials Interest Group*, Haworth, Binghamton, New York.

Rifkin, J (1987) *Time Wars: The Primary Conflict in Human History*, Henry Holt, New York.

Rifkin, J (1995) *The End of Work: The Decline of the Global Labor Force and the Dawn of the Post-Market Era*, Tarcher/Putnam, New York.

Ritzer, G (1995) *Expressing America: A Critique of the Global Credit Card Society*, Sage, Thousand Oaks, California.

Robertson, G (1979) *Obscenity: An Account of Censorship Laws and Their Enforcement in England and Wales*, Weidenfeld & Nicolson, London.

Robinson, D C, Buck, E B & Cuthbert, M (1991) *Music at the Margins: Popular Music and Global Cultural Diversity*, Sage, Newbury Park, California.

Roe, D B & Wilpon, J G (1994) *Voice Communication Between Humans and Machines*, National Academy Press, Washington, District Columbia.

Rolph, C H (1969) *Books in the Dock*, Deutsch, London.

Ronfeldt, D (1992) 'Cyberocracy is coming', *The Information Society*, vol. 8, no. 4, pp. 243–96.

Rose, N (1996) 'Governing "advanced" liberal democracies', in Barry, A, Osborne, T and Rose, N (eds) *Foucalt and Political Reason: Liberalism, Neo-Liberalism and Rationalities of Government*, Chicago University Press, Chicago, Illinois.

Rose, N (1999) *Powers of Freedom: Reframing Political Thought*, Cambridge University Press, Cambridge.

Rosell, S A (1992) *Governing in an Information Society*, Institute for Research on Public Policy, Montreal.

Rosen, H (2000) Testimony to Music on the Internet: Is There an Upside to Downloading?, Hearings of the Senate Judiciary Committee, 106th Congress, 2nd session, July 11, Washington, District Columbia.

Rosenbaum, D (1992) 'Resorts: Precast as big winner in Vegas', *ERN*, vol. 229, July 13.

Rosenberg, R (1991) 'Debunking computer literacy', *Technology Review*, vol. 94, no. 1, pp. 58–65.

Ross, A (1996) *Science Wars*, Duke University Press, Durham, North Columbia.

Ross, G (1995) *Jacques Delors and European Integration*, Polity, Cambridge.

Rossman, P (1992) *The Emerging Worldwide Electronic University: Information Age Global Higher Education*, Greenwood, Westport, Connecticut.

Roszak, T (1994) *The Cult of Information: A Neo-Luddite Treatise on High-Tech, Artificial Intelligence, and the True Art of Thinking*, 2nd edn, University of California Press, Berkeley, California.

Rourke, F E (1961) *Secrecy and Publicity: Dilemmas of Democracy*, Johns Hopkins Press, Baltimore, Maryland.

Rovizzi, L & Thompson, D (1991) *Price-Cap Regulated Public Utilities and Quality Regulation in the UK*, Centre for Business Strategy, London Business School, London.

Rule, J B (1973) *Private Lives and Public Surveillance*, Allen Lane, London.

Rust v Sullivan (1991) 500 US 354.

Sale, K (1995) *Rebels Against the Future: The Luddites and Their War on the Industrial Revolution; Lessons for the Computer Age*, Addison-Wesley, Reading, Massachusetts.

Salomon, J J (1994) *The Uncertain Quest: Science, Technology, and Development*, United Nations University Press, Tokyo.

Samuelson, P (1988) 'Modifying copyrighted software: Adjusting copyright doctrine to accommodate a technology', *Jurimetrics Journal*, vol. 28, pp. 179, 188–9.

Samuelson, P (1993) 'Fair use for computer programs and other copyrightable works in digital form: The implications of Sony, Galoob and Sega', *Journal of Intellectual Property Law*, vol. 1.

Samuelson, P (1996) 'The copyright grab', *Wired*, vol. 4, no. 1.

Samuelson, P (1997) 'Embedding technical self-help in licensed software', *Communications of the ACM*, vol. 40.

Samuelson, P (1999) 'Encoding the law into digital libraries', *Communications of the ACM*, vol. 41.

Samuelson, P (1999) 'Intellectual property and contract law for the Information Age: Foreword', *California Law Review*, vol. 87.

Sanders, B (1994) *A is for Ox: Violence, Electronic Media, and the Silencing of the Written Word*, Pantheon, New York.

Sardar, Z & Ravetz, J R (1995) 'Cyberspace: To boldly go', *Futures*, vol. 27, no. 7, pp. 695–796.

Schaffer, S (1992) 'Self evidence', *Critical Inquiry*, vol. 18, pp. 327–62.

Schaffer, S (1993) 'The consuming flame: Electrical showmen and Tory mystics in the world of goods', in Brewer, J and Porter, R (eds) *Consumption and World of Goods*, Routledge, London.

Schaffer, S (1997) 'Temporary contemporary: Some puzzles of science in action', in Farmelo, G and Carding, J (eds) *Here and Now: Contemporary Science and Technology Museums and Science Centres*, Science Museum, London.

Schement, J R & Curtis, T (1995) *Tendencies and Tensions of the Information Age: The Production and Distribution of Information in the United States*, Transaction, New Brunswick, New Jersey.

Schepp, D & Schepp, B (1995) *The Telecommuter's Handbook: How to Earn a Living Without Going to the Office*, 2nd edn, McGraw-Hill, New York.

Schiller, H I (1989) *Culture, Inc.: The Corporate Takeover of Public Expression*, Oxford University Press, New York.

Schiller, H I (1992) *Mass Communications and American Empire*, 2nd edn, Westview, Boulder, Colorado.

Schivelbusch, W (1977) *The Railway Journey: Trains and Travel in the 19th Century*, Urizen, New York.

Schlegel, J H (1995) *American Legal Realism and Empirical Social Science*, University of North Carolina Press, Chapel Hill, North Carolina.

Schlesinger, A S (1933) *The Rise of the City, 1878–1898*, Macmillan, New York.

Science Museum (1986) *Management Plan*, National Museum of Science and Industry, London.

Scientific American (1991) 'Communications, computers and networks: Special issue', *Scientific American*, vol. 265, no. 3, pp. 62–166.

Sclove, R (1995) *Democracy and Technology*, Guilford, New York.

Sheridan, T B (1992) *Telerobotics, Automation, and Human Supervisory Control*, MIT Press, Cambridge, Massachusetts.

Sheth, J N & Sisodia, R S (1993) 'Information mall', *Telecommunications Policy*, vol. 17, no. 5, pp. 376–89.

Shirer, W (1976) *20th Century Journey: The start: 1904–1930*, Simon & Schuster, New York.

Shortland, M (1987) 'No business like show business', *Nature*, vol. 328, p. 213.

Shrader, W K (1992) *Media Blight and the Dehumanizing of America*, Praeger, New York.

Shulman, S (1999) *Owning the Future*, Houghton Mifflin, Boston, Massachusetts.

Silverstone, R (1988) 'Museums and the media: A theoretical and methodological exploration', *International Journal of Museum Management and Curatorship*, vol. 7, pp. 231–41.

Silverstone, R (1992) 'The medium is the museum: On objects and logics in times and spaces', in Durant, J (ed.) *Museums and the Public Understanding of Science*, Science Museum, London.

Simmel, G (1997) 'The metropolis and mental life', in Frisby, D and Featherstone, M (eds) *Simmel on Culture*, Sage, London, pp. 174–85.

Sims, N (1979) *The Chicago Style of Journalism*, PhD dissertation, University of Illinois, Chicago, Illinois.

Sinclair, J (1987) *Images Incorporated: Advertising as Industry and Ideology*, Croom Helm, London.

Singer, J (1982) 'The legal rights debate in analytical jurisprudence from Bentham to Hohfeld', *Wisconsin Law Review*, vol. 975.

Slaton, C D (1992) *Televote: Expanding Citizen Participation in the Quantum Age*, Praeger, New York.

Slouka, M (1995) *War of the Worlds: Cyberspace and the High-Tech Assault on Reality*, Basic, New York.

Smith, A (1991) *The Age of Behemoths: The Globalization of Mass Media Firms*, Twentieth Century Fund Paper Priority Press, New York.

Smith, H J (1994) *Managing Privacy: Information Technology and Corporate America*, University of North Carolina Press Chapel Hill, North Carolina.

Smith, M H (1993) 'The limits of copyright: Property, parody, and the public domain', *Duke Law Journal*, vol. 42.

Snider, J (1994) 'Democracy on-line: Tomorrow's electronic electorate', *Futurist*, vol. 28, no. 5, pp. 15–19.

Snider, J & Ziporyn, T (1992) *Future Shop: How New Technologies Will Change the Way We Shop and What We Buy*, St Martin's, New York.

Social Text (1996) vol. 14, no. 1/2 (Special issue, 'Science wars').

Spanier, D (1992) *Welcome to the Pleasure Dome: Inside Las Vegas*, University of Nevada Press, Reno, Nevada.

Speier, H (1950) 'Historical development of public opinion', *American Journal of Sociology*, vol. 55, Jan.

Sproull, L & Kiesler, S (1991) *Connections: New Ways of Working in the Networked Organization*, MIT Press, Cambridge, Massachusetts.

St John-Stevas, N (1956) 'Obscenity, literature and the law', *Dublin Review*, vol. 230, pp. 41–56.

Stamper, J W (1989) 'The *galerie* of machines of the 1889 Paris World's Fair', *Technology and Culture*, vol. 30, no. 2, pp. 330–53.

Standage, T (1998) *The Victorian Internet*, Weidenfeld & Nicolson, London.

Star, S & Griesemer, J (1989) 'Institutional ecology, "translations" and boundary objects: Amateurs and professionals in Berkeley's museum of vertebrate zoology, 1907–39', *Social Studies of Science*, vol. 19, no. 3, pp. 387–420.

State Board of Insurance v Todd Shipyards Corporation (1962) 370 US 451, 456.

Steffens, L (1958) *The Autobiography of Lincoln Steffens*, Harcourt, Brace and World, New York.

Stefik, M (1996) 'Letting loose the light: Igniting commerce in electronic publication', in Stefik, M (ed.) *Internet Dreams: Archetypes, Myths, and Metaphors*, MIT Press, Cambridge, Massachusetts.

Stefik, M (1997) 'Shifting the possible: How trusted systems and digital property rights challenge us to rethink digital publishing', *Berkeley Technology Law Journal*, vol. 12.

Stein, J (1996) 'Annihilating space and time: The modernisation of fire-fighting in late nineteenth-century Cornwall, Ontario', *Urban History Review*, vol. 24, no. 2, pp. 3–11.

Stein, J (1999) 'The telephone: Its social shaping and public negotiation in late nineteenth- and early twentieth-century London', in Crang, M, Crang, P and May, J (eds) *Virtual Geographies: Bodies, Space and Relations*, Routledge, New York, pp. 44–62.

Stephens, C (1989) ' "The most reliable time": William Bond, the New England railroads, and time awareness in 19th-century America', *Technology and Culture*, vol. 30, no. 1, pp. 1–24.

Stephens, G (1995) 'Crime in cyberspace: The digital underworld', *Futurist*, vol. 29, no. 5, pp. 24–8.

Stevenson, J (1987) 'The philosophy behind launch pad', *Journal of Education and Museums*, vol. 8, pp. 18–20.

Stevenson, J (1994) 'Getting to grips', *Museums Journal*, May, pp. 30–2.

Steward, B (2000) 'Changing times: The meaning, measurement and use of time in teleworking', *Time and Society*, vol. 9, no. 1, pp. 57–74.

Stock, G (1993) *Metaman: The Merging of Humans and Machines into a Global Superorganism*, Simon & Schuster, New York.

Stoll, C (1995) *Silicon Snake Oil: Second Thoughts on the Information Highway*, Doubleday, New York.

Stone & McCarrick v Dugan Piano (1914) 210 F. 399.

Stone, A (1995) 'Innocence and awakening: Cyberdammerung at the Ashibe Research Laboratory', in Marcus, G (ed.) *Technoscientific Imaginaries*, Chicago University Press, Chicago, Illinois.

Stonier, T (1986) 'Intelligence networks, overview, purpose and policies in the context of global social change', *Aslib Proceedings*, vol. 38, no. 9.

Strathern, M (1992) *Reproducing the Future: Anthropology, Kinship and the New Reproductive Technologies*, Manchester University Press, Manchester.

Straw, W (1991) 'Systems of articulation, logics of change: Communities and scenes in popular music', *Cultural Studies*, vol. 5, no. 3, pp. 368–88.

Sussman, V (1995) 'Gold rush in cyberspace', *US News & World Report*, Nov. 13, pp. 72–83.

Sussman, G & Lent, J A (eds) (1991) *Transnational Communications: Wiring the Third World*, Sage, Newbury Park, California.

Talbott, S L (1995) *The Future Does Not Compute: Transcending the Machines in Our Midst*, O'Reilly, Sebastopol, California.

Tarr, J A & Dupuy, G (1988) *Technology and the Rise of the Networked City in Europe and North America*, Temple University Press, Philadelphia, Pennsylvania.

Thomas, D (1969) *A Long Time Burning: The History of Literary Censorship in England*, Routledge & Kegan Paul, London.

Thomas, G (nd) *The National Museum of Science and Industry: Facing the future*, mimeo.

Thompson, E P (1967) 'Time, work discipline and industrial capitalism', *Past and Present*, vol. 38, pp. 56–97.

Thrift, N (1981) 'Owners' time and own time: The making of a capitalist time consciousness, 1300–1880', in Pred, A (ed.) *Space and Time in Geography*, University of Lund, Lund, Sweden, pp. 56–84.

Thrift, N (1990) 'Transport and communication', in Dodgson, R A and Butlin, R A (eds) *An Historical Geography of England and Wales*, Academic, London, pp. 453–86.

Thrift, N (1995) 'A hyperactive world', in Johnston, R J, Taylor, P J and Watts, M J (eds) *Geographies of Global Change: Remapping the World in the Late Twentieth Century*, Blackwell, Oxford, pp. 18–35.

Thrift, N (1996) 'New urban eras and old technological fears: Reconfiguring the goodwill of electronic things', *Urban Studies*, vol. 33, no. 8, pp. 1463–93.

Tierney, J (1992) 'Sound bites become smaller mouthfuls', *New York Times*, Jan. 23, A1.

Tiffin, J & Rajasingham, L (1995) *In Search of the Virtual Class: Education in an Information Society*, Routledge, London.

Time Magazine (1995) 'Welcome to cyberspace', *Time*, special issue, Spring.

Toffler, A (1980) *The Third Wave*, Morrow, New York.

Toffler, A & Toffler, H (1993) 'Societies at hyper-speed', *New York Times*, Oct. 31, E17.

Toffler, A & Toffler, H (1993) *War and Anti-War: Survival at the Dawn of the 21st Century*, Little Brown, Boston, Massachusetts.

Toffler, A & Toffler, H (1995) 'Getting set for the coming millennium', *Futurist*, vol. 29, no. 2, pp. 10–15.

Tomlinson, J (1991) *Cultural Imperialism: A Critical Introduction*, Johns Hopkins University Press, Baltimore, Maryland.

Townsend, A (2002) 'Mobile communications in the twenty-first century city', in Brown, B, Green, N and Harper, R (eds) *Wireless World: Social and Interactional Aspects of the Mobile Age*, Springer, London, pp. 62–77.

Trachtman, J P (1996) 'The international economic law revolution', *University of Pennsylvania Journal of International Economic Law*, vol. 17.

Traweek, S (1988) *Beamtimes and Lifetimes: The World of High Energy Physicists*, Harvard University Press, Cambridge, Massachusetts.

Tsagarousianou, R, Tambini, D & Bryan, C (1998) *Cyberdemocracy: Technology, Cities and Civic Networks*, Routledge, London.

Tuman, M C (1992) *Word Perfect: Literacy in the Computer Age*, University of Pittsburgh Press, Pittsburgh, Pennsylvania.

Tunstall, J (1985) 'Deregulation is politicisation', *Telecommunications Policy*, vol. 9, no. 3.

Tyack, D & Cuban, L (1995) *Tinkering Toward Utopia: A Century of Public School Reform*, Harvard University Press, Cambridge, Massachusetts.

Ullman, E (1997) *Close to the Machine: Technophilia and its Discontents*, City Lights, San Francisco.

United States v Goss (1989) 803 F2d 638.

USCA (1987) *Constitution of the United States Annotated: First Amendment*, West Publishing, St Pauls, Minnesota.

Vajda, S A (1993) 'The growth and expansion of telecoms in Mexico', *InterMedia*, vol. 21, no. 4–5, pp. 8–13.

Valenti, J (1995) Testimony to the Copyright Term Extension Act: Hearing on H.R. 989 before the Subcommittee On Courts and Intellectual Property of the House Committee on the Judiciary, 104th Congress, 1st session, June 1, Motion Picture Association of America.

van Riemsdijk, J (1980) *The Science Museum*, Science Museum, London.

Vandevelde, K (1980) 'The new property of the nineteenth century: The development of the modern concept of property', *Buffalo Law Review*, vol. 29.

Vault Corp. v Quaid Software Ltd. (1988) 847 F2d 255.

Venturi, R (1991) *Learning from Las Vegas: The Forgotten Symbolism of Architectural Form*, MIT Press, Cambridge, Massachusetts.

Vinge, V (1993) 'Technological singularity', *Whole Earth Review*, no. 81, pp. 88–95.

Virilio, P (1990) 'Cateract surgery: Cinema in the year 2000', in Kuhn, A (ed.) *Alien Zone: Cultural Theory and Contemporary Science Fiction Cinema*, Verso, London.

Virilio, P (2000) *Polar Inertia*, Sage, London.

von Hayek, F A (1978) *Law, Legislation, and Liberty*, vol. 2, University of Chicago Press, Chicago, Illinois.

Ware, W H (1993) 'The new faces of privacy', *The Information Society*, vol. 9, no. 3, pp. 193–211.

Warwick, D R (1992) 'The cash-free society', *Futurist*, vol. 26, no. 6, pp. 19–22.

Washington, H A (ed.) (1854) *Writings of Thomas Jefferson, 1790–1826*, vol. 6.

Weatherford, M (1993) 'Where dreams come true', *Nevada*, Jan./Feb., pp. 10–14.

Weaver, R R (1991) *Computers and Medical Knowledge: The Diffusion of Decision Support Technology*, Westview, Boulder, Colorado.

Webster, F & Robins, K (1986) *Information Technology: A Luddite Analysis*, Ablex, Norwood, New Jersey.

Weinreb, L (1990) 'Commentary: Fair's fair: A comment on the fair use doctrine', *Harvard Law Review*, vol. 105.

Weiser, M (1991) 'The computer for the 21st century', *Scientific American*, vol. 265, no. 3, pp. 94–104.

Weizer, N (1991) *The Arthur D. Little Forecast on Information Technology and Productivity: Making the Integrated Enterprise Work*, John Wiley, New York.

Wesley-Tanakovic, I (1994) *Expanding Access to Science and Technology: The Role of Information Technologies*, United Nations University Press, Tokyo.

Wicklein, J (1981) *Electronic Nightmare: The New Communications and Freedom*, Viking, New York.

Widmer, K & Widmer, E (1961) *Literary Censorship: Principles, Cases, Problems*, Wadsworth, San Francisco.

Wiener, N (1948) *Cybernetics*, MIT Press, Cambridge, Massachusetts.

Williams, R (1974) *Television: Technology and Cultural Form*, Fontana, London.

Williams, R (1989) *Resources of Hope*, Verso, London.

Williams, R (1996) *Normal Service Won't Be Resumed: The Future of Public Broadcasting*, Allen & Unwin, Sydney.

Wines, M (1994) 'Washington really is in touch. We're the problem', *New York Times*, Oct. 16, E1.

Winston, B (1986) *Misunderstanding Media*, Harvard University Press, Cambridge, Massachusetts.

Woherem, E E (1991) 'Expert systems as a medium for knowledge transfer to less developed countries', *Science & Public Policy*, vol. 18, no. 5, pp. 301–9.

Wollen, T (1993) 'The bigger the better: From cinemascope to IMAX', in Hayward, P and Wollen, T (eds) *Future Visions: New Technologies of the Screen*, British Film Institute, London, pp. 10–30.

Woolgar, S (1976) 'Writing an intellectual history of scientific development: The use of discovery accounts', *Social Studies of Science*, vol. 6, no. 3/4, pp. 395–422.

Wright, R (1995) 'Hyper-democracy', *Time*, Jan. 23, pp. 15–21.

Wriston, W B (1992) *The Twilight of Sovereignty: How the Information Revolution is Transforming Our World*, Scribner, New York.

Wynne, B (1992) 'Misunderstood misunderstandings: Social identities and the public uptake of science', *Public Understanding of Science*, vol. 1, no. 3, pp. 281–304.

'Wynn's world: White tigers, blackjack, and a Midas touch' (1992) *Business Week*, March 30.

Yen, A C (1991) 'When authors won't sell: Parody, fair use and efficiency in copyright law', *University of Colorado Law Review*, vol. 62.

Zizek, S (1989) *The Sublime Object of Ideology*, Verso, London.

Zizek, S (1997) *The Plague of Fantasies*, Verso, London.

Zizek, S (1998) 'The inherent transgression', *Cultural Values*, vol. 2, no. 1, pp. 1–17.

Zizek, S (1999) 'You may!', *London Review of Books*, March 18, pp. 3–6.

Zysman, G I (1995) 'Wireless networks', *Scientific American*, Sept., pp. 68–71.

Index